Locke,
Wesley, and
the Method of
English Romanticism

Richard E. Brantley

Locke,
Wesley, and
the Method of
English Romanticism

University Presses of Florida

University of Florida Press
Gainesville

The section on Keats appeared in slightly different form in *Studies in Romanticism*, Volume 22, No. 3, Fall 1983.

Permission to use the quotations from the following books has been granted by the publishers: Colin Clarke, *Romantic Paradox: An Essay on the Poetry of Wordsworth* (New York: Barnes and Noble, 1963); Hugh Sykes Davies, "Wordsworth and the Empirical Philosophers," in *The English Mind: Studies in the English Moralists Presented to Basil Willey*, edited by Hugh Sykes Davies and George Watson (Cambridge: Cambridge University Press, 1964); Earl Wasserman, *The Subtler Language: Critical Readings of Neoclassic and Romantic Poems* (Baltimore: The Johns Hopkins University Press, 1959); and John Wright, *Shelley's Myth of Metaphor* (Athens: University of Georgia Press, 1970).

Library of Congress Cataloging in Publication Data

Brantley, Richard E.
  Locke, Wesley, and the method of English romanticism.
  "A University of Florida book."
  Includes bibliographies and index.
    1. Wesley, John, 1703–1791. 2. Locke, John, 1632–1704. 3. Romanticism—England. I. Title.
BX8495.W5B69 1984   942.07   83–26026
ISBN 0–8130–0783–6

University Presses of Florida is the central agency for scholarly publishing of the State of Florida's university system. Its offices are located at 15 NW 15th Street, Gainesville, FL 32603. Works published by University Presses of Florida are evaluated and selected for publication by a faculty editorial committee of any one of Florida's nine public universities: Florida A&M University (Tallahassee), Florida Atlantic University (Boca Raton), Florida International University (Miami), Florida State University (Tallahassee), University of Central Florida (Orlando), University of Florida (Gainesville), University of North Florida (Jacksonville), University of South Florida (Tampa), University of West Florida (Pensacola).

Printed in the U.S.A. on acid-free paper

Contents

Appendixes

Acknowledgments

I am happy to acknowledge as many debts as possible. The American Philosophical Society awarded me a travel grant for the summer of 1978. Thanks are due to the staffs of the British Library, the Evangelical Library, the Dr. Williams Library, and the Lambeth Palace Library. I wish to mention in particular David W. Riley of the John Rylands University Library of Manchester. The Rev. John C. Bowmer, the Rev. Kenneth Garlick, and Elizabeth Bostetter afforded me hospitality as well as good advice during my visit to England.

The Humanities Council of the University of Florida supported my research during the summers of 1978 and 1979.

In 1982, 1983, and 1984, I read portions of my manuscript to the Southeastern American Society for Eighteenth-Century Studies, the American Academy of Religion—Southeastern Region, the Conference on Christianity and Literature, and the American Academy of Religion.

Paul J. Korshin read the manuscript in detail and with generosity. The Keats section, in slightly different form, appeared in *Studies in Romanticism* 22 (Fall 1983). I am grateful for permission to use that material here. I thank the editor, David Wagenknecht, for his timely criticism of "Keats's Method."

For her perspective and support, I thank my wife, Diana. My daughters, Jessica and Justine, cared about this project. My parents encouraged it.

Colleagues proved invaluable. Harold Stahmer, Richard Hiers, and Sam Hill, Department of Religion, Wayne Conner, Department of Romance Languages, Eldon Turner and John Sommerville, Department of History, and Ray Jones, University Library, solved several problems of principle and procedure. Members of the Department of English helped often: Ronald Carpenter, William Childers, Peter Lisca, David Locke, Bernard Paris, John Perlette, Robert Ray, William Robinson, Robert Thomson, and James Twitchell contributed a range of lore to my deliberations, and Judson Allen, Carl Bredahl, John Cech, Ira Clark, Alistair Duckworth, Brandon Kershner, Brian McCrea, Marie Nelson, Greg Ulmer, and Aubrey Williams read and commented on various sections of the manuscript.

Special thanks, finally, are due to two persons in particular: Melvyn New, chairman of the Department of English, and the late T. Walter Herbert, who was Distinguished Service Professor of English, corrected error, sharpened terminology, improved prose, and insured, indeed, that I would finish the work. They accompanied my research for more than fifteen years, and the dedication is in lieu of what I owe to them.

Abbreviations

Cragg   John Wesley. *The Appeals to Men of Reason and Religion and Certain Related Open Letters.* Edited by Gerald R. Cragg. Vol. 11 of *The Works of John Wesley.* Edited by Frank Baker. Oxford: Clarendon Press, 1975. This edition is in progress.

Curnock   John Wesley. *The Journal of the Rev. John Wesley, A.M., Sometime Fellow of Lincoln College, Oxford, Enlarged from Original MSS., With Notes from Unpublished Diaries, Annotations, Maps, and Illustrations.* Edited by Nehemiah Curnock. 8 vols. London: Robert Culley, 1909.

Jackson   John Wesley. *The Works of the Rev. John Wesley, A.M.* 14 vols. London: Wesleyan-Methodist Book-Room, n.d. This edition and the London 1872 edition reissued by Zondervan in 1958 are reissues of the third edition, edited by Thomas Jackson, 1829–31.

Nidditch   John Locke. *An Essay concerning Human Understanding.* 1690. Edited by Peter H. Nidditch. Oxford: Clarendon Press, 1975.

Sermons   John Wesley. *Sermons on Several Occasions. First Series. Consisting of Forty-Four Discourses, Published in Four Volumes, in the Years 1746, 1748, 1750 and 1760 (Fourth Edition, 1787); To which Reference is Made in the Trust-deeds of the Methodist Chapels, As Constituting, with Mr Wesley's Notes on the New Testament, The Standard Doctrines of the Methodist Connexion.* London: The Epworth Press, 1944.

Telford   John Wesley. *The Letters of the Rev. John Wesley, A. M., Sometime Fellow of Lincoln College, Oxford.* Edited by John Telford. 8 vols. London: The Epworth Press, 1931.

The Procedure Peter Browne. *The Procedure, Extent, and Limits of Human Understanding.* 2d ed. London: W. Innys, 1729.

A *Note on Editions*

Quotations of Blake, Wordsworth, Coleridge, Shelley, and Keats are from the following editions:

Douglas Bush, ed., *Keats: Selected Poems and Letters*. New York: Riverside Editions, 1959.

Ernest Hartley Coleridge, ed., *Poetical Works of Coleridge, including poems and versions of poems herein published for the first time*. 1912. Reprint. London and New York: Oxford University Press, 1969.

David V. Erdman, ed., *The Poetry and Prose of William Blake*, with commentary by Harold Bloom. Garden City, N.Y.: Doubleday, 1965.

Roger Ingpen and Walter E. Peck, eds., *The Complete Works of Percy Bysshe Shelley*. 10 vols. London: Ernest Benn, 1965.

Ernest de Selincourt, ed., *The Poetical Works of William Wordsworth*. 5 vols. Oxford: Clarendon Press, 1940–49; 2d ed. of vols. 2 (1952) and 3 (1954) revised by Helen Darbishire.

Ernest de Selincourt, ed., *The Prelude: or, Growth of a Poet's Mind*. Oxford: Clarendon Press, 1959; 2d ed. revised by Helen Darbishire. Unless otherwise indicated, quotations from *The Prelude* are from the 1850 version.

*For T. Walter Herbert
and Melvyn New*

An Orientation

*Probably when our unified field theory of British Romanticism
finally arrives, the materials will be somewhat nearer at hand
than either the distant past of Milton or the far future of
Joyce. . . . Thinking about British Romanticism primarily in
connection with the eighteenth century may not taste quite so
sublime to our intellectual palates; but perhaps our taste has
become a bit depraved.*[1]

No matter how direct the attempt at revival, the near influence is always telling. For example, Hollywood's conception of Imperial Rome fluctuates according to "modern" rather than Roman styles of costuming: compare Claudette Colbert's Cleopatra in 1932 with Elizabeth Taylor's in 1963. The buildings of Balliol College, Oxford, attempt a direct reproduction of the medieval, but are finally Victorian: their designers saw the Romanesque through neo-Georgian and "gothick" eyes. Wordsworth begins his *Prelude* in the new world atmosphere of the end of *Paradise Lost*, but he could not escape what lay between him and Milton: the near influence on the Romantic revival of far-off things is the eighteenth century. I argue here that an important aspect of that century, and hence of the near influence on Romanticism, is John Wesley's dialectic of philosophy and faith.

The founder of Methodism, of course, did not think of himself primarily as a philosopher, but, according to my point of view, Wesley (1703–91) was decidedly philosophical, or at any rate philosophically theological: his theology, if not his faith, relates clearly to the empirical philosophy in *An Essay concerning Human Understanding* (1690) by John Locke (1632–1704). By exploring the intellectual atmosphere of Wesley's formative years and by drawing out the intellectual content of his prose, I have found that the experiential emphasis of his theology derives, in large measure, from the experiential emphasis of Locke. I can show, moreover, by pointing to disseminations of his works and by pursuing his specifically philosophical (as well as otherwise intellectual) influence that writers as well as readers within his revival responded not only to his spiritual experience but also to his philosophical theology. His methodology, among some followers, served as the model for putting experience into words.

Finally, and in accord with his intellectual influence, I apply a philosophically theological perspective to British Romanticism. Specifically, I reveal that Wesley's mediation of Locke's thought is an immediate context of English Romantic poetry: Blake, Wordsworth, Coleridge, Shelley, and Keats, whatever their differences from each other, resemble each other in their formulations of experience, which echo Wesley's. His works were prominent among models of intellectual synthesis available to Romantic England, and, in consequence, I show how English Romantic poetry (and some English Romantic prose and some writers as early as Cowper and as late as the Victorians) rests on the Wesleyan (and historicist) assumption that words and concepts arise from experience both natural and spiritual.

My thesis, in short, is twofold. First, Locke's theory of knowledge grounds the intellectual method of Wesley's Methodism. And second, Wesley's Lockean thought (i.e., his reciprocating notions that religious truth is concerned with experiential presuppositions, and that experience itself need not be non–religious) provides a ready means of understanding the "religious" empiricism and the English "transcendentalism" of British Romantic poetry.

My title suggests my interest in the eighteenth century. *Locke, Wesley, and the Method of English Romanticism* conveys not only the direction of my argument, but also the centrality of Wesley thereto. This book, then, contributes to Wesleyan studies as well as to studies in Romanticism.

For students of Romanticism, if not for eighteenth-century scholars, I affirm at the outset Wesley's more than merely pietistic stance. By epitomizing his theology, by outlining the basis for, and urgency of, aligning him with Locke's *Essay*, by countering, specifically, the view of Wesley (especially among students of the Enlightenment) as narrow-mindedly outside the intellectual moving force of his century, and, finally, by calling attention to his language as a study in its own right, I define my terms, and orient my reader (whether Romantic or "neoclassical," or whether a little of both) to my central figure.

The comprehensiveness of Wesley's understanding, if not the originality of his mind, is now well established. His thought, for example, presides over a range of doctrines, and derives from such traditions as his native Puritan, the continental Protestant, and even the Catholic.[2] Moreover, and accordingly, the boldly mediating quality of his "rationalist, traditionalist, and biblicist" (as well as simply "pragmatist") intellect is guided (if not determined) by the Anglican *via media* that lies between "the Scylla of Rome and the Charybdis of Wittenburg."[3] Students of Methodism have tended to see him as a significant but not significantly intellectual religious activist, but in *The Methodist Revolution* (1973) Bernard Semmel has laid to rest the assumption that Wesley's practice completely characterizes his historical contribution and his faith.[4] Wesley's religious feeling, though intuitional and in a sense distinct from his intellectual belief, is generally grounded in his spiritual discipline and particularly related to his intellectual tradition. Arminius's theology of free will, as opposed to Calvin's doctrine of predestination, strengthened Wesley's resolve to perform deeds of kindness. Arminius's theology of universal redemption, as opposed to Calvin's doctrine of election, generally deepened Wesley's fervor in the work of saving souls.

The force of Wesley's revival, then, derives in no small measure from the liberating energies of his thought: his strength of mind matches his work in the world. His revival remains revolutionary, of course, insofar as it reflects his sometimes antiecclesiastical disregard for Church order. Witness this exchange between the bold young clergyman and Joseph Butler, Bishop of Bristol:

Butler: You have no business here. You are not commissioned to preach in this diocese. Therefore I advise you to go hence.
Wesley: My lord, my business on earth is to do what good I can. Wherever therefore I think I can do most good, there must I stay so long as I think so. At present I think I can do most good here. Therefore here I stay.[5]

But Wesley was far from being mindlessly iconoclastic. Though his itinerant ministry led to the founding of a great world church, his thoughtful love of the Established Church kept his societies from ever formally separating during his lifetime.[6] And his love of all Christian thought steadied the momentum of his Methodism. The variety of views that all more or less insistently claim to characterize the essence of his religious thought reveals that the synthesizing range of his traditionalist imagination offered to his age not only the power and the form but also the substance of his Christian heritage.

A logical next step for the study of his theology, and the step that I am taking, is to answer the question of its philosophical dimension. "The Philosophy of Enthusiasm," by J. Clifford Hindley, links Moravian theology to Wesley's conversion but is also careful to speculate that Wesley's "philosophical studies partly supplied . . . the framework into which the teaching of the Moravians and his own experience was to be fitted."[7] Hindley's essay set me on the course I follow in the present book.

Here, in brief, is Hindley's point, together with some pertinent history. The conversion took place at "a quarter to nine" on the evening of May 24, 1738, "in Aldersgate Street," London, where, upon hearing William Holland, a Moravian brother, read "Luther's preface to the Epistle to the Romans," Wesley felt his heart "strangely warmed"; Holland "was describing," wrote Wesley, "the change which God works in the heart through faith in Christ."[8] Hindley argues that this experience, which was not only Wesley's conversion, but also the seed of Methodism, was facilitated by the Moravians' founding of their doctrine of assurance on Rom. 8:15:

> For ye have not received the Spirit of bondage again to fear; but ye have received the Spirit of adoption, whereby we cry, Abba, Father.[9]

But Hindley is concerned as well with whether Wesley's sudden conviction of grace was "largely determined" by the bold, but not so sudden, stroke of replacing the "metaphysical question" of knowledge of God with "the fundamentally epistemological question 'How can I know that I am saved?'" (Hindley, p. 99). "Only through experience," came the answer. What Hindley implies is that Wesley's "empiricist conditioning," if not his training in empiricism, taught him so much respect for experience as the necessary ground of knowledge that Wesley's quest for "a direct experience of the divine love" was necessarily quasi-philosophic (Hindley, pp. 107–8).

Thus, Hindley's essay announces a fresh approach to Wesley's entire career as well as to the central event of his life. His conversion has been thoroughly analyzed from exclusively theological points of view and even from the perspective of psychology.[10] Recently, a psychological approach to the entire career has proved especially fruitful: Robert L. Moore's *John Wesley and Authority* follows Erikson's *Young Man Luther* and *Gandhi's Truth* to "a psychological perspective" on the role of authority in Wesley's religious personality.[11] John Telford showed long ago that Wesley was simply expressing sincere fervor and not some psychologically based disrespect when he stood on his father's tomb and preached to more people than would fit inside the church at Epworth,[12] but one is tempted to see in this gesture, if not something Freudian, then in Moore's terms the dynamic influence of authority on Wesley's emergent religious identity. One may be equally attracted, though, to Hindley's disciplinary emphasis, for one is led by Hindley to draw a parallel between Wesley's conversion and such resurgences of empiricism as that of A. J. Ayer, whose "verification principle" demanded that "for a proposition to have meaning we must adduce some human experience by which its truth or falsity may be tested."[13] One is intrigued, too, by Hindley's preliminary conclusion that Wesley's appeal to experience, far from being "an odd idiosyncrasy with dangerous subjective tendencies," offered "an essentially right way" to reorient theology "in the face of philosophical empiricism" and therefore amounted to "the supreme apologetic for Christian faith in eighteenth-century England" (Hindley, pp. 202, 209).

Hindley, alas, is not concerned to search out Wesley's particular responses to philosophers and so does not confront the question of direct influence, but "The Philosophy of Enthusiasm" has more than sufficed to suggest to me that Wesley's language for "that faith which none can have without knowing that he hath it" (Curnock, 1:424) is not far from the experiential language of Locke. Hindley's essay, moreover, has accompanied my research into Wesley's experiential theology. Hindley's subtitle "A Study in the Origins of Experimental Theology" connotes like *experiential theology* the particular method whereby such religious problems as the knowledge of salvation (though not, to be sure, how far predestination extends) appear to arise from (if not always to be solved at) the times and places of one's sense-oriented as well as mental life. In this connection, it is worth mentioning that the term common in both Moravian theology and one of Wesley's most characteristic doctrines is also common in the experiential English philosophy of Locke's *Essay: "Assurance"* is Locke's name for the *"highest degree of Probability"* (*Essay* 4.16.6; Nidditch, pp. 661–62). It is worth noting too that Wesley's sometimes antiauthoritarian stance can be seen in the light of his philosophical background: Locke argued that "a Man shall never want crooked Paths to walk in . . . where-ever he has the Foot-steps of others to follow" (*Essay* 4.20.17; Nidditch, p. 719).

Alfred H. Body, unlike Hindley, is concerned with Wesley's responses to Locke's thought in particular; Body, for example, answers why Wesley required the *Essay* in the fourth year at Kingswood School.[14] Wesley's educational theory follows Locke's *Thoughts concerning Education* (1693) in holding that the design of education should counterbalance any bias of nature. Locke's very wording, as Body demonstrates, is reflected in Wesley's ban on holidays, his rules against play, and his insistence upon simplicity of diet and starkness of accommodation. The Lockean root of his educational theory is worthy of further examination, especially in view of *John Locke and Children's Books in Eighteenth-Century England*, in which Samuel Pickering, Jr., has recently explored *Thoughts concerning Education* in conjunction with the children's literature to which eighteenth-century evangelicalism, too, is surely pertinent; "I approached children's books," writes Pickering in his preface, "from the perspective of my earlier study of evangelicalism in the novel. Instead of finding religion on every page, however, I discovered the ideas of John Locke." [15] Finding the ideas of Locke on many pages of late eighteenth- and early nineteenth-century literature, adult if not children's, does not exclude but rather, as I demonstrate in chapter 4, all but signals the discovery of evangelical religion on those same pages. One might look, in this connection, at David Fordyce's *Thoughts concerning Education* (London, 1745), which applies Lockean premises to religious education.

The starting point for any further discussion of Wesley's Lockean thought, educational and otherwise, is obviously his denial of innate ideas. His sermon "On the Discoveries of Faith," for example, begins thus:

> For many ages it has been allowed by sensible men, *Nihil est in intellectu quod non fuit prius in sensu*: That is, "There is nothing in the understanding which was not first perceived by some of the senses." . . . [T]his point has now been thoroughly discussed by men of the most eminent sense and learning; and it is agreed by all impartial persons, that although some things are so plain and obvious, that we can very hardly avoid knowing them as soon as we come to the use of our understanding; yet the knowledge even of those is not innate, but derived from some of our senses. (Jackson, 7: 231; Yarmouth, June 11, 1788)

These sentences epitomize the main point in Book 1 of the *Essay* and indeed in the *Essay* as a whole. They make one wonder how far, and in what ways, not just this sermon but the generality of Wesley's works operates according to this particular Lockean premise and Lockean premises in general. My choice of works for discussion is announced as part of chapter 1. In the second chapter, I attempt to justify that choice. I am concerned in those chapters, and indeed throughout this study, not with Wesley's Lockean theory of education so much as with the Lockean aspect of all of his thought. I am interested in the impact thereon of the

Essay rather than *Thoughts concerning Education*, or, for that matter, any other works of Locke, each of which besides being less inclusive and less important than the *Essay* is of far less significance than the *Essay* to the history of Wesley's mind and the outpouring of his pen.

Martin Schmidt, in perhaps the broadest (and at any rate one of the most valuable) studies of Wesley's intellectual life, mentions Wesley's concurrence in Locke's denial of innate ideas.[16] And Gerald R. Cragg, in his recent edition of the two "Appeals to Men of Reason and Religion" (1743–45), observes that in the following passage from the first, "An Earnest Appeal," "Wesley's interpretation of the senses is a part of the epistemology he derived from Locke":

> [B]efore it is possible for you to form a true judgment of the things of God, it is absolutely necessary that you have a *clear apprehension* of them, and that your ideas thereof be all *fixed*, *distinct*, and *determinate*. And seeing our ideas are not all innate, but must originally come from our senses, it is certainly necessary that you have senses capable of discerning objects of this kind: Not those only which are called natural senses, which in this respect profit nothing, as being altogether incapable of discerning objects of a spiritual kind; but spiritual senses, exercised to discern spiritual good and evil. It is necessary that you have *the hearing ear*, and *the seeing eye*, emphatically so called; that you have a new class of senses opened in your soul, not depending on organs of flesh and blood, to be "the evidence of things not seen" [cf. Heb. 11:1], as your bodily senses are of visible things; to be the avenues to the invisible world, to discern spiritual objects, and to furnish you with ideas of what the outward "eye hath not seen, neither the ear heard" [cf. 1 Cor. 2:9]. (Cragg, p. 57)

(Wesley's second "Appeal" is "A Farther Appeal." Both "Appeals" and their announcement of the doctrine of the spiritual sense are discussed in chapter 2.) The sense-based origin of ideas, then, and hence the epistemology of Locke was what Wesley evidently took for granted as the first principle of philosophy. But Cragg neglects to listen for overtones of Locke's sense-based method in any passage other than the one just quoted. And Schmidt nowhere traces the connection between Wesley's "theological biography" and his denial of innate ideas.

This is not surprising, perhaps, in view of the fact that the *Essay*, like its precursors in Greek philosophy, and like its descendants in logical positivism, is skeptical enough to seem alien to theology of any kind.

Some orthodox thinkers, from its earliest reception, looked upon it as tending towards religious skepticism: Bishop Edward Stillingfleet, in "A Vindication of the Doctrine of the Trinity" (1696), attacked the *Essay* for being so general in its discussion of faith as to impugn an indispensable Christian tenet; and a sampling of titles—"The danger of corrupting the faith by philosophy" (1697) by William Sherlock; "Remarks upon Mr. Clarke's Sermons, preached at St. Paul's against Hobbs, Spinoza, and other Atheists" (1705) by William Carroll; and, on the continent, "Faith and Reason Compared . . . written . . . by a person of quality in answer to . . . theses drawn from Mr. Locke's Principles" (1713) by Metternich Freiher von Wolf—indicates how other turn-of-century polemicists-for-orthodoxy feared that religious skepticism, and even atheism, were unavoidable corollaries of what they took as Locke's failure to discern that faith and reason are drawn from distinct principles. This interpretation of Locke more or less directly anticipates the now usual reading of the *Essay* as a determiner of secular thought in the modern world. Geoffrey Hartman, for example, in his influential study of Wordsworth, relies upon Basil Willey's still heard argument that Locke left a demythologized world in which value and meaning had to be created.[17] Logical positivists are indeed so skeptical as to reject the claims of faith outright. Moritz Schlick, for one, in an argument reminiscent of Hume's, but even more inimical to religion, insists that since religious statements are simply expressions of attitudes, they are meaningless opinions and cannot be verified as knowledge.[18] Greek skepticism, similarly, was less than constructive with regard to faith. Pyrrho of Elis held that sense perception, since it is not known to be false, must not be distrusted on principle, but he was otherwise skeptical: he carried doubt and uncertainty to a greater extreme than either Democritus before him or Arciselaus and Carneades of the later New Academy, and as a result of traveling with Alexander the Great and observing differences between Greek religion and that of Indian fakirs Pyrrho concluded that religion and values are relative.[19]

One should bear in mind, however, that the skepticism of the *Essay* is not directed towards religion. Indeed, by founding a "knowledge" of God's perfection on the "general connexion" among "all parts of the creation," Locke shows himself in essential accord with the spirit of another philosopher, Francis Bacon, who makes the twofold observation in his essay "On Atheism" that "a little Philosophie inclineth to Atheism" but that "depth in Philosophie bringeth Men about to Religion."[20] By the same token, Locke was in agreement with Sir Thomas Browne, who came to faith as Bacon did by means of skeptical method. The *Essay*, far from insisting on religious skepticism, frequently acknowledges the Bible as source of religious knowledge and has been seen accordingly as the friend of revealed as well as natural religion. Since the *Essay* formed an element of the atmosphere in which Robert Boyle, Isaac Newton, John Ray, and Richard Bentley brought about a marriage of science and theology, it should come as no surprise that Socinians, Arians, and Deists regarded Locke as a believer in the God of natural religion. The Deist Matthew Tindal, in 1731, quotes *Essay* 4.16.10 as support for his emphasis on evidence in matters of faith; in 1713, the Deist Anthony Collins cites Locke as the authority for seeing a theological level of meaning in such terms as *evidence, understanding, judge, assent, know, proof,* and *will;* the Deist John Toland, in 1696, uses the language of Lockean epistemology to extol the concept of soul; and the compatibility between Locke and William Whiston, chief Arian and chief descendant of Socinianism, is seen in Locke's express admiration of Whiston's "New Theory of the Earth" (1696).[21] (Locke was a friend of Collins and an acquaintance of Toland.) For one who assumes that the secularist reading of Locke has always prevailed it may come as a surprise that not just proponents of natural religion, but even a proponent or two of revealed religion, were receptive to the *Essay* from the beginning. As early as 1691, for example, in "Reflections upon the Conduct of Human Life" (which incidentally was condensed and published by Wesley in 1735, just before he went to Georgia), the Anglican John Norris was drawn to the *Essay*'s denial of innate ideas; and in 1707, the Anglican Thomas Bray recommended the *Essay*, among other books, as "requisite to be perus'd . . . by the Reverend Clergy."[22]

Bishop Butler and Andrew Baxter, to be sure, are two orthodox apologists from mid-century who shared Bishop Berkeley's well-known view of Locke's philosophy as more or less explicitly materialist, but increasingly both the clergy and Christians in general summoned the *Essay* to defend the faith.[23] By 1747, when Catharine Cockburn linked her moral views to Lockean epistemology,[24] she almost had to do so since Locke was more and more assumed to be correct. Kenneth MacLean in his classic study of the *Essay*'s pervasiveness in eighteenth-century English thought and expression points out that even such conservative divines as William Law and Isaac Watts, and even the evangelical laureate William Cowper, consciously attempted to meet, in Hindley's words, "the philosophical demand for empiricism"; MacLean shows indeed that Bishop Butler, despite his Berkeleian discovery of materialism in the *Essay*, otherwise accepted its "sensational philosophy": Butler argued that the senses are "instruments of our receiving such ideas from external objects, as the Author of nature appointed those external objects to be the occasions of exciting in us."[25]

MacLean, it should be said, remains perhaps the most thorough twentieth-century definer of the *Essay*'s skepticism. It should also be said, however, that like other such definers, and despite his valuable demonstration of Locke's intellectual hegemony, MacLean leaves a somewhat biased impression of the *Essay*. He overemphasizes, or rather presents as the whole truth about Locke, Locke's admittedly major premise that, as MacLean paraphrases (p. 13), "human knowledge is limited." Locke was intent indeed upon tracing "the *cause of Obscurity* in simple *Ideas*" to "dull Organs," "weakness in the Memory," and all the other shortcomings inherent in sense perception (*Essay* 2.23.3; Nidditch, p. 363). MacLean has a sharp eye for such phrases,[26] and one may add to those he cites *Essay* 2.10.5, where Locke sounds this epistemologically elegiac note: "And our Minds represent to us those Tombs, to which we are approaching; where though the Brass and Marble remain, yet the Inscriptions are effaced by time, and the Imagery moulders away" (Nidditch, pp. 151–52). But the relentlessness of MacLean's emphasis can do scant justice to the sort of passage in which a more than expectant strain of rhapsodic optimism determines the tone of Locke's epistemology:

> Nor let any one think [simple ideas] too narrow bounds for the capacious Mind of Man to expatiate in, which takes its flight farther than the Stars, and cannot be confined by the limits of the World; that extends its thoughts often, even beyond the utmost expansion of Matter, and makes excursions into that incomprehensible Inane. . . . Nor will it be so strange, to think these few simple *Ideas* sufficient to employ the quickest Thought, or largest Capacity; and to furnish the Materials of all that various Knowledge, and more various Fancies and Opinions of all Mankind, if we consider how many Words may be made out of the various composition of 24 Letters; or if going one step farther, we will but reflect on the variety of combinations may be made, with barely one of the above-mentioned *Ideas*, *viz*. Number, whose stock is inexhaustible, and truly infinite: And what a large and immense field, doth Extension alone afford the Mathematicians? (*Essay* 2.7.10; Nidditch, pp. 131–32)

MacLean (p. 83) quotes the passage but does not dwell upon it. Consider also, for example, *Essay* 1.2.14 where Locke strikes an epistemologically robust note by speaking of the "very manifest difference between dreaming of being in the Fire, and being actually in it" (Nidditch, p. 537): Locke trusts sense perception to tell him of a non-illusory world.

It is remarkable to find MacLean touching on the *Essay*'s incorporation into Wesley's traditional theology. In recognizing that Wesley "followed Locke in denying innate ideas," that Wesley promoted Locke's view of animals as having degrees of reason and understanding, and that Wesley adopted Locke's principle of accepting as a matter of faith only what is consistent with reason, MacLean (pp. 28, 81, 154) includes Wesley among the Anglicans who represented the growing acceptance of Locke by all stripes of religious thinkers. Horton Davies argues persuasively that Wesley's theology is so squarely in the mainstream as to have been "the bridge that crossed the chasm between . . . Anglicanism and Dissent,"[27] but no one completes the connection MacLean begins to make between Wesley's mainstream theology and the Lockean assumptions of mainstream theology. Donald Greene notes the interaction between empiricism and the Augustan Anglicans, but does not discuss Wesley among them.[28] And V. H. H. Green in his study of Wesley's early life and thought recognizes Bishop Butler's attempt to establish the truths of Christianity on Lockean grounds of probability and even grants Butler's *Analogy* a significant position as "the ablest apologetic work" in Wesley's intellectual milieu, but nowhere mentions the fact that, despite Wesley's quarrel with the Bishop over Church order, Wesley fundamentally admired Butler's theology, and so could well have stood with him on its Lockean ground.[29]

MacLean, though, does not develop the parallels he points to and finally insists against his own evidence that Wesley simply "sought personal revelations of the divine will through bibliomancy and other forms of superstitious divination" (p. 154). Whenever Wesley practiced the *Sortes Liturgicae* to find out, for example, whether to go from Bristol to London, and whenever he indulged in divination by verses of the Bible, he was indeed as superstitious as when he entertained belief in ghosts and witches: all of his various forms of divination are so nonphilosophical as to hark back, if not to entrail-reading, then to the *Sortes Homericae* of the ancients. His bibliomancy, on the other hand, besides relating to eighteenth-century arguments for providence in "chance" events, regards the interrespondence of mind and externality, and may therefore be said to parallel, if not Jungian synchronicity in today's scheme of things, then the eighteenth-century Lockean view that discrete and casual perceptions form individual stages in the mind's growth and progress in the world.[30] I shall have little more to say of Wesley's bibliomancy, but I suggest, in the context of what I will say of his thought, that even his bibliomancy need not be seen apart from the intellectual context of its age.

I propose, then, affirmatively to answer whether Locke's emphasis on sense perception is what is needed just now in describing the ways of

Wesley's mind. Nidditch, in his introduction to his now standard edition of the *Essay*, defines the epistemology of Locke as an experiential continuum with understanding at one pole and physical sensation at the other: Nidditch formulates, and calls "sensationalistic," the assumption underlying Locke's view of mind as tabula rasa—"the ultimate source of all our ideas, and the ultimate required test of all our putative knowledge and beliefs, lie within the bounds of the workings of normal sense- or inner-experience"—and Nidditch rounds out his summary of Locke's thought by observing that in his epistemology the "modest potentialities" of the senses are "circumspectly approached" and "methodically elucidated" (Nidditch, p. x). Nidditch regards the *Essay* as in no small measure "rationalistic" (p. x), but this word, suggesting the dictionary's definition of rationalism (i.e., "the theory that reason is a source of knowledge in itself, superior to and independent of sense perceptions") is sufficiently reminiscent of Cartesian philosophy to be an ill-advised description of Lockean. To be sure, Locke's distinction between beliefs and knowledge, and his accentuation of ideas, amount to an emphasis on mind as complement to the operation of the senses: the senses are prior to mind, but mind responds to sense data. True, too, that Francis Gallaway long ago popularized a blunt claim: "Locke was a rationalist to the core."[31] And V. H. H. Green, in pointing to the presence of the *Essay* in Wesley's intellectual background, labels Locke's philosophy *empirical rationalism.*[32] But words like *rationalism, rationalist,* and *rationalistic* are not finally appropriate.

Locke's philosophy teaches, first, that ideas are the mind's record of what the senses bring; second, that the mind works on these ideas to produce general propositions; third, that these propositions take their place, with ideas, as what the mind works on; fourth, that the mind applies these propositions to problems it confronts; and fifth, that solutions to these problems occur. Anyone who goes through these stages uses his reason both inductively and deductively, and may be said, therefore, to behave reasonably, rationally. But to say that he exemplifies rationalism is to speak confusingly; I have not described what Descartes said *he* thought. I hasten to add, however, that it is not only well advised, but especially necessary at present, to call attention to Locke's emphasis on reason: this emphasis has been neglected, in recent years, by critics who regard his influence on eighteenth-century writers as largely confined to his sense-oriented methodology.[33] If one thinks of Lockean reason as sense-based, rather than independent of experience, then Gallaway's argument that Lockean reason accounts for the quality of reason in eighteenth-century England holds. *Rational empiricism*, rather than *empirical rational-*

ism, serves as a fuller and more accurate name for Locke's thought than *empiricism* alone. And *rational* and *reasonable*, rather than *rationalist* and *rationalistic*, are proper descriptions for an important component of his thought. While it is needful to draw a distinction between, say Shaftesbury, Francis Hutcheson, and David Hume, all of whom were sometimes nearly antirational as well as often nonrational, and such a priori (albeit English) rationalists as Richard Cumberland, Ralph Cudworth, and Samuel Clarke,[34] it is also needful to see that an ever increasing (though by no means innate) strength of reason formed such an important part of Locke's empiricism that it should regularly be said to include a specific appeal thereto.

I argue, at any rate, that Locke's rational empiricism (i.e., his epistemology of sense perception attended by induction and deduction) directly informs the religious "epistemology" whereby Wesley claimed the saving faith he felt was his. (*Perception*, distinct from *sense* alone, serves to signal the mental, rational element of Locke's epistemology.) By midcentury both poles of this broadly empirical and quintessentially English philosophy had become so commonplace that they entered, directly and indirectly, nonphilosophic forms of English expression: "Reason," writes Sterne, "is half of it, Sense."[35] Wesley, casually employing such phrases as "beyond all sense and reason" (e.g., Curnock, 6:6), and not so casually denouncing Rousseau's *Emile* as "grounded upon neither reason nor experience" (Curnock, 5:353), seems to think of sense-function as necessarily in concert with the distinguishing faculty of mind. The empirically rational assumption underlying these phrases could explain what Sir William Robertson Nicoll observes to be true of Wesley, namely, that while "detached" in "apostolical aloofness," he was at the same time "interested in everything."[36] Without necessarily following Hindley to his notion that empiricism engendered Wesley's conversion, I demonstrate that Wesley's Methodism derived a formal philosophic component from Locke's appeal to the senses and to reason.

This demonstration is sufficiently in line, I think, with just about all that is not ineffable regarding the conversion itself. It seems fair to say, even now, that when Wesley felt his heart warmed while thinking about the doctrine of faith, he (1) had an experience both rational and at least quasi-sensationalistic, and (2) came, then, to understand the experience along lines parallel to the Lockean view, namely, that experience is a complex process with elements each leading back to what the senses tell. I believe, in other words, that the experience of heartwarming was itself not entirely without rational as well as sense-like dimensions, and moreover that when he applied the experience in his further thinking, he was in his own view acting as a man "of reason and religion" indeed, i.e., not just as a man who in the general sense uses his mind critically and also worships God, but also as a man who, in a particular and historically appropriate sense, finds that his twice-born Christianity and his rational empiricism are strangely analogous to each other.

My view that Locke's influence on Wesley included an appeal to sense-based reason is implied only by Francis McConnell and V. H. H. Green. Green, exploring Wesley's intellectual background, mentions Locke's analysis of "the natural faculties," i.e., the senses, as a central part of his philosophy, but emphasizes that reason in general, i.e., "the exercise of the intellect and an orderly, logical process of thought," and "the harmonious relationship of faith and reason" in particular, also formed important elements of the *Essay*.[37] McConnell, in his biography of Wesley, identifies Locke with "the Age of Reason."[38] But McConnell, asserting that "the Age of Reason" came "to an end" because of "the Wesleyan Movement," implies that an Age of Reason cannot also be an Age of Religion. And Green does not pursue the possibility that a reasonable as well as deeply felt faith was both a Wesleyan and a rather Lockean property. Indeed Green does not at all attempt to establish the nature of the Lockean presence in Wesley's early intellectual milieu, but my first and third chapters, especially, further acknowledge Green's otherwise useful study. No student of Wesley's intellectual life, then, has hitherto specifically realized that insofar as his spiritual experience is, to recall Nidditch, "circumspectly approached" and "methodically elucidated" by his theological argumentation, his thought is intimately related to the methodology through which Locke granted to the mind a limited license to perceive the truth and entertain belief.

Reality appears to the reader of the *Essay* as a balance between matter and mind, or rather, to borrow M. H. Abrams's words, as an "interpenetration" and "coalescence" of subject and object.[39] Wesley's exclamation that "None can have general good sense unless they have clear and determinate ideas of all things" (Telford, 6:130) does more than simply paraphrase *Essay* 3's discussion of the causes of confusion among men: Wesley surely signals, in his remark, his agreement with Locke's argument that the mind forms a link with external reality. It cannot be said that Wesley attained to the sophistication with which Coleridge, for example, was to understand objective and subjective reality:

The groundwork, therefore, of all true philosophy [said Coleridge] is the full apprehension of the difference between . . . that intuition of things which arises when we possess ourselves, as one with the whole . . . and that which presents itself when . . . we think of ourselves as separated beings, and place nature in antithesis to the mind, as object to subject, thing to thought, death to life.[40]

But it can be said, with Hindley, that Wesley's doctrines of the "Direct Witness" and the "Witness of Our Own Spirit" amount to an understanding of subject and object, and hence to philosophical as well as theological components of his thought:

> [T]here is no . . . clear distinction in religious experience [writes Hindley] between the objective source of illumination and the subjective perception of that illumination. Insofar, therefore, as Wesley intended by "the Witness of Our Own Spirit" an immediate consciousness of God's working in the heart, we must conclude that it is *empirically* indistinguishable from what Wesley describes as the Witness of God's Spirit. (p. 204)

And it should be said, in line with this Wesleyan counterpart to Coleridge's "one with the whole," that Wesley was in the simultaneously "tough-minded" and "tender-minded" tradition of intellectual history. To that paradoxical tradition, William James notably assigns the *Essay*: it is "tender-minded," argues James, in being "rationalistic, intellectualistic, idealistic, optimistic, religious, free-willist, monistic, and dogmatical"; yet it is somehow also "tough-minded," i.e., "empiricist, sensationalistic, materialistic, pessimistic, irreligious, pluralistic, and skeptical."[41] Regardless of whether these sometimes wholly irreconcilable pairings can in every case be applied to the *Essay* (was Locke monistic? dogmatical? irreligious? pluralistic?), it can be argued, and will be argued here, that like Locke, Wesley was constructively skeptical; and it will also be argued that though he cannot any more than Locke be described as pluralistic and irreligious, though he was certainly not any more than Locke monistic, and though he was not even conceivably either materialistic or pessimistic, he was somehow sensationalistic and empiricist and at the same time free-willist, religious, optimistic, idealistic, intellectualistic, and generally reasonable though never quite rationalistic. Isaac Watts, incidentally, showed a similar blend of tough-mindedness and tendermindedness: his *Logic*, according to MacLean, "moderated and softened" Locke's philosophy, but it should be remembered, as MacLean points out, that in the preface to *Philosophical Essays* Watts speaks of the *Essay*'s many "truths" and emphasizes that they are "worthy of Letters of Gold."[42]

I know that my allusion to William James goes far towards implying that Locke and Wesley shared just about everything, but I run this risk of overstatement in order to cast my net as widely as possible. There is a particular need to do so, for it is the general rule that, notwithstanding such exceptions as Leslie Stephen, students of the Enlightenment don't read Wesley. Taking little or no notice of Wesleyan scholarship, they regard him as an unenlightened anachronism at worst and, at best, as a non-intellectual contrast to, and impediment of, Enlightenment thinkers.[43]

His own age, it is true, charged him with enthusiasm, or "a false pretension of an Extraordinary divine assistance"; Albert M. Lyles has amply documented the fact that Wesley-as-religious-fanatic was the polemicists' image of him.[44] But their image is wrong. "Wesley," as I have elsewhere argued, "though he conceded the occurrence of too many false claims to inspiration, defended the possibility of a 'genuine' Extraordinary witness, to be 'known by its fruits'"; and he could hardly have been both an enthusiast and a follower of John Locke: Locke's strictures against enthusiasm are well known.[45] From his congregations, to be sure, Wesley sometimes heard "loud cries," but by 1759 at least he was careful to judge such outbursts according to their measure of "love and joy" and to correct them when he found "sorrow and fear" (Curnock, 4:344). He everywhere inveighed, moreover, against the "false pretension" to "Extraordinary divine assistance"; the following instance is typical:

> I was both surprised and grieved at a genuine instance of enthusiasm. J[ohn] B[rown], of Tanfield Lea, who had received a sense of the love of God a few days before, came riding through the town, hallooing and shouting, and driving all the people before him, telling them God had told him he should be a king, and should tread all his enemies under his feet. I sent him home immediately to his work, and advised him to pray day and night to God, that he might be lowly in heart, lest Satan should again get an advantage over him.[46]

It is no wonder that Georges III and IV looked upon the revival as a force for stability. Especially when it came to political affairs and social order, Wesley rejected the extremes of Puritan fervor, despite the fact that he was affected by the character and sufferings of the Puritans: on his circuit riding, he customarily noted the destruction wrought by the "enthusiastic fury" of Cromwell's wars; Cromwell, said Wesley, was "as far from being a Christian as Henry VIII"; and, in December of 1768, because of increasing trouble in America, and because of the public outcry over the imprisonment of John Wilkes, Member for Middlesex, Wesley expressed

his fears concerning "a second Cromwell" and "a field of blood." [47] Finally, I see something detached and philosophic, if not William Jamesian
and scientific, in Wesley's straightforward accounts of such experiences
as that of Ann Thorn, "who had been several times in trances," and
"claimed" to have sojourned "in another world, knowing nothing that
was done or said by all that were round about" (Curnock, 4:344).

It is an indication of my view of Wesley that the blend of English mind
and religious temper with which he was endowed assured him a place in
the Enlightenment of which Locke's theological as well as philosophical
Essay was a major manifesto. In addition to the "natural faculties" of the
senses and the thereby aided reason, the *Essay* includes revelation as a
means of understanding, and, insofar as Wesley mastered the *Essay*, followed its principles, spread its message, reconciled it with his faith, and
incorporated it into his philosophical theology, he not only participated
as such an enlightened man in that Enlightenment but also contributed
to it.

I am far from meaning by this subthesis that Wesley approved of the
continental Enlightenment. At worst, he was unaware of the *philosophes*,
for he nowhere mentions Kant, and at best he was ambivalent: admiring
Voltaire as "a very lively writer, of a fine imagination," and respecting the
"judgment" of both Voltaire and Rousseau, Wesley nevertheless denounced them because they "contributed all their labours" to "extol *humanity* to the skies, as the very essence of religion." [48] It is no wonder, in
view of this denunciation, that in his usage *this enlightened age* was ironic
and satirical. [49] The *philosophes*, as Henry May puts it, "could not get out
of their systems . . . the deductive method of Descartes"; [50] and Wesley's
more negative than positive attitude toward Cartesian thought is further
evidence, if evidence is needed, of his distance from the continental Enlightenment. Insofar as he admired Nicolas Malebranche, who owed a
debt to Descartes's deductive powers, Wesley undoubtedly recognized
both those powers and, at least subconsciously, Descartes as wielder of
them, but insofar as Wesley approached Cartesian thought at all, he
should be said to have approached it from his English perspective: the
works of John Norris, who was influenced by Descartes as well as Locke,
and Berkeley's *Alciphron*, which, besides counterinterpreting Locke's *Essay*, assimilates Malebranche and hence in part Descartes, were objects of
Wesley's praise. [51] Wesley, far from being in any essential sympathy with
Cartesian philosophy, was finally, and from an empirical point of view,
more than dubious about the results of Cartesian method, for he attacked
Cartesian astronomy for being, like Ptolemaic, incapable of "solid, convincing proof" (Jackson, 13:490–91), and, by way of challenging the

Cartesian view that self-knowledge, presumably "the most useful, the most necessary" kind, is certain and inevitable, he cast doubt on the *cogito* (Jackson, 13:497). (Wesley specifically scorned Descartes's notion that "the soul is lodged in the pineal gland.") Hindley is correct, then, to assert that Descartes, when present in Wesley's thinking, "is very much in the background of it" (Hindley, p. 209).

But Wesley was necessarily near the *Essay*-dominated Anglo-American Enlightenment. Though Nidditch points to important channels of the early "diffusion of Locke's epistemology in Europe," and though Peter Gay and Paul Hazard demonstrate that the *Essay* remained a staple of the continental Enlightenment until, as Hazard puts it, "Kant came on the scene,"[52] the *Essay* enjoyed a more long-lasting acceptance, and a greater one, in the English-speaking world. "Colonial readers of modern philosophy," writes May, "started with Locke's *Essay*, which they knew much better before the Revolution than his *Two Treatises on Government*"; and May points out that Locke, as representative of the "Moderate or Rational Enlightenment," continued to be admired in America well after, say, 1815, when such representatives of the "Skeptical Enlightenment" as Hume and Voltaire, and such an epitome of the "Revolutionary Enlightenment" as Rousseau, had begun to come under attack.[53] J. G. A. Pocock, for one, is not entirely comfortable with the notion of an English Enlightenment, but the *Essay*'s influence on such varied English thinkers as Isaac Newton, Anthony Collins, Bernard Mandeville, George Berkeley, Lord Bolingbroke, David Hume, Lord Kames, Adam Smith, Horace Walpole, Joseph Priestley, Edmund Burke, and Thomas Paine justifies calling Locke, if not the father of the English Enlightenment, then the progenitor of an eighteenth-century intellectual tradition at many points linked to the continental Enlightenment.[54] Without denying Gay's view of the continental Enlightenment as "the rise of modern paganism," and indeed by way of cooperating with Gay's effort to avoid "compact" definitions of the Enlightenment ("Hume's scepticism," "Diderot's vitalism," "Rousseau's passion"), I suggest in these pages that Wesley helped to assure both depth and breadth in the Anglo-American Enlightenment, which, largely because of him and Jonathan Edwards, lacked the narrow-if-not-benighted anticlericalism of the Enlightenment on the continent.[55] Insofar as a methodology of the entire Enlightenment, i.e., the Lockean, illuminates Wesley's method, he is part of the Enlightenment as generally understood, and I shall demonstrate that, besides playing an essential role in the spiritual enlightenment of England (if not America) during the eighteenth century, he fostered a particularly Lockean as well as generally intellectual kind of illumination and was thus an Enlightenment figure indeed.[56]

His definition of logic (he published a *Logic*) as "a proper use of deductive and inductive reasoning and of accurate evidence" (Curnock, 3:391) can serve, in advance of further argument, to epitomize his place in the Enlightenment. The definition's element of deduction is at once distinctly continental and sufficiently Lockean. The element of induction, though distinctly Lockean, coexists with a continental spirit, for, though nothing in the *Essay* supports the *cogito* as a decent place to start, a *cogito* that follows actualities imported into the mind through, say, the eye, is warmly embraced by Locke,[57] and Lockean reason relates to Cartesian rationalism insofar as even Lockean reason, making sense of sense-data through reflection, or intuition, is of the mind's very nature. In other words, Wesley's place in the Anglo-American Enlightenment is necessarily also in, or rather quite near, the Enlightenment as a whole. Since he rejected the doctrine of innate ideas, he regarded ideas as datable impressions on the mind's white paper, but, despite doubting the *cogito*, he sympathized with a Malebranchian metaphysic and, therefore, undoubtedly (if subconsciously) entertained the notion that ideas possess what Malebranche called "a most real [i.e., Platonic] existence": they are, said Malebranche, "beings and beings spiritual."[58] For Wesley, I suggest, as for Norris and Berkeley, and even as for Locke (insofar as Locke scattered through the *Essay* tinctures of Cartesian thought), ideas are somehow both independent mental entities and the products of shaping forces. Lockean ideas, after all, not only clarify the world, but also themselves become quasi-objective, for "Ideas," in Locke's twofold understanding, are not only "Perceptions in our Minds" but also "modifications in the Bodies that cause such Perceptions in us" (*Essay* 2.8.7; Nidditch, p. 134).

My argument that Wesley's thought is at once rigorous in its conformity to Lockean criteria and important in its impact, direct and indirect, upon English life and letters entails an explicit concern with the various strengths and characteristics of his language. His tones, it is clear, are quite deliberate in their precision and their variety. George Lawton, for example, examines such topics as Wesley's adjectives, his scriptural idiom, his use of familiar speech and aphorisms, his grasp of narrative vocabulary, his figures of speech, and even his lexicography; and T. Walter Herbert points to the "resonance and force" of the diction in Wesley's hymns and poetry.[59] Wesley's words, moreover, are carefully placed within divers forms. Herbert goes beyond an emphasis on tone, and beyond an emphasis on the poetry and hymns, to demonstrate the grasp of genre underlying Wesley's journals, his letters, and his editions of fiction and biography. His mastery of nonreligious as well as religious genres, to say nothing, for the moment, of his virtual invention of certain genres, provides the organizing principle of the long-needed and now-in-progress *Oxford Edition of Wesley's Works*.[60] Wesley's structuring powers, like his verbal choices, form an emphasis in Samuel J. Rogal's forthcoming contribution of *The Wesleys* to the Twayne English Author Series.[61] Small wonder, in view of what is being written about Wesley's style, that he admired Swift's description of good writing as "proper words in proper places."[62]

Thus Wesley's standing as a literary figure, i.e., his words in structures, has begun to receive the attention it deserves: his two million published words reward attention to form and style as well as content. His blend of his intellectual heritages, i.e., Anglican, Dissenting, Puritan, Arminian, Calvinist, Lutheran, Thomistic, Catholic, and Anglo-Catholic, emerges not only from his command of theme but also from his richness of diction, his complexity of tone, his trenchancy, and, in general, his production of such formal and informal, conventional and original genres as diaries, journals, letters, advice to the Methodists, Methodist polity and principles, polemics, appeals, open letters to exponents of religion, apologetics, expositions of doctrine, biblical exegesis, homilies, devotionals, hymns, prayers, and poems. If not from his flexible range of genres and tones, then from my argument in chapter 2, moreover, it should be clear that his language-as-language, though not the language, surely, of every writer, serenely but markedly plays with differing possibilities and so flatters even the theory of literature as paradox.

The record of his conversation, for one good example now, suggests that his language, if not paradoxical, is never quite predictable in expressing Christian truth, for his responses to his associates on August 1, 1745, at the New Room in Bristol, reveal his flair for distinctions and his sensitivity to nuance:

Q. Does not the truth of the gospel lie very near both to Calvinism and Antinomianism?

A. Indeed it does; as it were, within a hair's breadth: So that it is altogether foolish and sinful, because we do not quite agree either with one or the other, to run from them as far as ever we can.

Q. Wherein may we come to the very edge of Calvinism?

A. (1) In ascribing all good to the free grace of God. (2) In denying all natural free-will, and all power antecedent to grace. And, (3)

In excluding all merit from man; even for what he has or does by the grace of God.

Q. Wherein may we come to the edge of Antinomianism?

A. (1) In exalting the merits and love of Christ. (2) In rejoicing evermore. (Jackson, 8:284–85)

This language is theologically adventurous. Wesley's joy of salvation, to be sure, like his Christological reference, his emphasis on grace, and his animadversion on the natural state, is sufficiently orthodox. But his Delphic replies are not just bluntly authoritative: they evince his respect for doctrines that he usually found uncongenial (they run counter to his rather more characteristic strictures against Calvinism's "particular" redemption and the antinomian smugness of its "irresistible grace").[63] And his joy, though hardly anything so heretical as the *fröhliche Wissenschaft* of Nietzsche, i.e., the latter-day "antinomian" headiness of seeing beyond good and evil,[64] exceeds Arminian bounds: Wesley's joy becomes a controlling and almost more than merely theological tone of his replies, which gain in energy from the exuberance of his appreciation for shades of meaning and elements of soundness in a range of doctrines. His thought, in this passage, is rich and complex; for his mind, if not exactly philosophic, is almost so in its synthesizing powers and in its discovery of truth wherever truth is to be found; and his language, though keeping to the Christian-moral interpretation of life, and expressing nothing like Nietzschean nihilism, is nonetheless sufficiently susceptible to the nihilistic and Nietzschean criticism whereby Deconstructionists see all modes of expression as playful and life-affirming, but amoral and anything but Christian, acts of joyful wisdom.[65] It is logical, in any case, to read this particular record of Wesley's conversation as at once an illustration of his theological, nay, even philosophic, intelligence, and a token of his primal and literary sense of the antithetical.

Students of his language, despite recognizing it as allusive, have hardly begun to listen for either his generally philosophic or his particularly Lockean voice. They are aware, of course, of his theology: Lawton establishes the conceptual referents, and conceptual resonances, of Wesley's religious vocabulary.[66] But when they focus on his vocabulary, they are not concerned to relate it to his thought so much as to argue that it is well selected: his diction is indeed the boast of his style. Herbert, in pointing out (p. 41) that Wesley published an abridgment of the *Essay*, connects one of his most characteristic "genres" with the philosophy of John Locke: the abridgment, and Wesley's accompanying remarks on the *Essay*, form foci of my argument. But not even Herbert specifically raises the question of Wesley's Lockean echoes. And no one has asked whether Lockean language is included among his conscious and other than exclusively religious allusions. James L. Golden acknowledges that Wesley admired Locke's style (philosophy, as Golden also notes, was part of "*belles lettres*" for Wesley);[67] but Golden overlooks the fact that the most important background to Wesley's familiarity with such "new rhetoricians" as Alexander Gerard and Hugh Blair was none other than Locke's *Essay*;[68] and no one has hitherto been in a position to see whether the timely and more than theologically intellectual component of Wesley's expression owed any of its force to the forceful accents of Locke's philosophy. Perhaps the neglect of this question is due to the fact that only one student of Wesley's language, and only a few students of his thought, have looked for his relation to any nonreligious eighteenth-century disciplines whatever;[69] but for whatever reason, students of his language have not specifically asked whether either his form and diction or the concepts to which his words refer derive in part from the particularly Lockean context of his age.

It is time, then, to be specifically concerned with the form of his thought and to ask whether a Lockean idiom is central to his discourse. To Lawton's argument that "Wesley's prose is a stout three-fold cord having Scriptural, Classical, and colloquial strands interwoven" (p. 14), I add the thesis of a fourth and further reinforcing strand: the Lockean. While it is true that by the end of the nineteenth century Locke's style was considered dull, wooden, and unelevated, rather than anything like a model of good prose, it is my contention that Wesley shared the typical eighteenth-century evaluation as represented, say, by Goldsmith, who saw as much clarity and simplicity in Locke's writing as in his understanding.[70] It is my assumption that Locke's emphasis on clarity and simplicity—"[M]ethinks those, *who* pretend *seriously to search after*, or maintain *Truth*, should think themselves obliged to study, how they might deliver themselves without Obscurity, Doubtfulness, or Equivocation, to which Men's Words are naturally liable, if care be not taken" (*Essay* 3.11.3; Nidditch, p. 509)—not only gave Wesley a principle for criticizing terms like *legal* and *legality* as "odd, indeterminate, troublesome, silly and unmeaning" (Telford, 5:222; Jackson, 10:369), but also provided him with a guide for avoiding equivocation (though not, to be sure, multivocalization) in his own prose. His predilection for similes rests on the fact that as "miniature proverbs" "their basis is the facts of experience" (Lawton, p. 132); and it is specifically Lockean language of experience, as well as experiential language in general, which I think enabled him to raise his ineffable experience of grace to graceful and cogent expressions of methodology.

Experience, of course, is in one sense preverbal. I am thinking of Theodore Roszak's recent definition: "Let me, arbitrarily then, limit experience here to that which is not a report, but knowledge before it is reflected in words or ideas: immediate contact, direct impact, knowledge at its most personal level as it is lived."[71] But Wesley verbalized his experience. And *experience*, throughout this study, is conceived as a continuum from things, through ideas, to words. This conception is in line with Hans Aarsleff's recent book, *From Locke to Saussure: Essays on the Study of Language and Intellectual History*, which argues that even so continental a principle as Saussure's structuralist distinction between *signifier* and *signified* derives from such French *idéologues* as Condillac and, through these French Lockeists, from Locke's "double conformity" thesis that things may conform to ideas and that ideas may conform to words.[72] Experience, in Chomsky's neo-Cartesian view, is in no sense prior to language, but Derek Bickerton's recent book, *Roots of Language*,[73] concludes that prior to language is the experience of distinguishing between the specific and the nonspecific, between state and process, between boundedness and unboundedness in events, and between the causative and the noncausative. I argue, in other words, that John Wesley's method, if not always self-conscious, is assuredly present throughout his writings: his defenses of faith are enhanced by Locke's experiential idiom, which, though hardly so pervasive in Wesley's works as, say, his scriptural reference, is nonetheless so clearly a major feature of them as to demonstrate that besides being syncretic and steeped in tradition his theology *articulates* his understanding of empiricism.

I understand *literature*, then, in an inclusive sense indeed. In 1887, pursuant to arguing for English literature as a regular course of study at Oxford, Edward Dowden gave the following view of literary study in general:

> The study of literature, English or other, is not a study solely of what is graceful, attractive, and pleasure-giving in books; it attempts to understand the great thoughts of the great thinkers. To know Greek literature we must know Aristotle; to know French literature we must know Descartes. In English literature of the eighteenth century, Berkeley and Butler and Hume are greater names than Gray and Collins.[74]

Thus Dowden, though biographer of Shelley and critic of Shakespeare, seeks a broader literary canon than the works of major authors such as these, let alone such minor ones as Gray and Collins. E. D. Hirsch, Jr., distinguishing between "the narrower, more decadent conception expressed by *les belles lettres*" and the "grand, broad, and noble conception" expressed by "*les bonnes lettres*," quotes Dowden's remarks.[75] For Hirsch defines *literature* as including both conceptions and even as emphasizing *les bonnes lettres*: "Literature," declares Hirsch, is "everything worthy to be read, preferably the best thoughts expressed in the best manner, but above all the best thoughts." Exploring *les bonnes lettres* through the prose of Wesley and *les belles lettres* through English Romantic poetry, I relate the poetry to the prose and describe the link between the two as not so much hierarchical (is *bonnes* "better" than *belles*?) as dialectical: Romantic poetry, in England, is sufficiently broad and hardly decadent.

With respect to Wesley's prose there is much of "best manner": unfailing readability and no little grace. But there are "best thoughts" above all: I am concerned more with what it says than with the fact that it is written well. Conveying its attractiveness, but stressing its content, I show that empiricism is both a formative influence on it and a constant presence in it. I demonstrate that *theology* is neither so inclusive nor so accurate a label for it as *philosophical theology*. And I suggest that the breadth and substance of the prose together give Wesley a place in *les bonnes lettres* of eighteenth-century England at least as great as that of "Berkeley and Butler and Hume": Berkeley and Butler blend theology and philosophy, but Wesley is theological where Hume is not.

I propose, finally, that perhaps especially in its philosophical dimension the prose is a means of seeing the influence steadily and whole. I bring Wesley's thought, and even his manner, to bear on the manner and especially the thought of William Blake, William Wordsworth, Samuel Taylor Coleridge, Percy Bysshe Shelley, and John Keats. Thus affirming, with Dowden, that *les belles lettres* find intellectual contexts in *les bonnes lettres* ("To know Greek literature we must know Aristotle; to know French literature we must know Descartes"), I assume that to know English Romanticism one should know Wesley. His method, or rather the methodology of his Methodism, is traceable from its Lockean origins to its echoes in *les belles lettres*; for I reveal that the testimonial idiom of such a representative Romantic as Coleridge coexists with, and subtly transfigures, his empirical language; and I indicate, consistent with the lasting popularity of Wesley's works, that the Wesleyan blend of philosophy and theology is not simply available to, but significantly discernible in, the discourse of all five major poets.

These poets have never been read against this particular background, but this particular background, surely, is the next one that they should be read against. Wesley's faith, as I contend in *Wordsworth's "Natural Methodism,"* is more than simply prelusive to Wordsworth's theme of spiritual experience, and my essay on "Johnson's Wesleyan Connection," besides demonstrating that "the religious imagination for which Wesley was largely responsible relates directly to the history of Samuel Johnson's mind" (p. 144), suggests that, especially in England and conceivably in America and Germany, Romanticism is not so much "spilt religion" (in the phrase of T. E. Hulme) as religion "freely poured from renewed sources of spirituality" in the "age of spiritual awakening" (p. 168). (This age led, say, from Wesley's first itinerant steps to the partly Wesley-inspired Oxford Movement.) Despite the fact, however, that English Romantic religion is sufficiently strong, and sufficiently precise, to have shaped the faith of Victorian England, no one has attempted systematically to characterize the collective faith of English Romanticism in both the first and second generations.[76] And no one has systematically pursued what English Romantic faith has to do with English Romantic philosophy. It is well known, of course, that the poetry of English Romanticism has to do with Lockean thought so much as to fit Robert Langbaum's label for both the Romantic and the Victorian dramatic monologue: *The Poetry of Experience*;[77] Langbaum, and a host of other scholar-critics (see chapter 4), acknowledge that the priority of experience in English Romantic poetry derives, ultimately, from Locke's *Essay*. It is time, now, to test the experiential emphasis of Wesley's thought, i.e., his philosophical theology, as a means of exploring the experiential common ground of English Romantic faith and English Romantic philosophy; I argue, in so doing, that the primarily natural experience of Locke, and the primarily spiritual experience of Wesley, not only come together in Wesley's philosophical theology, but thence inform, directly and indirectly, a central dialectic of the poets. Not only does the almost religious quality of their emotion relate to Wesley's emotional faith, but a Wesleyan blend of "spiritual sense" and a posteriori reason forms part of what they all retained from the century and the place in which all of them were born.

Thus Wesley's method, in the pages of this book, is a sufficiently high-minded (if not always sublime) antecedent to Romanticism, for these major Romantics (if not other Romantics in England and elsewhere) reflect in their formulations of experience the Wesleyan alignment of theology with a standard philosophy of their age. Besides placing Wesley's thought in a mainstream current of Western philosophy from the late seventeenth century to the mid-nineteenth, I lay out an approach to Romanticism along lines of the following premises in their cumulative effect: the history of Wesley's mind features the philosophy of Locke; Locke's continuum from physical sensation to "human understanding" contributes method to Wesley's account of saving faith; Wesley's religious "epistemology," i.e., his philosophy of religion, helped to assure a theological as well as philosophical tone among formulations of experience in late eighteenth- and early nineteenth-century England; the Wesleyan mode of experience defines a criterion of truth in the most important genre of British Romantic literature; the quality of experience in English Romantic poetry is spiritual as well as natural; Wesley's philosophical theology is a satisfyingly complex, appropriately interdisciplinary, aptly inclusive, and almost only available model for the broad concept of experience everywhere implicit in English Romantic epistemology; the priority of experience in the empirical philosophy, and the importance of experience in the Wesleyan faith,[78] of eighteenth-century England provide, together, a sufficiently synoptic background to British Romanticism; English "Romantic origins" are discoverable on the Wesleyan, i.e., most broadly experiential, ground of British Romantic exemplars;[79] and *British Romanticism*, finally, is yet a conceivably single concept. Insofar, in sum, as I advance towards "our unified field theory of British Romanticism" by offering a perspective on English Romantic poetry at once empirical and evangelical, Wesley's place in literary history rivals his place in the history of religion and in the history of ideas.

One

Young Man Wesley's Lockean Connection

It is feasible, here, as prologue to listening for Lockean overtones in Wesley's prose, to search out Lockean roots of his theology. Overlooking the fact that many of the theologians whom "the young Mr. Wesley" studied, to wit, Benjamin Hoadly, Isaac Barrow, John Tillotson, Nicolas Malebranche, John Norris, George Berkeley, William Wollaston, William Derham, Samuel Clarke, Richard Fiddes, and Isaac Watts, were often philosophical, and even sometimes Lockean, theologians, V. H. H. Green does not ask whether Locke, through the spectrum of theologians whom he influenced, exerted a formative influence on the century's most influential religious thinker.[1] I demonstrate that the *Essay*'s effect on theology, and even the *Essay* itself, were unmistakable presences in Wesley's early milieu and, thence, his early thought.

His understanding of revelation, for example, some thirteen years before Aldersgate, was expressed in terms of Locke. Lockean reason had been described by Richard Fiddes as in no small degree responsive to *traditional* revelation; for Fiddes, in his argument that scripture is the most substantial reason for faith, had drawn upon Locke's view of faith as "reasonable"; and "That definition of Faith which Dr. Fiddes sets down," i.e., "a firm persuasion built upon substantial reasons," had been accepted by Wesley as "the only true one."[2] Then, on June 18, 1725, in a letter to his mother Susanna, he exclaimed that he wanted to "perceive" the graces and "be sensible of" the indwelling spirit of Christ (Telford, 1:20). To "be sensible of," of course, means to be conscious of, but, together with Wesley's desire to "perceive" the graces, the phrase is more than merely reminiscent of Lockean sense perception. His yearning for *immediate* revelation, in other words, like his endorsement of scriptural priority in rational experience, connotes Lockean method.

That method, indeed, in that same year, was described by him as more than merely conducive to faith; for on July 29, 1725, he wrote to Susanna that "there is . . . no Belief, and consequently no Faith," "without Rational Grounds";[3] and *rational grounds* is unmistakably Lockean phraseology. *Grounds*, for example, denoting terrene reason as distinct, say, from the relatively ungrounded (if not necessarily groundless) mentalism of Descartes, is Locke's very word:

> The *grounds* of [probability] are, in short, these two following:
>
> First, The conformity of any thing with our own Knowledge, Observation, and Experience.
>
> Secondly, The Testimony of others, vouching their Observation and Experience. (*Essay* 4.15.4; Nidditch, p. 656. My italics—RB.)

And *rational*, far from merely describing just anyone's process of thought, whenever and however one thinks, labels Locke's sense-grounded method of mind: "Mind[,] if it will proceed *rationally*, ought to examine all the grounds of Probability" (*Essay* 4.15.5; Nidditch, p. 656. My italics—RB).

As early as 1725, then, working apparently with the *Essay*'s formulations, Wesley reached for a philosophically satisfying faith. "Faith," he wrote in the letter of July 29, is a "Species of Belief," and in that same letter he defined belief as "Assent to a Proposition upon Rational Grounds." Locke, similarly, not only taught that sense perception gauges beliefs (belief, he writes, is "the entertainment the Mind gives to Propositions" of probability: *Essay* 4.15.3; Nidditch, p. 655), but also suggests that sense perception relates to faith: "Faith" consists with the "Dictates of Reason" and rests on the "Testimony" of "undoubted Witnesses," i.e., on their sense-based as well as rational experience (*Essay* 4.18.10; Nidditch, p. 696). Nowhere, though, does Locke associate faith with belief, whereas Wesley, in so doing, all but states that belief can be a ground of faith as well. At any rate, his phrasing suggests that his faith in One who acts within, yet is other than the world, derives in part from the *Essay*; for Locke's "fundamental theism," his view of God as transcendent and indwelling, rests on sense perception of order among cosmic and quotidian phenomena; and Wesley's theism rests not on the Bible alone, at least insofar as in this letter he everywhere indicates his inclination towards the Lockean, and moderate because theistical, form of natural religion.[4]

His study of the *Essay* was all but direct at least by October 12, 1725, when he finished reading *Anti-scepticism: or, Notes upon each chapter of Mr. Locke's Essay* (1702) by Henry Lee, D. D., Rector of Tichmarsh in Northamptonshire (see *The Young Mr. Wesley*, p. 71n); Wesley knew that the *Essay* can be taken as inimical to any sort of faith. The letters to Susanna, however, seeking a Lockean means of encompassing saving and speculative faith, give reason to think that he saw faith as compatible with the *Essay*'s skeptical method. The letters even give reason to think that he saw faith as reconcilable with the *Essay*'s view of matter, for, on November 22, 1725, in a third letter to his mother (Telford, 1:23−25), he opposed Berkeley's anti-Lockean denial of matter. Wesley was fair in his summary of Berkelian argument: "no sensible thing can exist but in a mind . . . no idea exists but in some mind." But he found immaterialism over-ingenious: "How miserably does he play with the words 'idea' and 'sensation'!" Perhaps Lockean sensation in conjunction with Lockean idea, i.e., the Lockean balance between subject and object, forms the underlying assumption of his strictures. At any rate, he concluded that in *Three Dialogues between Hylas and Philonous* (1713) Berkeley "said nothing at all," or rather "advanced a palpable falsehood": Wesley knew that matter had often seemed correspondent to the "things" of God.

If, then, young Wesley did not take the *Essay* as completely true, he more than merely took it into account, and, if he did not regard it as a "canonical" object of study, he nonetheless showed that as a man of distinctively religious temperament he was especially capable of a Lockean point of view. Whether or not he accepted the *Essay*'s argument that objects correspond to particular ideas in the mind, and whether or not he directly drew upon the *Essay*'s form of natural religion, he evidently tried to employ Lockean method to articulate, or at least to intimate, a correspondence between sense perception and receptivity to immediate and traditional forms of grace. His search was for an inclusive and intellectually up to date form of faith.

The search went on. During the early weeks of 1727, for example, as though to follow through on the letters to Susanna, Wesley devoted part of Friday mornings to direct study of the *Essay* (*The Young Mr. Wesley*, p. 116n). And on "Xtmass Eve, 1730," with a flourish of his pen, he finished filling a 103-page bound quarto notebook with his abridgment of *The Procedure, Extent, and Limits of Human Understanding* (1728) by Peter Browne (d. 1735), Bishop of Cork and Ross.[5] The bishop's title, and his title as bishop, indicate what his treatise is: a theologizing of the *Essay*. Wesley's abridgment, more than three months in the making,[6] marks the resumption of his all but direct study of the *Essay*, for the manuscript abridgment by its very existence demonstrates that *The Procedure* held his attention. Perhaps his flourish of the pen was his mark of satisfaction with the coincidence of Christmas Eve and intellectual synthesis.

The manuscript, though obscured among uncatalogued particulars, is clearly important: it stands out in a category of its own among the letters, diaries, accounts, and sermon registers in the J. J. Colman Collection, an individual gathering within the Methodist Archives at the John Rylands University Library of Manchester.[7] It was written, moreover, at an early point of the sixteen years (1725–41) covered in Colman and so promises to shed light on the pre-revival period of Wesley's ministry and the formative stages of his intellectual life. Richard Heitzenrater, currently engaged in decoding the Colman diaries, will publish much of Wesley's preconversion thought,[8] and I am convinced that the Colman abridgment forms the basis for a parallel undertaking, namely, determining the origin, nature, and impact of the evangelist's philosophical theology. It is time, in other words, to read the abridgment as an index to Wesley's understanding of Locke and to see it as a turning point in young man Wesley's quest: the years from 1725 through 1730, covering his ordination as deacon, his graduation as Master of Arts from Christ Church, Oxford, his election as Fellow of Lincoln College, his curacy at Wroot, his ordination as priest, and his return to Lincoln, where as tutor he remained until 1735, were pivotal not simply for his particularly theological and generally religious kinds of development, but especially, through *The Procedure*, for his education in philosophical theology. I propose, specifically, on the circumstantial but intriguing and admissible evidence of the manuscript that if Wesley did not find in *The Procedure* a philosophically satisfying faith, he found therein a Locke-derived theology with which he was more than merely comfortable. The manuscript, according to Hindley, indicates that Wesley "imbibed" Browne's "presuppositions."[9] But neither Hindley nor anyone else fully uses either *The Procedure* or the manuscript as documents in the background of Wesley's thought. It is time, by way of asking to what extent his Methodism derived from the method of the *Essay*, to identify Browne's presuppositions and to lay bare their configuration in the manuscript. It is possible, thereby, to create after Wesley his more than merely distilled, i.e., his representative, understanding of a theological and philosophical continuum from knowledge and belief to natural and revealed religion.

As part of Church history and the history of ideas, if for no other reason, it is important to remember Browne's contribution to philosophical theology. A. R. Winnett in by far the most thorough study of Browne's thought demonstrates that *The Procedure* expanded the room Locke saved for mystery in religion: Browne follows the *Essay*'s philosophical and theological principle that there are things beyond reason in the rationally attested system of Christianity.[10] Winnett demonstrates, moreover, that Brownean reason infers divine order from sense impression: *The Procedure*, like the *Essay*, argues that the eye anchors the mind at once to "see" into the spirit of things and to rise, with a measure of assurance, to an immediate and accessible (i.e., theistical) form of natural religion.[11] Winnett's study, then, showing Browne's Lockean contribution to natural as well as revealed religion, establishes a full perspective on the way the *Essay* was employed to provide philosophical substance for eighteenth-century religious thought. *The Procedure* everywhere maintains that human understanding, though limited to a wise passiveness in regard to Christian mystery, is well designed to acquire a philosophy of faith.

Winnett, in demonstrating that the full range of Lockean method pervades Browne's "procedure," suggests that Browne is if anything more consistent than Locke in adhering to the sensationalistic and rational theory of belief and knowledge.[12] Be that as it may, Browne's consistent adherence to the theory and his adaptation of it to faith are especially implicit in his characteristic citations of Heb. 11:1: "Now faith is the substance of things hoped for, the evidence of things not seen."[13] This verse, to be sure, concludes with the suggestion that sense experience is of no help in acquiring faith. But faith, as access to the un*seen*, is nonetheless depicted in relation to sense-based method. For the definition alludes to physical vision not simply to reject it but to intimate the appearance of God's things. Faith, according to this definition, relates to reason as well; a statement of Hindley, despite his term *rationalism* (which hardly names the place of reason in eighteenth-century England), is helpful in this regard: "Hebrews 11:1 has a philosophical cast peculiarly in tune with eighteenth-century rationalism, and suggests at once that the definition of faith which these philosophers could accept was the one which the Bible offered: faith is primarily the attitude of mind which believes truths about an unseen spiritual world which reason is unable to discover but which satisfies the demands of reason for evidence" (p. 208). *Evidence*, in the definition if not precisely in Hindley's usage, implies that human *feeling* can be interpreted by human understanding as a basis of faith: "things *hoped* for" are data of experience and so provide an at least quasi-sensationalistic grounding for the rational method implicit in the verse. Heb. 11:1, then, in its "epistemological" dimension, sanctions and largely underlies Browne's always philosophical theology.

His doctrine of analogy, among those who have deemed his thought worthy of attention, is his most distinctive theme,[14] but no one notices his theme's nearby source in the *Essay*. Locke argues that "Analogy is the only help we have" in inferring unseen causes:

Thus finding in all parts of the Creation, that fall under humane Observation, that there is a gradual connexion of one with another, without any great or discernible gap between, in all that great variety of Things we see in the World, which are so closely linked together, that, in the several ranks of Beings, it is not easy to discover the bounds betwixt them, we have reason to be perswaded, that by such gentle steps Things ascend upwards in degrees of Perfection. . . . Observing . . . gradual and gentle descents downwards in those parts of the Creation, that are beneath Man, the rule of Analogy may make it probable, that it is so also in Things above us, and our Observation; and that there are several ranks of intelligent Beings, excelling us in several degrees of Perfection, ascending upwards towards the infinite Perfection of the Creator, by gentle steps and differences. . . . [A] wary reasoning from Analogy leads us often into the discovery of Truths . . . which would otherwise lie concealed. (*Essay* 4.16.12; Nidditch, pp. 665–67)

Thus Locke emphasizes the transcendent otherness of the Creator; but Locke also intimates, in this passage, the accessibility of divine truth; and he implies that just as there is unity among things above, and just as there is unity among things below, so there is correspondence, if not continuity, between the natural and the spiritual worlds. *Essay* 4's advocacy of analogy is anticipated by *Essay* 3's reservations about metaphor: Locke's fledgling theory of language devalues metaphor because of the arbitrary nature of its comparisons.[15] The *Essay's* linguistic position, then, proposes analogy as a nonfigurative and philosophically correct means of expressing a proportion of things. And Locke even recommends analogy as his "great Rule of Probability" in theological inquiry: Lockean analogy, i.e., the principle of using what is known to reach partial understanding of what otherwise lies entirely outside the range of human knowledge, establishes on the relative certainty of natural knowledge the probable truth of at least a natural religion. Browne's doctrine, however much it works against that of St. Thomas,[16] grows immediately out of the *Essay* insofar as Locke's predilection for analogy forms a recognizable part of what Browne has to say:

Metaphor is mostly in Words, and is a Figure of Speech; Analogy a Similis Ratio or Proportion of Things, and an excellent and necessary Method or Means of Reason and Knowledge. Metaphor uses Ideas of Sensation to express Immaterial and heavenly Objects, to which they can bear no real Resemblance or Proportion [e.g., "I am the Good Shepherd"]; Analogy substitutes the Operations of our Soul, and notions mostly formed out of them, to represent Divine Things to which they bear a Real tho' Unknown Correspondency and Proportion [e.g., "God is love"]. In short, Metaphor has no real Foundation in the Nature of the Things compared; Analogy is founded in the Very Nature of the Things on both Sides of the Comparison. (*The Procedure*, pp. 141–42)

Browne's doctrine constitutes a distinctive result of his agreement with the *Essay*; had Winnett, for example, linked his discussion of this particular theme to its counterpart in the *Essay* he would have strengthened his argument for the philosophical roots of Browne's thought.

Browne's content, though, is finally his, for his doctrine extends beyond natural to revealed religion. The above passage, for example, suggests that the doctrine embraces immediate as well as traditional revelation, for Browne not only alludes to the biblical language for God's nature but also implies divine self-disclosure in "the Operations of our Soul," wherein love, for example, is known preverbally and hence with no mediation indeed as both divine in origin and human in possession.

In other words, and this is especially what no one notices, Browne's most original contribution to Lockean thought, and to Anglican, is his by no means antirational and almost sense-like intimation that the Spirit continues to witness. Churchmen just preceding Browne can hardly be said to have distinguished themselves by their theology of the Spirit: spiritual theology occupies a minor place in the works of such Cambridge Platonists as Henry More, Ralph Cudworth, George Rust, and Henry Hallywell, and an even smaller place in the works of such Latitudinarians as Edward Stillingfleet, John Tillotson, and Robert South; for these "Anglican rationalists," or rather these reason oriented Anglicans, specifically reacted against the Puritans' antirational emphasis on spiritual experience.[17] Browne, for his part, though a rational enough Anglican, makes bold to suggest throughout *Procedure* 2.7–9 that the Spirit acts in the present. The opening passage of 2.7 admits of "those relations we bear to God, and he to us, which are entirely new and indiscoverable by reason" (p. 291); and it is clear from the emphasis on these relations as nonrational and current and from the use of the first person that the reference is to immediate revelation distinct from the long-established and rationally attestable Word of God. *Procedure* 2.8, moreover, not only alludes to Pentecost, where the Spirit conferred "grace and favours" upon the Apostles, but also asserts that the Spirit "lifts men into service" (p. 309); thus Browne points to the effect of grace that continues in the present. Finally, the beginning of 2.9 presents *The Procedure*'s most explicit expression of the Spirit's ways with living men:

> [W]e are temples of the Holy Ghost . . . he dwells in us . . . by him the love of God is shed abroad in our hearts . . . he helps our infirmities . . . and enables us to mortify the deeds of the body; and . . . he fills us with righteousness, and peace, and joy. (p. 334)

The passage is replete with scriptural allusions (cf. Rom. 5:5, 8, 13, 26; 1 Cor. 6:19; and James 3:8). But Browne calculates his *us*'s, his *our* (the *our* in *our hearts* is the only first person in the biblical language), and his *we*: he introduces an affective rhetoric to bring home to his readers the Spirit's postbiblical activity.

Browne's spiritual theology, then, pivotal in Anglican thought, signals the Anglican emphasis on spiritual experience during the rest of the eighteenth century and into the nineteenth. As late as 1762, of course, it was possible for a prominent Anglican to devalue immediate revelation altogether: Bishop Warburton, mid-century inheritor of Latitudinarian thought, took the position that the Spirit's operations do not extend beyond the apostolic age.[18] But Wesley's announcement of a second apostolic age was the dominant influence in the Church of England from the rise of the Evangelical Movement through the time of the Clapham Sect.

Browne's theology of immediate revelation, significantly, by no means entirely departs from the *Essay*. It is true that no less a rational Anglican than Locke fostered the received idea that claims to immediate revelation are likely nothing more than dangerous enthusiasm:

> This I take to be properly Enthusiasm, which though founded neither on Reason, nor Divine Revelation, but rising from the Conceits of a warmed or over-weening Brain, works yet, where it once gets footing, more powerfully on the Perswasions and Actions of Men, than either of those two, or both together: Men being most forwardly obedient to the impulses they receive from themselves; And the whole Man is sure to act more vigorously, where the whole Man is carried by a natural Motion. (*Essay* 4.19.7; Nidditch, p. 699)

Locke remembered the Civil Wars and, like Latitudinarians and Cambridge Platonists, reacted against what he regarded as pretentions to spiritual access among the Puritans. But while very far from encouraging any expectation of direct disclosures, he is also far from ruling them out.

For the *Essay* makes bold to suggest that Englishmen, among God's chosen, are potential recipients of extraordinary communication:

> God I own cannot be denied to be able to enlighten the Understanding by a Ray darted into the Mind immediately from the Fountain of Light: This . . . he has promised to do, and who then has so good a title to expect it, as Those who are his peculiar People, chosen by him and depending on him?[19]

Browne means to draw out Locke's implication that spiritual influx can supplement biblical truth and natural knowledge: the Spirit, besides inspiring the Apostles "with the gift of tongues and miracles," gave them "wisdom and knowledge," and led them "into all truth" (*The Procedure*, p. 334). Although *truth, knowledge,* and *wisdom* exemplify general vocabulary and are common in the Bible (cf. Acts 6:3; 1 Cor. 12:8; Eph. 1:8, 17; and 1 Tim. 2:4), this particular diction resonates within the largely philosophical context of *The Procedure* and therefore takes on a philosophic connotation. The sequence parallels the stages of empirical method: *wisdom* arising from sense experience makes up *knowledge* of whatever *truth* is possible to attain to.

Browne, in reaffirming the Spirit's witness, ran the risk of seeming enthusiastic, especially since he specifically addressed *Procedure* 2.7–9 to "Deists" and "unbelievers of all ranks and degrees" (*The Procedure*, p. 329); but his purpose was clear enough: he used the "philosophical" language of the Bible to describe the Spirit, in relation to philosophical method, as a pararational and parasensationalistic means of acquiring truth. Thus *The Procedure* suggests that the philosophy of experience prepares one for an emotional and intellectual acceptance of the Spirit's ministrations as theological equivalents for distinct impressions from without. Browne implies that spiritual experience, though taking up where reason and the senses leave off, is precisely analogous to natural experience: with Lockean phraseology he concludes that immediate revelation not only "greatly enlarges our intellect," but also "gives an immense scope to human understanding" (pp. 334–35). He invites his readers to consider Locke's philosophy as so much the right way to knowledge that it even corresponds to, if not resembles, how one "perceives" and "senses" God's ongoing work in the world. Subtly, but with no apology, *The Procedure* attempts nothing less than the translation of the *Essay* into the idiom of divine self-disclosure. For Browne carried the warmest Christian heritage into the otherwise largely dispassionate discourse of early modern thought.

Epistemological language, then, or rather proto-epistemological language, enabled Bishop Browne to encompass revelation in particular and theism in general. Browne attempted, thus, to resolve an emergent dualism between speculative and saving faith, a dichotomy that threatened to obscure the Anglican *via media*. Not simply was he undisturbed by any skepticism in the *Essay*, he was also intent upon canonizing the *Essay* by linking its method to the open mind and receptive spirit of faith in One who speaks directly as well as through the Bible and the book of nature. Small wonder, in view of Wesley's attraction to the *Essay*, that soon after *The Procedure* appeared he mastered it with a scribal fidelity.

The manuscript not only shows that Wesley considered the *Essay* in relation to faith, but also offers clues to how he did so. The mere existence of the manuscript, of course, does not necessarily indicate that Wesley endorsed *The Procedure*: he often objected to works he carefully read; and some of his more than two hundred abridgments include matter with which he disagreed.[20] As for the abridgment in question, he hardly swallowed Browne's prose whole: not only did Wesley excise prolixity, he also omitted *Procedure* 3.[21] His abridgment, however, by its very existence, demonstrates his interest in, if not subscription to, *The Procedure*'s attempt at synthesis; and his omission of *Procedure* 3 suggests that he especially approved what he included of Browne's argument.[22] Wesley's response to *The Procedure*, at any rate, and hence his early understanding of the *Essay* as imprimatured philosophy, can be inferred from the amount and arrangement of what he chose to represent. The abridgment amounts to an edition, or even an indirect commentary, and it is time, as a means of fully determining young Wesley's perspective on Locke's sometimes theological philosophy, to correlate *The Procedure* with the manuscript.

For one thing the abridgment gives pride of place to *The Procedure*'s philosophical view of revelation. *Procedure* 2.7–9, which everywhere tries to reconcile immediate as well as traditional revelation with Lockean method, is fully represented in the final thirty-three pages of the manuscript, which, like this central section of *The Procedure*, elaborate Locke's definition of revelation as "natural Reason enlarged by a new set of Discoveries communicated by God immediately, which Reason vouches the truth of, by the Testimony and Proofs it gives, that they come from God."[23] The abridgment, indeed, highlights the passages from 2.7–9 already quoted here for their thematic and structural significances.[24] Thus the accident or rather coincidence of the abridgment suggests that *The Procedure* was an intellectual source for Wesley's emphasis on the Holy Spirit. Young Wesley, in accordance with Locke's implication and Browne's argument, stressed in his abridgment that the Bible and the Spirit's witness supplement natural knowledge without violating a fundamental philosophic principle: reason, of the specifically philo-sophical kind so receptive to evidence as to be grounded therein, is re-moved from revelation but construes it, nonetheless, as logical, cohesive, and true. And revelation, in the manuscript as in *The Procedure*, meets the sensationalistic criterion insofar as Browne suggests that as one sees a shepherd, so one feels the love of God: the abridgment allots five pages to the two brief chapters, 1.6 and 1.9, in which *The Procedure* formulates the doctrine of analogy.[25]

The abridgment, moreover, thoroughly reflects the theistical character of Browne's natural religion. *Procedure* 2.6 is an exhaustive commentary upon Locke's definition of reason as "natural Revelation, whereby the eternal Father of Light, and Fountain of all Knowledge communicates to Mankind that portion of Truth, which he has laid within the reach of their natural Faculties"; and the manuscript devotes thirty-four pages to this chapter of *The Procedure*, a chapter arguing that through the "natural faculties," i.e., the faculties of sense, reason draws knowledge of God's existence and partial knowledge of His nature from the book of crea-tion.[26] Here, for example, in a passage construing Heb. 11:1, is 2.6's sug-gestion that even "Evangelical Faith," i.e., complete trust in New Testa-ment Revelation, is somehow dependent on or at least strengthened by the rational empiricism of theistical natural religion, i.e., natural objects as "Symbols and Representatives" of "Things Inconceivable":

> Thus we see that Men must Know, before they can rightly Believe; and have a full Conviction of their Judgment upon sufficient Evi-dence, before there is any closing of the Will to Complete the Na-ture of Evangelical Faith; which is literaly as the Apostle defines it, the Evidence of Things not seen, or the Assent of the Understand-ing to the Truth and Existence of Things Inconceivable, upon cer-tain and evident Proof of their Reality in their Symbols and Repre-sentatives. (*The Procedure*, p. 250)

Young Wesley, then, understood rational and sensationalistic method as an indirect access to God and even as a precondition of belief in the Bible.

And finally, the abridgment fully represents Browne's endorsement of Locke's philosophy for its own sake. The following principles of the *Es-say* are seconded throughout *Procedure* 1: "ideas of sensation," or rather, ideas acquired through the senses, being simple, immediate, direct, clear, and distinct, form the basis of knowledge; and reason, raising sense impression to the level of knowledge, completes empirical method.[27] The manuscript gives twenty pages to *Procedure* 1.[28] Wesley, then, in 1730 if not before, understood the full range of Lockean empiricism as an intellectual given, and it seems fair to go further and say that he would hardly have committed so much space to a system of inquiry with which he differed in any significant way.

The themes of reason and evidence are universally acknowledged as central to *The Procedure*, but no one notices that the theme of evangelical faith, at least in the passage above from 2.6, somehow synthesizes them: *Evangelical Faith* occupies the pivot of the passage and is conditioned by such diction as *Know, Judgment, Evidence, Will, Assent, Understanding, Evidence, Proof,* and *Reality*. This philosophical context suggests that Browne was attempting to define evangelical faith, as well as faith in general, according to the model of empirical thought. However defined, evangelical faith epitomizes what must have appealed to the founder-to-be of the Evangelical Movement: although Wesley does not include the passage above, he renders thirteen lines of the thirty-eight-line paragraph in which it appears, and he represents eight of the twelve other passages from 2.6 in which Browne uses empirically rational language to explore the nature of "Evangelical Faith."[29] I propose, at any rate, that if Browne's attempt to understand such faith in the context of philosophy is not the most pervasive or even the most original part of his thought, it is the part that most directly points to the philosophical underpinnings of Wesley's faith. For a full understanding of faith in eighteenth-century England, in other words, it is desirable to concentrate on Browne's use of this particular phrase not only in these lines near the center of his central chapter, but also elsewhere among *The Procedure*'s important structural points, to encompass the experiential and even particularly Lockean scope of revealed as well as natural religion.

With regard, first, to what Browne means by *Faith*, he suggests in the 2.6 passage that it raises sense impression to the level of religious knowledge. Asserting that men must "have a full Conviction of their Judgment upon sufficient Evidence," he associates a philosophical faculty, i.e., judgment, with a religious emotion, i.e., conviction, and thereby certifies the religious as well as philosophical validity of "Evidence." Faith, then, a mind based sixth "sense" receiving and interpreting sense data, extends Lockean reason.

Thus, the passage builds upon Locke's intimation that the mind's experience of nature informs the faculty of faith and strengthens it to conceive of God and the unseen spiritual world. It bears reiteration, here, that though faith and empiricism appear mutually exclusive, the one referring to observation and experience of the natural world, the other to spiritual apprehension of religious concepts, Locke was not concerned to advocate his philosophy at the expense of religious tradition. Rather, seeking to reconcile religion with his method, he broadened the definition of faith to include the spiritual interpretation of natural objects as "Symbols and Representatives" of God. *Belief, Conviction*, and even *Faith*—these occur in the *Essay* along with what Wordsworth, in "Lines Composed a Few Miles above Tintern Abbey on Revisiting the Banks of the Wye During a Tour, July 13, 1798," calls "the language of the sense" (line 108). Locke distinguished between philosophy and religion not to devalue religion, but to recognize where the two disciplines merge, and where faith takes up: faith, he felt, expands the range of knowledge. Thus the philosophical climate favored what one finds in Browne's passage, namely, the suggestion that faith is partly "natural": the constructive intent of Lockean method is consistent with Browne's effort to understand faith in the context of philosophy.

Indeed, the passage especially well represents his concept of that method as faith's precondition, if not accompaniment. At the beginning, "Men must Know, before they can rightly Believe," the passage suggests that knowledge causes faith, or rather that faith is a product of the mind's interaction with the world. Thus Browne assumes that reasoned synthesis of experiential data must equip the mind before there can be any "reasonable" expectation of faith: faith is no more innate than ideas written by experience on the mind's blank tablet—and no less dependent than reason upon the nourishment of experience. In short, he held natural knowledge to be at once a ground of faith and a continuing ingredient thereof. To put it another way: he held that faith, following upon disciplined pursuit of natural knowledge and far from being the result of a blind leap, partly consists of such knowledge.

The passage, however, goes beyond the *Essay* at last, and recognizes that faith overflows the bounds of empiricism: Browne suggests, for example, that in bringing one to the pitch of natural philosophy, the "Will" arrives where faith alone continues the quest for truth; and in the allusion to Heb. 11:1—"[F]aith is literaly as the Apostle defines it, the Evidence of Things not seen"—*Evidence* refers not so much to sense data, and hence not so much to empiricism per se, as to the paraempirical theology of Browne, wherein data of spiritual influx impress the mind and constitute faith's unsensuous, ineffable essence. The passage, in other words, understands faith nonempirically and empirically: Browne affirms a continuum from one kind of meaning to another. In an age when seeing had almost the religious quality of believing, he found grounds for religious belief in the things he naturally saw. He thereby extended empirical standards to a distinctively eighteenth-century understanding of faith wherein faith is partially grounded in the senses and virtually equivalent to the shaping of intellect. In this particular historical sense, faith is something natural: it grows with the mind's outward reach and thus accords with accumulative wisdom. In this same sense, however, faith is something spiritual: it conceives of things beyond this world, i.e., of what Wordsworth in "Elegiac Stanzas Suggested by a Picture of Peele Castle, In a Storm, Painted by Sir George Beaumont" (1807) calls "The light that never was, on sea or land" (line 14), but does so in relation to natural things. Thus Browne implies that empirical philosophy is analogous to faith: as reason perceives what the senses grasp, so faith apprehends the things of God; and Browne's faith is never antiempirical; for even his nonempirical faith is included in the catalogue of experience.

And finally, his passage confers Lockean meaning upon *Evangelical* as well as *Faith*. It is true that, unlike *Faith*, *Evangelical* occurs nowhere in the *Essay*. It is true, too, that Carl F. H. Henry's recent description of "evangelical faith" as "biblical essentials"[30] suffices for general understanding. Browne's passage, however, with such sense-related phraseology as "sufficient Evidence," and "certain and evident Proof . . . in . . . Symbols and Representatives," causes *Evangelical* to connote sense experience. This connotation, this usage, is consistent with at least one evangelical tradition: the Great Commission, with which Matthew closes his Gospel, urges Christ's followers to spread the good news; and such evangelism, like Locke's philosophy, assumes that one infers from what one sees and hears a knowledge otherwise inconceivable, a certainty with unique and pivotal bearing upon one's subsequent life and development. Browne's use of *Evangelical*, though, is linked not so much to the Bible as to the empiricist state of philosophic art: his language is more Lockean than scriptural; and his definition of evangelical faith can be said to extend both spiritual validity and philosophical authority to such "Representatives" of present experience as, presumably, eighteenth-century spreaders of the Word. *Evangelical*, in other words, "fundamental" to Browne's language, not only points in the historic Evangelical direction of English faith, but also raises the distinct possibility that such faith included an experiential component describably philosophical and even precisely Lockean. At any rate, his passage is a concentrated means of grasping his juxtaposition of Locke's thought and a kind of faith not ever before so explicitly associated with philosophy; experience, for reasons philosophical as well as theological, retains for Browne the potential for revelation.

Small wonder, then, that in *Procedure* 2.9 Browne culminates this theology of immediate revelation with a second, and I think similarly philosophical, definition of "Evangelical Faith": "an Assent to a revealed and express Proposition upon the Testimony of God" (p. 335). Since Browne's argument tends towards this definition, and, above all, since Wesley's abridgment closes with it (see the manuscript, pp. 102–3), it, too, should bear no little weight of consideration.

The definition, like the one in 2.6, is informed by Lockean thought and all but duplicates, indeed, Locke's definition of faith as "the Assent to any Proposition, not . . . made out by the Deductions of Reason; but upon the Credit of the Proposer, as coming from God, in some extraordinary way of Communication" (*Essay* 4.18.2; Nidditch, p. 689). *Assent*, in this definition and in Browne's, is neutral, formal, and official, and denotes mental acceptance and approval of a proposal that does not concern oneself. The mind, then, is according to this denotation a detached and passive recipient of external and objective truths of revelation, whether immediate or traditional. However else he thought of faith, Browne evidently accepted Locke's view of it as an intellectual and nonpassional acknowledgment of religious truth; thus, part of what makes Browne's theology philosophical is his objective Lockean tone. But early-century significations, in the air as well as the *Essay*, suggest that his language includes subjective as well as objective levels. *Assent*, besides denoting response to stimuli and besides indicating acquiescence to objective truth, signifies concurrence of the will and so connotes mental activity. According to this connotation, the mind sanctions possibilities of truth and so becomes a location thereof. *Assent* implies subjectivity in possession of unseen objects of faith.

This rich doubleness of implication is borne out by other language in Browne's second passage. *Testimony*, for example, meaning *evidence* as well as *attestation in support of a fact*, is both subjective and objective, and points to the mind's affinity for and appropriation of external reality. Locke employs the term in both senses. Not only does he argue that "the Testimony of others" vouches "their Observation and Experience" of the objective world; he also suggests that, in and of itself, testimony is an avenue to knowledge: "A credible Man vouching his Knowledge of [the Being and Existence of the thing it self], is a good proof."[31] Thus Locke accords full methodological validity to the concept of testimony; and Browne, in extending the concept to the realm of faith, suggests that religious attestation participates in, as well as corresponds to, revealed truth.

The two levels of *express Proposition* particularly imply correspondence between mind and nonmental religious truth—or even a near identity of seeking and finding. Both words, during the early century, carried specifically Christological, and therefore especially objective and mind independent, freight: *express* was reminiscent of Heb. 1:3, in which Christ, the "express image of [God's] person," is held to resemble his Father exactly; and *Proposition*, following upon such subliminally Christological diction, goes beyond Locke's usage and, connoting the "loaves of proposition" in Jewish ritual, implies the sacramental loaves and Christ's body.[32] The phrase, moreover, besides remembering in the treatise of a bishop incarnated Christian truth, comes from a *philosophical* theologian and so denotes a distinct and explicit statement of a truth to be demonstrated: his mind, assuming the importance of objectivity, declares a determination to search it out. And finally, coming from a philosopher-theologian, the phrase exhibits a subjective sense suggesting that Browne's mind is confident in conceiving what has not yet reappeared and even what has not yet appeared: he reveals himself as quasi-autonomous propagator of Christian knowledge or at least as perpetuator of it by imaging to himself a truly depicted presentation of Christ and thus internalizing far horizons of religious truth.

Browne's language, in short, implies subjective and objective levels of *Evangelical Faith*.

Such faith is eminently objective insofar as *evangelical* means "of or pertaining to the Gospel narrative" (*OED*); and the context of Browne's second definition shows that part of its intended meaning is indeed the objective, Gospel idea of faith as the gift of salvation. In the previous paragraph, for example, he marvels at "the Renovation of [human nature] by pardon of Sin, the washing us from Guilt, and the Sanctification of the Whole Man in Body and Soul" (*The Procedure*, p. 334). Immediately following the definition, moreover, he observes that no one could "believe [God's] express Word before he spoke to us by the prophets and his son" (p. 335). Thus Browne reflects Locke's objectivist assumption that since the mind can claim no innate idea, knowledge of whatever kind, religious or natural, is so independently objective as to enter untransformed like images in the camera's eye. Browne implies, then, that evangelical faith is grounded in the received object of scripture, as opposed to being in any way self-originated.

On the other hand, *evangelical faith*, both in Browne's passage and outside it, can be interpreted subjectively as inward inspirations distinct from outward causes. Berkeley, in 1730, used *evangelical* as a synonym for *inward*, and in 1875, Henry Edward Manning described "the gift of the Holy Ghost" as "the one great evangelical gift."[33] By 1875, of course, the word had to some degree been qualified by the whole Wesleyan history which made it refer, in part, to the inner spiritual experience of postbiblical man. But it is tempting to think that since *Testimony of God* in Browne's passage refers to the still, small voice as much as to the Gospels, his second definition delineated, for the first time, revelation's inward as well as outward setting and hence its commensurability with empirical philosophy's subject/object emphasis. It is tempting, too, to speculate that since Berkeley read *The Procedure* closely, he was influenced in his usage by Browne's suggestion of an internalist signification for what was, after all, a most distinctive term of *The Procedure*: Browne associated *Evangelical Faith* not only with the express Word of God, but also with the realm of immediate revelation, i.e., with the ongoing process whereby the whole man, body and soul, participates in his santification. Thus Browne reflects the subjective assumption whereby Locke grants the mind an a posteriori power to shape the world without and the world within.

In sum, then, Browne's second definition implies subjective assurance and objective confirmation that God's redeeming love is real, and both definitions taken together show that *Evangelical Faith* was the name Browne gave to his experientialist blend of rational empiricism with religion both natural and revealed. The second definition, more inclusive than the first, and more explicit in associating evangelical faith with immediate and traditional revelation, is no less philosophical, and no less Lockean, than the definition in 2.6, for the second definition accords with the categories of subjectivity and objectivity and so completes the bold new enterprise of making saving faith a part of philosophical theology. Thus *The Procedure* serves, if nothing else, to expand today's accepted views of what *evangelical faith* has meant. The *OED* acknowledges that *evangelical* in part denotes "the school of theology which [the Methodist] movement represents,"[34] but this definition, though including an intellectualist component, does not recognize that in *The Procedure* and the abridgment, and hence in the embryonic consciousness of Methodism, *Evangelical* included philosophical along with theological meanings. Wesley, choosing to conclude his manuscript not only with Browne's second definition but with its preceding argument as well gives it even more prominence than does Browne, whose anticlimactic repetitions in *Procedure* 3 reduce the definition's effect. The abridgment, then, suggests that Wesley's understanding of evangelical faith was informed from the beginning by the early-century philosophic intimation that subjectivity corresponds with, and commands, objective truth. Perhaps Browne's grasp of outward and inward reality suggested to Wesley that for an evangelical to feel at one with God was more philosophically correct than unavoidably enthusiastic.

The abridgment, in sum, indicates that by 1730, *Evangelical Faith* sig-

nified to Wesley's mind if not a synthesis of revelation and rational empiricism then an intellectually as well as passionally experiential emphasis
in religion both revealed and natural. His manuscript if not a landmark of
his thought is a guide thereto, for it not only copies out Browne's depth
of understanding but shapes it as well, and emphasizing Browne's use of
Evangelical Faith, the abridgment points to theological and philosophical
ramifications of what it meant to be an evangelical in the early modern
era. Matthew Arnold's definition of an evangelical as "a good Christian with a narrow understanding"[35] does not apply to such an early
modern evangelical as Browne, for whom knowledge based on experience amounted to faith that was nonetheless saving for being couched in
the language of philosophical theology, and Arnold's definition is no
more accurate for Wesley, whose claim to inner experience rested in large
part upon his knowledge of the external sources of religious truth. What
needs demonstration is the extent to which Wesley's thought, and his
evangelical faith, fit his emphases in the abridgment, for if there should
be a correlation, then Wesley would have to be seen as an early modern
evangelical of the same philosophic stripe as Browne, and Arnold's definition would have to be qualified at least insofar as Wesley's influence was
intellectual. The abridgment, closely following *The Procedure*'s reconciliation of Christian faith and what many since Henry Lee have regarded
as the skeptical and secular manifesto of British empiricism, mirrors at
just one remove the religious as well as philosophical dimensions of the
Essay, and the abridgment therefore not only discloses young Wesley's
thorough (even if only indirect) understanding of the *Essay* as an aid to
faith, but is also a potentially indispensable guide to the *Essay*'s presence
in his later theology. His reading of the *Essay* culminated, perhaps, with
his abridgment of it in 1781, but his religious understanding of it appears
to have crystallized in a much earlier abridgment, some eight years before the day of his New Birth. This abridgment, together with the record
of his reading in the works of sometimes Lockean as well as often philosophical theologians, and together with his own philosophically theological sallies and assays in the letters to his mother, collectively constitute young man Wesley's Lockean connection, but the abridgment is
chief within this strange constellation of Lockean Wesleyana, for whereas
Wesley had yearned to "perceive" the graces and "be sensible of" the indwelling spirit of Christ, Browne argued that adherence to empiricism
somehow disciplines and even somehow prefigures the beholding of
revelation's mystery.

Young man Wesley's encounter with *The Procedure* was evidently formative enough to have assured his lifelong elaboration of Heb. 11:1[36]—
and hence of its analogy between, almost its interinvolvement of—reve-

lation and sense perception. Young man Wesley's Lockean connection is sufficiently strong and sufficiently important to demand investigation of how far his theology of experience, if not his experience of faith, derived from Lockean philosophy. The abridgment, if it did not necessarily inform the intellectual content of a major expression of Christianity in eighteenth-century England, was nevertheless a prelude to what can now emerge as the Lockean aspect not simply of Wesley's conversion but indeed of his thought and perhaps of his revival.

It is essential to look more closely than Hindley does at the two "Appeals to Men of Reason and Religion," and to add such other methodologically promising titles of the 1740s as the Preface to *Primitive Physick* (1747).

Hindley quotes from just one method oriented title after the 1740s: he observes (p. 100) that "The Case of Reason Impartially Considered" (1788) represents an especially strong effort of Wesley's "long struggle" to satisfy the "demand for 'reason' and 'evidence'." It is essential to look more closely at this sermon and to add such other empirically oriented works as the Preface to *Desideratum: or Electricity Made Plain* (1760), "Thoughts upon Necessity" (1774), the introductory and concluding essays in *A Survey of the Wisdom of God in the Creation: or a Compendium of Natural Philosophy* (1777), "A Thought on Necessity" (1780), and "The Imperfection of Human Knowledge," from the Second Series of *Sermons on Several Occasions* (1788). These very titles indicate that like Locke and Browne Wesley applied empirical method to the natural realm in an argument for the deity as sustainer of creation. The tough-mindedly nature-oriented faith to be found, say, in Old Testament wisdom literature, is at least indirectly related to Wesley's Christian experience, but what remains to be explored is how far the philosophy of experience, distinct from other influences, located his experience of faith within as well as outside nature. (The abridgment, incidentally, fully represents *The Procedure*'s use of the *Essay*'s theistical natural religion to explicate the monotheism of Old Testament revelation.[37]) It proves proper to place the emphasis upon his constant and self-generated acquisition of knowedge and even to see this aspect of his mind as a forceful antecedent of Romantic natural religion.

The "wise passiveness" of Romantic faith, moreover, is anticipated by Wesley's reactive receptivity to what he took to be the condescensions of Spirit. Such receptivity, to be sure, despite its inductive thoughtfulness, seems hardly Lockean insofar as Lockean theology stresses a Latitudinarian leveling more than the Spirit's ministrations. When Isaac Watts, in a poem from *Horae Lyricae* (1709), has Locke say from heaven,

> Forgive . . . , ye Saints below
> The wav'ring and the cold Assent
> I gave to Themes divinely true,[38]

Watts is clearly with Bacon, Pascal, Sir Thomas Browne, and Dryden, all of whom, more or less intentionally, divorced faith from reason and clearly against Locke who evidently seemed to Watts to emphasize reason at the expense of such nonrational Christian traditions as that of immediate spiritual experience. Browne, however, as philosopher-theologian and bishop, gave young Wesley a model of spiritual theology at once nonrational and, because hardly antirational, undivorced from rational empiricism, and it is a contention of the present study that because of Browne and even because of Locke in Locke's most fully theological moments Wesley's assent to revealed truths was at once warm (i.e., sufficiently sense-like) and prorational—and hence in line with all due rigor of both theological and philosophical methodology. MacLean long ago pointed out that Lockean analogy was perhaps the most popular concept of eighteenth-century English thought, and MacLean also mentioned that Wesley, along with Watts and Edward Young, was among those of the English conservative right who agreed with Locke that analogy is "man's surest guide below."[39] What needs to be explored is to what extent Wesley saw, with the help of Browne as well as Locke, that analogy could be an aid not only to a theistical natural religion but also to faith in immediate as well as traditional revelation.

One suspects, then, that like Jonathan Edwards, Wesley sought to apply empirical method even to the extranatural realm of faith, i.e., that the already mentioned works and others like them pertain in their empirical methodology to the substance of his works in general. One imagines, in advance of exploration, that like *The Procedure* his works caution against sensation as a direct avenue to religious knowledge; but one anticipates them drawing a Brownean analogy: as the sight of a man is to the man, so the feeling of love is to the nature of God. And one predicts, with confidence, that such an analogy of proportionality helped Wesley to think that what is felt is a theologically satisfying substitute for what is seen philosophically—that as the intellect remains convinced of what the senses have to tell, so the intellect trusts emotion to be not illusory but spiritually veridical, i.e., to correspond to religious fact.[40] One expects from Wesley's prose the intimation that even as what is felt surpasses what is seen, so what is thought approaches, without dispelling the mystery of, what has been and is being revealed. The abridgment urges the question whether Wesley, with the help of Locke and Browne, came to believe that spiritual actuality, like natural, is inward as well as outward, for Wesley's strange warming of the heart and his view of God's love as shed abroad therein parallel the view of sense perception as sufficiently accordant with the nature of the thing itself.

One expects, in short, that Wesley worked with empiricist methodology to develop his "epistemology" of Christian experience. The next chapter shows how his Brownean reading of the *Essay* facilitated his testimony, nay, provided the method for his testament, of real and living faith.

Two

Wesley's Philosophical Theology

From the 1740s, when Wesley first formulated his thought, to the last year of his life, when he spoke Lockean language with the ease of exhalation, he more or less consciously followed the Brownean procedure for making Lockean method the method of theology.

Formulations

"An Earnest Appeal," first of all, is so Lockean as to suggest that Wesley had the *Essay* in view. Observe, for example, the following paragraphs, both of which are obviously Lockean, the first manifestly enough to deserve quotation here as well as in my introduction:

> You know . . . that before it is possible for you to form a true judgment of the things of God, it is absolutely necessary that you have a *clear apprehension* of them, and that your ideas thereof be all *fixed*, *distinct*, and *determinate*. And seeing our ideas are not innate, but must all originally come from our senses, it is certainly necessary that you have senses capable of discerning objects of this kind —not those only which are called "natural senses," which in this respect profit nothing, as being altogether incapable of discerning objects of a spiritual kind, but *spiritual* senses, exercised to discern spiritual good and evil. . . .
>
> And till you have these internal senses, till the eyes of your understanding are opened, you can have no apprehension of divine things, no idea of them at all. Nor consequently, till then, can you either judge truly or reason justly concerning them, seeing your reason has no ground whereon to stand, no materials to work upon. (Cragg, pp. 56–57)

The sensationalistic diction, i.e., *materials, ground, eyes, internal senses, spiritual senses, natural senses, objects, senses,* and *things,* constitutes perhaps the fullest statement of what Hindley, if not Wesley in so many words, calls Wesley's "doctrine of the spiritual sense": by this doctrine, "the philosophical demand for empiricism appeared firmly met" (Hindley, p. 202).[1] The demand for rational empiricism, indeed, is met in the far from anti-rational concept of inspiration: witness *reason, understanding, discern, ideas, apprehension,* and *judgment.* Wesley, then, as though to maintain Lockean balance between reason and its ground, implies a more than metaphorical relationship between spiritual "senses" and almost more than quasi-rational "apprehension" by the spirit. Thus, besides endorsing tabula rasa and besides making it the first principle of theology he signals his affinity for, dependence on, Lockean method.

"An Earnest Appeal," moreover, is so Brownean that Wesley must have had *The Procedure* in view. For one thing, he emphasizes Heb. 11:1:

> Now faith (supposing the Scripture to be of God) is . . . the demonstrative evidence of things unseen, the supernatural evidence of things invisible, not perceivable by eyes of flesh, or by any of our natural senses or faculties. Faith is that divine evidence whereby the spiritual man discerneth God and the things of God. (Cragg, p. 46)

This mixture of commentary and quotation is the chief particular of "An Earnest Appeal" 's general admiration for the Book of Hebrews: "Neither do we know," writes Wesley, "in all the productions of ancient or modern times, such a chain of reasoning or argumentation, so close, so solid, so regularly connected, as the Epistle to the Hebrews" (Cragg, p. 56).

For another thing, Wesley draws an analogy between faith and empirical observation: "[Faith] is with regard to the spiritual world what sense is with regard to the natural" (Cragg, p. 46). Cragg acknowledges that throughout "An Earnest Appeal" "Wesley argues by analogy from our senses and knowledge based on their reports, to faith and the assurance based on its testimony" (p. 56n); but it is needful to go further and point out that "An Earnest Appeal" is therefore explicitly, or at least perspicuously, Brownean. The sentence just quoted, for example, is in its very structure precisely analogistic, as though Wesley, like Browne, intends more than a merely metaphorical and hence arbitrary identification of faith with the natural senses. In suggesting, however, that sense perception is analogically and therefore really related to faith, Wesley is careful to avoid implying that one can easily, or even ever, know the common ground between faith and empiricism, for "An Earnest Appeal," like *The Procedure*, is careful to stress that natural understanding cannot apprehend spiritual truth:

> What then will your reason do here? How will it pass from things natural to spiritual? From the things that are seen to those that are not seen? From the visible to the invisible world? What a gulf is here! By what art will reason get over the immense chasm? (Cragg, p. 57)

Passage from visible to invisible cannot occur, declares Wesley, "till the Almighty come in to your succour, and give you that faith you have hitherto despised":

> Then, upborne as it were on eagles' wings, you shall soar away into the regions of eternity, and your enlightened reason shall explore even "the deep things of God", God himself "revealing them to you by his Spirit" [cf. 1 Cor. 2:10]. (Cragg, p. 57)

Wesley remains sufficiently Lockean, and sufficiently methodological, in applying the criterion of "enlightened reason" to this particular realm of faith; and his grounding of immediate revelation in biblical authority is circumspect enough; but he appeals to traditional revelation as Browne does, i.e., in order to underscore the Spirit's continuing witness. Elsewhere in "An Earnest Appeal," moreover, Wesley assumes, or rather appears to assume, the Brownean concept of immediate revelation as a gift analogous to if not somehow continuous with sense experience:

> Can *you* give yourself this faith? Is it now in your power to see, or hear, or taste, or feel God? Have you already, or can you raise in yourself, any perception of God or of an invisible world? . . . Is it in your power to burst the veil that is on your heart and let in the light of eternity? You know it is not. You not only do not but cannot (by your own strength) thus believe. The more you labour so to do, the more you will be convinced, "it is the gift of God." (Cragg, p. 48)

It can even be said, and should be, that "An Earnest Appeal" goes beyond *The Procedure*, for whereas Browne tends to shrink from flight to the heavenly regions, Wesley envisions such flight; and so he elaborates the Brownean, and indirectly Lockean, understanding of immediate

revelation. He defines faith, for example, not simply according to scripture, but even in accordance with the rational and sensationalistic balance:

> It is the *feeling* of the soul, whereby a believer *perceives*, through
> the "power of the Highest overshadowing him" [cf. Luke 1:35]
> both the existence and the presence of him in whom he "lives,
> moves, and has his being" [cf. Acts 17:28], and indeed the whole
> invisible world, the entire system of things eternal. And hereby, in
> particular, he feels "the love of God shed abroad in his heart" [cf.
> Rom. 5:5]. (Cragg, p. 47. My italics—RB)

It is hardly news that if Wesley did not quite identify faith with feeling,
he nonetheless anticipated the late eighteenth- and early nineteenth-
century tendency, on the continent at least, to regard faith as "a trend"
thereof;[2] but it may come as a surprise to learn, from the context of the
definition above that in associating such faith with specific senses he pro-
ceeded in a manner so far from either non- or anti-intellectual as even to
outdo Browne, to say little of Locke, in applying a philosophically theological and peculiarly eighteenth-century principle to the selection and
quotation of almost more than merely quasi-sensationalistic passages
from scripture:

> Faith, according to the scriptural account, is the eye of the new-
> born soul. Hereby every true believer in God "seeth him who is
> invisible" [cf. Heb. 11:27]. . . .
>
> [Faith] is the ear of the soul, whereby a sinner "hears the voice of
> the Son of God and lives" [cf. John 5:25]; even that voice which
> alone wakes the dead, saying, "Son, thy sins are forgiven thee" [cf.
> Mark 2:5].
>
> It is (if I may be allowed the expression) the palate of the soul.
> For hereby a believer "tastes the good word, and the powers of the
> world to come" [cf. Heb. 6:5]; and hereby he both "tastes and sees
> that God is gracious" [cf. Psalms 34:8], yea, and "merciful to him a
> sinner" [cf. Luke 18:13]. . . .
>
> [Faith] is with regard to the spiritual world what sense is with
> regard to the natural. It is the spiritual sensation of every soul that is
> born of God. (Cragg, pp. 46–47)

The penultimate sentence, worth reiterating, is almost more than merely
Brownean in its Browne-derived yet now sufficiently Wesleyan analogy
between sense perception and immediate spiritual experience.

Wesley's definition, finally, by its diction ("whereby a believer *perceives*") and by its development throughout "An Earnest Appeal," intimates his more than merely Brownean and quite other than Lockean (though still finally Locke-derived) view that religious feeling is so far from complete mindlessness as, like sense data, to constitute matter for the mind to work upon. His contention, in other words, that "So far as [a man] departs from true genuine reason, so far he departs from Christianity," rests on a sense-based concept, for, when Wesley next describes reason both as consonant with "the nature of things" and as "the faculty . . . of inferring one thing from another" (Cragg, p. 55), he intends a rational empiricism distinct from the a priori, innate rationalism of Descartes and say the Cambridge Platonists. Wesley's definition, in short, is more than exclusively sensationalistic in its language: "This [faith] we *know* and feel" (Cragg, p. 47. My italics—RB). And it is worth pointing out in this connection that the definition anticipates late eighteenth- and early nineteenth-century ones not simply in its sensationalistic, but also in its rational dimension. Schleiermacher is of course a notable exponent of faith as feeling:

> As regards Feeling [writes Schleiermacher], . . . it is not only in its duration as a result of stimulation that it is an abiding-in-self: even as the process of being stimulated, it is not effected by the subject, but simply takes place in the subject, and thus, since it belongs altogether to the realm of receptivity, it is entirely an abiding-in-self; and in this sense it stands alone in antithesis to . . . Knowing and Doing.[3]

But no more than Wesley did the fully theological Schleiermacher entirely depart from traditional views of faith as knowledge and action. And his largely philosophic description of religious feeling as produced from without, rather than as self-originated, is of the same far from insufficiently thoughtful order of faith as Wesley's nonenthusiastic, responsive, and by no means entirely antirational emotion-in-religion.

In such other works of the 1740s as "A Farther Appeal to Men of Reason and Religion," "Letters to Mr. John Smith," "The Great Privilege of those that are born of God," "The Character of a Methodist," "A Letter to the Rev. Dr. Conyers Middleton," and the Preface to *Primitive Physick*, the themes of "An Earnest Appeal" are further developed. In conjunction therewith, in other words, or at least derivative therefrom, these works constitute convenient boundaries of evidence for Wesley's relatively early desire fully to adapt to his theology Brownean procedure in particular and Lockean method in general.

"A Farther Appeal," to advance chronologically, is primarily concerned to prove that the "technical terms" of Methodism "coincide exactly with . . . the official pronouncements of the Church of England" (Cragg, p. 95), but Wesley is also concerned, therein, to use the language of Lockean method, and he insists in so doing that the kind of religion he espouses is not "religious madness" but

> *rational* as well as scriptural; it is as pure from enthusiasm as from superstition. It is true that the contrary has been continually affirmed. But to affirm is one thing, to prove another. Who will prove that it is enthusiasm to love God, even though we love him with all our heart? to rejoice in the *sense* of his love to us? (Cragg, pp. 97–98. My italics—RB)

The Brownean analogy between sense perception and revelation, then, underlies the latter "Appeal" as well as the former. The two "Appeals," taken together, argue that Methodism is so far from enthusiasm as to be methodologically distinguished, for even the latter "Appeal," in this instance, respects empirical criteria.

A philosophical theology in line with and derived more or less perspicuously from *The Procedure* and the *Essay* is reflected in "Letters to Mr. John Smith." (Over the two and a half years from September 28, 1745, to March 22, 1748, Wesley addressed six letters to "John Smith"; "Smith," the assumed name of a person who sent a series of letters to Wesley, was probably Thomas Secker, Bishop of Oxford and later Archbishop of Canterbury.[4]) "To this day," Wesley tells "Smith" on June 25, 1746, "I have abundantly more temptation . . . to be . . . a philosophical sluggard, than an itinerant Preacher" (Telford, 2:68). It is accordingly the case that evangelistic goals are combined, throughout this series of letters, with an evident love of philosophical theology.

It is intriguing, for example, if not surprising, to find Wesley applying to traditional revelation the Lockean as well as Cartesian skepticism whereby the mind remains open even after systematically searching for, and apparently finding, what is not subject to doubt: "I am as fully assured to-day, as I am of the shining of the sun, that the scriptures are of God. I cannot possibly deny or doubt of it now; yet I may doubt of it to-morrow; as I have done heretofore a thousand times, and that after the fullest assurance preceding" (Telford, 2:92).

With regard to Lockean method, moreover, the letters to "Smith" acknowledge both of its poles, for the sense-based nature of mind is everywhere suggested in Wesley's phraseology, e.g., "so far as men can *judge* from their *eyes* and *ears*" (Telford, 2:44. My italics—RB). "Perceptible inspiration," writes Wesley, forms part of what "the Methodists preach" (Telford, 2:62, 74); and though unsure exactly what Robert Barclay means by this originally Quaker doctrine, Wesley is sure of what *he* means by it: "No man can be a true Christian without such an inspiration of the Holy Ghost as fills his *heart* with peace, and joy, and love; which he who *perceives* not, has it not. . . . This I take to be the very foundation of Christianity" (Telford 2:64. My italics—RB). Wesley suggests, both here and elsewhere in the letters, that the mind is immediately conscious of the graces; for he makes no claim that one perceives "the *manner* in which [the Spirit] operates" (Telford, 2:74. My italics—RB). The implication of the letters, therefore, includes rational response to, if not participation in, the Spirit's witness. On the other hand, the image of the heart emphasizes feeling, and this image is allied to Wesley's overt selection of "sensationalistic" diction from the Bible, e.g., "we stir up the gift of God by earnestly and continually *watching* unto prayer [cf. Eph. 6:18]" (Telford, 2:103–4. My italics—RB). "Perceptible inspiration," then, like the "spiritual sense," contains language both sensationalistic and rational.

The letters, in their view that spiritual experience fills the mind, recall Locke's general argument that understanding depends upon sense experience. *The rise and progress of*, a phrase characteristic of eighteenth-century England, assumes the English philosophy of experience,[5] and, when Wesley writes that "we are speaking, not of the progress, but of the first rise, of faith" (Telford 2:48), he suggests, for one thing, that no more than knowledge does faith exist innately, and for another that faith, like knowledge, must be datable by precise moments in personal history. The letters imply elsewhere that just as one knows what one experiences naturally so one has faith in what one encounters spiritually: "[I]t cannot be, in the nature of things, that a man should be filled with this peace, and joy, and love, by the inspiration of the Holy Spirit, without perceiving it as clearly as he does the light of the sun" (Telford 2:64). And here is another such implication of the letters, complete with Lockean blend of irrepressible knowledge claim and careful distinction:

> [T]hough I allow that some may fancy they have [the Spirit's witness], when in truth they have it not; I cannot allow that any fancy they have it not, at the time when they really have. I know no instance of this. When they have this faith, they cannot possibly doubt of their having it; although it is very possible, when they have it not, they may doubt whether ever they had it or no. This was Hannah Richardson's case; and it is, more or less, the case with many of the children of God. (Telford, 2:59–60)

Wesley's gathering of instances, here, and indeed his willingness throughout the letters to rely upon testimony, recall Locke's allowance of undoubted witnesses among the kinds of evidence on which knowledge may be induced from experience. To "Smith"'s objection to the Methodists' "working of Apostolic signs and wonders," Wesley replied that he "waited three years before I told the story," until convinced "by the only *method* which I can conceive . . . that the matter of fact was just as it is . . . related" in the Journal (Telford, 2:44. My italics—RB); and whatever one might think of the conclusion Wesley reached, the means by which he reached it seem hardly less than philosophically correct:

> I am acquainted with more than twelve or thirteen hundred persons, whom I believe to be truly pious, and not on slight grounds, and who have severally testified to me with their own mouths that they do know the day when the love of God was first shed abroad in their hearts, and when his Spirit first witnessed with their spirits, that they were the children of God [cf. Rom. 5:5, 8:15–16]. Now, if you are determined to think all these liars or fools, this is no evidence to you; but to me it is strong evidence, who have for some years known the men and their communication. (Telford, 2:47)

The letters, finally, like the two "Appeals," are Brownean as well as Lockean. The letters' epistemologically satisfying examination of faith begins, for example, with two allusions to *The Procedure*'s chief proof-text, Heb. 11:1 (Telford 2:45, 48); and not only does Wesley's emphasis on immediate revelation parallel that of *The Procedure*, but his choice of theme, like *The Procedure*'s, seems due to an estimation of what the age needed to hear: the letters are directed not just to "Smith," but, perhaps with the expectation that they would eventually be published, to Anglicans in general and Deists in particular (Telford, 2: 59, 96). Thus the letters, like *The Procedure*, speak to the extremes of natural and revealed religion in the hope that method would make them meet.

This is not to say, of course, that the letters are Brownean slavishly, for, just as they add a Wesleyan flavor to Lockean thought, so they go beyond *The Procedure*. For one thing, their theology of immediate revelation is not only more elaborate, but also more epistemologically specific than that of *The Procedure*: the doctrine of perceptible inspiration led Wesley to the cognitive and quasi-philosophic conclusion that "the inward witness . . . is the proof, the strongest proof, of Christianity" (Telford 2:135). For another thing, the letters' doctrine of analogy goes beyond *The Procedure*'s, for whereas *The Procedure*'s relates to spiritual theology chiefly by extension from traditional revelation and natural religion, the letters' doctrine is everywhere implicit even in spiritual theology:

> [S]upposing a man to be now void of faith, and hope, and love, he cannot effect any degree of them in himself by any possible exertion of his understanding, and of any or all his other natural faculties, though he should enjoy them in the utmost perfection. A distinct power from God, not implied in any of these, is indispensably necessary, before it is possible he should arrive at the very lowest degree of Christian faith . . . [H]e must be created anew, thoroughly and inwardly changed by the operation of the Spirit of God; by a power equivalent to that which raises the dead, and which calls the things which are not as though they were. (Telford, 2:71)

This is very far from saying that the unaided understanding and the unaided senses are capable of apprehending the spiritual graces. But the passage draws an extended, if not self-conscious, analogy between spiritual experience and sense perception. For Wesley, though he preserves herein a Brownean recognition of the limits of the natural man, avers that spiritual reality, to the spiritual man, can appear actual. If this passage does not quite acknowledge a more-than-Brownean power in natural concepts to approach the mysterious yet strangely accessible Creator, and if the passage does not finally imply interdependence of, and affinity between, the spiritual and natural kinds of experience, the letters elsewhere go beyond implication and assert for one thing that sense perception depends for its operation upon the life of the spirit: "[W]ithout God we can do nothing; . . . we cannot think, or speak, or move a hand or an eye, without the concurrence of the divine energy; . . . all our natural faculties are God's gift, nor can the meanest be exerted without the assistance of his Spirit" (Telford, 2:71). For another, and even more boldly, the letters suggest that spiritual reality is in a way dependent on sense perception, for, as Wesley writes therein, as long as a twice-born man "continue sound in mind and memory," he cannot doubt that he received the witness, but, if his "understanding is now darkened," "the very traces of that divine work" can be "well-nigh erased out of his memory" (Telford, 2:90).

Thus, far from making a false and arbitrary, i.e., merely metaphorical, identification between the way one perceives the natural world and the way one feels the influxes of grace, Wesley implies that these two ways of "knowing" are analogous to each other, i.e., founded in the same creation, derived from the same Source and therefore really related. The letters to "Smith," though never specifically employing the term *analogy*, describe the Spirit analogically, for, like *The Procedure*, but more systematically, they suggest that the Spirit is both wholly other and dimly apprehensible according to the degree of His contact with the world, and their doctrine of perceptible inspiration, therefore, is both different from Barclay's and original in part because it not only presupposes but also grows out of and advances Browne's doctrine of analogy.

Wesley's doctrine, finally, is all but explicit in the letters' view of language, which is introduced in their full quotation of Lib. 7, cap. 10, of Augustine's *Confessions*:

> Under thy guidance and direction, I entered into my inward parts: And I was enabled to enter, because thou wast my Helper. I entered, and saw, with the eye of my soul, (such as it is,) the unchangeable light of the Lord above this very eye of my soul, and above my mind. I perceived that the light was not of this common kind, which is obvious to all flesh: Neither did it appear as if it was a larger light of the same kind. It was not a light of this description, but of another; a light that differed exceedingly from all these. Nor was it above my mind, in such a manner as the heavens are above the earth: But it was superior, because it made me. He who knows the truth is acquainted with this light; and he who knows it, knows eternity. Love knows it.
>
> O eternal Truth! Thou art my God. Day and night I sigh after thee. And when I obtained my first knowledge of thee, thou didst take me to see that there was something which I might behold. Thou didst likewise beat back the weakness of my own sight, and didst thyself powerfully shine into me. I trembled with love and with horror; and I found myself at a great distance from thee.—I exclaimed, "Is truth a nonentity?"—And thou didst reply from afar, "No, indeed! I AM THAT I AM"—I heard this, as we are accustomed to hear in the heart; and there was no ground whatever for doubting. Nay, I could more easily doubt of my existence itself, than that it was not the Truth.[6]

Of this passage, Wesley says that Augustine "does not appear, in writing this confession to God, to have had any adversary in view, nor to use any rhetorical heightening at all; but to express the naked experience of his heart, and that in as plain and unmetaphorical words as the nature of the

thing would bear" (Telford, 2:70–71). The letters, then, state an explicitly antimetaphorical view of language. No more than Browne, and no
more than Locke, is Wesley naive, for he knows that "the nature of the
thing," i.e., the essence of language, is in one sense metaphorical, but he
admires "plain" words nonetheless, which relate to the thing signified directly and with as little figurativeness as possible. From the standpoint of
Lockean rhetoric he reads into the *Confessions* the Lockean relation between word and idea: mental experience is laid bare in language.

These expressive and mimetic functions of Augustine's language may
be its priorities, as Wesley suggests, but its pragmatic, affective function
is strong enough to have conveyed to him the important point that an
implicitly analogical, because explicitly nonmetaphorical, way of speaking can be identical to a methodologically decorous language of spiritual
experience. Augustine's language is of course metaphorical: "I entered,
and saw, with the eye of my soul." But the passage is finally analogical.
In Brownean terms: when he says that the Spirit "entered into my inward
parts," Augustine substitutes for "Ideas of Sensation" "the Operations of
our Soul"; and when he refers to "the unchangeable light of the Lord," he
does not speak metaphorically; for he writes, after all, that "the light was
not of this common kind, which is obvious to all flesh." Rather, and still
to use Brownean terms in reading him, he represents "Divine Things"
analogically by suggesting that this divine light bears "a Real tho' Unknown Correspondency and Proportion" to the inner life of man. He
affirms both the strange accessibility of the light and its exceeding difference. In such a way, at any rate, he seems to have been understood by
Wesley. "I cannot have so full and certain a knowledge of a writer, as of
one I talk with face to face," writes Wesley with a Lockean distinction
(Telford, 2:60); but he adds, in this same letter to "Smith," that the passage from the *Confessions* is "exceeding clear and strong"; and it is evident that he thinks so for Lockean and Brownean reasons: not only does
Augustine show a proto-Brownean, if not proto-Lockean, preference for
particular, unprecedented, and unrepeated experiences, distinct, say, from
any proto-Cartesian preference for self-existence as the foundation of
truth, but he also shows a proto-Lockean and proto-Brownean preference for analogy over metaphor.

In "The Great Privilege of those that are born of God" (1748), Wesley's
doctrine of analogy is further elaborated, especially at the beginning.
First asking "what is the proper meaning of that expression, 'Whosoever
is born of God'" (1 John 3:9), Wesley then announces his theme that "the
circumstances of the natural birth" provide "the most easy way to understand the spiritual" (*Sermons*, p. 175). This implication of analogy is in

precisely Brownean terms insofar as his exclamation that "there is *so near a resemblance* between the circumstances of the natural and of the spiritual birth" (*Sermons*, p. 175. My italics—RB) should be linked with Browne's argument that analogy is founded in a "real Resemblance" between the things compared. No more than Browne does Wesley pretend to make the resemblance fully known. But he does affirm a real correspondency between this universal natural experience and a spiritual experience that would remain quite ineffable were it not for the linguistic instrument of analogy. Here is Wesley on "the circumstances of the natural birth":

> The reason why he that is not yet born is wholly a stranger to the visible world, is not because it is afar off (it is very nigh, it surrounds him on every side); but, partly, because he has not those senses, they are not yet opened in his soul, whereby alone it is possible to hold commerce with the material world; and partly, because so thick a veil is cast between, through which he can discern nothing. (*Sermons*, pp. 175–76)

As with the natural, so with the spiritual birth: the entire sermon is an extended Brownean analogy insofar as it teaches that the invisible world is familiar to twice-born men whose spiritual sense corresponds to the limited but sufficient a posteriori operation of the natural faculties.

Wesley's analogy, in other words, rests on empiricist epistemology and hence on the assumption that mind is tabula rasa. Note the faith in experience and the rational as well as sensationalistic diction in two important passages linked by parallelism. First,

> Before that great change [i.e., the New Birth] is wrought, . . . [one] is not *sensible* of God; he does not *feel*, he has no inward consciousness of His presence. He does not perceive that divine breath of life, without which he cannot subsist a moment: nor is he sensible of any of the things of God: they make no impression upon his soul. . . . He seeth not the things of the Spirit of God; the eyes of his understanding being closed, and utter darkness covering his whole soul, surrounding him on every side. It is true he may have some faint dawnings of life, some small beginnings of spiritual motion; but as yet he has no spiritual senses capable of discerning spiritual objects: consequently, he "discerneth not the things of the Spirit of God; he cannot know them, because they are spiritually discerned" [cf. 1 Cor. 2:14]. (*Sermons*, p. 176)

And second,

> The child which is not yet born subsists indeed by the air, as does
> everything which has life; but *feels* it not, nor anything else, unless
> in a very dull and imperfect manner. It *hears* little, if at all; the
> organs of hearing being as yet closed up. It *sees* nothing; having its
> eyes fast shut, and being surrounded with utter darkness. There
> are, it may be, some faint beginnings of life, when the time of its
> birth draws nigh, and some motion consequent thereon, whereby it
> is distinguished from a mere mass of matter; but it has no *senses*;
> all these avenues of the soul are hitherto quite shut up. Of conse-
> quence it has scarce any intercourse with this visible world; nor any
> knowledge, conception, or idea, of the things that occur therein.
> (*Sermons*, p. 175)

The italicized words, and such other words as *impression*, *seeth*, *eyes*,
senses, *organs*, *avenues*, and *intercourse*, are balanced by such concepts of
consciousness as perception, understanding, discernment, knowledge,
awareness, and idea.

"The Great Privilege," then, in conjunction with its implication of
analogy, can be read as a more or less deliberate blend of subjective and
objective diction. In the following passsage, for example, the sensationalistic language in my italics expresses contact with divine objects,
and the rational and spiritual language in my small capital letters denotes
assimilation of those objects:

> But when [one] is born of God, born of the Spirit, how is the
> manner of his existence changed! His whole SOUL is now *sensible* of
> God, and he can say, by sure experience, "Thou art about my bed,
> and about my path" [cf. Ps. 139:8]; I *feel* Thee in all my ways:
> "Thou besettest me behind and before, and layest Thy hand upon
> me" [cf. Ps. 139:5]. The spirit or breath of God is immediately in-
> spired, breathed into the new-born SOUL; and the same breath
> which comes from, returns to, God: as it is continually received by
> faith, so it is continually rendered back by love, by prayer, and
> praise, and thanksgiving; love, and praise, and prayer being the
> *breath* of every SOUL which is truly born of God. And by this new
> kind of spiritual respiration, spiritual life is not only sustained, but
> increased day by day, together with spiritual strength, and motion,
> and *sensation*, all the *senses* of the SOUL being now awake, and capa-
> ble of DISCERNING spiritual good and evil. (*Sermons*, p. 177. My
> capital letters and italics—RB)

The subject/object blend in "The Great Privilege" is more than casually related to that same blend in Locke's philosophy. For one thing, the phrase *sure experience* in its context of empirically methodological language is not far from Locke's philosophy in general: the intimation of "faint dawnings of life before birth" is somewhat other than exclusively Lockean, if not necessarily therefore Cartesian; but the gist of these passages is other than narrowly Wesleyan, for they epitomize the methodologically unexceptionable and broadly Wesleyan modus of the sermon. And if the sermon is not specifically intent upon grounding the doctrines of perceptible inspiration and the spiritual sense upon the Lockean formulae of philosophical theology, such a possibility seems more than merely implicit in say the following passage, wherein "The Great Privilege" draws upon the especially "philosophical" second chapter of 1 Cor. to conclude that the invisible world of the spirit is not only conceivable in the language of a theologized empiricism, but even available to all:

> The *other world*, as we usually term it, is not far from every one of us; it is above, and beneath, and on every side. Only the natural man discerneth it not; partly, because he has no spiritual senses, whereby alone we can discern the things of God; partly because so thick a veil is interspersed as he knows not how to penetrate. (*Sermons*, p. 177)

For another thing, and more importantly to the subject/object connection, "The Great Privilege" waxes all but Lockean with regard to the interpenetrations of sense perception and the natural world:

> [N]o sooner is the child born into the world, than he . . . . *feels* the air with which he is surrounded, and which pours into him from every side, as fast as he alternately breathes it back, to sustain the flame of life: and hence springs a continual increase of strength, of motion, and of sensation; all the bodily senses being now awakened, and furnished with their proper objects. (*Sermons*, p. 176)

The mind's wakeful involvement with sense data is just as clear in this passage as in whole sections of the *Essay* where Locke insists that the mind's response to sense experience puts man almost at one with what he needs to know about the world.

It should be said, finally, that the sermon's description of "*senses*, whereby alone we can DISCERN the things of God," bespeaks a vital interaction: what is "continually received," is "continually rendered back." Or as Wesley puts it elsewhere in the sermon, "God does not continue to act upon the soul, unless the soul reacts upon God" (*Sermons*, p. 184). At the mental level, then, and by analogy with the senses, spiritual experience is depicted as a coalescence at least, and at most as an almost total identification, with the condescensions of God:

> [One's] *ears* are now opened, and the *voice* of God no longer calls in vain (cf. Ezek. 1:24; Isa. 32:3]. He *hears* and OBEYS the heavenly calling; he KNOWS the voice of his Shepherd. All his spiritual *senses* being now awakened, he has a clear *intercourse* with the invisible world; and hence he KNOWS more and more of the *things* which before it could not "enter in to his heart to conceive" [cf. Isa. 64:4; 1 Cor. 2:9]. He now KNOWS what the peace of God is; what is joy in the Holy Ghost; what the love of God which is shed abroad in the hearts of them that believe in Him through Christ Jesus [cf. Rom. 5:5]. Thus the veil being removed which before intercepted the light and *voice*, the KNOWLEDGE and love of God, he who is born of the Spirit dwelleth in love, "dwelleth in God, and God in him!" (*Sermons*, pp. 177–78. My capital letters and italics—RB)

The alternation, and indeed the oscillation, between rational and sensationalistic diction signifies again that through immediate revelation God and man are ensphered, or rather that "a clear intercourse" occurs not only between man as object and God as Subject, but also between man as subject and God as Object.

  "The Great Privilege," in sum, both akin and strikingly contributory to both the *Essay* and *The Procedure*, develops the letters to "Smith" and the two "Appeals," for not only does the sermon exceed what *The Procedure* says about immediate revelation, and not only does the language, here, draw out what the *Essay* implies about subject and object, but the sermon also goes further than both the *Essay* and *The Procedure* in extending the concept of analogy from the realms of nature and the Bible to the realm of the spirit. Furthermore, Wesley outdoes Browne in selecting "philosophical" language from the Bible: *The Procedure* draws primarily upon Heb. 11:1; but "The Great Privilege" adds such other books as 1 John, Isa., Ezek., and 1 Cor.; and this sermon is also careful, in its delineation of the New Man's power to "see," to suggest methodology in three other scriptures replete with empirical nuance: " 'The *eyes* of his UNDERSTANDING' are now 'open' [cf. Eph. 1:18], and he '*seeth* Him that is invisible' [cf. Heb. 11:27]. God 'doth shine,' in his *heart*, to ENLIGHTEN him with 'the KNOWLEDGE of the glory of God in the *face* of Jesus Christ'" [cf. 2 Cor. 4:6] (*Sermons*, p. 177. My italics and capital letters—RB). "The Great Privilege," in short, breaks ground in quasi-empirical theology.

This sermon, moreover, is not the only one among Wesley's works of the 1740s in which he ventured to combine homiletical purpose with philosophical method; a Lockean view of language, for example, is featured in "The Character of a Methodist" (1742), which, like "The Great Privilege" but unlike "Letters to Mr. John Smith" and the two "Appeals," is more message than intellectual treatise. Compare the following passages, the first from "The Character," and the second from the *Essay*:

> The most obvious, easy, common, words, wherein our meaning can be conveyed, we prefer before others, both on ordinary occasions, and when we speak of the things of God. We never, therefore, willingly or designedly, deviate from the most usual way of speaking; unless when we express scripture truths in scripture words, which, we presume, no Christian will condemn. (Jackson, 8:340)

> To conclude this Consideration of the Imperfection, and Abuse of Language; the *ends of Language in our Discourse with others*, being chiefly these three: *First, To make known* one Man's Thoughts or *Ideas* to another. *Secondly,* To do it with as much ease and *quickness,* as is possible; and *Thirdly,* Thereby to *convey* the *Knowledge* of Things. Language is either abused, or deficient, when it fails in any of these Three. (*Essay* 3.10.23; Nidditch, p. 504)

Locke's view that the word corresponds to the thing, albeit through the idea, leads him to advocate a simple style, i.e., with as little as possible of the arbitrariness of metaphor, and his passage, though nowhere mentioning analogy, is nonetheless so nearly antimetaphorical as to be sufficiently analogical and fully consistent with his analogy between the things of this world and spiritual things. Wesley's passage, like that of Locke, implies an antimetaphorical and hence analogical view of language and of truth: describing "scripture words" as desirable, of course, hardly excludes metaphor from either truth or language; but the simplicity and clarity of his writing, both here and generally, are due in part to Locke's argument that metaphor can too easily undermine the capacity of language for communicating and representing truths of whatever kind, whether natural or spiritual. It is clear, at any rate, from "The Character of a Methodist" as well as from "Letters to Mr. John Smith," that Wesley derives much of his style more or less directly from the analogical method of both Locke and Browne.

"Letters to Mr. John Smith" and the two "Appeals" are not the only nonhomiletical works of the 1740s in which philosophical theology lies near the heart: "A Letter to the Rev. Dr. Conyers Middleton" (1749) is more explicit than *The Procedure* in drawing upon the *Essay* for a theology of immediate revelation. The Bible, to be sure, is given "its due honour" as "traditional evidence" (Jackson, 10:75). Thus Wesley observes epistemological criteria, i.e., the rules of evidence, to suggest that reading the Book with an eye of understanding is a sure access to the truth of Christianity. But that same epistemology leads him to contend that "internal evidence" of Christian truth, i.e., immediate revelation, is superior even to scripture:

> Traditional evidence is of an extremely complicated nature, necessarily including so many and so various considerations, that only men of a strong and clear UNDERSTANDING can be *sensible* of its full force. On the contrary, how plain and simple is this; and how level to the lowest CAPACITY! Is not this the sum: "One thing I KNOW; I was blind, but now I *see*"? [cf. John 9:25]. An argument so plain, that a peasant, a woman, a child, may feel all its force.
>
> The traditional evidence of Christianity stands, as it were, a great way off; and therefore, although it speaks loud and clear, yet makes a less lively *impression*. It gives us an account of what was transacted long ago, in far distant times as well as places. Whereas the inward evidence is intimately present to all persons, at all times, and in all places. (Jackson, 10:75–76. My italics and capital letters—RB)

The diction here, sensationalistic and rational, is precisely Lockean and signals a deliberate, if not a deliberately Brownean analogy between sense perception and immediate revelation. Wesley is once again careful of course to manifest Brownean reticence regarding how much one knows even from spiritual sense and spiritual discernment: "Consider, not only how little you know of the immensity of the things that are beyond sense and time, but how uncertainly do you know even that little!" (Jackson, 10:74). It is important to hear, however, the fully epistemological tone of his relative confidence in immediate revelation; he emphasizes what "senses suitable to invisible or eternal objects" will bring "to the rational, reflecting, part of mankind": "A more extensive knowledge of things invisible and eternal; a greater certainty in whatever knowledge of them we have; and in order to both, faculties capable of discerning things invisible" (Jackson, 10: 74).

"A Letter to the Rev. Dr. Conyers Middleton" rises to an especially characteristic height in presenting experiential faith as counterpart to courageous though skeptical empiricism:

Is it not so? Let impartial reason speak. Does not every thinking man want a window, not so much in his neighbour's, as in his own, breast? He wants an opening there, of whatever kind, that might let in light from eternity. He is pained to be thus feeling after God so darkly and uncertainly; to know so little of God, and indeed so little of any beside material objects. He is concerned, that he must see even that little, not directly, but in the dim, sullied glass of sense; and consequently so imperfectly and obscurely, that it is all a mere enigma still.

Now, these very desiderata faith supplies. It gives a more extensive knowledge of things invisible, showing what eye had not seen, nor ear heard, neither could it before enter into our heart to conceive [cf. 1 Cor. 2:9]. And all these it shows in the clearest light, with the fullest certainty and evidence. For it does not leave us to receive our notices of them by mere reflection from the dull glass of sense; but resolves a thousand enigmas of the highest concern by giving faculties suited to things invisible. (Jackson, 10:74–75)

This statement, couched in the doubly "empirical" context of a telescope metaphor (witness "*resolves* a thousand enigmas") and a quasi-philosophic allusion to the Bible, is in keeping with both *The Procedure* and the *Essay*, for if the telescope image is a rather more self-conscious trope than Locke, Browne, or even Wesley himself would usually allow, both this passage and the entire letter to Middleton nonetheless constitute Wesley's most pronounced dilation upon Brownean and Lockean analogy as an at once natural and spiritual mode of knowing and of speaking.

During the 1740s, then, Wesley completed his philosophically theological formulation of method: not only did he draw a Brownean analogy between sense perception and revelation, but he also signaled an interest in bridging the gap between revealed and natural religion. The letter to Middleton, though lamenting that one can know but little of God through the "sullied glass of sense," suggests that material objects indicate a divine original. The letters to "Smith" are addressed to Deists as well as Anglicans. And the definition of faith in "An Earnest Appeal" insists that the believer perceives and feels the existence of God as well as His presence: God's existence was what the argument of natural religion set out to prove. Finally, *Primitive Physick* (1747) suggests that a theistical natural religion is not just consistent with, but even demanded by, empirical method. For one thing, Wesley's endorsement of empirical method as the only guide in medicine is made clear by the bluntness of his delightful Preface, in which he praises the Greeks for their healing arts: "The Trial was made. The Cure was wrought. And Experience and Physick grew up together."[7] And for another, although he deplores the legacy of much subsequent medical practice, in which in general "Men of Learning began to set Experience aside," he rejoices that

> there have not been wanting from Time to Time, some Lovers of Mankind . . . Who have laboured to explode out of [physick] all Hypotheses, and fine-spun theories, and to make it a plain intelligible Thing, as it was in the Beginning: Having no more Mystery in it than this, "Such a Medicine removes such a Pain." (pp. ix, xii)

When Wesley asks "has not the Author of Nature taught us the use of many . . . Medicines?" he implicates an undeistical because intervenient God of nature in the very process of scientific inquiry (p. vii).

Applications

Wesley's methodology, at once theological and philosophical, continued to operate throughout his mind's long history. After the 1740s, it is true, when his thought was formulated to his satisfaction and he hoped to the satisfaction of fair-minded readers at large, he wrote more and more with his followers in mind; but it is feasible here, from a sampling of the broadly directed writings characteristic of his years of greatest fame, to show that if anything he grew more intellectually rigorous as his audience increased. It is true too that unlike the writings of the 1740s, or at any rate unlike the ones just discussed, the later works are more often sermons than not; but this does not mean that the later sermons, of which I shall discuss a number, are necessarily any less fully methodological; for the writings of the 1740s, of which the ones just discussed form a large sample, demonstrate the philosophically theological procedure of his homiletical as well as nonhomiletical genres.

What Cragg says of the "Appeals," namely, that they are "primarily directed to a constituency outside his own societies" (Cragg, p. 34), can be said as well about the letters to "Smith" and Dr. Middleton; but if one is less than completely surprised to find Wesley being philosophically theological with intellectually inclined divines and "men of reason," one should not shrink from seeing in "The Great Privilege," notably, the possibility of a broadly methodological dimension in even his most specifically kerygmatic language for common people. Moreover, and this may come as a surprise, his works after the 1740s include many nonhomiletical and intellectually ambitious titles intended for, if not read by, Methodist readers in particular and common readers in general. These typically "public" and less narrowly directed writings of his fullest literary maturity, in other words, are describable as either simultaneously theological and philosophical or exclusively philosophical. In sum, then, it is feasible to indicate that regardless for the moment of whether his intention was to show respect for the common reader's intellect or to improve it or both and far from countering the spirit of the earlier works by sacrificing quality of thought to broad appeal, the later mode of discourse, i.e., the sermons and such mass audience matter for the mind as Wesley's popularizations of electrical science and natural philosophy, his reviews of philosophical books, and, clearly not least, his annotations to the *Essay*, reflects his consistently functioning and often explicit theologizing thereof.

So Lockean is "The Case of Reason Impartially Considered" that this sermon requires attention first. One recognizes, for example, the range of empirical method in the definition of reason:

> [R]eason is much the same with *understanding*. It means a faculty of the human soul; that faculty which exerts itself in three ways;—by simple apprehension, by judgment, and by discourse. *Simple apprehension* is barely conceiving a thing in the mind; the first and most simple act of the understanding. *Judgment* is the determining that the things before conceived either agree with or differ from each other. *Discourse*, strictly speaking, is the motion or progress of the mind from one judgment to another. The faculty of the soul which includes these three operations I here mean by the term *reason*. (Jackson, 6:353)

The third operation, i.e., discourse, reserves for the mind the a posteriori but active function of Lockean reason: for Locke's similar use of the term *discourse*, see *Essay* 2.4.5; Nidditch, p. 126 (see also 2.9.1; p. 143). The second operation, judgment, reserves for the mind the still active, yet more explicitly sense-grounded, function of Lockean reason: for Locke's similar use of the term *judgment*, see *Essay* 4.14.3; Nidditch, p. 653. And the first operation, apprehension, reserves for the mind the most intimately sense-related, and least active, function of Lockean reason: for Locke's similar use of the term *apprehension*, see *Essay* 4.11.9; Nidditch, p. 635 (see also 2.9.1; Nidditch, p. 143). Wesley's equation of reason with understanding clinches, or at least further indicates, the Lockean context of his definition.

Specifically Lockean too is "The Case of Reason"'s view of reason's relation to faith. Whereas some proponents of revealed religion, such as

Latitudinarians and Cambridge Platonists, perhaps, "lay it down as an undoubted principle that reason is the highest gift of God" and whereas others, i.e., "those enthusiasts who suppose the dreams of their own imagination to be revelations from God," "despise and vilify reason," and
finally, whereas proponents of natural religion, e.g., Socinian and Deist,
overvalue reason in their way, viz., "They that are prejudiced against the
Christian revelation, who do not receive the Scriptures as the oracles of
God, almost universally run into this extreme: I have scarce known any
exception: So do all, by whatever name they are called, who deny the
Godhead of Christ," Wesley, for his part, asks whether there is no "medium between these extremes," and answers his own question, to wit,
"Certainly there is," by emphasizing that Locke points to such a medium:
"But who is there to point it out?—to mark down the middle way? That
great master of reason, Mr. Locke, has done something of the kind,
something applicable to it, in . . . his Essay concerning Human Understanding" (Jackson, 6:351–52).

Thus, Wesley not only employs an explicitly Lockean means of moving from philosophy to theological method, but he also implies that
Locke's model of sense-based reason, i.e., the view of reason as entailing
what Browne calls "limits," as well as what Browne calls "extent," is the
way reason should be thought of in religion. Taking as text Paul's exhortation to the Corinthians, to wit, "Brethren, be not children in understanding: Howbeit in malice be ye children, but in understanding be
men" (1 Cor. 14:20), and in the context of equating understanding with
sense-based reason, Wesley upholds a Lockean concept of reason-in-
religion. For he implies that such reason is object-oriented and other-
directed: it tells "what it is to be outwardly holy," and it "enables us to
understand what the Holy Scriptures declare concerning the being and
attributes of God" (Jackson 6:354–55). Not only, he concludes, can reason "do much, very much, in the affairs of common life," and not only
can it "assist us in going through the whole circle of arts and sciences,"
but it can also "do exceeding much, both with regard to the foundation
of [religion], and the superstructure" (Jackson, 6:353–54).

"Exceeding much." But by no means all. Wesley's emphasis on the
"Godhead of Christ," and the "oracles of God," as objects of a rational
and almost Lockean understanding, makes his view of reason-in-religion
more broadly "grounded" than the less biblical understanding of the
Deists. But Wesley's understanding, though expanding the range of natural religion's methodological rigor, makes no pretense of being an all-
sufficient method of faith: "Let reason do all that reason can. But, at the
same time, acknowledge it is utterly incapable of giving either faith, or

hope, or love; . . . . Seek and receive them, not as your own acquisition, but as the gift of God" (Jackson, 6:360). "The Case of Reason" takes reason to the boundary of its usefulness, namely, where immediate takes over from traditional revelation; and this is consistent with the positions of Locke and Browne regarding the limits of human understanding. Far from being mystical, anti-intellectual, or wrong-headed, Wesley's recognition of reason's limit is sufficiently Brownean and sufficiently Lockean insofar as he advocates constant and quasi-sensationalistic contact with the data base of spiritual experience: the influx of grace, for him, is non-rational but not antirational; and since it is more or less analogous to sense impression, it is more or less in line with an important component of Lockean methodology.

The purest and least religiously motivated form of Wesley's empiricism is to be found in his preface to *Desideratum; Or, Electricity made plain and useful* (1760), a "tract" in which, as Wesley puts it, "I have endeavoured to comprise the sum of what has been hitherto published on this curious and important subject, by Mr. Franklin, Dr. Hoadly, Mr. Wilson, Watson, Lovett, Freke, Martin, Watkins, and in the Monthly Magazines" (Jackson, 14:241). This preface, it is true, evinces a marked faith in electricity as panacea, and one must regard as hardly rigorous the "method" of hearsay and incomplete observation whereby Wesley concludes that electricity is among such "simple remedies" as that of Berkeley in *Siris* (1744): "The ingenious and benevolent Bishop of Cloyne brought tar-water likewise into credit for a season; and innumerable were the cures wrought thereby, even in the most desperate and deplorable cases" (Jackson, 14:242). It is worth pointing out, however, that the disposition to regard remedies as "simple," or rather to expect them to be so, is shared today by no less an experimental observer than Lewis Thomas, who holds that "genuine understanding of disease mechanisms" produces medical technology which is "relatively inexpensive, relatively simple, and relatively easy to deliver."[8] At any rate, the Preface to *Desideratum*, like the Preface to *Primitive Physick*, evinces a firm grasp of empirical principles; it is even the case, for example, that on the strength of his up-to-date knowledge of electrotherapy Wesley advances a hypothesis of his own. Here he is on the relation between electricity and anatomy:

> Perhaps if the nerves are really perforated, (as is now generally supposed,) the electric ether is the only fluid in the universe which is fine enough to move through them. And what, if the nervous juice itself be a fluid of this kind? If so, it is no wonder that it has always eluded the search of the most accurate naturalists. (Jackson, 14:243)

This empirical understanding is intellectually and perceptively inquisitive.

"Thoughts upon Necessity" (1774), a reaction to Lord Kames's *Essays on the Principles of Morality and Natural Religion* (1751) and David Hartley's *Observations on Man* (1749), reveals that Wesley's understanding of empiricism extended to some of its most radical post-Lockean developments. As empiricist versions of the Manichean and Stoical view that "man is not self-determined" (Jackson, 10:457), these titles attracted Wesley's careful attention.

"Thoughts upon Necessity" pays Kames the compliment of letting him speak for himself; "Man," says Kames (as Wesley quotes him)

> imagines himself to be free in all his actions. . . . But all this is an entire mistake; it is no more than a pleasing dream: . . .
>
> In the moral world, whatever is a cause with regard to its proper effect, is an effect with regard to some prior cause, and so backward without end. Events, therefore, being a train of causes and effects, are necessary and fixed. Every one must be, and cannot be otherwise than it is. . . . We are necessarily determined. (Jackson, 10:460. Cf. p. 157 of Kames's *Essay*)

This argument, that freedom is an illusion, is supported with the suggestion that illusion is the state of man; Kames insists, for example, that sense impressions are no more than a dream. Here is Wesley's quotation:

> The impressions which man receives in the natural world, do not correspond to the truth of things. Thus the qualities called secondary, which we by natural instinct attribute to matter, belong not to matter, nor exist without us; but all the beauty of colours with which heaven and earth appear clothed, is a sort of romance or illusion. (Jackson, 10:460)

To present Hartley's argument, Wesley blends quotation, paraphrase, and even favorable comment:

> [Hartley] lays it down as a principle, (and a principle it is, which cannot reasonably be denied,) that as long as the soul is vitally united to the body, all its operations depend on the body; that in particular all our thoughts depend upon the vibrations of the fibres of the brain; and of consequence vary, more or less, as those vibrations vary. In that expression, "our thoughts," he comprises all our reflections and passions; yea, and all our volitions, and consequently

our actions, which, he supposes, unavoidably follow those vibrations. He premises, "But you will say, this scheme infers [*sic*] the
universal necessity of human actions;" and frankly adds, "Certainly
it does. I am sorry for it, but I cannot help it." (Jackson, 10:458)

Wesley goes so far, indeed, as to agree expressly with much of what
Hartley says:

> [*Observations on Man*] certainly contains a great deal of truth, as will
> appear to any that considers it calmly. For who can deny, that not
> only the memory, but all the operations of the soul, are now depen-
> dent on the bodily organs, the brain in particular? insomuch that a
> blow on the back part of the head (as frequent experience shows)
> may take away the understanding, and destroy at once both sensa-
> tion and reflection; and an irregular flow of spirits may quickly turn
> the deepest philosopher into a madman. It must be farther allowed,
> that . . . our judgments . . . will and passions also, . . . alternately
> depend on the fibres of the brain. (Jackson, 10:469–70)

Thus, despite its determinism, Hartley's highly sensationalistic point of
view receives a more than fair hearing from Wesley; perhaps what he
liked in Hartley and in Kames was their Lockean presuppositions.

Among what Wesley did not like, of course, were their determinism
in general and in particular the methodological timidity on which it was
based. Again he is careful to let them speak for themselves; here, for example, is his quotation of Kames's determinism, which, oddly enough, is
developed from the perspective of Deism:

> The Deity is the First Cause of all things. He formed the plan on
> which all things were to be governed, and put it in execution by
> establishing, both in the natural and moral world, certain laws that
> are fixed and immutable. By virtue of these, all things proceed in a
> regular train of causes and effects, bringing about the events con-
> tained in the original plan, and admitting the possibility of no other.
> This universe is a vast machine, winded up and set a-going. The
> several springs and wheels act unerringly one upon another. The
> hand advances and the clock strikes, precisely as the Artist deter-
> mined. (Jackson, 10:461)

Hartley's determinism, also grounded in Deism, is paraphrased by Wesley thus:

[Hartley] indirectly ascribes the necessity of all human actions to God; who, having fixed the laws of this vital union [of the soul and body] according to his own good pleasure, having so constituted man that the motions of the soul thus depend on the fibres of the body, has thereby laid him under an invincible necessity of acting thus, and in no other manner. (Jackson, 10:462)

Wesley, for his part, "would fain place mankind in a fairer point of view . . . as I cannot believe the noblest creature in the visible world to be only a fine piece of clockwork" (Jackson, 10:457). For his part, too, Wesley should be called epistemologically adventurous or at least epistemologically vigorous: witness his animadversion that "Wherever [in Hartley's *Observations* and Kames's *Essay*] this argument occurs, (and it occurs ten times over,)—'The natural world is all illusion; therefore, so is the moral,'—it is just good for nothing" (Jackson, 10:471).

The empiricism in "Thoughts upon Necessity" in other words leaves no doubt of the natural world's actuality, and seems intent indeed upon correcting the overingenious extreme, I had almost said the post-Berkeleian decadence, of such post-Lockean developments in the theory of perception as, especially, that of Kames. "I infer," writes Wesley,

> that colour is just as real as size or figure; and that all colours do as really exist without us, as trees, or corn, or heaven, or earth.
>
> "But what do you mean by colour?" When I say, "That cloth is of a red colour," I mean its surface is so disposed as to reflect the red (that is, the largest) rays of light. When I say, "The sky is blue," I mean, it is so disposed as to reflect the blue (that is, the smallest) rays of light. And where is the delusion here? Does not that disposition, do not those rays, as really exist, as either the cloth or the sky? And are they not as really reflected, as the ball in a tennis-court? It is true, that, when they strike upon my eye, a particular sensation follows in my soul. But that sensation is not colour; I know no one that calls it so. Colour therefore is a real material thing. There is no illusion in the case, unless you confound the perception with the thing perceived. And all other secondary qualities are just as real as figure or any other primary one. So you have no illusion in the natural world to countenance that you imagine to be in the moral. (Jackson, 10:470–71)

This empiricism, sophisticated in its awareness of the *esse est percipi* and scientific in its Newtonian optics, is in its untroubled realism more or less directly beholden to Locke, for, as the one British empiricist often able to think that things exist which correspond to particular ideas in the mind, Locke is often pleased to expatiate within the limits of knowledge.

The empiricism of "Thoughts upon Necessity" is especially beholden to what Locke says of secondary qualities. Writing, for example, of "the Idea of White and Red," Locke defines "Idea" as "the Object of the Understanding when a man thinks"; and he speaks of "Light" not only as "the Idea which is produced in us by it," but also as "the Cause of that Sensation in us" (*Essay* 1.1.8, 3.4.10, 16; Nidditch, pp. 47, 424, 427): thus, he suggests that not just things-in-themselves, but even secondary qualities, have external existence. Wesley, writing after it became smart if not fashionable to think that not even things, much less their secondary qualities, exist outside the mind, seems intent upon countering over-Berkeleian subtleties; compare, for example, the comment of Kames that "all the beauty of colours with which heaven and earth appear clothed, is a sort of romance or illusion" with paragraph thirty-eight of Berkeley's *Treatise concerning the Principles of Human Knowledge* (1710):

> But after all, say you, it sounds very harsh to say we eat and drink ideas, and are clothed with ideas. I acknowledge it does so; the word "idea" not being used in common discourse to signify the several combinations of sensible qualities which are called "things". . . . But this does not concern the truth of the proposition, which in other words is no more than to say, we are fed and clothed with those things which we perceive immediately by our senses. The hardness or softness, the color, taste, warmth, figure, or suchlike qualities, which combined together constitute the several sorts of victuals and apparel, have been shewn to exist only in the mind that perceives them. . . .

In apparent concert with Berkeley, Kames denies that a world exists without mind to observe it, but Wesley reaffirms Locke's indication that not just the thing sensed, but the sense image as well, is almost mind-independently real.

With regard not just to the natural but also to the moral world, "Thoughts upon Necessity" offers implicitly Lockean reproof of Kames. When Kames contends, for example, that the will "necessarily obeys" the judgment, Wesley replies, "Indeed it does not" (Jackson, 10:472); and this reply accords with, if not derives from, Locke's argument that "uneasiness of *desire* . . . determines the will" (*Essay* 2.21.39; Nidditch, p. 256. My italics—RB). In any case, Wesley's view of free will is indebted

to Locke's: Locke's view that "Liberty . . . [pre-]Supposes the Understanding, and Will" (*Essay* 2.21.9; Nidditch, p. 238) underlies Wesley's
insistence that

> God created man an intelligent being; and endued him with will as
> well as understanding. Indeed, it seems, without this, his under-
> standing would have been given to no purpose. Neither would ei-
> ther his will or understanding have answered any valuable purpose,
> if liberty had not been added to them, a power distinct from both; a
> power of choosing for himself, a self-determining principle. It may
> be doubted whether . . . these three faculties . . . are not implied in
> the very nature of a spirit. Certain it is, that no being can be account-
> able for its actions, which has not liberty, as well as will and under-
> standing. (Jackson, 10:468)

In their views of "moral good and evil," moreover, Wesley and Locke are
precisely similar. Here is the *Essay*:

> That God has given a Rule whereby Men should govern them-
> selves, I think there is no body so brutish as to deny. He has a Right
> to do it, we are his Creatures: He has Goodness and Wisdom to di-
> rect our Actions to that which is best: and he has Power to enforce it
> by Rewards and Punishments, of infinite weight and duration, in
> another Life: for no body can take us out of his hands. This is the
> only true touchstone of moral Rectitude; and by comparing them
> to this Law, it is, that Men judge of the most considerable Moral
> Good or Evil of their Actions; that is, whether as Duties, or Sins,
> they are like to procure them happiness or misery, from the hands
> of the Almighty. (*Essay* 2.28.8; Nidditch, p. 352)

And here is "Thoughts upon Necessity":

> It follows, if there be no such thing as virtue or vice, as moral good
> or evil, if there be nothing rewardable or punishable in the actions
> or passions of men, then there can be no judgment to come, and no
> future rewards and punishments. (Jackson, 10:464)

Wesley, like Locke, regards good and evil as the results of voluntary disagreement with, or conformity to divine as well as civil and natural law;
and insofar as "Thoughts upon Necessity," in this instance, draws upon

the *Essay* (as indicated by both content and wording), Wesley's argument for liberty rests upon an epistemological as well as religious foundation.

"Thoughts upon Necessity" in other instances adds to Lockean method and is no more simply derivative from it than, say, "The Great Privilege of those that are born of God" is slavishly dependent upon *The Procedure*. Not only, for example, is discussion of secondary qualities in "Thoughts upon Necessity" illuminated by Newtonian optics and Berkeleian refinements, but there is also something almost nonrational, if not para-Humean, about its highly sensationalistic regard for the power of belief: "It is not easy," writes Wesley, "for a man of common understanding, especially if unassisted by education, to unravel these finely woven schemes [of Kames and Hartley], or show distinctly where the fallacy lies. But he knows, he feels, he is certain, they cannot be true" (Jackson, 10:463). Or again (and more elaborately) there is more than merely Lockean argument (for there is quite decidedly Wesleyan passion) in the linkage of sense impression and free will in "Thoughts upon Necessity":

> [I]t is certain I can trust none of my senses, if I am a mere machine. For I have the testimony of all my outward and all my inward senses, that I am a free agent. If therefore I cannot trust them in this, I can trust them in nothing. Do not tell me there are sun, moon, and stars, or that there are men, beasts, or birds, in the world. I cannot believe one tittle of it, if I cannot believe what I feel in myself, namely, that it depends on me, and no other being, whether I shall now open or shut my eyes, move my head hither and thither, or stretch my hand or my foot. If I am necessitated to do all this, contrary to the whole both of my inward and outward senses, I can believe nothing else, but must necessarily sink into universal scepticism. (Jackson, 10:471–72)

Wesley's conviction that "the idea of freedom is essential to the moral feeling" (Jackson, 10:465) is so strong as to cause him to diverge from Locke when Locke (uncharacteristically from Wesley's point of view) borders on the mechanistic. "In bare naked Perception," says Locke at one point, "the Mind is, for the most part, only passive; and what it perceives, it cannot avoid perceiving" (*Essay* 2.9.1; Nidditch, p. 143). But this view, as drawn out by Kames, is denounced by Wesley, for when Kames observes that "Man is passive in receiving the impressions of things," Wesley replies in certain terms: "Not altogether. Even here much depends on his own choice. In many cases he may or may not receive the impression; in most he may vary it greatly" (Jackson, 10:472).

"Thoughts upon Necessity," in other words, like everything else he wrote, is finally religious; a theology of sin and guilt, for instance, is what decisively persuades him against necessity:

> Certainly the pain, the remorse, which is felt by any man who had been guilty of a bad action, springs from the notion, that he has a power over his actions, that he might have forborne to do it. . . . On the system of universal necessity, there could be no place for blame or remorse. And we struggle in vain to reconcile to this system the testimony which conscience clearly gives to freedom. (Jackson, 10:465)

To put it more precisely: "Thoughts upon Necessity" offers a theological defense of free will in concert with an informed and largely sympathetic consideration of philosophical issues. Wesley, after all, does not deny the usefulness, indeed implies the validity (up to a point), of even the most technical Hartleian understanding:

> I am not careful therefore about the flowing of my blood and spirits, or the vibrations of my brain; being well assured, that, however my spirits may flow, or my nerves and fibres vibrate, the Almighty God of love can control them all, and will (unless I obstinately choose vice and misery) afford me such help, as, in spite of all these, will put it into my power to be virtuous and happy for ever. (Jackson, 10:473)

The particular importance of "Thoughts upon Necessity" is indicated by Wesley's revisitation of its themes in "A Thought on Necessity" (1780; see Jackson, 10:474–80); moreover, the blend of philosophy and theology explicit in these companion pieces is, if anything, even more marked in the introduction and conclusion of his two volume anthology of scientific empiricism, *A Survey of the Wisdom of God in the Creation: or a Compendium of Natural Philosophy* (1777). In other words, the period from 1774, when "Thoughts upon Necessity" appeared, to the appearance of "A Thought on Necessity" in 1780, constitutes an especially intense stage of his philosophically theological emphasis. The beginning and end of the *Survey* deserve thorough consideration here not only because they were written at the midpoint of this period, and so bid fair to represent his method well, but also because they make for some of the Wesleyan canon's most memorable reading. "Natural philosophy," writes Wesley in the introduction, "treats both of God himself, and of his creatures visible and invisible" (Jackson, 13:482); the conclusion, entitled "Remarks on the Limits of Human Knowledge," so stresses "the invisible things of God" that Wesley uses it extensively in a sermon, "On the Imperfection of Human Knowledge" (cf. Jackson, 6:337–50, especially 339–42, with Jackson, 13:488–99); and both "Remarks on the Limits" and the introduction (the introduction is entitled "Of the Gradual Improvement of Natural Philosophy") stress "the visible things of God" so much that they constitute, in part, empiricism outright.

With respect to the empiricism, it is so extensive as to be complete. Note, for example, in "Of the Gradual Improvement" the tough-mindedness, if not the proto-positivist perspective of the surprising conviction that "moral philosophy" and "divinity," as understood by the ancient Greeks, were part of what kept all but Aristotle from advancing scientific knowledge:

> [W]hen the four Greek sects, the Platonic, Peripatetic, Epicurean, and Stoic, divided the western world between them, the Platonists almost confined themselves and their opinions to the subject of divinity; the Peripatetics regarded little but logic; the Stoics little but moral philosophy; and the Epicureans had small concern about any, being immersed in sensual pleasures: So that none of them made any considerable improvement in any branch of natural philosophy. (Jackson, 13:483)

These essays hereafter referred to collectively as the *Survey* were written, like those on necessity, from the perspective of post-Lockean yet still Locke-oriented empiricism, and, unlike those on necessity, from the perspective of a prescient yet still sufficiently Lockean empiricism.

With regard first to the latter perspective, just as "Thoughts upon Necessity" shows awareness of Newton as well as Berkeley, so the *Survey* is at least as much scientific as philosophical, and it may even be said that Wesley's scientific insights were ahead of his time. His treatment of "spontaneous generation," and his insistence that "none that dwells in a body" "knows when the spirit returns to [God]," parallel today's attempts to define death and the inception of life (Jackson, 13:495, 498). His queries regarding the nature of light—"Is light subject to the general laws which obtain in all other matter; or is it a body *sui generis*, altogether different from all other bodies? Is it the same, or how does it differ from ether, Sir Isaac Newton's subtile matter? . . . Wherein does [ether] differ from the electric fluid?" (Jackson, 13:491)—amount to an understanding of the classic but still lively question whether light is particulate or undulant. When Wesley asks "Whence arise the different qualities and tempers, not only in different kinds and species, but even in the individuals of one species . . . ?" (Jackson, 13:496), he anticipates an issue of Darwinian science. And when he asks "What is at the center of the earth?" and "What, for that matter, does one know of its surface?" (Jackson, 13:492–93), he anticipates an issue of Lyellian science.

With regard now to eighteenth-century science, which grew in large measure from the *Essay*'s immediate influence, the *Survey* is fully informed. Wesley's enumeration of the atmosphere's constituent parts, for example, dew, rain, and "other vapours," and his awareness that "not only various diseases, but often death itself ensues" from incomplete knowledge of the air (Jackson, 13:491–92), reflect his recognition of the then still young science of atmospherics. As an instance of how far this science advanced in the time, say, from 1728, when Ephraim Chambers's *Cyclopaedia* appeared, to the appearance of Shelley's *Queen Mab*, in 1815, compare Shelley's still accurate understanding with Chambers's quaint usage of *atmosphere* and *diffusion*. Here is Chambers:

> According to [modern scientists], there is no other *Diffusion*, but that of corporeal substance, emitted in minute effluvia, or particles, into a kind of atmosphere all around the body; which Diffusion of corpuscles some call *atmospherical*, as being supposed to be terminated by a circle, whereof the diffusing body is the centre.[9]

And here is Shelley:

> Beyond our atmosphere, the sun would appear a rayless orb of fire in the midst of a black concave. The equal diffusion of its light on earth is owing to the refraction of the rays by the atmosphere, and their reflection from the other bodies. (Note to *Queen Mab*)

The *Survey*'s inquiry into sea life and the nature of vegetables (Jackson, 13:493–94), not to mention its anthologizing of Charles de Bonnet's proto-evolutionary theories,[10] illustrates Wesley's discernment of the other ascendant branch of eighteenth-century science, i.e., biology. Finally, Wesley's familiarity with established, early-century science was thorough, for he knew that a central question arising from the microscope was whether "microscopic tribes" are "animals" (Jackson, 13:494); and his knowledge of Newton extended not only to the *Opticks*, but also to the theory of planetary motion and the post-Newtonian body of re-finements and queries that arose in response:

> What is it that contains [the planets] in their orbits? And what is the principle of their motions? By what created power, what outward or inward force, are they thrown forward to such a point, and then brought back again to a determinate distance from the central fire? Dr. Rogers has evidently demonstrated that no conjunction of the centrifugal and centripetal force can possibly account for this, or even cause any body to move in an ellipsis. Will light moving outward, and returning inward in the form of spirit, account for them? Nay, if they take away some, they plunge us into other difficulties, no less considerable: So that there is reason to fear that even the Newtonian, yea, and Hutchinsonian system, however plausible and ingenious, and whatever advantage they may have in several particulars, are yet no more capable of solid, convincing proof, than the Ptolemaic or Cartesian.[11]

The *Survey*'s perspective, not simply empirical scientifically, is philosophically so, to the edge of sympathy with Hume; for despite Wesley's strictures against Humean attitudes towards religion, his sophistication regarding proof of scientific theory rests on evident acceptance of Hume's critique of causation in Section 7 ("Of the Idea of Necessary Connection") of *An Enquiry concerning Human Understanding* (1748). "I endeavour throughout" the *Survey*, Wesley writes therein,

> not to account for things, but only to describe them. I undertake barely to set down what appears in nature; not the cause of those appearances. The facts lie within the reach of our senses and understanding; the causes are more remote. That things are so, we know with certainty; but why they are so, we know not. In many cases we cannot know; and the more we inquire, the more we are perplexed and entangled. God hath so done his works, that we may admire and adore; but we cannot search them out to perfection.
> . . .
> [A]s to the reasons of almost everything which we see, hear, or feel, after all our researches and disquisitions, they are hid in impenetrable darkness.
> I trust, therefore, the following sheets may . . . be a means . . . of humbling the pride of man, by showing that he is surrounded on

every side with things which he can no more account for, than for immensity or eternity. (Jackson, 14:301, 302)

Wesley's perspective, here, insofar as it is indeed Humean, incorporates the latest and some of the subtlest issues of empirical epistemology; and his drift aligns him with the increasingly problematical status of that epistemology's rational hemisphere.

His method, however, only incidentally Humean, is primarily Lockean. The *Survey*'s brief history of empiricism, from Thales Milesius and Aristotle through Roger Bacon and Albertus Magnus to Francis Bacon and the Royal Society (Jackson, 13:482–83), extends, significantly, to the period of that philosophy's prescient as well as culminating manifesto, *An Essay concerning Human Understanding*.

The *Essay*'s epistemology, for example, is strikingly consistent with the *Survey*'s understanding that proper method, whether philosophical or scientific, is a systematic process of sense perception. Wesley's power of perception, i.e., his active mind, is sufficiently evident from the hypothesizing tone of passages quoted already; and his recognition of the mind's inquisitive role in scientific enterprise is implicit in his comment that Aristotle's "observations" "led the way" in natural history (Jackson, 13:483). Wesley's salute to telescopes, microscopes, burning glasses, barometers, thermometers, air pumps, diving bells, and diving machines (Jackson, 13:484–85) discloses his assumption that the senses, if extended, yield the base of knowledge. "The knowledge of nature," in short, "diligently cultivated" by Aristotle, is phraseology epitomizing the objective and subjective criteria whereby one knows when one has "searched out the properties of particular things" (Jackson, 13:487). Or as Wesley also phrases it, "reason" and "experiment" bring about "gradual improvement of natural philosophy"; note in particular the blend of object and subject in the *Survey*'s suggestion that mind and matter meet in the realm of modern experiment: "[N]ot single persons only, but whole societies apply themselves carefully to make experiments; that, having accurately observed the structure and properties of each body, they might the more safely judge of its nature" (Jackson, 13:483).

The *Survey*'s understanding of scientific method, then, is shaped at least in part by Lockean empiricism. Indeed, Wesley pays due attention to the Locke related work of such English scientists as William Harvey and Robert Boyle: Wesley cites Boyle for his rigorously skeptical method and Harvey for his improvements in natural philosophy (Jackson, 13:484, 494). Moreover, the *Survey* not only echoes but also agrees with Locke's proto-biological as well as proto-behaviorist argument that animals "reason" and "feel" as humans do:

> Do they reason, or do they not? . . . Are they mere machines? If we assert they are it inevitably follows, that they neither see, nor hear, nor smell, nor feel. For of this mere machines are utterly incapable. Much less can they know or remember anything, or move any otherwise than they are impelled. But all of this, as unnumbered experiments show, is quite contrary to matter of fact. (Jackson, 13:496–97)

It would appear, from all that Wesley says in the *Survey*, (1) that he viewed natural philosophy as complex and intellectually satisfying because of its delineation in the robust but not simplistic pages of the *Essay*, and (2) that he looked upon natural philosophy not just as one of the three medieval divisions of thought, *metaphysical* and *moral* describing the other two, but, more in line with an age of Locke, as the discipline whereby one takes the way things seem to be as the sometimes equivocal, or even sometimes paradoxical, but not ever quite finally indeterminate indication of the way things are. As Wesley had written in 1774, and this statement is worth repeating, "None can have general good sense unless they have clear and determinate ideas of all things" (Telford, 6:130); here, and in his natural philosophy generally, he bespeaks not only his awareness of the effort required to gain certain knowledge, but also his ambition to gain it.

The Lockean language of the *Survey*'s methodology is matched by what may legitimately be described as its specifically Lockean form. To make this point, I quote at length:

> How far does the universe extend, and where are the limits of it? . . . what do we know of the fixed stars? . . . what are comets? planets not fully formed? or planets destroyed by a conflagration? . . . What is the sun itself? . . . who knows of what substance it is composed? or even whether it be fluid or solid? What are those spots on his surface that are continually changing? . . . How many satellites, secondary planets, move around Jupiter or Saturn? are we sure even of their number? . . . Why do some substances conduct the electric matter, and others arrest its course? Why does a globe of glass and another of sulphur just counteract each other? Why is the coated phial capable of being charged just to such a point, and no

farther? O *crux philosophorum*! . . . Do we thoroughly understand
the nature and properties of the atmosphere that surrounds us? . . .
Whereof consists the inner parts of the globe? . . . And who knows
what is contained in the broad sea? . . . Who can clearly determine
even the fundamental question concerning the general nature of
vegetables? Does the sap perform a regular circulation through
their vessels, or not? . . . where is the soul lodged? in the pineal
gland? the whole brain? in the heart? the blood? in any single part of
the body? Or, is it (if any one can understand those terms) all in all,
and all in every part? . . . Are the nerves pervious or solid? How do
they act? By vibrations, or transmission of the animal spirits? . . .
By what token then can we surely know? (Jackson, 13:488–98)

This form is reminiscent of the general and time-honored philosophic
form of "elenctic disputation," i.e., a debate in which each contestant
could use only questions to advance his argument;[12] but whereas the opponent in elenctic disputation is limited to yes or no answers, Wesley's
form of debate is open-ended: his questions are intended not so much to
dispose of an opponent, or even to persuade one, as to implicate the
reader in truth-seeking. The questions, then, are less elenctic than Lockean: like Locke, and in the context of his thought, Wesley generates an
atmosphere of the searching question, in the hope of finding answers that
would "satisfy our need" to know (Jackson, 13:496) and gradually improve our knowledge.

It cannot be said, though, that the hope is fulfilled. Despite the air of
expectancy with which the questions are framed, the *Survey* is not finally
so confident in its empiricism as, say, "Thoughts upon Necessity." "All
we can attain to," he concludes, "is an imperfect knowledge of what is
obvious . . . [E]nough to satisfy our need, but not our curiosity" (Jackson, 13:496). Or again: "[God] has so exactly proportioned our knowledge to our state! We may know whatever is needful for life or godliness,
whatever is necessary either for our present or eternal happiness. But how
little beside can the most penetrating genius know with any certainty!"
(Jackson, 13:498–99). Thus stressing the limits of understanding, the *Survey* evinces an empiricism modest enough to complement Wesley's religious nature. The *Survey*'s view that "we can neither depend upon reason
nor experiment" to learn of "God and spirits" and its view that "what-
soever men know or can know concerning them must be drawn from the
oracles of God" (Jackson, 13:487) leave room for immediate while denoting traditional revelation and imply that revelation supplements sensa-

tionalistic and rational ways of knowing. Thus the *Survey*'s means of transcending the limits of sense perception is analogical method.

To put it another way, the *Survey* is implicitly Brownean. *The Procedure*'s view that language is problematical, because metaphor is arbitrary, is arguably corollary to the *Survey*'s lament that "we cannot order speech by reason of darkness" (Jackson, 13:497). The *Survey*'s concluding essay is specifically Brownean in the diction of its title: "Remarks on the *Limits*" (my italics—RB). And above all, the *Survey*'s empiricism is so entirely lacking in pride of intellect as to resemble *The Procedure* almost more than the *Essay*. Small wonder, then, and note this well, that immediately preceding "Remarks on the Limits" is Wesley's abridgment of *The Procedure*, which, along with "Remarks on the Limits," occupies pride of place in his ambitious and wide-ranging encyclopedia for the English common reader. The abridgment, entitled "An Appendix on the Human Understanding written chiefly on the plan of Dr. Brown [*sic*], late Bishop of Cork," was evidently composed with the 1730 version at hand: just three of the manuscript's nine sections are left out, and discrepancies in wording and punctuation are rare.[13]

During the final years of his life, Wesley maintained the philosophically theological intensity of the *Survey*, "A Thought on Necessity," and "Thoughts upon Necessity." On May 28, 1781, for example, and this deserves notice indeed, the seventy-eight-year-old Wesley completed "Remarks upon Mr. Locke's 'Essay on Human Understanding'" (see Jackson, 13:455–64). These remarks were more than a month in the making; Wesley began them on April 28, after "some days" spent in studying the *Essay* (Jackson, 13:455). And they are substantial.[14]

They suggest, moreover, that besides having known the *Essay* intimately ("a careful consideration of this whole work" lies behind the "Remarks," writes Wesley therein: see Jackson, 13:454), Wesley accepted it in the main. The more than 1,800 words given over to Books 1 and 2, despite some trenchant demurrers to particular points, include no hint of any problem with Locke's affirmation of the origin of ideas in sensation and reflection; Wesley's denial of innate ideas is already established. Wesley makes the point that Books 3 and 4 are "by no means equal" to Books 1 and 2; he objects to the "inadequate definitions" in Book 3 and the bias against Aristotle's logic in Book 4.[15] Book 4, however, is deemed of sufficient importance to merit more than five hundred words of annotation, none of which, despite demurrers, records objection to the Book's main emphases, i.e., its classification of knowledge into identity and diversity, relation, coexistence or necessary connection, and existence, its classification of the ways of knowing into intuition, demonstration, and sensation, its distinction between knowledge and belief, and, finally, its ranking of beliefs according to such degrees of probability as assurance, confidence, and assent. The nearly eight hundred words given over to Book 3, moreover, include no objection to its distinction between words and ideas, its recognition that almost all thinking is in words, its principle of getting from words back to ideas as the cure for confused thought, and its reconciliation of the fact that words are, and must be, general, with the fact that each word is a particular: the attention to Book 3 suggests that Wesley, like Locke and Browne but unlike Berkeley and Hume, was aware that the problems of philosophy are linguistic.

Last, and far from least, the remarks show approval. Wesley disassociates himself, to be sure, from "that immoderate attachment to [Locke] which is so common among his readers" (Jackson, 13:464). And Wesley laments such "mistakes" as Locke's "attack upon logic" (Jackson, 13:463–64); logic formed part of the Oxford training that stayed with Wesley. But emphasizing that no error of Locke is of "any great importance," Wesley concludes that the *Essay* "contains many excellent truths, proposed in a clear and strong manner, by a great master both of reasoning and language" (Jackson, 13:464). Wesley begins, in fact, with an encomium:

> I do not now wonder at [the *Essay's*] having gone through so many editions in so short a time. For what comparison is there between this deep, solid, weighty treatise, and the lively, glittering trifle of Baron Montesquieu? As much as between tinsel and gold; between glass-beads and diamonds. (Jackson, 13:455)

The "Remarks," then, devoting close attention to Locke's philosophy, themselves indicate Wesley's regard for it, and, though miscellaneous, and though not particularly helpful in explaining his larger reasons for writing them (see, however, my third chapter), the "Remarks" are guides to his thinking about individual points: see occasional references in my subsequent argument and especially Appendix C. Moreover, while falling short of clarifying the nature of his debt, since, after all, that can only be done by such as the present study, the "Remarks" self-evidently constitute a high watermark not only of his fascination with the *Essay*, but also of his dependence on it.

Wesley's late method obtains not simply among such far from overtly evangelistic works as the "Remarks," but even among such overtly religious, and more typical, works as sermons.

Like "The Case of Reason Impartially Considered," for example, "The Imperfection of Human Knowledge" is wide ranging in content as well as broad in appeal: this sermon, besides quoting from "Remarks on the Limits," develops in a message of its own the continuum from natural to revealed religion. "Natural and revealed religion," indeed, is the sermon's very phrase (Jackson, 6:348). And the Lockean-Brownean attempt to blend even immediate revelation with a theistical natural religion is everywhere reflected in the full statement with which the sermon founds its comprehensive view of religion on the denial of innate ideas:

> If indeed God had stamped (as some have maintained) an idea of himself on every human soul, we must certainly have understood something of . . . his . . . attributes; for we cannot suppose he would have impressed upon us either a false or an imperfect idea of himself; but the truth is, no man ever did, or does now, find any such idea stamped on his soul. The little which we do know of God, (except what we receive by the inspiration of the Holy One,) we do not gather from any inward impression, but gradually acquire from without. "The invisible things of God," if they are known at all, "are known from the things that are made" [cf. Heb. 11:3]; not from what God hath written in our hearts, but from what he hath written in all his works. Hence then, from his works, particularly his works of creation, we are to learn the knowledge of God. But it is not easy to conceive how little we know even of these. (Jackson, 6:339)

The Brownean flavor of this central passage grows piquant elsewhere in the sermon: not only does Wesley argue that knowledge is "confined within very narrow bounds; abundantly narrower than common people imagine, or men of learning are willing to acknowledge," but he also waxes interjectional about one of *The Procedure*'s main themes: "How astonishingly little do we know of God!—How small a part of his nature do we know! of his essential attributes!" (Jackson, 6:337, 338). The central statement's Lockean flavor is further accented in the sermon's biblical allegiance to sensationalistic and rational methodology: "The desire of knowledge," writes Wesley, is "constant in every rational creature. . . . And it is insatiable: the eye is not satisfied with seeing, nor the ear with hearing [cf. Eccles. 1:8]; neither the mind with any degree of knowledge which can be conveyed into it" (Jackson, 6:337). And finally, the statement's theistical natural religion is elsewhere explicit; there is no more complete indication of Wesley's blend of natural religion and orthodoxy than the following combination of biblical and scientific references:

> The omnipresence or immensity of God, Sir Isaac Newton en-
> deavours to illustrate by a strong expression, by terming infinite
> space, "the Sensorium of the Deity." And the very Heathens did not
> scruple to say, "All things are full of God:" Just equivalent with his
> own declaration:—"Do not I fill heaven and earth? saith the Lord"
> [cf. Ps. 33:5; Jer. 23:24]. How beautifully does the Psalmist illustrate
> this! "Whither shall I flee from thy presence?" [cf. Ps. 139:7]. (Jack-
> son, 6:338)

Perhaps the most peculiarly *Wesleyan* flavor of the sermon, its central statement included, is its implication that faith is somehow a corollary of skeptical philosophy: "A full conviction of our ignorance," says Wesley, "may teach us (what is not always so easy as one would conceive it to be) to trust the invisible God, farther than we can see him" (Jackson, 6:349). The turn of phrase is Wesley's, though the thought is sufficiently Brownean. Another passage—"[T]here will be some future state of being, wherein that now insatiable desire [for knowledge] will be satisfied, and there will be no longer so immense a distance between the appetite and the object of it" (Jackson, 6:337)—is not only sufficiently Brownean: there is something proto-Sartrean, or at least para-Blakean, in his hover-ing insight that man's anxiety, i.e., his seemingly infinite desire, derives in part from his keen sense of his condition as one of lack. "More! More!" exclaims Blake in "There is no Natural Religion" (1788), "is the cry of a mistaken soul, less than All cannot satisfy Man." "Kierkegaard," writes Sartre in *Being and Nothingness* (1943),

> in describing anxiety in the face of what one lacks, characterizes it
> as anxiety in the face of freedom. But Heidegger, whom we know
> to have been greatly influenced by Kierkegaard, considers anxiety
> instead as the apprehension of nothingness. These two descriptions
> of anxiety do not appear to us contradictory; on the contrary the
> one implies the other.[16]

Wesley's passage above has the ring of a decidedly Wesleyan assurance. And the sermon's central statement, certainly one of the most inclusive summations of his philosophical theology, contains something even truer to his mentality than any prescience regarding developments in religious thought and expression: his statement suggests that the immense distance between man and God is bridgeable in the present insofar, though only insofar, as "we know of God" through "the inspiration of the Holy One." It is characteristic of Wesley to heighten Browne's spiritual theology and broaden its appeal without reducing its methodological sophistication.

As a final sign of the philosophical as well as theological continuity even in Wesley's sermons, consider briefly just three others. "On Faith" takes as text Heb. 11:1, the chief scriptural basis of Browne's philosophical theology (Jackson, 7:326). "Human Life a Dream" draws upon Locke's conception of dreams: Locke's argument that "the Dreams of sleeping Men" are "all made up of the waking Man's Ideas, though, for the most part, oddly put together" (*Essay* 1.1.16; Nidditch, p. 113) is largely in accord with Wesley's argument that "we are many times not able to determine" which dreams "arise from natural, which from supernatural, influence," and with Wesley's conclusion that many are due to the "constitution of the body" and the "passions of the mind" (Jackson, 7:318). As for the text of "On Faith," Heb. 11:1 is the only scripture expounded more than once among the 141 printed sermons; and of the many times it is alluded to therein, the following instance from "The Scripture Way of Salvation" includes the most sustained empirical associations and so deserves complete quotation as perhaps the best single illustration and summation of Wesley's thought as I see it:

> *An evidence*, a divine *evidence and conviction* (the word [i.e., *elenchos*] means both) *of things not seen*; not visible, not perceivable either by sight, or by any other of the external senses. It implies both a supernatural *evidence* of God, and of the things of God; a kind of spiritual *light* exhibited to the soul, and a supernatural *sight* or perception thereof. Accordingly, the scripture speaks of God's giving sometimes light, sometimes a power of discovering it. So St. Paul: "God, who commanded light to shine out of darkness, hath shined in our hearts, to give us the light of the knowledge of the glory of God in the face of Jesus Christ" [cf. 2 Cor. 4:6]. And elsewhere the same Apostle speaks of "the eyes of" our "understanding being opened" [cf. Eph. 1:18]. By this two-fold operation of the Holy Spirit, having the eyes of our soul both *opened* and *enlightened*, we see the things which the natural "eye hath not seen, neither the ear heard" [cf. 1 Cor. 2:9]. We have a prospect of the invisible things of God; we see the *spiritual world*, which is all round about us, and yet no more discerned by our natural faculties than if it had no being: And we see the *eternal world*; piercing through the veil which hangs between time and eternity. Clouds and darkness then rest upon it no more, but we already see the glory which shall be revealed. (Jackson, 6:46–47)

This blend of sensationalistic and rational diction, i.e., Wesley's subject/ object playfulness, evinces, particularly in his dual translation of *elenchos*, an almost more than distinctively eighteenth-, even a nineteenth- and twentieth-century, critical acumen. "On Faith" and "Human Life a Dream," finally, like most other works considered in this chapter, expand upon a Lockean and Brownean conception of analogy as the method of connecting heaven and earth. Here is "Human Life a Dream":

> Now, considering that every child of man who is yet upon earth must sooner or later wake out of this dream, and enter real life; how infinitely does it concern every one of us to attend to this before our great change comes! . . . How advisable, by every possible means, to connect the ideas of time and eternity! so to associate them to-gether, that the thought of one may never recur to your mind, without the thought of the other! It is our highest wisdom to asso-ciate the ideas of the visible and invisible world; to connect tem-poral and spiritual, mortal and immortal being. Indeed, in our common dreams we do not usually know we are asleep whilst we are in the midst of our dream. As neither do we know it while we are in the midst of the dream which we call life. But you may be conscious of it now. (Jackson, 7:324)

And here is "On Faith":

> [I]f we know so little of [these objects that surround us], what can be now known concerning objects of a quite different nature? con-cerning the spiritual world? It seems it will not be possible for us to discern them at all, till we are furnished with senses of a different nature, which are not yet opened in our souls. These may enable us both to penetrate the inmost substance of things, whereof we now discern only the surface; and to discern innumerable things, of the very existence whereof we have not now the least perception. (Jackson, 7:329)

The philosophical theology of "On Faith," "Human Life a Dream," "The Scripture Way of Salvation," "The Imperfection of Human Knowl-edge," "The Case of Reason Impartially Considered," and "The Great Privilege of those that are born of God," holds as well for many of Wesley's 135 other printed sermons, early and late; and the philosophical theology of the "Remarks," "Thoughts upon Necessity," "A Thought on Necessity," the *Survey*, the Preface to *Desideratum*, the Preface to *Primitive*

Physick, "A Letter to the Rev. Dr. Conyers Middleton," "Letters to Mr. John Smith," and the two "Appeals" holds not only for many of the other nonhomiletical titles, early and late, but also for much of the vast material in the journal and letters. In view of the philosophically theological overtones of "The Character of a Methodist," for example, it is reasonable to expect similar overtones in the many nonhomiletical titles relating to Methodist polity and principles, e.g., "Rules of the Band Societies," "Minutes of Several Conversations between the Rev. Mr. Wesley and others," "Advice to the People Called Methodists," and "The Principles of a Methodist"; and the very titles of "A Short History of Methodism," "A Plain Account of the People Called Methodists," and "A Scheme of Self-Examination Used by the First Methodists in Oxford" indicate histories of individuals as well as the group, and reflect, therefore, an emphasis on experience reminiscent, at least, of the similar emphasis in Locke's philosophy. Moreover, at least the following dozen sermons are by their titles self-evidently pertinent to either the empirically philosophical dimension of his thought, or the religious emphases that I have shown to be particularly related thereto, or both: "The Witness of the Spirit," "The Witness of our Own Spirit," "On the Holy Spirit," "Free Grace," "The Means of Grace," "Awake, Thou that Sleepest," "The Marks of the New Birth," "The Nature of Enthusiasm," "The Unity of the Divine Being," "On a Single Eye," "Walking by Sight, and Walking by Faith," and, clearly not least (in view of Locke's pioneering theories in the area), "On the Education of Children."

An Overview

In sum, then, or rather as an overview of Wesley's career, his continuum from empirical philosophy to natural and revealed religion provides the means of drawing together much of what has been written about the quality of his mind.

Many, for example, have recognized his interest in and thorough knowledge of science,[17] but what should now be recognized is that his interest in science necessarily flowed from, or at any rate intimately related to, British empiricism as best represented in his day by Locke. Wesley's general trust in experience, e.g., his ranking of travel literature above other forms of secular writing and his citation of Proverbs and Ecclesiastes more than any other biblical books, is a partly Lockean trust: he spoke, experientially, of "solid wisdom" and "solid philosophy"; he gave high praise to Addison's thoroughly Lockean, and thoroughly experiential, "Pleasures of the Imagination";[18] and such unmistakably Lockean trust surely underlies his application of experimental method. In other words, his participation in "The Hunt of Pan," i.e., the practice of science by individuals in all walks of life,[19] exists in the larger context of philosophic method, for no more than Johnson's love of chemistry and Berkeley's belief in tarwater could Wesley's practice of medicine and electrotherapy have occurred apart from Lockean method. The rationally empirical basis of his practice is indicated, for example, at once by his claim through "primitive [i.e., both early and foundational] physick" to have rescued a child from "death and the doctors" and by his characteristic complaint against the nonempirical and not very rational medical profession: "When physicians meet with disorders which they do not understand, they commonly term them nervous; a word that conveys to us no determinate idea, but it is a good cover for learned ignorance" (Jackson, 6:378; 11:286; Curnock, 5:496).

V. H. H. Green, in *The Young Mr. Wesley* (p. 76), recognizes that Wesley's well-known concern for animals (he often cautioned his preachers to be kind to their horses) dates from his days at Christ Church, Oxford, where in 1726, he made "the problem of reasoning in the brute creation" part of his master's degree. Such concern, however, is specifically philosophic as well as generally humanitarian: what should be recognized, now, is that Lockean methodology, sensationalistic as well as rational, underlies his view of animals: "Set aside that ambiguous term [i.e., reason]; exchange it for the plain word understanding, and who could deny that brutes have this? We might as well deny that they have sight or hearing."[20] He saw a relation, then, between the human mind and what Hartley, following Locke, called "the intellectual principles of brute animals." Wesley's attitude with respect to this particular development of Lockean methodology links him more closely to such radically Lockean thinkers as Bolingbroke, Voltaire, Swift, Pope, and Hume, than to such moderate Lockeans as Addison, Young, Watts, and Johnson.[21]

Wesley's consistent denial of innate ideas is another indication of the radical bent of his empiricism: Watts's effort to soften this doctrine—"I take the Mind or Soul of Man not to be so perfectly indifferent to receive all Impressions, as a Rasa Tabula, or *white paper*; and 'tis so framed by its Maker as not to be equally disposed to all sorts of Perceptions, nor to embrace all Propositions, with an Indifferency to judge them true or false"[22]—finds no parallel in Wesley's writings. Leslie Stephen's suggestion that Wesley's denial of innate ideas made what had been radical opinion into conservative doctrine[23] seems wide of the mark; Wesley's denial, rather, associates him with radical opinion and puts distance between him and conservative doctrine.

Wesley's familiarity with natural religion and his mastery of traditional revelation need no further demonstration, but it bears reiterating here that empirical method specifically allowed him to embrace both the Bible and an up-to-date theism. Locke anticipated that experiments would increase conveniences without reducing the mystery of nature; Swift and Sterne learned from Locke that nature baffles inquiry; Berkeley sensed that spiritual circumnavigations of the world form the final truth about it; and all of these attitudes show the interdependence of natural knowledge and religious aspiration.[24] Such a spirit of natural religion is everywhere implicit in Wesley's theistical view that nature, though "of itself . . . unevangelical, corrupt, and somnolent," "is indeed an organic system, wonderful and divine in origin and continuance"; and this natural religion is what allows him at once to associate human understanding with the understanding of animals and to hold that religion is what sets man apart from them.[25] It is with similarly Lockean reason that he describes traditional revelation; for since he speaks of "standing revelation" as "the best means of rational conviction," since he distinguishes, in the same breath, between "standing revelation" and "impressions" or "frames and feelings," and since, in other words, he suggests that a "rational conviction" of traditional revelation is methodologically akin to quasi-sensationalistic convictions of immediate revelation, he indicates that scripture is the basis of a far from a priori, if not all but sense-related, reason-in-religion.[26]

Green's view of Wesley as a "nonrational fideist," i.e., as one who rejects natural religion and approaches revelation from an all but antirational stance (*The Young Mr. Wesley*, pp. 11 ff.), is wrong. Or rather not completely right: Wesley's approach to traditional revelation was rational; his approach to immediate revelation, never antirational to my knowledge, was often sufficiently rational as well as often nonrational; and rather than resolving the debate between revealed and natural religion by rejecting natural in favor of revealed, and far from retreating by taking an antirational or even immovably nonrational stance, he drew a connection between rational empiricism and the entire range of early-century faith. Just as he was comfortable with sensationalistic and quasi-sensationalistic methodologies, so he was comfortable with reason in religion both natural and revealed, for he advocated revelation as well as theistical natural religion according to, and by analogy with, Lockean criteria. He realized, in other words, that insofar as natural religion was theistical, the natural and revealed manifestations of religion in eighteenth-century England were not inimical to each other. Green's view rests on his assumption that the fideism of William Law was the decisive influence on Wesley. But

Wesley parted company from Law: Law, according to Wesley, was too much attracted to "[Jacob] Behmen and an whole army of Mystic authors"; and since Wesley warned against mysticism as "superfluous, uncertain, dangerous, irrational, and unscriptural philosophy," he implied that the right kind of philosophy to mix with faith was the decidedly unmystical rational empiricism which, as received by him and Browne, complements scripture as a resource of knowledge and thus constitutes a safe and needful guide for the religious minded in their search for certainty.[27]

Green is right to stress Wesley's indebtedness to Law's conviction that faith consists in personal experience and its assurance of truth and salvation; but Green is wrong to conclude from this that such faith is completely alien to Lockean method, for Wesley keeps Lockean emphases in mind even in his historic exploration of immediate revelation. In the letter to Middleton, for example, the means of describing the inward search reflect the generally scientific and specifically empirical diction and methodology of early modern biblical studies:

> I have sometimes been almost inclined to believe, that the wisdom of God has, in most later ages, permitted the external *evidence* of Christianity to be more or less clogged and incumbered for this very end, that men (of *reflection* especially) might not altogether rest there, but be constrained to look into themselves also, and attend to the light shining in their hearts. . . . It seems . . . that, particularly in this age, God suffers all kinds of objections to be raised against the traditional evidence of Christianity, that men of *understanding*, though unwilling to give it up, yet, at the same time they defend this evidence, may not rest the whole strength of their cause thereon, but seek a deeper and firmer support for it. (Jackson, 10:76. My italics—RB)

Immediate revelation emerges from this passage as a sufficiently rational and quasi-sensationalistic means of acquiring religious knowledge. The definition of *inspiration* in Wesley's *Dictionary*, viz., "that secret influence of the Holy Ghost which enables man to love and serve God" (see the discussion in Lawton, *John Wesley's English*, p. 97), gives no such indication of methodological basis, but the letter to Middleton, and much else studied here, reveal that Wesley's spiritual theology, if not his claimed experience of the Spirit, rests in part upon quasi-Lockean methodology.

It is true, of course, that Locke includes "*Grace*" among his instances of "certain Words, that, if they be examined, will be found, in their first

Original, and their appropriated Use, not to stand for any clear and distinct Ideas;"[28] but Locke also holds that words for such immaterial and complex ideas may be defined by enumerating the simple ideas they contain (see, for example, *Essay* 3.11.15; Nidditch, p. 516); and this is not only what Johnson does in his *Dictionary*:[29] this is also akin, at least, to what is done by Wesley when he thinks of grace according to Locke's full methodological range. Though Wesley admits, in "The Case of Reason Impartially Considered," that reason neither produces faith nor gives "clear satisfactory evidence of the invisible world," he elsewhere both associates reason with immediate revelation and implies affinity between the two: his view of Christian vocation, viz., "To steer our useful lives below / By reason and by grace" (Telford, 5:163), recalls Aristotle's figure of the human chariot under Reason's control, but the personification of grace as *joint*-charioteer is quite distinctive.[30] Wesley's distinctively sensationalistic language of immediate revelation is best distilled, perhaps, in his employment of the Lockean terms *sealing* and *impression* when commenting upon the Spirit's Direct Witness: newborn Christians, in Wesley's England, were sometimes known as "seals."[31] Finally, the Lockean basis of Wesley's spiritual theology is well captured in perhaps his most technically conspicuous, and certainly his most uncharacteristically arcane, terminology: "*plerophory*" (or fullness), he wrote in uncharacteristically mystical mood, is "a kind of mystical consciousness of unhindered, unclouded [i.e., unmediated] favour with God"; "*elenchos*," he wrote, denotes "an unmistakable sense, the origin of which is supernatural, of God's forgiveness, love, and power to renew the soul"; and these terms, taken together, express his at once quasi-sensationalistic and sufficiently mind-oriented apprehension of immediate revelation (see Telford, 1:347; 7:57; and the discussion in Lawton, *John Wesley's English*, pp. 18–19).

Ernest Lee Tuveson, in his influential study of eighteenth- and early nineteenth-century English sensibility, analyzes

> how it was necessary to reconstruct . . . the "means of grace" in terms of a theory of the mind that denied the possibility of occult and supernatural influences on the personality. By a natural process, I conclude, imagination came to be a means of grace within the world of actual, physical sense impressions.[32]

I conclude, on the other hand, that at least for Wesley, if not for those who came within his sphere of influence, it was not a question of either empiricism or grace. His was a both/and logic.

In other words, though it was not quite "by a natural process," i.e., not quite "within the world of actual, physical sense impressions," that Wesley's theology of spiritual experience was achieved, his defense of "supernatural influences on the personality" was nonetheless more than merely reminiscent of empirical methodology, for not just his doctrine of assurance, of which *elenchos* is a key term, but also several other concepts of his experiential faith, bring up to his time and place the interpretation of New Testament times wherein Locke, true to his subject/object theory of perception, admits that "outward Signs" commended the Spirit's witness to early Christian mentality (*Essay* 4.19.15; Nidditch, p. 705). Wesley's missionary zeal, his quest for perfection, and his Arminian joy, for example, may even be said to find justification in Locke's *Essay*: a corollary to Locke's denial of innate ideas, namely, virtue is not natural to man, is a more or less direct precursor of Wesley's as well as Berkeley's missionary spirit; Isaac Watts, anticipating Wesley's emphasis on Christian perfection, follows Locke in envisioning perfect knowledge after death and agrees with Locke's admonition "to spend the days of this our pilgrimage with industry and care, in the search and following of that way which might lead us to a state of greater perfection"; and Locke, in philosophic as well as theological anticipation of Wesleyan joy, speculates that God "scattered up and down several degrees of pleasure and pain," "that we, finding imperfection, dissatisfaction, and want of complete happiness, in all the enjoyments which the creatures can afford us, might be led to seek it in the enjoyment of Him with whom there is fullness of joy, and at whose right hand are pleasures for evermore."[33] There can be little doubt, moreover, of the broad but instructive parallels between Locke's and Wesley's views of time: the journal of Wesley and the spiritual autobiographies of his followers are so particularized and so precisely dated as to be founded at least indirectly upon Locke's view that "the complex ideas, or modes, of time and eternity, originate in the simple idea of duration we discover by reflecting upon the succession of ideas in our own minds";[34] Locke further psychologizes time by arguing not only that while sleeping there is no time, but also that there could be no time at all if it were possible, while waking, to focus on just one idea (*Essay* 2.14.3, 4; Nidditch, pp. 181–82); and one thinks, in this connection, not only of Wesley's God-preoccupation as a more or less directly Lockean attempt to focus on just one idea, and thus to envision, while on earth, timelessness and hence eternity, but also of both his dislike of sleep and his constant tracking of the time as more or less directly Lockean attempts to evoke eternity in a state of wakefulness and hence to promote a state of spiritual awakening.

With regard, then, to Wesley's "empiricist conditioning" (Hindley, p. 108), Hindley is right to say that it sets him apart from most other figures in Christian history. St. Francis de Sales, for example, took a Spartan and Quietist, and decidedly nonempirical, stance towards religious experience, for he was fond of saying that, if Christians are constantly attending to the sensible consolations of the prayer life they become as a bride, "who should keep her attention on her wedding-ring, without looking upon the bride-groom who gave it her." [35] Wesley, insofar as his receptivity to spiritual influx is so emotionally grounded as to be all but sense-related, is willing, non-Quietistically, to look at the ring.

With regard to the implications of Wesley's "empiricist conditioning" for the subsequent development of philosophical theology, it is instructive to note the experiential, if not exactly "empiricist," thought of F. H. Jacobi (1743–1819). Whereas Kant, for example, "remains a rationalist in his effort to derive God, freedom, and immortality as implications of a rational moral law," Jacobi "finds their reality directly guaranteed by the mind's inner experiences, which carry with them the feeling of immediate certainty or faith": "Jacobi's faith rests on direct experience of the supersensible: the ultimate realities are immediately revealed to us in our consciousness; in such experience, we come face to face with spirit, freedom, and the divine Being: we believe in these things because we experience them directly." [36] Wesley's experiential emphasis is anticipatory.

And finally, Wesley's Lockean-Brownean analogy between empirical method and religion both natural and revealed is grounded in his Lockean-Brownean striving towards, or rather assumption of, unmetaphorical language. The OED gives Tristram Shandy (1767) as the earliest instance of unmetaphorical: "I am got," writes Sterne, "into a cold unmetaphorical vein of infamous writing"; but Wesley's use of the term in "Letters to Mr. John Smith," specifically the one dated June 25, 1746, was both twenty-one years earlier and honorific; for Wesley's defense of Augustine's style, to wit, that it is without "rhetorical heightening . . . but in as plain and unmetaphorical words as the nature of the thing would bear," not only attacks metaphor as mere ornament, but also implies that Lockean-Brownean analogy underlies Wesley's conception of language. His works, of course, besides being unavoidably metaphorical, are metaphorical in being deliberately scriptural: "The Bible is my standard of language" (Telford, 5:8); but his favorite biblical style is that of 1 John, which he singles out for the easy words and obvious sense of its "plain," i.e., unmetaphorical, language (Telford, 6:15); and Wesley is even capable, as though mindful of Locke and Browne, of murmuring apologetically about the metaphor-bound anthropomorphisms of the Bible; it speaks, he writes, "after the manner of men" (Jackson, 6:379; 7:210, 230). Lawton, then, is perceptive in characterizing Wesley's metaphors as "colloquial, proverbial, and scriptural" (*John Wesley's English*, pp. 133– 41): in his philosophic, i.e., linguistically rigorous, mood, he does, or rather tries, not to breathe among them. Small wonder that *analogy of faith*, as Lawton (p. 16) demonstrates, is characteristic of evangelical discourse.

An Epitome

The headnote to the *Survey*'s version of *The Procedure* and the first of the "Remarks" on the *Essay* epitomize what I have argued in chapter 1 as well as here, namely, that the *Essay*, as interpreted by *The Procedure*, not only informed young Wesley's understanding, but also settled into Wesley's philosophical theology.

The headnote, hitherto unquoted except to identify the abridgment for bibliographical purposes,[37] announces the abridgment's divisions and hence Wesley's view of *The Procedure*'s emphases:

> It is needful, first, to trace out the bounds and extent of human understanding. These bounds being fixt, we are next to consider, how the mind dilates itself beyond them: how it supplies the want of direct ideas, by raising up secondary images in itself: insomuch that things, otherwise imperceptible, grow familiar and easy: and we meditate and discourse even on those beings, whereof we have not the least direct perception. (*Survey*, 2:438)

The beginning of this passage reflects the attitude of Browne, and for that matter Locke, regarding both the limits and the reach of what one can know philosophically. Wesley assumes both the modesty and the program of empiricism. Next, affirming the mind's capacity for fashioning ideas from internalized experience, he still speaks as an empiricist: memory is indirectly sense-grounded. And towards the end of the passage, the "things otherwise imperceptible" and the "beings whereof we have not the least direct perception" are simply remembered objects whereof we had perception. The entire headnote, like the abridgment and *The Procedure*, notably endorses rational empiricism; Wesley holds to the method of Locke.

The headnote, however, not only captures the methodological gist of the *Essay* and *The Procedure*, but also reflects the supernatural tone and content to be found in *The Procedure* and to a less developed extent in the *Essay*. *Things*, to be sure, exemplifies diction commonplace in the philosophy of matter. But *beings*, on which *we meditate*, refers in part to spiritual objects, such as "Spirits, Angels, Devils" (see *Essay* 4.16.12; Nidditch, p. 665). And even *things* refers to the substance of revealed knowledge, as in "things of the Spirit," and therefore serves as a central, though quasi-philosophic, term of religious language. At any rate, taking for granted the rightness of Browne's argument, the last of Wesley's passage suggests a decidedly spiritual and implicitly revelationist level of meaning: the headnote, like *The Procedure*, is hardly glib about what cannot be cited by the senses; but the passage is understandable as more than simply a verbally consistent philosophical statement; for though Wesley makes no overt, enthusiastic claim to otherworldly truth, he denominates *discourse*, i.e., the rational argumentation of homily, as conceivable response to the extrasensory or para-empirical; and when he implies that one can know through indirect or spiritual perception what exceeds the fixed and sensate bounds of human understanding, i.e., when, far from leaving off empirical language, he employs a negative form thereof: "Whereof we have *not* the least direct *perception*," he relies on philosophic language even as he seeks to utter what lies beyond philosophy's ken. His implication, in other words, is that whatever knowledge does not come through the senses is generally spiritual and particularly revealed; the headnote rings with rather more than simply the theistical overtones of natural religion.

The headnote, then, endorses Browne's philosophical theology thus: the first sentence points approvingly to Wesley's version of *Procedure* 1, in which Browne accepts rational empiricism; and the second recommends Wesley's version of *Procedure* 2.6–9, in which Browne modulates from a Lockean natural religion to a philosophical understanding of revelation. Though an infinitesimal product of Wesley's pen, the headnote emerges as his tribute to the human mind, which he evidently held to possess a capacity not simply for knowledge of nature as divine, but even for otherworldly knowledge, i.e., knowledge underived from, though congenial with, what reason learns from the senses. Browne's doctrine of analogy, in other words, forms the underlying assumption of Wesley's passage, which, like his version of *Procedure* 1.6 and 1.9, is more than accordant with the instrument of religious knowledge whereby Browne remembered empirical method even in his search for more than sensory truth. The headnote symbolizes the tough-mindedly philosophical quality of Wesley's lifelong spirituality.

From the vantage point of the early 1780s, when, in his seventies,

Wesley was still looking forward to perhaps his most influential decade, he relished in his first remark on the *Essay* the strangeness of Locke's fundamental premise to faith as well as philosophy:

> I think that point, "that we have no innate principles," is abundantly proved, and cleared from all objections that have any shadow of strength. And it was highly needful to prove the point at large, as all that follows rests on this foundation, and as it was at that time an utter paradox both in the philosophical and the religious world. (Jackson, 13:455)

Wesley was disturbed during the 1720s perhaps by the fact that Locke's denial of innate ideas was alien to received, sense-independent rationalism, and undoubtedly by the fact that the denial was at variance with a fundamental religious view, namely, that man, made in the image of God, comes "trailing clouds of glory" (if I may be permitted to read into the 1720s this image from Wordsworth's "Ode: Intimations of Immortality from Recollections of Early Childhood"). It occurred to young Wesley that no theology could reflect the *Essay*'s philosophy without seeming so nearly of this world as to be indifferent or skeptical regarding worlds elsewhere. Yet the annotation itself is undisturbed by any such logic; only "at that time" was Locke's point a paradox. By the 1780s, clearly, Wesley savored the paradox for its complexity, or rather resolved it into a rich unity. Well before the 1770s, indeed, when he published his abridgment of *The Procedure*—perhaps as early as Christmas Eve, 1730, when he finished filling the bound quarto notebook, and certainly by the 1740s, when he first formulated his philosophical theology—he learned from *The Procedure* to base the mind's capacity for religious knowledge not by any means upon some innate or inherent idea of self-transcendence, but assuredly upon the mind's quasi-empirical acquisition of immediate as well as traditional revelation. His thought, then, unlike the Roman Church's nonrational mass, and unlike the all but antirational German mysticism with which, on at least one occasion, he has been associated,[38] but very like the Locke-based religious philosophy of the mid-century mainstream, appears to have posited rational, sensationalistic, and quasi-sensationalistic bases of theology, for mature Wesley confessed to the uncanny conviction (to anticipate Wordsworth again) that man remembers nothing of God who is his home, yet through his sensuous and mental experience in

> the very world which is the world
> Of all of us, the place in which, in the end,
> We find our happiness, or not at all,
>   (1805 *Prelude* 10. 726–28)

somehow finds himself not quite knowing but almost rationally persuaded of a world of the spirit. The annotation, at any rate, suggests that
Wesley regarded a philosophical faith as not finally contradictory, and
even as requisite: the single *world* is simultaneously *religious* and, not just
generally *philosophical*, but according to context specifically Lockean.

Wesley's cross disciplinary intuition in the remark and the headnote is
an immediately suggestive means of clinching my demonstration that regardless of whether the manuscript represented his thinking from the
start it points beyond itself to a lifelong philosophical quality of his faith.
Not only did he think well enough of *The Procedure* to publish his version
of it, but he also thought well enough of the *Essay* to publish "Remarks"
upon it, and even without the argument already here advanced, the fact
that he set about writing the annotations only some four years after the
appearance of *The Procedure* in the *Survey* indicates not simply that he
thought of *The Procedure* and the *Essay* together, but even that *The Procedure*'s view of the *Essay* was his view of it too.

His Lockean assumptions, at any rate, were effortless and natural at
the last. On July 6, 1790, just eight months before his death (on March 2,
1791), he preached at Rotherham that, even as a creature "destitute of
sensation" is necessarily "destitute of reflection," so a man "without God
in the world" (cf. Eph. 2:12) is necessarily without discernment of "the
invisible world" (Jackson, 7:360–61). This sermon, entitled "On Living
Without God," speaks in extremely, i.e., literally, Lockean terms about
the hypothetical creature "destitute of sensation":

> It must be very little, if at all, that it could be acquainted even with
> the general sense,—that of *feeling*: As it always continued in one
> unvaried posture amidst the parts that surrounded it, all of these,
> being immovably fixed, could make no new impression upon it; so
> that it had only one feeling from hour to hour, and from day to day,
> during its whole duration. (Jackson, 7:350)

Thus, "On Living Without God" aspires to harmony between faith and
what was still at the end of the century a rationally empirical standard of
truth; Wesley never wavered in regarding the denial of innate ideas as a

principle of right thinking, whether in philosophy or in religion. The sermon, finally, by comparing the godless life to the utter mental blankness that would result from lack of contact with the world, teaches the need for experience of God:

> But the moment the Spirit of the Almighty strikes to the heart of him that was till then without God in the world . . . all things around him are become new, such as it never before entered into his heart to conceive. He sees, so far as his newly-opened eyes can bear the sight,
>
> > The opening heavens around him shine,
> > With beams of sacred bliss. . . .
>
> At the same time he receives other spiritual senses, capable of discerning spiritual good and evil. He is enabled to *taste*, as well as to see, how gracious the Lord is. . . . He *feels* the love of God shed abroad in his heart by the Holy Ghost which is given unto him. . . . (Jackson, 7:351–52)

Wesley's "spiritual sense," a deep and central doctrine paralleling Edwards's "religious sense" and anticipating the method of Schleiermacher,[39] is both the all but lifelong and the all but final analogy with Locke's finite, sensate means of knowing by which Wesley, in his more than Brownean way, attempted to apprehend the religious unknown. A major contention of my next chapter is that this "spiritual sense" of his is a major English antecedent of the Romantic imagination, which, according to Kant and Sartre, is in the world but not of it:

> [I]magination [writes Sartre] is not an empirical and superadded power of consciousness; it is the whole of consciousness as it realizes its freedom. . . . The imagination . . . is the necessary condition for the freedom of empirical man in the midst of the world. . . .

> Though the imagination . . . [writes Kant] finds nothing beyond the sensible world on which it can lay hold, still this thrusting aside of the sensible barriers gives it a feeling of being unbounded; and that removal is thus a presentation of the infinite. As such it can never be anything more than a negative presentation—but still it expands the soul.[40]

To conclude: Wesley's access to empiricism, i.e., his mastery of *The Procedure* as well as the *Essay*, led to the philosophically theological nature

of his thought and expression. As for his language, his abridgment prepares one to see that the literary merit of his writings rests in part on the
detailed design by which his revelationist and theistically natural reli-
gionist themes flourish on a rationally empirical framework: his writings,
that is, besides showing his religious temperament in both its spontaneity
and its various theological moorings, require inspection as interdisciplinary structures, for they disclose his study of philosophy in relation to saving as well as speculative faith. As for his thought, moreover, his abridgment prepares one to perceive fully a hitherto only partially recognized
dimension thereof: on the positive evidence of strong parallels between
his ideas and those of Browne and on the negative evidence of no major
disparities, it should be said that Wesley's selective presentation of *The
Procedure*'s point of view not only foreshadows, but also unlocks, the
Brownean and Lockean nature of his theological method. The abridgment, that is, as his compendium of a theologized *Essay*, marks a turning
point not only in the story of his early philosophical researches but also in
the entire history of his mind, for the manuscript's lingering presence
therein, and the palpable care with which he first thought through *The
Procedure*, reveal that young Wesley not only recognized its broad importance, but also entered it as a large deposit in the fund of lore from which
he would draw for creative thought. Insofar, in other words, as the
abridgment sets an interdisciplinary pattern that recurs throughout, and
tends to unify, Wesley's intellectual and spiritual lives, *The Procedure*
exerted a formative influence. Browne, though acknowledging limits of
human understanding, dilated beyond them; and both he and Wesley, in
their argumentation, were hardly ill-informed anachronisms and should
now stand out as precise dialecticians of rational empiricism and Christian faith. Insofar as *The Procedure* showed Wesley how a theistical natural
religion could be acceptable to orthodox faith and insofar as *The Procedure* informed his deep sense of grace, it must be said that however sudden
or culturally uninformed were some of the influxes he "felt in the blood,
and felt along the heart" (cf. Wordsworth's "Lines: Composed a Few
Miles above Tintern Abbey, on Revisiting the Banks of the Wye during a
Tour, July 13, 1798," line 28), his spiritual experience relates to the life of
his mind and, for that matter, contributes to the English Enlightenment.
Insofar as his works reflect in particular *The Procedure*'s emphases on immediate revelation, they reveal what has not hitherto been widely acknowledged, namely, that his analogy between Methodist experience and
Lockean method, i.e., between sense perception and the mind's response
to the feeling of faith, constitutes an especially distinctive early modern
blend of religion and philosophy.

In short, then, Wesley more or less intentionally formulated the experiential common denominator of mainstream British thought and mainstream British faith: his was a most thoroughly English language of experience.

Three

Wesley's Intellectual Influence

The pervasiveness of Wesley's influence, outside as well as within the Wesleyan community, is hardly news. W. E. H. Lecky, thinking of social history, asserted that Wesley's conversion "meant more for Britain than all the victories of Pitt by land and sea."[1] Wesley's message reached even the *literati*: "Among those who heard him preach were James Boswell, Samuel Johnson, George Crabbe, William Cowper, Sir Walter Scott, Horace Walpole, and Henry Crabb Robinson."[2] What has not been fully addressed is the nature and extent of his *intellectual* influence; few, that is, have found occasion to build upon the twofold recognition of Augustine Birrell, i.e., not only that "no single voice touched so many hearts" as Wesley's did, but also that "no single figure influenced so many minds."[3] In March 1791, soon after his death, a reporter for *The Gentleman's Magazine* was able to observe that Wesley's personal effectiveness "was greater, perhaps, than that of any other private gentleman in any country."[4] This statement implies that the effects of his career were more than merely religious and more than merely cultural; accordingly, I argue that his influence was centrally, if not fundamentally, intellectual. The question of such influence on the literary world, of course, is finally decided on the basis of literary texts, but, at present, I focus on the Wesleyan community to demonstrate that his intellectual effect thereon was sufficient to form an aspect of his influence generally. I submit, specifically, that his philosophical theology impelled a cross-section of his followers, laymen as well as ministers, women as well as men, in a more or less philosophically theological direction, for I show that due in large measure to more or less direct emulation of his methodological example they practiced methods correlative to his.

Appearing on the inside front cover of the bound quarto notebook containing his manuscript abridgment of *The Procedure* is "Mrs Pendarves," in his youthful hand. This instance of his personal interest in sharing *The Procedure* is an early, and especially pertinent, indication of his influence, for his friendship with Mary Pendarves, young widow and member his Cotswold circle of friends, is seminal to the manuscript. True, the hiatus in his diary from February 1727 through May 1729 makes it difficult to sort out the nature of the Cotswold circle. The diary reveals, however, that at least by June 1729, the conversation was significantly Lockean: in June, and again in August, he engaged in discussions of the *Essay* with Sally Kirkham, and such other Cotswold friends as Anne Granville, Bernard Granville, Nancy Griffiths, Robin Griffiths, and Harry Yardley provided Wesley with a congenial atmosphere in which to consolidate his philosophic thought.[5] His friendship with Mary Pendarves, reaching a high plateau in April 1730 and continuing strong through the end of that year, represented an intensification and indeed a culmination of the Cotswold discussions of the *Essay*'s relation to faith: in September, he was engaged in his diligent reading of *The Procedure*; and it was clearly a topic between him and Mrs. Pendarves, for on October 3 he wrote "to beg leave to present you with an abridgment of it" (Telford, 1:57). Nine days later she replied and reflected his evident curiosity to see how a bishop would respond to Locke: "I shall wait with impatience for the Abstract you promise me, which I am sure will very well deserve the time I shall bestow in reading of it" (Telford, 1:58). The idea of giving her the manuscript is undoubtedly what Wesley had in mind when, on December 12, 1730, he wrote to her mother and spoke thus glowingly: "To be the instrument of *some advantage* to a person from whom I have received *so much*, as it would be the truest instance of my gratitude, is the utmost wish I can form."[6] This statement, to be sure, shows something of a swain's ingratiating flourish, but it also indicates both their common ground of compatible minds and his indebtedness to her mind.

The abridgment, then, as the main fruit of his Cotswold associations, and as his most graphic contribution to the Cotswold discussions of the *Essay*, was important in the first instance because it was both the symbol of and the tribute to the mutually recognized intellectual essence of his friendship with Mary, but it must be said that, though their friendship was primarily intellectual, it was partly romantic: he labored until Christmas Eve, energized no doubt by her genuine interest in the project and perhaps in him. Maldwyn Edwards, though describing her as "well able in talk and correspondence to discuss serious topics," emphasizes that Wesley found increasing "delight" in her company,[7] and the feeling was undoubtedly mutual; she was thirty, he twenty-seven. V. H. H. Green, though emphasizing Sally Kirkham, pays considerable attention to Mary and says that the Granville sisters, Mary and Anne, "offered him an opportunity to relax enjoyably, to pass the time in riding and walking, in cards and quadrille, in singing and dancing."[8] This description does not quite ring true, of course, since Wesley abhorred relaxation except insofar as he found it in great purposive energy, but it is clear that romantic feeling and loving regard underlay the intellections of those salad days. The abridgment, as things turned out (and whatever its impact on his and her intellects), was hardly the pitch for a man to woo with: perhaps Wesley's enthusiasm for *The Procedure* and the *Essay* was unrelieved; or rather, perhaps his oral reading of them and of his own sermons was beginning (after the nearly two years of their friendship from June, 1729, to May, 1731) to tire her out; but whatever the reason, the friendship faded as she moved more and more toward London society.[9] The friendship, then, tells something already known about Wesley's personality, namely, that he was awkward at love.[10] But the episode's most significant aspect, as biography and as an example of the social milieu, is the evidence it gives of one man's taking the intellect of a woman seriously indeed: his feeling for Mary Granville Pendarves was catalyst for an intellectual advance that, though nonetheless real for being partially a sublimation, was all the more dramatic for being addressed to her. He intended the abridgment as a Christmas token of his love, and his approach to philosophical theology, therefore, as represented by his work on the abridgment, was emotional and deeply motivated as distinct from exclusively academic.

His interest in the subject continued as it began, i.e., publicly and even socially; Wesley was nothing if not evangelical in every sense of the word. As early as three years after abridging *The Procedure*, for example, he found it effective to enlist empiricism in his effort to persuade members of the Holy Club to his way of thinking: in 1733, he talked to Tom Grieves and John Robson "about the communion, and to help their faith read [John] Wynne's commentary on Locke's Essay on Human Understanding to them."[11] This approach worked at least on Grieves, who, by February of 1739 if not before, appeared "affected" by the linkage of Locke's philosophy to the eucharistic sacrament (see Green, pp. 191–92). Wesley did not say how Grieves was affected, and Wynne's "commentary," an abridgment, in fact, is so extensive[12] as not to give more clues than the *Essay* itself. It is inferrable, however, from the *Essay* as from Wynne's abridgment, that the sacrament has at least the one philosophic-religious property of elevating to the level of religious significance certain sense impressions.

Wesley's intellectual influence, of course, though evident in Claphamite Anglicanism and even in the Oxford Movement,[13] was greatest among the men of God he actually knew, and, of all of his fellow-ministers, the Rev. Vincent Perronet (1693–1785) deserves the most attention here. For one thing, as Curnock long ago observed (4:493n), "Vincent Perronet, vicar of Shoreham, John Fletcher, vicar of Madeley, and William Grimshaw, incumbent of Haworth, were Wesley's closest friends among the clergy of the English Church." For another, Perronet (if not quite Methodist) was more than Anglican: Charles Wesley went so far as to call him "the Archbishop of Methodism" (Telford, 2:292). But most importantly: this son of a French Huguenot member of the Royal Society was born into the early-century world of empiricism and Protestantism and so was in a position to become, with Wesley and in the same way as he, an intellectual leader of the revival. Indeed, Perronet developed a philosophical theology parallel to that of Wesley, for from 1736 to 1740, he wrote three books in which he attempted to go even further than Browne did in aligning empiricism with Christian faith. The titles, in eighteenth-century fashion, give good indication of what the books seek to do, and I quote them, therefore, in my text:

> *A Vindication of Mr. Locke, from the charge of giving Encouragement to Scepticism and Infidelity, and from several other Mistakes and Objections of the Learned Author of the Procedure, Extent, and Limits of Human Understanding. Wherein is likewise Enquired, Whether Mr. Locke's True Opinion of the Soul's Immateriality was not mistaken by the Learned Mons. Leibnitz* (London: James, John, and Paul Knapton, 1736). . . .
>
> *A Second Vindication of Mr. Locke, Wherein his Sentiments relating to Personal Identity are clear'd up from some Mistakes of the Rev. Dr. Butler, in his Dissertation on that Subject. And the various Objections rais'd against Mr. Locke, by the learned Author of an Enquiry into the Nature of the Human Soul, are consider'd. To which are added Reflections on some Passages of Dr. Watts's Philosophical Essays* (London: Fletcher Gyles, 1738). . . .
>
> *Some Enquiries, Chiefly relating to Spiritual Beings: In which the Opinions of Mr. Hobbes, With Regard to Sensation, Immaterial Substance, and the Attributes of the Deity, Are taken Notice of. And wherein likewise is examined, how far the Supposition of an Invisible Tempter, is defensible on the Principles of Natural Reason. In Four Dialogues* (London: F. Gyles; J. and P. Knapton; J. Roberts, 1740).

A full exploration of these titles as part of the revival's intellectual background and even as background to English Romantic consciousness is matter for another treatise. What needs to be stressed now is that in theologizing Locke, Wesley had an ally in Perronet. Perronet, taking even Browne to task for *The Procedure*'s few reservations about the *Essay*, is more Lockean than any other early-century Anglican, not excluding Wesley himself, for Perronet nowhere objects to any part of Locke's philosophy, and whereas Dr. Watts, Andrew Baxter, Bishop Butler, and for that matter Edward Young and Samuel Johnson, were concerned that one may find in Locke the materialism of a Hobbes or a Leibniz, Perronet not only found no materialism in the *Essay* but also remained unperturbed even by the *Essay*'s strange hypothesis that matter thinks.[14] This hypothesis, from the time of Voltaire's *Letters concerning the English Nation*, Letter 13,[15] aroused more criticism than any other notion of the *Essay*. Lord Bolingbroke, of course, embraced the idea, but Johnson, through Imlac, scorned it,[16] and Young, in *Night Thoughts*, rejects its materialistic implications for the mind: "Her ceaseless flight, tho' devious, speaks her nature / Of subtler essence than the trodden clod" (1.99–100). "It is not necessary," wrote Locke, "to suppose that [the soul] should be always thinking, always in action" (*Essay* 2.1.10), and Voltaire, and Bolingbroke again, agreed, but the Cartesians, Berkeley, and Watts contended that the soul "always thinks even without our consciousness of the fact" (see MacLean, p. 49). Watts, besides defending innate ideas, and hence elevating the mind above Locke's estimation of it, disagrees "with this great Writer"

> by asserting that the soul always does think, even in that profound sleep which leaves no record of thought. The soul in this respect . . . [in the words of Watts] "bears a very near Resemblance to God, and is the fairest Image of its Maker, whose very Being admits of no Sleep nor Quiescence, but is all conscious Activity."[17]

Perronet, emphasizing as the heart of Locke's philosophy "identity," which "stands independent of the particles of matter that compose the body," illustrates a largely tender-minded approach to the *Essay*.[18]

There can be no doubt that Wesley influenced Perronet to turn evangelical, for example, but it is also clear, from Perronet's spirited defense of Methodism, if from nothing else, that the influence was intellectual, and it is even likely that the influence, in this case, was two-way, i.e., from Perronet to Wesley as well as from Wesley to Perronet. In religion, at any rate, the two shared an undogmatic but nonetheless intellectual and, indeed, almost Latitudinarian principle of tolerance: in 1749, in a letter to Perronet published as *A Plain Account of the People called Methodists*, Wesley emphasized his view that "Orthodoxy or Right Opinions is, at best, but a very slender Part of Religion, if it can be allowed to be any Part of it at all";[19] and Perronet, on April 19, 1764, wrote to Wesley and remarked that "It has always been a leading principle with me . . . to love all those labourers of Christ, who give proof by their diligence, their holy and heavenly behaviour, that they love our Lord Jesus Christ in sincerity, even though their sentiments in many things should differ from mine" (as quoted in Curnock, 5:65). There can be little doubt of William Hunt's thesis that Perronet, at least after 1746 or so, was Wesley's "most intimate friend."[20] Beginning with *Some Reflections, By Way of Dialogue, on the Nature of Original Sin, Baptismal Regeneration, Repentance, the New Birth, Faith, Justification, Christian Perfection, or Universal Holiness, and the Inspiration of the Spirit of God* (1747), Perronet published at intervals for the rest of his life titles defending the Methodists and reflecting further their emphases of faith.[21] In the Calvinist/Arminian controversy, Perronet cogently defended the Arminian position.[22]

Another part, though, of the intellectual foundation of this friendship was the similar nature of their searches and researches, i.e., their common, long-held interest in philosophical theology. Hunt remembers that "at one time" Perronet "took some interest in philosophical works so far as they bore on religion," and, though neither Hunt nor anyone else has asked whether Perronet's three earliest, i.e., his philosophically theological, books are both essential to his mind and a possible basis of his appeal to John Wesley,[23] it should be clear by now that any "philosophical works" bearing on Perronet's "religion" would necessarily constitute an important reason for his friendship with Wesley. For a decade or so before they met, Perronet engaged in the same sort of inquiry that marked the first stages of Wesley's career. Their early intellectual development, along similar lines of methodology, made it all but certain that they would hit it off, for they shared a passion for reconciling faith and philosophy.

Perronet's philosophical theology, at any rate, besides being of interest in itself, as a neglected element of intellectual history, should serve not simply as parallel but perhaps as index to Wesley's. Emphasizing, in his open letter to Perronet, an intellectual dimension of faith, Wesley defines religion as "nothing short of or different from the Mind that was in Christ, the image of God stampt upon the Heart, Inward Righteousness, attended with the Peace of God, and Joy in the Holy Ghost";[24] and this mid-century selection of biblical language (cf. especially 1 Cor. 2:16) is in accord with the then standard philosophy of mind. The philosophical theology of Isaac Watts, moreover, is part of what both Wesley and Perronet admired: Perronet did not think Watts Lockean enough; but Watts

and Perronet agreed with each other, at last, that they held Locke in common; and Wesley, of course, praised Watts's thought as early as 1725.[25]
Finally, the similarity between the mind of man and "the Souls of Brutes"
is a philosophically theological and Lockean tenet that Wesley not only
held in common with Perronet but also derived from the same source as
he: Perronet, in *Some Enquiries* (p. 78), cites Humphry Ditton's *A discourse concerning the resurrection of Jesus Christ . . . Together with an appendix
concerning the impossible production of thought from matter and motion: the nature of humane souls, and of brutes* (London, 1712); and Wesley, between his
ordination in September 1725 and his election to the Fellowship of Lincoln on March 17, 1726, read "Ditton of Matter's Thinking, and the
Souls of Brutes" (Curnock, 1:66).

The philosophical theologies of Wesley and Perronet, when considered together, should add to the understanding of evangelical method.
Perronet's methodological books are not always cohesive: they consist of
too much quotation and too little commentary, whereas Wesley's essays
are sustained and therefore better for studying philosophical theology in
the revival. One must add to their analysis, however, scattered bits of
thought, which, though valuable for conveying the life of the man, remain inherently fragmentary, whereas Perronet's titles are a handy part of
the revival's intellectual background. And they are no more disjointed
than the considerable quotation and the random commentary in Wesley's
"Remarks upon Mr. Locke's 'Essay on Human Understanding,'" which
is helpful, nonetheless, as a guide to revival method. Perronet's three earliest works, as anthologies of empiricist passages conformable to faith,
anticipate what was most substantial in experiential religion. It was not
just Wesley who sought to merge philosophy and theology with an entire
way of life, for Perronet's trilogy, if not commonplace books of a methodology more or less explicit in the revival, are confirmations nonetheless of the revival's philosophically theological beginnings.

The leadership of Perronet was sufficiently methodological. *Some Reflections*, to be sure, was published not so much as method but rather as a
simple sign of "having received the Gospel in its power and purity": "[H]e
began to think it likewise his duty," writes the editor of his "Memoirs," "to
bear witness to the Truth, and to make an open profession of it before the
whole world."[26] Like Wesley, Perronet was finally a man of more faith
than philosophy; in *Some Reflections* (pp. 101–2), to allude, again, to his
first "Methodist" work, he exclaimed against philosophy thus: "How
dry and sapless are all the voluminous Discourses of Philosophers, compared with this Sentence,—Jesus Christ came into the world to save Sin-

ners! 1 Tim. 1:15." I suggest, however, that philosophical theology is
naturally assimilated into his evangelical message: the very text of *Some
Reflections*—

> For the Jews require a sign, and the Greeks seek after wisdom: But
> we preach Christ crucified, unto the Jews a stumblingblock, and
> unto the Greeks foolishness; But unto them which are called, both
> Jews and Greeks, Christ the power of God, and the wisdom of
> God. Because the foolishness of God is wiser than men; and the
> weakness of God is stronger than men. (Cf. the title page of *Some
> Reflections* and 1 Cor. 1:22–25)

—contains the implication that Perronet's faith is founded upon equal
parts, namely, the power of spiritual signs and the detachment of philosophic wisdom. Empiricism, at any rate, combines the rigor and method
of ancient wisdom with a new trust in the power of human senses to read
aright the signs of nature. The fact that "Christ crucified" was the center
of Perronet's preaching, as of every other evangelical's from the histrionic
Whitefield's to the learned Romaine's, should not suggest blinkered nar-
rowness; the Evangelical Anglicanism of Romaine included, as instances
of his learnedness, his mastery of and subscription to the "complete system of natural history, theology, and religion" in John Hutchinson's
weighty, and ponderous, *Moses's Principia* (1724).[27] Rather, the image indicates breadth of inquiry: the context of "Christ crucified" implies that
marriage of Hebraic and Hellenic which in every age has accounted for
Western humanism.

In this sense, incidentally, evangelicals are eighteenth-century con-
tinuators of the effort made from Augustine to Milton and the Puritan
ideologues, namely, to transmit culture and keep civilization healthy by
following the intellectual example of Paul for whom Christ was synthesis
of faith and philosophy. Perronet, it is true, made a distinction between
scientific and spiritual kinds of experience; one, he said, is from books
and the other from a higher power within: "Spiritual experiences cannot
be learnt like human Sciences: these are taught by books, and the instruc-
tions of others; but the former can no man know, unless a much higher
power work them within him" ("Memoirs," p. 3). This contrast is no
sharper, though, than the one Paul draws between Greek and Jewish temperaments. And the drawing of the contrast does not prevent Perronet
from seeing, as did Paul, the possibility of a common denominator between potentially disparate traditions of human culture. For just as Paul's
testimony of conversion to Christ seems to grow out of, and then to re-

lieve, the tension of his philosophico-religious awareness, so Perronet's entire life and thought are the more dramatic for his cultivation of both book learning and receptivity to signs and signals of God. His career is of a piece because his theology and his philosophy were unified, or so he felt, in his experience of Christ.

To return now to Wesley and to hark back for a moment to Mary Pendarves, it is possible to see in their friendship the setting of a lifelong pattern: Wesley combined personal concern with pedagogical purpose in his consistent and recurring enterprise of promoting *The Procedure*. The manuscript abridgment, one remembers, was almost certainly at his hand when he published his abridgment of *The Procedure* in 1777; it seems likely, therefore, that he was in possession of the notebook on December 6, 1756, when from his personal version undoubtedly he read *The Procedure* to his preachers: "I began reading to our preachers the late Bishop of Cork's excellent Treatise on Human Understanding" (Curnock, 4:192). The aim of filling philosophical as well as theological needs of both his associates and his followers evidently formed his purpose. *The Procedure*, if not the manuscript, was at hand on the several occasions from the 1750s through the 1770s when he praised the thought of Bishop Browne.[28] And judging from the date at the end of the notebook, i.e., "Jan 6 1788," it is clear that the manuscript and hence *The Procedure* as Wesley saw it was in his aging hands that day when significantly he spent time in study before meeting with his preachers.[29]

(Since the manuscript is in excellent condition, it is reasonable to think that Wesley had always cherished it, and, incidentally, it seems likely that he was once more in possession of it by at least the mid-1730s. He had presented it to Mrs. Pendarves some time between February 1, 1731, when he and Charles found her and her sister Anne at home, and February 13, when Mary wrote him a thank-you note.[30] It is possible, of course, given the postscription, and assuming for the moment that the abridgment of *The Procedure* was *not* published with the help of the manuscript, that she returned it as her death approached in April of 1788. But "Jan 6 1788" accompanies his transcription of a German hymn and so seems intended to record when he wrote the hymn in the notebook, rather than, say, the time of the notebook's return; perhaps the hymn, in addition to or even instead of *The Procedure*, was what he read that morning, to himself, if not to his preachers. It is also possible given the dates of his explicit references to *The Procedure* that he recovered the notebook from her in the 1750s, but there is no record of any contact between him and her for the fifty-four years of her life remaining after July of 1734, when he wrote the last of his letters to her.[31] A possible reason, at any rate, for Wesley's forty-seven-year wait before publishing his abridgment of *The Procedure*, besides his fear of confusing common people with philosophical theology, was his hesitation to cast in print a private document associated bittersweetly, in his mind alone, with Mary Pendarves.)

Thus, throughout his life, Wesley was intent upon conveying his enthusiasm for *The Procedure*: both *The Procedure* and the notebook, as present objects or simply as parts of his mind, turned up at intervals to bespeak a religious and philosophical pattern of his activity, namely, the professing of Browne's thought in conjunction with and as part of the spread and practice of Methodism. Penultimate in the *Survey* is Wesley's published version of *The Procedure*; and this conspicuousness is an especially suggestive part of his relation to Browne's thought; for although the manuscript contains more than the published version and is therefore privileged for purposes of studying the Brownean aspect of Wesley's thought, the published version shows him so haunted by *The Procedure* that he needed, after living with it for forty-seven years, to impart it not simply to his preachers but, through his encyclopedia for common readers, to everyone else he could. He had been advocating *The Procedure* since the 1750s and before, and when he judged that the time was right, he made available in handsome printed form what he had well thought out and valued. The abridgment had gone with him from the beginning, and he took steps before the end to assure that a full portion of it would go with those fit few among his people who were ready for Browne's difficult argument. Browne's view of the *Essay*, then, was meant to inform their spiritual experience. It is true that when his preachers heard him read *The Procedure* he told them it was "in most points far clearer and more judicious than Mr. Locke's [*Essay*], as well as designed to advance a better cause" (Curnock, 4:192); but this remark need not be interpreted either as a proscription of the *Essay* or as a statement that the *Essay* and *The Procedure* are irreconcilably contrasting; for although Wesley wanted the preachers to prefer *The Procedure* for having explicitly put philosophy in the service of faith, he was also willing for them to think of *The Procedure* and the *Essay* together, presumably as grounded in empirical method. To show the *Essay*'s commensurability with orthodox religion was undoubtedly part of his purpose in promoting *The Procedure*.

His efforts on behalf of *The Procedure*, at any rate, are paralleled by as well as implicit in his explicit and direct interest in sharing the *Essay*. In his theological access to the *Essay*, i.e., *The Procedure*, he found a lifelong appeal that must have led him, fifty-one years after first looking into it, to serialize the *Essay* and to recommend it as filled with "a deep fear of God, and reverence for his word" (Jackson, 13:455): "Extracts from Mr.

Locke," along with "Remarks upon Mr. Locke's 'Essay on Human Understanding'" appeared in *The Arminian Magazine* from January, 1782, through June, 1784.[32] Not only, in other words, did Wesley publish sustained responses and annotations to the *Essay*, but he also and at the same time published an abridgment of it. Five years after publishing much of *The Procedure* and after twenty-six years and more of recommending the *Essay* indirectly, i.e., from *The Procedure*'s point of view, he deemed it not merely safe but salutary as well to give his readers as heavy a dose of the *Essay*: Locke, thought Wesley, was a sufficiently scriptural philosopher and a sufficiently God-fearing one to strengthen the mind's part of faith. Thus the "Remarks" were published soon after they were written, not, indeed, as a full accounting of Wesley's debt to the *Essay* but rather as his commendatory and more than adequate introduction of it to the Methodists. His "Remarks" conclude with the point that the *Essay* might especially "be of admirable use to young students" (Jackson, 13:464); but it is clear from his extensive serialization that he intended it to reach adults as well; and, if not little short of astonishing, it is noteworthy that he apparently expected at least some of them to appreciate such nuanced commentary as this:

> [I]t is evident, Mr. Locke thinks, "consciousness makes personal identity;" that is, knowing I am the same person, makes me the same person. Was ever a more palpable absurdity? Does knowing I exist make me exist? No; I am before I know I am; and I am the same, before I can possibly know I am the same. Observe, "before" here refers to the order of thinking, not to the order of time.[33]

Wesley recognized, of course, that both the "Remarks" and the "Extracts" might be objected to as "not intelligible to common readers": "I know it well."[34] But he counted on reaching not just "the learned," but "the unlearned": "What they do not understand, let them leave to others, and endeavour to profit by what they do understand." Thus he wanted his abridgment to find a broad readership. Though he surely entertained little hope that many of the unlearned would appreciate the *Essay*, he nonetheless optimistically and stubbornly insisted upon making it available to them, for some of them he knew would appreciate it: the assumption of serial publication, as Herbert observes, is that "the reader is often caught by what he least likes."[35]

Wesley, then, regarded the *Essay* and *The Procedure* together as orthodox and vital books for anyone who would respond to his call for methodological understanding of faith. It is feasible now to determine that many responded if not directly to these twin sources of his philosophical theology then indirectly to them and directly to the method of his message, written and spoken.

To focus first and briefly on his fellow ministers and to hark back for a moment to Perronet: Perronet's prominence in presectarian Methodism is in line with revival leadership in general insofar as Wesley, regardless of how much he influenced Perronet to be a philosophically theological leader, influenced other fellow ministers to be sufficiently intellectual, and even methodological, leaders. In "Address to the Clergy," for example, finished on February 6, 1756, he urges each of his preachers to study not only philosophy per se but also natural philosophy, logic, geometry, and psychology (Jackson 10:492 ff.). It seems likely, therefore, especially in view of his advocacy of *The Procedure* during the 1750s and thereafter, that not just theology in general and not even just philosophical theology but philosophical and scientific empiricism in particular were part of what he had in the back of his mind when, on July 15, 1764, he wrote to Samuel Furly and declared that a clergyman should be able to "think with the wise" as well as to "speak with the vulgar" (Telford, 4:258). By century's end, the former ability was sufficiently strong to enable his ministers to continue his denunciations of "roving charlatan preachers" who caused "gospel sermons" to become a cant term and who gave a bad but undeserved name to the generality of Methodist preachers.[36] That their good name was due to their generally intellectual if not specifically methodological attainments was the theme of a tribute to them by James Lackington, who, as a layman well educated by Methodism, testified in his *Confessions* of 1804 that the preachers had "great natural abilities" and were often "learned men."[37]

By sampling times when Wesley, to say little of his preachers, exerted intellectual influence on his flock, it is possible to delineate or at least to envision a genealogy not simply of the English common reader but specifically of the intellectual commoner. "Thinking with the wise," for Wesley, was not inconsistent with "speaking with the vulgar": indeed, as Lackington's testimony suggests, these two activities of Wesley—and of those ministers most like him in mental ability and intellectual interest (e.g., Perronet, Furly, William Romaine, and George Story)—formed an enterprise of universal education. It is possible, moreover, not only to discover an auspicious beginning of the well informed but middle class audience to which belles–lettres were increasingly addressed, but also, and more remarkably (from the present chapter's point of view), to observe that philosophical theology formed an explicit part of the wisdom with which Wesley attempted to equip his followers.

Take for example and at some length the case of women in his revival. "A Letter to the Rev. Dr. Conyers Middleton," to be sure, in holding that immediate revelation presents "an argument so plain, that a peasant, a woman, a child, may feel all its force," rings oddly nowadays. But such a statement is capable of being read as "ahead of its time." So well into the century as 1752, Lady Mary Wortley Montagu lamented that even women as highly placed as she "are educated in the grossest ignorance and no art omitted to stifle our natural reason." [38] And for Wesley to have included all women among recipients of divine argument was for him to have dignified them, albeit along with children and peasants, in a way most unusual. In a time, for example, when Samuel Johnson was sure to get a laugh with his comment that "a woman's preaching is like a dog's walking on his hinder legs. It is not done well; but you are surprised to find it done at all," [39] it was most unusual for anyone to be receptive to this particular idea. But Wesley was so far receptive to it as to be the first man in history to encourage it considerably. "He was a pragmatist" on this question, writes Maldwyn Edwards, "and dealt with each case as it came along," but, when women proved their preaching abilities, he gave them his blessing: Sarah Crosby, with his blessing, traveled "over the North Yorkshire moors and dales . . . holding meetings in the afternoons and evenings," and, with his blessing, Mary Bosanquet, later Fletcher, wife of John, preached in the open air. [40]

Methodist women played quite a variety of leadership roles. Witness, for example, Mary Bosanquet's acting as book agent, Nancy Bolton's and Elizabeth Ritchie's serving as Society founders at Witney and Olney, respectively, and remarkably Hannah Ball's overseeing of meetinghouse construction at High Wycombe. [41] Wesley even asked the women to oversee the preachers. Witness his letter to Ann Bolton in November of 1772:

> Sammy Wells will always be useful, for he can take advice. But how is it with Billy Brammah? Does he follow the advice I gave him concerning screaming and the use of spirituous liquors? If not, he will grow old before his time, he will both lessen and shorten his own usefulness. Drop a word whenever you find an opportunity. He is upright of heart. He enjoys a good deal of the grace of God, but with a touch of enthusiasm. (Telford, 5:347)

And witness his letter to Hannah Ball, in April, 1774, with regard to Joseph Bradford: "He is plain and downright. Warn him gently not to speak too fast or too loud, and tell him if he does not preach strongly and explicitly concerning perfection" (Telford, 6:79). Wesley's confidence in

Hannah Ball's knowledge of doctrine reveals that the cause of his proto-feminism was not so much his regard for the general abilities of women as his respect for their intellects specifically. (The first male feminist, of course, was Shelley,[42] but this was thanks in part though not directly to Wesley's forerunning.)

Wesley set about deliberately to increase women's learning, and far from teaching easy subjects, he chose to impart philosophical theology. He talked with Miss March about both Norris and Browne (Telford, 5:237, 270). He requested his niece Sarah to read Locke's *Essay* and Malebranche's *Search After Truth* (Telford, 7:82). Perhaps most amazingly, he advised Mary Bishop to teach these two books to her schoolchildren. On August 10, 1784, she wrote to Wesley and asked, "Are there any unexceptionable novels [for my schoolchildren] besides [Henry Brooke's] the *Fool of Quality?*" Wesley replied on August 18 not only by recommending Brooke's *The History of the Human Heart* but also by making these rather startling suggestions: "For the elder and more sensible children, Malebranche's *Search after Truth* is an excellent French book. Perhaps you might add Locke's *Essay on the Human Understanding*, with the Remarks in *The Arminian Magazine*" (Telford, 7:227–28). In line with this methodological tinge in Wesley's converse with women there are (1) empirical implications in his description of Hannah Ball as full of "understanding . . . and experience" (Telford, 5:216), (2) Lockean overtones to his assurance of Anne Foard that it "is right" "to cultivate your understanding," though "wrong," of course, "to *lean* on it" (Telford, 7:278), and (3) quasi-methodologic elements in Damaris Perronet's revival-inspired concentration on the development of her mind.[43]

I sum it up this way: Wesley was ready to establish with all women the intellectual and indeed the philosophically theological relationships he enjoyed with Mary Granville Pendarves and his mother. Not only Maldwyn Edwards but also Grace Elizabeth Harrison (and others) have offered insight into Wesley as son and would-be lover,[44] but the psychological approach, though fascinating, is reductive, for the women in his life and in his sphere of influence are of more than passing interest in his intellectual biography. His sister Mehetabel remarked that he liked "Woman merely for being woman,"[45] but applied to him this remark signifies not simple addiction to gallantry so much as the love of women as sisters in Christ and hence as fellow human beings and intellectual equals. Wesley's friendship for Mary Pendarves, together with his sonship to Susanna, set the pattern for a lifetime of intellectual relationships with Methodist women, and these relationships, take them all together, are nothing short of historic. Although early Methodist women are hardly describable as feminist, they were the first women in England to assume much leadership, whether intellectual or social. Thus, the proto-feminist element of Methodism's incubation stages underscores the allure of proto-feminist material at the Rylands Library: diaries, journals, autobiographies, and commonplace books by Mary and Eliza T. Tooth, Martha Hall, and Mary Bosanquet attract one's immediate attention as timely features of the Methodist Archives, and on the assumption of more such material in the Archives and elsewhere, one must speculate that progress in cataloguing will provide a means of validating women's studies historically (see Appendix B). Affording a unique opportunity to examine the beginnings of "female" self-awareness, the Archives reflect the milieu of Mary Wollstonecraft: she had Nonconformist roots and can be seen to have gained her ideological momentum from the inherently activist evangelical atmosphere which encouraged women too to be active and even to write. Perhaps it is not quite true that "scribbling women," from Wollstonecraft and Hannah More to Charlotte Yong, got a certain impetus from John Wesley,[46] but it is surely true that because of Wesley's efforts on behalf of women's intellects in general Thomas Jackson's *Lives of the Early Methodist Preachers* (1846) should now be balanced by scholarly re-creations of the lives of early Methodist women.[47]

What Wesley did for women, he did for the laity in general and indeed for the rising commoner. All Methodists and all who came near the revival more or less directly benefited from his efforts to improve the common mind; "a sense that the individual man was infinitely valuable," writes Herbert,

> merely from the fact of his humanity, was an integral and dominating part of the religious conviction which furnished the driving force of his whole life. . . . In a day when a poor man, in the eyes of the cultivated world, was a mere atom in the body of a great beast, or, at best, a caricature of a human being, John Wesley wrote in such a manner as to make his characteristic symbol of respect appropriate: when a poor man thanked him for a favor, he always removed his hat.[48]

Wesley, in other words, suited his language to his audience but did not dilute his thought. He respected the intellects of his readers as part of what made them "infinitely valuable." And he did not talk down to his hearers either. W. L. Doughty, to be sure, suggests that Wesley's spoken sermons differed from his published ones,[49] but Lawton for one feels that "there is something to be said on the other side: . . . Wesley's words . . .

'I now write, as I generally speak, *ad populum*' assert that there was little or no difference between his written and his extempore styles."[50] The Rev. William Gurley, moreover, testifies that on May 1, 1785, standing on a table at the end of the Mall in Waterford, Wesley preached on 1 Cor. 13 "a most able discourse, just the same as is printed."[51] Perhaps even the philosophically theological sermons (if not especially them) were "just the same" delivered as printed.

Print, though, was important to Wesley's purposes. "Reading Christians," he wrote, "will be knowing Christians" (Telford, 6:201). As R. Wilberforce Allen observes, "nothing can be more calculated to stimulate a man intellectually than a spiritual experience such as was shared by the early Methodists,"[52] but they were also thus stimulated by their leader's desire for them to read, for Wesley said that "newly awakened people should . . . be plentifully supplied with books. Hereby the awakening is both continued and increased" (Telford, 7:294). To this end, he became a bookseller and, as Leslie Shepard points out, had such "an abiding faith in the impact of the printed page" that he insisted on his preachers' being "colporteurs or book agents": the preachers "travelled on horseback with a saddlebag filled with Wesley's publications."[53] Not only in London, but also in York and Stourbridge, such late eighteenth- and early nineteenth-century Methodists as Robert Spence, Richard Burdekin, Henry Bickers, James Nichols, Joseph Thompson, and, clearly not least, James Lackington followed the preachers' example and became booksellers themselves.[54]

Among Wesley's chief concerns as bookseller was to make books affordable. *Primitive Physick* was so cheaply printed that it was among the dozen or so most widely read books in England from 1750 to 1850.[55] *A Survey of the Wisdom of God in the Creation*, despite its five-volume bulk, was also reasonably priced. On March 25, 1775, as he was completing the third edition, Wesley praised Oliver Goldsmith's similar venture, *A History of the Earth, and Animated Nature*,[56] but adding that Goldsmith's "minute descriptions" (the venture went to seven volumes) were "useful only to the book-seller, by swelling the bulk, and consequently the price" (Jackson, 14:303), Wesley went ahead with the smaller, less "minute" set. His chief means of lowering costs emerged in 1771, when as publisher of *The Arminian Magazine*, he set up his own printing press, and as a result *The Arminian Magazine* enjoyed a circulation of 7,000 by 1791, compared, for example, with 4,550 for *The Gentleman's Magazine* in 1797.[57] Wesley made and gave away £30,000 by selling books.

Lackington, beneficiary of the preachers' saddlebags, not only explored additional means of lowering book prices, but also succeeded materially in doing so. "It was he," writes H. F. Mathews, "who introduced the sale of publishers' remainders at a cheap price, instead of destroying books which were not selling in order to keep up the price." [58] Lackington took pleasure, as Wesley would have done, both in this innovation per se and in the consequences of it:

> And you may be assured that it affords me the most pleasing satis-
> faction, independent of the emoluments which have accrued to me
> from this plan, when I reflect what prodigious numbers in inferior
> or reduced situations of life have been essentially benefited in conse-
> quence of being thus enabled to indulge their natural propensity for
> the acquisition of knowledge, on easy terms: nay I could almost be
> vain enough to assert, that I have thereby been highly instrumental
> in diffusing that general desire for reading now so prevalent among
> the inferior orders of society. [59]

Lackington claims, moreover, that "four times the number of books are sold now than were sold twenty years ago," i.e., 1771, and he adds that "I now sell more than one hundred thousand volumes annually" (pp. 255, 259–61). The year of Wesley's death, then, to the extent that these statis-tics are correct, is a culmination of his ministry in more ways than one.

As to the nature of his reading program, *The Arminian Magazine*'s high circulation, the *Survey*'s cheap price, and their popularization of *The Pro-cedure* and the *Essay* imply what I stress, now, that Wesley disseminated good, substantial, and challenging books. In 1782, of course, thirteen years before Hannah More's establishment of Cheap Repository Tracts, Wesley directed his societies to distribute religious tracts among the poor, and these broadside and chapbook forms of popular literature were hardly sophisticated. [60] His tracts, however, unlike most others, did not condescend to readers, and his goal, unlike that of tracts in general, went beyond literacy for the purpose of achieving political stability and basic religious instruction. His blending of tract distribution with the dispersal of difficult titles, moreover, recalls and goes beyond Thomas Bray's early-century Society for the Propagation of Christian Knowledge which first distributed tracts, and which founded libraries placing human knowledge alongside divinity. [61] Thus, as the first to encourage ambitious reading among the generality of people, Wesley was "ahead of his time" indeed and perhaps of the nineteenth century as well. He was not so much inter-ested in diluting ideas in popular formats as in transporting, or rather "colporting," his readers to the world of such elite and sophisticated books as would do them good intellectually as well as spiritually. Consider, in this connection, the *Essay* abridgment. Herbert concludes that *The Arminian Magazine* was "one of Wesley's most effective instruments of religious and cultural enlightenment," and *enlightenment* seems the *mot juste* for such features as the abridgment, which represents as Herbert understates it "articles . . . of texture sufficiently tough to exercise the teeth of his readers."[62]

As for the 200-plus abridgments in general, the revival, observes V. H. H. Green, necessarily "lacked originality and profundity" because "much of what [Wesley] wrote consisted of abridgments or condensations of books already in print,"[63] but it should be said in counterpoint that the collective consciousness can only have been deepened by the publication of such abridgments as those of the *Essay* and *The Procedure*, and indeed that such a deepening of consciousness, though accomplished by ideas not Wesley's, was "original" not only in the sense of being his configuration of them but also in being an unprecedented experiment in education. Moreover, though it may be true (as Douglas Elwood argues) that the American contemporaries of Jonathan Edwards "misunderstood" him because even "his own disciples lacked his genius for maintaining the delicate distinctions and for balancing the logical poles necessary to his theology," it fails to follow from this that "Edwards did not appreciably affect the mainstream of eighteenth-century thought,"[64] for, in England at least, Wesley's abridgment (1773) of Edwards's *Treatise on the Religious Affections* (1746) affected many. As Richard Green observes, in his bibliography of the Wesleys' works (p. vii), "It is indeed [John] who deserves the credit of having been the first in this country to provide and diffuse cheap popular literature of a useful kind." Wesley raised abridgment to an art anticipating and even rivaling the un-"original" disseminations of modern popularizers: Isaac Asimov, Jacob Bronowski, Carl Sagan, and *The Reader's Digest*.

As to the effects of Wesley's reading program, one can assume, perhaps, that just as Methodism grew from one meetinghouse, at Bristol in 1739, to seventy throughout England in 1771, to 359 in 1784, and just as the number of Methodists jumped from 241,319 in 1816, to 451,286 in 1843 (by 1852, one in sixteen in Yorkshire and one in three in Cornwall were Methodist),[65] so the number of reading Methodists, if not intellectual ones, increased geometrically. "That Mr. Wesley's people," wrote Lackington in 1804, "are a comparatively ignorant people I am fully convinced is not true; that the reverse is the fact may be easily shown. . . . As the Methodists do not waste their time in idleness and diversions, they have more time to read than others. . . . So that the difference in degree of knowledge between the poor Methodists and the poor in general is very remarkable."[66] This view is supported, for example, by A. E. Dobbs, who in *Education and Social Movements, 1700–1850* concludes that "an exceptional degree of intelligence and attainment was not uncommon among the Methodists in humble station."[67] And J. H. Rigg discovered, in Mousehole, Cornwall, "such a spirit of reading, including a sort of club supply of books, as is seldom found":[68] reading circles grew out of the Methodist class meetings.

But Sunday schools, evangelical in general as well as Methodist in particular, undoubtedly deserve most credit both for immediate literacy and for intellectual attainment. "The Sunday-schools," declared Lackington in 1791,

> are spreading very fast in most parts of England, which will accelerate the diffusion of knowledge among the lower classes of the community, and in a very few years exceedingly increase the sale of books.—Here permit me earnestly to call on every honest bookseller (I trust my call will not be in vain) as well as on every friend to the extention of knowledge to unite (as *you* I am confident will) in a hearty AMEN.[69]

The Methodist Magazine, indulging in 1818 in wishful thinking, ejaculated that Sunday schools "will raise Great Britain to a distinction above all Greek, above all Roman fame."[70] Something is to be said, though, for such hyperbole: Sunday schools were phenomenal. The number they educated went from 250,000 in 1787, to 1.5 million in 1833, to 7.5 million in 1898; therefore, despite the fact that in Lancashire and Cheshire, for example, 40 percent of the men and 68 percent of the women married or witnessing marriages were unable to sign their names as late as 1839–41, it seems fair to conclude with Mathews that "much of the inspiration for the elementary education was the religious movement of the eighteenth century and the ambitions for culture which were evoked by the revival."[71] Among the enterprises of early Methodist women were Sunday schools, which were begun indeed not by Robert Raikes in the 1780s, but rather in 1769 by Hannah Ball; upon corresponding with Wesley, she did not shrink from the task at hand: "The children meet twice a week, every Sunday and Monday. They are a wild little company but seem willing to be instructed. I labour among them earnestly . . ." (Curnock, 5:104n). The Methodist Sophia Cooke first suggested the idea to Raikes.[72] Dorothy Wordsworth participated in the Sunday school movement.[73]

Wesley's intellectual influence, then, is everywhere evident. Intellectual awakening meant first of all spiritual leadership from the laity: "So wide was the scope of the [Methodist] layman's activity," writes Mathews, "that Dr. Arnold, when he drew up his proposals for the reform of the Church of England, wanted the Church to imitate the Methodist plan for the employment of laymen in its chief offices."[74] But the intellectual awakening was not exclusively religious in nature. Lackington's testimony—

> [I]f I had never heard the Methodists preach, in all probability I should have been at this time, a poor, ragged, dirty cobler, peeping out from under a bulk, with a scruffy nose and long beard. . . . It was by their means also that I was excited to improve my little intellectual faculties. (*Confessions*, p. 180)

—finds counterparts in the autobiographies of William Potter, Thomas Jackson, W. E. Adams, Samuel Barnford, Thomas Carter, Thomas Cooper, Thomas Holcroft, William Hone, William Hutton, Charles Knight, Robert Chambers, G. J. Stevenson, William Kent, Kenneth Young, William Lovett, Francis Place, and G. L. Craik—all of whom were late eighteenth- and early nineteenth-century evangelicals more or less directly educated by Methodism.[75] And quite directly educated by it were such Chartist leaders as William Lovett, Thomas Cooper, Samuel Barnford, Robert Owen, and Thomas Burt: Methodist influence is responsible for the fact that the Chartist Movement was concerned not merely with higher wages and better working conditions but also with the question of education and "the rights of citizenship and culture for every working man."[76] Cooper, reports Mathews, "studied languages or history from waking until seven, breakfasted with a book in his hand, did the same at dinner, and, after he had worked until eight or nine at night, spent the last hour committing *Hamlet* to memory 'until compelled to go to bed by sheer exhaustion.'"[77]

Most noteworthy, perhaps, is the empiricist effect of Wesley's influence. Because of him empiricism per se is found among evangelicals as early as the late 1740s at least: witness the popularity of his preface to *Primitive Physick*. By the turn of the century, a large minority of Methodists was not only "highly cultured and intellectual," but also scientifically trained: Dobbs, and Amy Cruse, and Elie Halévy have pointed out, for example, that the Methodist Joseph Caine of Penzance was a Fellow of the Royal Society in the 1840s and that Dr. Thomas Lovell Beddoes of Bristol

> founded the "Pneumatic Institute" and lectured to crowds of middle-class folk who flocked to hear his popular expositions of chemistry. He was assisted in his work of managing the Institute by a young

Cornishman who hailed from a humble Methodist family, and who afterwards became famous—Humphry Davy.[78]

Wordsworth knew Davy and shared with him an empirical temper.[79]

Did then a self-consciously philosophical theology, traceable from the late seventeenth and still in force during the early nineteenth century, find its way into the English popular imagination? I think so. "Life means for us," wrote Nietzsche, "constantly to transform into light and flame all that we are or meet with."[80] "To be a philosopher," wrote Thoreau, "is not merely to have subtle thoughts, or even to found a school, but so to love wisdom as to live, according to its dictates, a life of simplicity, independence, magnanimity, and trust."[81] In such fundamental senses as these, at least, Wesley's followers were good practitioners of philosophy, for many of them led lives of compassion, energy, and self-control, thus reflecting the light of truth as much as, if not more than, hot subjective claims to truth. Wesley, moreover, taught them a reliance upon experience. This reliance derived from Locke as well as from Wesley's own proclamation of a second apostolic age.

It is needful, therefore, despite the fact that Methodists emphasized faith more than the purely rational and were usually empirical only in "the religious sense" of being grounded in their spiritual experiences, to recognize the philosophical ramifications of what it meant to be an evangelical in the early modern era. Insofar as theological issues were developed in the light of Locke's *Essay*, two fields of thought came together, and insofar as the force of Locke's ideas continued to be felt in the dominant form of late eighteenth- and early nineteenth-century Anglicanism, theology and philosophy extended their influence as one single force beyond the world of print. Wesley's philosophical theology thus represents a crucial point where theological history ceases to be a subspecies of the history of ideas and becomes a part of cultural history; on at least this one occasion, difficult philosophy indirectly and directly wrought its fascination upon the broad popular life of a country. Richard Green, in his biography of Wesley, concludes that Wesley "deflected the course of historical development," and that he delayed only for a while both the ascendancy of secularism and the consequent declining role of religion in modern life and thought.[82] It can just as well be argued, and has been argued here, that Wesley was in the mainstream of historical development, and that he founded a world church precisely because of his modernity of outlook. V. H. H. Green, in his more recent biography, concludes that Wesley "offered in fact nothing that could satisfactorily meet the intellectual difficulties of his times" (pp. 11–12). But quite the reverse is true. Wesley

should be said to have made his most substantial, and hence most significant, contribution to Christian history in precisely this area of equipping
his followers to exploit philosophical challenges and counterparts to
faith.

The latter Green, moreover, despite recognizing that the revival was
"originally promoted" by an "intellectual challenge," i.e., rational criticism of the Church and Christianity, concludes that the revival finally
lacked intellectual substance because Wesley became a man of "increasingly circumscribed intellectual pursuits": "the remainder of his work"
(after "An Earnest Appeal") "lacked originality and profundity" (pp. 11–
12). This assertion is unaccountable. Wesley's Journal alone, ranging over
every tradition and every trend of thought, constitutes a work of more
substance than multiple titles by most authors. Together with "An Earnest Appeal" and all the other works of philosophical theology, the Journal not only is original in almost every sense of the word but also renders
absurd any implication, Green's included, that the revival was not intellectually stimulated by its leader. The impact of the Journal needs no
demonstration, and "An Earnest Appeal" also enjoyed wide distribution
(a distribution enjoyed as well, undoubtedly, by other methodological
titles). Wesley often sent it ahead of him to prepare a town for his message.[83] Francis Gilbert, who had been introduced to Wesley by Perronet,
sent a copy to his brother Nathaniel in Antigua, West Indies.[84] Nathaniel,
in turn, was so impressed by this intellectual manifesto of the revival that
he returned to England primarily to meet its author.

Flatly stated, Wesley's intellectual influence surpassed that of all other
intellectuals of his century, for he popularized as well as contributed to
almost any field that one can name. His prescience with regard to de Bonnet's biology, for example, helped to prepare the ground for Darwin's
theory, and certain early twentieth-century descendants of the revival remembered this: they point to Wesley's abridgment of de Bonnet's theory,
namely that God gradually but progressively develops nature through
organic and human forms.[85] Thus, as recently as some sixty years ago,
the effects of Wesley's intellectual example were yet being felt; there lived
the memory of him as one who did not hide his methodology.[86] Since,
however, a scholar as sympathetic to and as informed about Wesley as
V. H. H. Green was apologetic as recently as 1961, it is clear that scholars
in general need to grasp more firmly Wesley's intellectual importance to
cultural, to say little of literary history. Reassessing in earnest, accordingly, I recall what Alfred Caldecott knew in his 1909 study of Methodist
spiritual autobiography: Caldecott, Professor of Moral Philosophy in
King's College, University of London, extends to the lives of early Meth-

odist preachers and their hearers a William Jamesian interest in the varieties of religious experience, and Caldecott emphasizes that "intellectual sentiment" and "the love of truth and knowledge" were primary marks of Wesley's most notable followers.[87] Besides noticing their "Social Sentiment," their force of will, and their vicissitudes after the first victory, moreover, Caldecott points to their "Aesthetic Sentiment," i.e., their attraction to external nature as the symbolic form of spiritual being, and thus he implies their theistical form of natural religion. He seems, finally, to apprehend their methodology of immediate revelation, whereby subjectivity was pure joy, for of what Caldecott says of Methodist joy, Eayrs remarks that

> the steady health of the whole mental nature is seen in the presence and pre-eminence of Joy. Not only occasional ecstasy, but a fund of solid happiness came to be theirs. Nor was this the result of physical conditions or organic sensations. Only in a few instances was there any seeming connexion between the outward and the inward conditions. Often the natural tendencies were reversed. They rejoiced in tribulation. The reference of the self to the Infinite . . . touched the very centre of the mental nature of these men. (p. 263)

The revival, in sum, reflected the Lockean trend of early modern sensibility. Wesley's recommendations of the *Essay* and *The Procedure*, his published abridgments of both, and above all the Brownean and Lockean quality of his writing, bespeak his purpose of popularizing as the methodology of his movement a broadly religious interpretation of the *Essay*. His philosophy of religion, occupying the experiential ground of rational empiricism and revealed as well as natural religion, affords a way to see steadily and whole not simply his life of the mind, but even his intellectual influence. Green, in discussing the early-century response to Lockean method and Newtonian science, goes perhaps a bit too far when he speculates that "the Methodist movement was possibly less of a reaction to contemporary religious activity, or the lack of it, than an answer to a problem the outward expression of which was theological and philosophical in content."[88] But Green does not go far enough, and indeed beats a too hasty retreat from his intriguing speculation, when he adds that the "answer [was] expressed in practical rather than in intellectual terms." Judging by the Methodists' awareness, indirect when not direct, of Locke's importance to religion, I conclude that Wesley's revival was like him in being intellectual as well as practical, or rather practically intellectual and intellectually practical.

His manuscript, accordingly—that notebook in which he cast his version of *The Procedure*—is important not just because it contributes to what is known of his thought. The manuscript is important, for another reason, because it is undoubtedly the most painstaking of his abridgments: it is true that on at least some other occasions during his sixty-one years of abridging, he copied out the passages he chose to excerpt, but he often simply gave the printer his marked copy of the book.[89] And for still another reason the manuscript is important as the *first* of his abridgments: the notebook antedates by four years the first-to-be-published of his abridgments.[90] Thus, as prototype and model of his style and organization in abridgment, the notebook points to the nature and quality of a whole genre of his writing, and as what became one of the longest abridgments he ever published (the *Essay* serialization is another of his longest), the manuscript not only well represents the content but also fully anticipates a major form of his lifelong determination to make philosophically challenging religious literature an explicit part of his message for the common reader. Wesley, from the beginning of his career, taught numbers of his associates to read the *Essay* as he did, so that by the end his ministers spoke his consciously Lockean language of spiritual experience, and insofar as his flock heeded this particular language, his influence emerged as that of a theologian and philosopher whose well-thought-out message built upon the complex compromise Locke had tried to negotiate between the power of mind and the force of sense experience. Wesleyan Methodists, when they followed the philosophical lead of their instructor and guide, were Methodists in more ways than one: they were methodologically rigorous, i.e., in accord with a method of philosophy, in their implicit credo and their sometimes conscious attitude that experience is not so much a fleeting and shadowy means of searching for the truth as the only possible and an immediate and sufficiently reliable means of finding out the truth, whether spiritual or temporal. "I look upon all the world as my parish," said the itinerant Wesley (Curnock, 2:218); but it should be added that as a way of saving souls the peripatetic Wesley searched for minds to be enlightened at once by the quasi-philosophic perception of spiritual things and by the quasi-spiritual perception of natural things. It should also be said, and is said most emphatically now, that since some of his people were philosophically informed in their approach to faith they were the English common reader's most advanced embodiments.

Methodism, then—harking back to "medieval science through Ramist homiletic,"[91] designating the devotional exercises of the Holy Club, referring thence to the systematic practice of one's religion and naming somehow whatever it was that warmed the hearts and caught the imaginations of many—connotes the philosophic induction of religious knowledge from spiritual and natural experience. The revival can be thought of simply as eighteenth-century English Methodism.[92] Or not so simply, the revival can be broadly understood as extending in space to America's Great Awakening, in breadth to the Dissenting as well as Anglican branches of England's Evangelical Movement, and in time to the mid-nineteenth century and after.[93] Though it is too much to claim that the larger revival exactly paralleled Browne's patterning of *The Procedure* after the timely method of Lockean thought, it is nonetheless logical to settle on the evidence presented here (and even without taking Jonathan Edwards's movement into account) that early modern revival faith remythologized Christianity partly on the model of a theologized empiricism.

Wesley's Brownean reading of the *Essay*, finally, was "in the air" of pre–Romantic and Romantic England. Thomas McFarland, in describing his historical approach to Romanticism, writes that

> Creeks and branches of individual discovery or originality, though arising at different points along the banks, all flow inevitably to a common mingling in the larger current of the age. Indeed, the very idea of "an age" or "a time" tends to repudiate the importance of smaller temporalities and priorities within the larger entity. . . . [The Romantics] participated in that frequent and varied interchange, that intense interweaving of thought, that raised certain matters . . . beyond the conception of source and influence to the status of being "in the air."[94]

Important as being "in the air" is, and without speaking of source, I include influence, direct and indirect, in my historical approach.

Either part of or close to the first generation of English Romantics, for example, were two figures, at least, who were sufficiently aware of the revival's methodological dimension to write about it. Joseph Priestley, for one, carried into print his philosophically theological debate with Joseph Benson, headmaster of Kingswood School: Benson entered the fray with Wesley's encouragement, for on March 10, 1787, Wesley wrote to Benson that Benson was "quite equal to the task" of countering Priestley's skeptically oriented but theologically informed *History of the Corruptions of Christianity* (1781).[95] Benson issued a two-volume response, in 1788 or 1789, and 1791, and Priestley thought well enough of Benson's method of argument to reply with respect.[96] The second figure, though, is more to the present purpose. Robert Southey, in his *Life of Wesley; and the Rise and Progress of Methodism*, drew upon Methodist lore from the 1790s to the waning years of Romanticism in England and noticed the affinity between Methodism and empiricism. Southey's study, to be sure, though especially valuable as one of the first nonsectarian signs of sympathetic interest in Wesley, and as one of the first nonsectarian sources of information about him, hastily concludes that he "laid no stress" upon the Church of England's intellectual tradition (2:166), but in emphasizing his belief that nothing contradictory to reason should be accepted as a matter of faith, Southey implicitly acknowledges the Lockean basis of Wesley's theology.[97] Southey emphasizes, moreover, the following more or less precisely Lockean elements of Wesley's life and influence: George Story, one of the most studious of the preachers, came to his faith by working through his "old skepticism"; Wesley "entertained some interesting opinions concerning the brute creation," e.g., that animals resemble men in reason and understanding; and "Wesley was an excellent physician" to such as Story because Wesley himself went through a skeptically methodical "stage of doubt in early life" (2:152, 189, 410). In other words, as one who (unlike Priestley) was close to the Anglican circle of Wesley's revival, Southey admired (as well as knew about) the methodological center of the revival as well as the revival in general. It is not quite true that he "had no private sources of information in composing the present work" (1:v), for he was helped by Wesley's sister Martha Hall and Coleridge's friend the Rev. John Prior Estlin of Bristol (2:411n); but it is certainly the case that *The Life of Wesley* "derived chiefly," as Southey put it, not only from Wesley's *Works*, but also from a wide variety of other, no less "empirical," revival books.[98]

Southey's scholarly, two-volume biography, the first major view of Methodism from the non-Wesleyan British community, would suffice, even if it had not been in Wordsworth's library,[99] and even if it had not triggered a signal instance of Coleridge's penchant for writing marginalia,[100] to anticipate perhaps the most important point of my next chapter, namely, that the intellectual (distinct, say, from some mind-independently emotional) aspect of the revival was indeed present to the English Romantic mind.

Four

Romantic Method

The method of John Wesley, i.e., his progress from empiricism through quasi-empirical apprehension to faith, applies, *mutatis mutandis*, to Blake, Wordsworth, Coleridge, Shelley, and Keats. Their crossovers from observation of nature through imagination to poetic faith, in other words, are more than merely reminiscent of Wesley's relation to John Locke. I argue here that the Lockean-Wesleyan continuum is background to, if not context for, Romantic thought and expression. By interpreting much Romantic practice and some Romantic theory, both against and with Wesley's thought and language, I show specifically that his experiential range illuminates Romantic passages from experience into words. I address, then, the paradox of Romanticism's mundane and otherworldly points of view. The "tension," therein, between "Transcendentalism and a resurgent, neo-empiricist, organic naturalism" is "irreconcilable," if one follows John Kinnaird.[1] In counterpoint, however, and by way of generating critical method, I announce a program for studies in Romanticism whereby one finds, *mirabile dictu*, that Romantic tension in England at least is both partially reconcilable and fully understandable along clear lines of Wesley's philosophical theology.

Blake

Consider, before I delineate Blake's philosophical theology, his connections to Wesley in particular and Methodism in general. Margaret Bottrall, it is true, avers that Blake was never "obsessed by that need for the personal assurance of divine pardon which characterized the Methodists."[2] But Bottrall recognizes that in Nights 8 and 9 of *The Four Zoas* he evinces his need for, and testifies to the fact of, personal assurance of divine self-disclosure. And both Bottrall and Morton D. Paley, not only in their parallelings of Blake's emphasis on forgiveness with Wesley's on conversion, but also in their references to Blake's view of regeneration as an attainable state incorporated into common life in the secular world, mean to suggest an at least indirect relation between him and such a range of English religious figures as Wesley, Whitefield, William Law, other evangelicals, and Dissenters.[3] Useful, though preliminary, arguments have been made not just for parallels but even for direct links between the revival and Blake. Martha England, in her study of *Jerusalem*, *Milton*, and *Songs of Innocence and of Experience* against the background of Wesleyan hymnography, has shown "enthusiasm without mysticism" to be a concept that Blake was more or less explicitly aware of holding in common with Wesley.[4] And Jacob Bronowski, against one's expectation in his case of an empirico-scientific approach, has pinned down specific comparisons between evangelical practical charity and Blake's social consciousness.[5]

Blake's relation to the revival, then, was too close for one to conclude that he was merely generally informed about it or even that he was only incidentally sympathetic to it. Witness, now, the Preface to the third chapter of *Jerusalem* ("To the Deists"):

Voltaire Rousseau Gibbon Hume. charge the Spiritually Religious with Hypocrisy! but how a Monk or a Methodist either, can be a Hypocrite: I cannot conceive. . . . [Samuel] Foote in calling Whitefield, Hypocrite: was himself: for Whitefield pretended not to be holier than others: but confessed his Sins before all the World; . . . (Plate 53)

And witness *Milton*:

But then I [i.e., Rintrah] rais'd up Whitefield, Palamabron raisd up Westley,
And these are the cries of the Churches before the two Witnesses[']
Faith in God the dear Saviour who took on the likeness of men:
Becoming obedient to death, even the death of the Cross
The Witnesses lie dead in the Street of the Great City
No Faith is in all the Earth: the Book of God is trodden under Foot [i.e., Samuel?]:
He sent his two Servants Whitefield & Westley; were they Prophets
Or were they Idiots or Madmen? shew us Miracles!

Can you have greater Miracles than these? Men who devote
Their lifes whole comfort to intire scorn & injury & death
Awake thou sleeper on the Rock of Eternity Albion awake
The trumpet of Judgment hath twice sounded: all Nations are
    awake
But thou art still heavy and dull: Awake Albion awake! (Plates 22
    and 23)

Bernard Blackstone's comment, namely that Blake had "the greatest respect for true devotion and evangelical zeal, whether in the Church or
out of it" (*English Blake*, p. 375), is true as far as it goes but does not
indicate what is also true that Blake had the highest regard for the revival's
leadership. The passages above shade over from respect and fellow feeling
into a sense of identity between the author, whose lines amount to a third
"trumpet," and the two other true prophets of the early modern era.

    J. G. Davies's study of Blake's theology is close to the mark in record-
ing, albeit without elaboration, that Blake specifically "approved" and
"defended" Whitefield as well as Wesley;[6] like Samuel Johnson, however,
Blake identified with Wesley more than Whitefield. The passages above
mention Whitefield more often, but it should be noted, perhaps, that
Blake's praise of Whitefield is qualified by recognition of the "Sins" he
had to confess, and it is clear, from Paley's study of "Cowper as Blake's
Spectre," that an erroneous, if not sinful, belief in God as Urizen and
Nobodaddy, i.e., in God the punisher and judge, was what Blake objected to in Cowper, another Evangelical Anglican of the Calvinistic
stripe.[7] As late as May 24, 1804, in a letter to Hayley, Blake wrote of his
"happiness" in "seeing the Divine countenance in such men as Cowper,"[8]
but "the Spectre" in Plate 10 of *Jerusalem*, for which as Paley shows Cowper is the original, is comforted by Los for feeling, as Cowper did to the
point of madness, that God "is not a Being of Pity & Compassion" and
"cannot feel Distress," and Blake's pity for God-tormented Cowper together with Blake's admiration for Cowper as God-intoxicated may well
be an accurate characterization of his attitude toward Whitefield. Toward
Wesley, evidently, he had no such ambivalence. Wesley's God, as I have
elsewhere sketched him, was primarily an Arminian God of pity, who
desired nothing less than redemption for all,[9] and this conception undoubtedly formed the basis of Blake's admiration for Wesley: it is Palamabron, or Pity, who raises Wesley up, and though both Palamabron
and Rintrah, or Wrath, are children of Los, or Imagination, and though
Blake, therefore, evinces a mood somehow both Arminian and Calvinistic, there can be little doubt that a most un-Calvinistic conception of divinity occupies the center of his emphasis:

> I am not a God afar off, I am a brother and friend;
> Within your bosoms I reside, and you reside in me:
> Lo! we are One; forgiving all Evil; Not seeking recompense!
>
> (*Jerusalem*, Plate 4)

Bottrall's main conclusion, namely that the "triumph" of Blake's interpretation of Christianity "was to incorporate the gospel of liberty into the profounder gospel of love" (*The Divine Image*, p. 11), is a good way to understand the Arminian, as distinct from the exclusively political, quality of his vision, for his God is a personal God of forgiveness, who like the God of Wesley appeals to the free will of all people. Bottrall, though, is wrong to suggest that sin-and-damnation constitutes the only emphasis of the revival, just as Blackstone is wrong to suggest that "prudential maxims" do.[10] Despite their respective interests in Blake's Christianity and his English roots, they do not pursue his relation to the revival; clearly they mistake it as finally Calvinistic and, hence, finally uncongenial with his temperament.

His self-disclosing God, i.e., almost necessarily the God of immediate revelation, could hardly be more reminiscent of Wesley's. Blake's protracted "conversion," culminating at Felpham in November 1802, is followed by the decidedly orthodox turn of *The Four Zoas, Milton,* and *Jerusalem*: "He writes" therein, say D. J. Sloss and J. P. R. Wallis, "of the cardinal Christian doctrines, the Incarnation, the Atonement, and the Resurrection, . . . as facts in the spiritual history of man";[11] the experience at Felpham, then, prelusive to embrace of traditional revelation, is Immediacy. It may be, as Paley says, that "for Blake . . . the redemptive power [in these later works] is the Imagination" (*Energy and Imagination*, p. 147). But Paley goes too far in adding that this "account of regeneration differs from" that of the evangelicals. For the particular place and the immediacy of Blake's regeneration are at once in line with the subject/ object base of Romantic imagination and strongly reminiscent of Wesley's partly Locke-derived emphasis on possible spiritual influx for postbiblical man. The near identity, indeed, of evangelical and Blakean accounts of regeneration is indicated by the fact that, at least by 1816, an uncannily Blakean terminology entered into evangelical language; Samuel Greatheed, minister of Newport Pagnell, defends Cowper against the charge of religious madness by implicitly identifying the witness of the Spirit with what even Paley, in quoting Greatheed, calls "a rather Blakean definition of sanity," and with what all students of Blake might recognize as a sufficiently Blakean usage of the term *imagination*:

The Enthusiast [writes Greatheed] is merely an individual in whom the passions are more habitually in a state of excitation, and the imagination operates with the force of a stimulus. The man's sanity must be determined by the course his reason takes, by the nature of the object which engages all this enthusiasm, by the steadiness and consistency with which he presses forward in its attainment. And if the object chosen be infinite, surely it is the enthusiast alone that is altogether sane.[12]

Consider, now, the prospect of Blake's philosophical theology. Insofar as both the evangelical enthusiast and Blake attained to their respective spiritual objects, i.e., insofar as each conceived of a divine spirit as one and the same with his immediate self-consciousness,[13] each conceived an at least quasi-philosophical, and at any rate far from madly religious, methodology of spiritual experience. Blake's idea of "the Spirit of Prophecy," which he sometimes called "the Poetic Genius," is for him "the first principle of perception, actively building a reality from the materials of sensation" (Paley, *Energy and Imagination*, pp. 221–22); this principle, Paley adds, "has an antecedent in the philosophy of David Hume. . . . Hume argues that belief is not produced by abstract reason but by the imagination acting upon either memory or sensation." Paley recognizes an even greater congeniality between Blake's thought and the philosophy of Berkeley: both men held that "the phenomena are dependent upon Mind active in perception."[14] As for Locke, and for that matter scientific empiricism, it should be pointed out that despite Blake's well-known and admittedly wonderful diatribe against Newtonianism and Lockeanism (in *Jerusalem*, Plate 15), to wit,

I turn my eyes to the Schools & Universities of Europe
And there behold the Loom of Locke whose Woof rages dire
Washd by the Water-wheels of Newton. black the cloth
In heavy wreathes folds over every Nation; cruel Works
Of many Wheels I view, wheel without wheel, with cogs tyrranic
Moving by compulsion each other: not as those in Eden: which
Wheel within Wheel in freedom revolve in harmony & peace,

he did not simply reject these systems, but, in the case of Newton, turned him "inside out," and in the case of Locke, translated his emphasis on the five senses into the analogical language of "Imagination or Spiritual Sensation."[15] "Bacon & Newton & Locke," though *bêtes noires* in Blake's mythic pantheon, were not only recognized by him as genuine truth seekers but also admired by him as such: even in *Jerusalem*, for example, he places them among "the Innumerable Chariots of the Almighty."[16] The Lockean as well as Wesleyan dimensions of his thought, then, are sufficiently evident in the works of his maturity to warrant alertness to them, taken together, as a means of understanding his entire career.

Despite the widespread assumption that a simple rejection of the rationally empirical tradition was strongly evident as early as January 1788, when he wrote "There is No Natural Religion," I suggest that even then empirical method formed a model for his religious thought, for Wesley's doctrines of perceptible inspiration and the spiritual sense comprise self-evidently accurate glosses upon Blake's conclusion, in this tractate, that "Mans perceptions are not bounded by organs of perception. he perceives more than sense (tho' ever so acute) can discover." Attempting, from the start, a kind of writing at once peculiarly religious and peculiarly empirical, Blake therein implies that if there is no natural religion of a Deistic kind, then there is nonetheless revealed religion with room for both natural theism and quasi-empirical methodology.

Though one accepts, moreover, E. D. Hirsch's view that the language of such early works as *Poetical Sketches* (1783) is only casually religious and is indeed intended merely to contribute to the purity of a fundamentally secular pastoral landscape, one may resist Hirsch's implication with regard to *Songs of Innocence and of Experience* (1789–94) that the intensively religious language whereby Blake therein sacramentalizes pastoral landscape is exclusively Miltonic.[17] What Hirsch calls the "radically immanent Christianity" of such poems as "A Cradle Song" and "The Divine Image" has as much to do with Wesley's all but worldly faith as with the faith of Milton. And the earnestness of evangelical practical charity informs such poems as "The Little Black Boy" and "The Chimney Sweeper"; witness, for just two examples of these poems' contexts, Wilberforce's efforts against the slave trade and the evangelical Jonas Hanway's *Sentimental History of Chimney-Sweeps in London* (1788).

Thus, insofar as the content of Blake's *oeuvre* is understandable as not only evangelical on the one hand and Lockean on the other, but also at once Lockean and evangelical, Wesley's philosophical theology is almost certainly à propos. Although full establishment of this point lies beyond the present program, one may see even now that the evangelical thought of Blake, deriving not so much from rejecting sense as from cleansing doors of perception, is more than merely reminiscent of Wesley's methodology which adheres either to sense perception per se or to a model thereof: Blake characteristically looks at the sun both to discover heavenly hosts singing "Holy Holy Holy" and to see a coin-sized disk, and because "Imagination" is for him "Spiritual Sensation," he feels, with equally Wesleyan sensibility, both that "This World is all One continued Vision" and that "a Man may be happy in This World" (to the Rev. Dr. Trusler, August 23, 1799). In short, Blake "perceives" along the continuum from natural to spiritual. The experiential basis of his method links him to Wesleyan thought, though not, of course, to the abuse of Lockean method during the Industrial Revolution; Wesley was Blake's access to Locke.

It is not inadvisable, then, to be alert even to other than merely thematic parallels. Consider, as concluding indications of what can be done, form and phraseology.

First, as to phraseology, Wesley's view of spiritual experience as identification with the condescensions of God is so strikingly like Blake's radically immanent Christianity that it is justifiable both to quote Blake in full and to repeat an important quotation of Wesley. Here is "The Great Privilege":

> [One's] *ears* are now opened, and the *voice* of God no longer calls in vain [cf. Ezek. 1:24; Isa. 32:3]. He hears and OBEYS the heavenly calling; he KNOWS the voice of his Shepherd [cf. John 10:1–16]. All his spiritual *senses* being now awakened, he has a clear *intercourse* with the invisible world; and hence he KNOWS more and more of the things which before it could not "enter in to his heart to conceive" [cf. Isa. 64:4; 1 Cor. 2:9]. He now KNOWS what the peace of God is; what is joy in the Holy Ghost; what the love of God which is shed abroad in the hearts of them that believe in him through Christ Jesus [cf. Rom. 5:5]. Thus the veil being removed which before intercepted the light and *voice*, the KNOWLEDGE and love of God, he who is born of the Spirit dwelleth in love, "dwelleth in God, and God in him!" (*Sermons*, pp. 177–78 [cf. 1 John 3:24]. My italics and capital letters—RB)

And here is "The Shepherd":

> How sweet is the Shepherds sweet lot,
> From the morn to the evening he strays:
> He shall follow his sheep all the day
> And his tongue shall be filled with praise.
>
> For he *hears* the lambs innocent call,
> And he *hears* the ewes tender reply,

> He is *watchful* while they are in peace,
> For they KNOW when their Shepherd is nigh.
> (My italics and capital letters—RB)

In "The Shepherd," as in "The Great Privilege," the alternation and oscillation between rational and sensationalistic diction suggest that, through immediate revelation, God and man are ensphered, and since as Hirsch points out, there is in Blake a radical identity between man, as shepherd, and God, as Shepherd,[18] it should be said that in Blake as in Wesley a "clear intercourse" occurs not only between man as object and God as Subject but also between man as subject and God as Object.

And finally, as to form: Wesley's aphorisms, according to Lawton, "express the empiricism in his spirit" (*John Wesley's English*, p. 226), but considering their source, I suggest that they also express the spirit in his empiricism, and I suggest too that a similar combination of inductive wisdom and spiritual receptivity informs the proverbial forms wherein Blake often blends his prophetic mode of utterance with a tough-minded respect for experience per se. Here, for example, is Blake:

> Dip him in the river who loves water.
>
> . . . .
>
> Think in the morning, Act in the noon, Eat in the evening, Sleep
>   in the night.
>
> > (*The Marriage of Heaven and Hell*)

And here is Wesley: "Let him who must die tomorrow live today" (Curnock, 4:402). Here again is Blake: "I sunned [my anger with my foe] with smiles, / And with soft deceitful wiles" ("A Poison Tree"). And here, in shorter compass, is Wesley: "Stabbing my friend with a smile" (Telford, 1:104). Here, finally, is Blake:

> Prudence is a rich ugly old maid courted by Incapacity.
> > (*The Marriage of Heaven and Hell*)

> God keep me from the Divinity of Yes and No too[,] The Yea Nay Creeping Jesus[,] from supposing Up & Down to be the same Thing as all Experimentalists must suppose. (To George Cumberland, April 12, 1827)

And here is Wesley, in a similar mood of letting one's light shine: "God deliver me, and all that seek him in sincerity from what the world calls Christian prudence" (Curnock, 2:101).

Wordsworth

Wordsworth's "Methodism," like that of Blake, is complementary to, even when not fully consistent with, empiricism. Charles Lamb's characterization of Wordsworth's *Excursion* as "natural methodism," in other words, applies to Wordsworth's works in a way broader than I was sufficiently aware of in 1975 when in *Wordsworth's "Natural Methodism"* I wrote of Lamb's phrase that "the word *methodism* suggests the religious quality of [Wordsworth's] thoroughgoing reliance on . . . experience as a basis for knowing the true and the good" (p. 8). Now I realize that whatever Lamb meant by his phrase,[19] *natural methodism* indicates the continuum from empiricism to faith and denominates even the strange, experiential simultaneity of Wordsworth's religious and philosophical assumptions. The quality of his reliance on experience, I argue, is at once philosophical and religious, for I show here that *Wordsworth's "Natural Methodism"* is an apt phrase for the empiricist as well as evangelical dimensions of his thought-and-language, and I state at the outset that his evangelical and empiricist hemispheres of mind interact through its corpus callosum of experience both natural and spiritual. Recognizing, in 1977, that he not only "breathed in the Evangelical atmosphere of Anglican faith," but also "stood on the ground of empirical philosophy," I suggested that "he sought . . . a way of transcendentalizing Locke and Hume" ("JWC," pp. 164–65); now, in the light of Wesley's methodology, I realize that such a transcendentalizing process was near, if not built into, Wordsworth's quasi-Wesleyan faith. It is time, by way of reconciling his religious urge with his philosophic bent, to explore the likelihood that his empiricist and "Methodist" propensities are two sides of the same coin. It is feasible, specifically, to draw out Wesleyan implications of the most presently pertinent historical approach to his mind and art, i.e., the Lockean. This approach, still standard, is notably represented by Hugh Sykes Davies and Colin Clarke, and by engaging their arguments I reveal that the one thing lacking therein, and hence in the Lockean approach generally, is the realization that for a sampling at least of Wordsworth's major poetry and for at least a smattering of his prose the most immediate, and a quite explanatory, context is not so much the philosophy of Locke as Wesley's philosophical theology.

Clarke's approach, worthy of no brief rehearsal here, emphasizes the subject/object complexity of Wordsworth's blank verse. "Assumptions about the mind and its place in nature," writes Clarke at his outset, "are concealed in every act of human perception. We take it for granted, merely by perceiving or being aware, that the given world both is and is not extrinsic to our selves. . . . It is implied in . . . perceptual experience

. . . that the place of mind in the natural world is equivocal, or a paradox," and he goes on to argue, persuasively, that "a more or less latent
awareness of this paradox, a feeling for the ambiguity and the strangeness
of perception, a largely unconscious perplexity in fact, was the 'cause' of
some of Wordsworth's finest poetry."[20] In "The Boy of Winander," for
example, which Wordsworth published both separately and as part of
Prelude 5, Clarke finds an especially apt illustration of his subthesis,
namely, that Wordsworth's "landscapes often exist simultaneously as
prospects within the mind, as outward scenes, and as configurations of
solid objects" (*Romantic Paradox*, p. 6). Here are the final lines of Wordsworth's poem-within-a-poem:

> . . . and, when a lengthened pause
> Of Silence came and baffled his best skill,
> Then sometimes, in that silence while he hung
> Listening, a gentle shock of mild surprise
> Has carried far into his heart the voice
> Of mountain torrents; or the visible scene
> Would enter unawares into his mind,
> With all its solemn imagery, its rocks,
> Its woods, and that uncertain heaven, received
> Into the bosom of the steady lake.
> (*Prelude* 5.388–97)

And here is the final observation in Clarke's discussion of these lines:
"The uncompromising apposition, '. . . its solemn imagery, its rocks, Its
woods' implies a simple equivalence of imagery and outward objects and
suggests that if it is not quite the rocks and woods themselves that enter
the mind neither is it a mere picture or representation of them" (*Romantic
Paradox*, p. 7).

Clarke is at his best, I think, in his discussion of "Tintern Abbey," in
which, as he puts it, "[Wordsworth] resolves the apparent contradiction
that the natural world is extrinsic to the self and yet a modification of it":

> Resolves it, however—if I may be allowed to labour the point a
> little—in the manner of a poet. . . . The "mystical" moments in
> *Tintern Abbey* . . . are validated by, and find their primary analogue
> in, quite ordinary sensory experiences in which the visible scene
> and the observer's mind at once confront each other (preserving
> their distinctions) and interpenetrate deeply. (*Romantic Paradox*,
> pp. 12–13)

The poem, accordingly, becomes for Clarke a well-sustained, well-integrated series of wordplays in which "rigid distinctions between outer and inner . . . fall into abeyance"; Wordsworth repeats such terms as *murmur, impress, motion, quiet, deep, lofty, lone, wild, gleams, behold, lead, wander, world, bless, eye, sublime, heart, language, harmony, light, sky, form,* and *life* to establish subjective and objective contexts, and hence objective and subjective meanings, for each (*Romantic Paradox*, pp. 41, 46–48). *Life*, for example, despite seeming an exclusively subjective word, includes an objective denotation: "the life of things" and "the living air" are as prominent, in the poem, as "a good man's life" and "a living soul." Here is Clarke's conclusion:

> If cliffs and thoughts are both "lofty"; if the sky and the human eye are alike "quiet"; the soul and the air both "living"; if both river and human observer wander; if the light of setting suns is a "dwelling", and the memory a "dwelling-place"; if the spirit or presence is "a motion" and "our human blood" also felt as "motion", etc. etc., then it becomes difficult for the reader to sustain without radical qualification a normal, common-sense distinction between the living and the lifeless. (*Romantic Paradox*, p. 48)

Clarke's approach, though broad enough to take Wordsworth's transcendentalist diction into account, is refinable in my terms, for despite Clarke's nod to "Tintern Abbey"'s "mystical," and hence at least quasi-religious, moments, the poem's vision of unity, for him, is achieved entirely on the horizontal, empirical plane. With regard, it is true, to Wordsworth's description of Dorothy's memory as "a dwelling-place / For all sweet sounds and harmonies," Clarke recognizes, in *sweet*, spiritual meaning, viz., "free from taint or corruption" (*Romantic Paradox*, p. 43), but he is far from interpreting her, thereby, as in tune with another realm. Rather, through the alchemy by which language suggests interpenetration of subject and object, *sweet*, for him, finally evokes "the actual *process* of sensing" (p. 43), and, although he appears at one point to take seriously the religious dimension of Wordsworth's language, to wit, "The flashes of insight into an invisible or more ultimate world seem an inevitable consequence of the way substance and spirit are ambiguously and mysteriously implicated in the simplest act of perception," Clarke neither here (p. 44) nor anywhere else asks whether such visionary language includes, in its unity, the vertical with the horizontal. This question is logical from the standpoint even of Clarke's both/and method: not only is the poem objective and subjective, both together, but it is also philosophical and theological, both together, and, as *sweet* is largely spiritual, and as *mystical* is an all but unavoidable term of analysis, so "Tintern Abbey" is often more biblical, moral, and spiritual, and hence more religious, than anything else; witness these words and phrases:

> *purer mind; portion; good man's life; little, nameless, unremembered, acts / Of kindness and of love; gift; sublime; blessed; soul; belief; spirit; recognitions dim and faint; gifts; abundant recompense; chasten; moral being; heart; prayer; cheerful faith; ecstasies; mansion; exhortations; worshipper; service; zeal;* and *holier love.*

The poem's interpenetrations, in other words, to say nothing for the moment of interpenetrations in Wordsworth's other works, are up-and-down as well as in-and-out; the cohesive vision here is a good bit more ambitious and a good bit more inclusive than Clarke allows.

In *Wordsworth's "Natural Methodism,"* I argued that "the emphasis [in "Tintern Abbey"] lies not so much on the doubt, diffidence, and desperation of the speaker . . . as on his mature experience of grace" (pp. 126–27), and it is time, now, in the light of Wesley's methodology, to see that the richness of the poem depends finally on its exploration of the common ground between transcendental and empirical modes of thought. The poem, in other words, is one in which "the simplest act of perception" is such a mysterious blend of subject and object as to prefigure, if not cause, "flashes of insight into an invisible or more ultimate world," for I argue that "the 'mystical' moments" in "Tintern Abbey" are not so much mystical as quasi-empirical: they are modes of spiritual experience that reinforce, and resemble, the uncanny oneness-in-multiplicity of sensory experience. This poem brings one round, in short, to the realm of Wesleyan analogy. Clarke observes that "though the analogy between spiritual and sensory vision is an ancient one ('We see into the life of things') in the context of this poem it has special force" (*Romantic Paradox*, p. 49). He means by *spiritual* nothing in addition to *living* or *mental*, but if one takes *spiritual* to refer, however dimly, to that part of the mind in touch with a world elsewhere, then one may take Clarke's statement of the poem's "analogy" as appropriate to a philosophically theological as well as simply philosophical argument. Indeed, with regard not only to "Tintern Abbey," but also, as I shall indicate, to the entire canon of which it is so representative, one is justified in qualifying Clarke's perspective from the standpoints not only of Wesley's philosophical theology, but also, more narrowly, of Wesley's empiricism per se.

Relative, for example, to Clarke's naturalistic emphasis on subject and object, I hold out that in "Tintern Abbey," as in the works of Wesley and Locke, it is not so much a matter of balance as of an at least slightly greater emphasis on the objective. Such an emphasis, certainly, is evident in the *Essay*, in which the term *idea*, far from being exclusively subjective, includes an objective dimension: "the numerous indications," writes Mac-Lean, "that [Lockean] ideas were closely associated with external, sensible objects, begin with the significant use of the word 'idea' itself, which in some instances [in the *Essay*] is made to stand for an object outside the mind in a connection which now seems unusual" (*John Locke and English Literature of the Eighteenth Century*, p. 54). It is true, of course, that Addison, in his interpretation of Locke, dilates on Locke's subjective side: Addison expatiates "delightfully lost and bewildered," "like the enchanted hero of a romance," in the "pleasing delusion" of "light and colours" that do not exist "in the objects themselves" (*Spectator*, No. 413, as quoted in MacLean, p. 94). But it is also the case that in the "distinction between primary and secondary qualities of [material] substance, which was peculiarly suggestive to the literary mind" (MacLean, pp. 93–94), the primary qualities of solidity, extension, figure, and mobility receive the emphasis during the remainder of the century: Pope and Sterne, for example, tended to stress the objective, decidedly unromancelike side of the distinction,[21] and a passage from "Thoughts upon Necessity," quoted earlier, reveals that Wesley, though recognizing the distinction and though acknowledging a subjective character in the "sensation" of secondary qualities, was so far objective as to insist, going further than Sterne, Pope, and Locke, that "colours" finally "exist without us." Wesley's bias, in "Thoughts upon Necessity," is so extreme in its objectivity that it is of course at no small distance from the often romancelike, and hence often subjective, orientation of English Romantics. But a glance at the Wordsworth *Concordance* reveals that in his poetry, at least, primary qualities occur more frequently than secondary, by a ratio of $6\frac{3}{4}$ to $5\frac{1}{2}$.[22] And it is clear, from an apposition in "Tintern Abbey" fully as "uncompromising" as the one in "The Boy of Winander," that the secondary qualities of color and form are closely associated in the mind of Wordsworth with the objective world:

> The sounding cataract
> Haunted me like a passion: the tall rock,
> The mountain, and the deep and gloomy wood,
> Their colours and their forms, were then to me
> An appetite; . . . .

> (lines 76–80)

This resembles radical, Lockean realism, rather than the imaginary, if not visionary, romance of Addison.

By way of adding philosophical theology to philosophy, i.e., by way of further broadening Clarke's focus, I maintain relative to "Tintern Abbey" that the methodological, Brownean-Wesleyan continuum from natural to revealed religion is so far from being merely a propos that it is, indeed, an inclusive gloss. With regard first to natural religion: Clarke implies that a radical, if not Spinozistic, pantheism informs "Tintern Abbey," and H. W. Piper argues that pantheism is central thereto,[23] but one should remember the English context of the poem, i.e., one should realize that "Tintern Abbey" is close to natural religion. Not only did John Toland's *Pantheisticon* (1720) coin the term, i.e., not only was pantheism, in England, associated with Deism, but also, and more importantly for my emphasis on theistical natural religion, Wordsworth's letter of December 1814, to Catherine Clarkson, wife of his Evangelical Anglican friend Thomas, specifically rejects pantheistic interpretations of the poem, and does so, moreover, in terms reminiscent of Wesley's natural religion, i.e., his theistical view of nature. The poet begins the letter, as I have said,

> by refuting [Patty Smith's] contention that the poem fails to distinguish "between Nature as the work of God, and God himself." He goes on [in the letter] to clarify his beliefs about God's precise relationship to nature, first by rejecting (as did the Evangelicals) the deistic notion of "the Supreme Being as bearing the same relation to the Universe, as a watch-maker bears to a watch," and then by implying, through as strong an association between nature and the Bible as can be found among the Evangelicals, that God relates to nature as an author relates to his book: he speaks of "the innumerable analogies and types of infinity . . . which I have infused into that poem from the Bible of the Universe, as it speaks to the ear of the intelligent, and as it lies open to the eyes of the humble-minded." (*W*"NM," p. 149)

What I did not say, but what I add, is that the poem's central passage, for example, should be thought of as fully consistent with and sharply reminiscent of the Wesleyan and quintessentially English form of natural religion whereby God is seen to be present in, but not equivalent to, the text and texture of his second book. The "presence that disturbs" Wordsworth "with the joy / Of elevated thoughts," since it "impels / All thinking things, all objects of all thought," stands outside and pushes the blended worlds of animate and inanimate. And since it "rolls through all things," it not only permeates them but also emerges from them: it rolls not only throughout but also all the way through.

Finally, with regard to revealed religion, Clarke is right, I think, to shy away by means of his quotation marks from *mystical* as description of the moments in "Tintern Abbey," but he is also right in believing that some such vocabulary is needed, and I contend specifically that Wesley's analogy between sense perception and immediate revelation is a precise means of elaborating Geoffrey Hartman's point that the poem is "a statement on revelation."[24] Just as Wesley was more empirically rational than mystical in his approach to this most potentially un-"philosophic" dimension of faith, so Wordsworth, far from leaving off the Lockean language of images, includes it towards the end of his testimony of vision:

> And I have felt
> A presence that disturbs me with the joy
> Of elevated thoughts; a sense sublime
> Of something far more deeply interfused,
> Whose dwelling is the light of setting suns,
> And the round ocean and the living air,
> And the blue sky, and in the mind of man: . . .
>
> (lines 93–99)

From this passage, though, one has the impression that the "presence," albeit inferrable from a theistical attitude towards nature, and albeit linked therefore to sense images per se, is felt not so much through the senses as through a perception, quasi-Wesleyan, unmediated by any images at all and related to them, indeed, only if nonetheless really, by analogy.

Wordsworth's "sense sublime," then, is in its historical context essentially akin to Wesley's "spiritual sense" and "perceptible inspiration," or, to put the matter in even more inclusively Wesleyan terms, the subject-object, empirically rational dimension of "Tintern Abbey" is consistent with its "sense sublime" in the same way that Wesley's theology of immediate revelation is consistent with his Lockean methodology. One recalls, in this connection, Wesley's view as expressed in "A Letter to the Rev. Dr. Conyers Middleton," i.e., that "senses suitable to invisible or eternal objects" will bring "to the rational, reflecting, part of mankind" "a more extensive knowledge of things invisible and eternal," for it is clear that Wordsworth claims cognition of the "presence" in accordance with methodology sufficiently philosophic, as well as emotionally charged and poetically transformed. The poet's desire "to *connect* / The landscape

with the quiet of the sky," for example, amounts to a poetic response to
Wesley's injunction, in "Human Life a Dream," "by every possible means
to *connect* the ideas of time and eternity," my italics, for just as Wesley, in
that sermon, pleads with his audience "so to associate them together, that
the thought of one may never recur to your mind, without the thought
of the other," so "Tintern Abbey," as it seems, bespeaks what Hartman
might call an "identity" between the transcendent "presence" and the
time-bound perceiver of that "presence": "We would," writes Hartman,

> distinguish and sum up the attributes of this [Wordsworthian]
> power whereby the human mind may perceive, and the poetic fac-
> ulty express, mystical ideas. . . . [The possibility of symbols] re-
> sults from the mind's immediate, sustained perception of an iden-
> tity between itself and the thing perceived. . . . [A final] attribute
> concerns the object sought by the understanding and revealed to it
> as a pure principle of love sustaining and moving that by which it is
> sought. (*The Unmediated Vision*, p. 45)

Wordsworth's awareness of a "paradox," i.e., "that the given world both
is and is not extrinsic to our selves," led indeed, if "Tintern Abbey" is any
indication, to the "perplexity" that caused some of his finest poetry, but
the poetry is not for that reason exclusively philosophical in tone. In the
Preface to the *Survey*, Wesley is "perplexed and entangled" because "we
cannot know" the "why" of things, yet for him this perplexity is a more
theological than quasi-Humean condition, for he adds, in his Preface,
that "God hath so done his works, that we may admire and adore; but we
cannot search them out," and his relishment of two strange, all but simultaneous truths, namely tabula rasa and the divine origin of mind (see
his first remark upon the *Essay*), together with his denomination of this
two-edged truth as "an utter paradox," uncannily parallel the genius
whereby Wordsworth celebrates in "Tintern Abbey," and generally, the
curious but incontrovertible fact that one is defined by the passing of
time, viz., "Five years have passed . . . ," yet interinvolved also with the
timelessness, and even the extraspatiality, of transcendence.

The approach of Hugh Sykes Davies addresses in particular the theme
of free will, but Davies's emphasis on this theological as well as philosophical theme is exclusively philosophical, and his approach, therefore
like Clarke's, is refinable in my terms.

Davies's interpretation of Wordsworth's blank verse, like Clarke's, is
so useful for present purposes that it deserves a hearing here. Davies's
discussion is grounded first of all in the empiricists' tendency to see the

mind as a more passive than active participant in experience: "Experience," he writes, in the philosophy of Hartley and Hume, and even of Berkeley and Locke,

> tends to be continuous and homogeneous: . . . it flows in through the senses upon the mind with an unremitting and undifferentiated force, no one piece of it being of greater importance than another. It is further stated [by the empiricists] . . . that the more complex mental structures made up from sensations are not the product of any autonomous activity in the mind, but are suggested to it by the frequent recurrence of some sensations in "gangs" and "clusters" amid "the constant vicissitude of things." To the mind conceived as quite passive, without any power to choose among or to modify sensations, all sensations must be equal, save that mere frequency of occurrence would draw attention to some rather than others.[25]

Moreover, Davies argues that, though Wordsworth "wrote in general harmony with [the empiricists'] formal doctrines," he "was in sharp disagreement with what they implied" about human experience (*The English Mind*, p. 157): especially in *The Prelude*, for example, "his own mode of experiencing things was specially sensitive to the isolated" (pp. 162–63), and his "spots of time," therefore, are distinguished from the empirical account of experience "by their capacity for isolated and instant action, with long continued effects" (p. 166). Davies, it seems to me, is at his best in showing how Wordsworth's mode of experiencing anticipates Freud's conclusion that "certain perceptions or sensations have a far greater power on the growth of the spirit than others" (p. 167), and Davies is equally stimulating in his observation that "a writer who is at all concerned with the growth of human spirits cannot but plump" either for Freud and Wordsworth or for "the empirical philosophers" (p. 169). Virginia Woolf and James Joyce, adds Davies, are attracted to the philosophers insofar as their "stream of consciousness" or interior monologue represents "the undifferentiated flow of sensations."

Where Davies goes astray, I think, is in his hasty conclusion:

> If it is commonly true, at least of some people, that the growth of the mind is discontinuous, depending often on comparatively few crucially formative involutes [i.e., the sensations, feelings, and thoughts present in certain experiences]; and if these experiences are indeed correctly described as depending upon some special conjunction of an inner state and some outward circumstance, then it

follows that chance, destiny, fate—whatever synonym seems most euphemistic—has the power of intervening in the very formation of the human personality. . . . It seems to be an unavoidable consequence of Wordsworth's view of experience, however he may have tried to avoid it, that sometimes it may matter very much what we chance to be seeing, hearing, or touching at a crucial moment of thought and feeling. (*The English Mind*, pp. 172, 174)

Thus Davies goes against much of his own drift and implies that Wordsworth's mind finally is under the control of, if not overborne by, circumstance.

I suggest, however, that Wordsworth's crucial experiences, despite their preponderant objectivity, present the mind as more active than passive and more free than circumscribed. I hold indeed that the "spots of time" are finally distinguished from the empirical account of experience not simply by their philosophical "capacity for isolated and instant action, with long continued effects," but especially by their strangely simultaneous philosophical and theological preservations of free will. Not only have I recognized, in *Wordsworth's "Natural Methodism,"* that "the nature of perception" is "an important theme" of the "spots of time," but I have also indicated therein that in their "resistance to solipsism" they draw upon "philosophical as well as spiritual contexts" (pp. 55 ff). I do not compete here with that full-scale discussion, but I reiterate its thesis that the "spots of time" recount "the awakening of conscience," and hence of free will, by means of "early chastening of guilty passion" (*W*"NM," pp. 53–54). I realize now that Wordsworth's theme of guilt is in Wesleyan terms proof positive of his assumption of free will, since Wesley, to repeat a passage from "Thoughts upon Necessity," finally objects to "the system of universal necessity" because there could be therein "no place for blame or remorse": "Certainly the pain, the remorse, which is felt by any man who had been guilty of a bad action, springs from the notion, that he has a power over his actions, that he might have forborne to do it."

It is worth pointing out, for still further purposes of refining Davies's approach and of announcing this direction for Wordsworth studies that the likely way in which Wordsworth's theological and philosophical themes come together in the "spots of time," and generally, is illuminated by Wesley's particular equilibrium in "Thoughts upon Necessity," where Wesley's theological emphasis on free will, for example, coexists with his qualified sympathy even for the extreme empiricism of Hartley. "Let the sensation *A*," writes Hartley, be often associated with each of the sensations B, C, D, &c. . . . A, impressed alone, will, at last, raise b, c, d, &c. all together, i.e. associate them with one another. . . . All compound impressions A + B + C + D, &c. after sufficient repetition leave compound miniatures a + b + c + d, &c. which recur every now and then from slight causes. (*Observations on Man*, 1, prop. 12)

"I am not careful," responds Wesley, "about the flowing of my blood and spirits, or the vibrations of my brain; being well assured, that, however my spirits may flow, or my nerves and fibres vibrate, the Almighty God of love . . . will put it in my power to be virtuous and happy for ever." Thus, not even Hartley's most absolute statement of the undifferentiated force of sense impressions is enough to disturb Wesley's faith in free will, but Wesley, to cite "Thoughts upon Necessity" once more, emphatically denies that sense impressions are the undifferentiated destroyers of free will: "[I]n receiving the impressions of things," he writes, "much depends on [one's] own choice. In many cases he may or may not receive the impression; in most he may vary it greatly." The context of philosophical theology in which Wesley understood free will was undoubtedly a condition that favored the particularly inclusive thematic achievement of the "spots of time," for Locke's notion that there would be no time if it were possible, while waking, to focus on just one idea, and Wesley's preoccupation with precisely datable moments of spiritual access, are analogous, as well as historically related, to the infinite but particularized moments suspended, in *The Prelude*, by Wordsworth's creative act of will.

It is time now in the context not only of Davies's and Clarke's approaches, but also of all other critics who tend to see Wordsworth in exclusively philosophical terms,[26] to determine just how far Wesley's philosophical theology, in its implications for both the methodology of sense perception in Wordsworth and Wordsworthian free will, explains the blank verse in particular and the poetry in general. What follows is a sample of what one finds.

With regard first to the poetry in general, L. J. Swingle has observed that Wordsworth's peculiarly English development of Descartes's skeptical method led not just to the *cogito*, i.e., not just to the fact that the mind thinks and can no more help thinking than the eye can keep from seeing but especially to how the mind thinks, i.e., what its differences are among all ages and types.[27] But Wesley's comment (in "A Letter to the Rev. Dr. Conyers Middleton") that "a peasant, a woman, a child" may feel all the force of immediate revelation, and Wesley's implication that this mode of knowledge gives such people an at once sensationalistic and rational rhetoric of spiritual discovery (to wit, "One thing I KNOW; I was blind, but now I *see*") both strongly suggest that spiritual as well as empiricist levels of inquiry converge to underlie poems as otherwise diverse as "The Idiot Boy," "She Was a Phantom of Delight," and "The Leech-Gatherer." From the beginning of "She Was a Phantom of Delight," for example, is a blend of empirical and spiritual diction, viz., "She was a *phantom* of *delight*, / When first she *gleamed* upon my *sight*" (my italics—RB).

With regard specifically to Wordsworth's contribution to the literary ballad, one thinks immediately of

> A slumber did my spirit seal;
>   I had no human fears:
> She seemed a thing that could not feel
>   The touch of earthly years.
>
> No motion has she now, no force;
>   She neither hears nor sees;
> Rolled round in earth's diurnal course,
>   With rocks, and stones, and trees.

Locke's identification of motion as a primary quality, i.e., as something which exists whether it is perceived or not (see MacLean, p. 93), and Wesley's association of motion with "spiritual strength" and "the senses of the soul" (see "The Great Privilege of those that are born of God"), hover near the meaning of the word in this most familiar of the Lucy poems. Wordsworth's usage of *motion*, to be sure, in the context of *force* and *diurnal*, relates to Newton's laws of gravity and planetary movement:[28] though Lucy, in death, is quite still, she is translated onto the cosmic plane and "survives" at least insofar as she participates in the revolutions of the earth. The context of Wesley's philosophical theology, however, is also pertinent, for it heightens, though not the consolatory dimension of the poem, its poignancy of tone: if Lucy has no motion, part of what she has lost is her spiritual sensation and her spiritual strength, and by the same token, she has lost her identity as it is in itself, without regard to what the speaker perceives, or has ever perceived, about her. Much of the second stanza's uncompromising tragedy, then, lies in its implication that she has lost not just her physical presence, i.e., her gravity, but her philosophically spiritual and spiritually philosophical reality as well.

The philosophically theological overtones of the poem are especially Wesleyan in the first line, in which Wordsworth appears somewhat to undercut the speaker. If "a slumber" sealed his spirit, then his state before Lucy's death seems blind, if not spiritually moribund: is he the one who is "dead"? One's spirit, according to Wesleyan signification (in the doctrine of the Spirit's witness), is properly sealed by the Spirit and hence by the opposite of an illusory slumber. The persona, perhaps, has been blind to the spiritual strength-and-motion of Lucy, whose name, of course, connotes spiritual illumination: part of his dirge-like cadence, at any rate, derives from his belated realization of the more than merely physical beauty of what he had but has no longer. The Wesleyan idiom of being "sealed by the Spirit" derives from the New Testament (see, for example, Lawton, *John Wesley's English*, p. 209). But especially when one considers the frequently Lockean motivation underlying Wesley's choice of scripture texts, his word *seal* resonates within the cluster of diction associated with Locke's central metaphor of the mind as wax tablet, and *impression*, as another example of such diction, was commonplace in Wesleyan parlance: religious experiences were generally spoken of as "impressions" (see Lawton, p. 16). Accordingly, the former insouciance of Wordsworth's speaker, regarding mortality both in particular and in general, is so devoid of experience of the spiritual kind or rather so apparently unreceptive to any such experience that he is doomed not to know Lucy as she is, until, through the cruel revelation of death, he is all too late informed about her.

Consider just two additional, but two similarly representative, examples of Wordsworth's non blank verse forms, namely, the sonnet "Surprised by Joy" and "Ode: Intimations of Immortality from Recollections of Early Childhood."

The great Ode's metaphor of preexistence, i.e., "trailing clouds of glory do we come / From God, who is our home" (lines 64–65), amounts to at least as much a Platonic as a theological emphasis, and Wordsworth himself, in a note dictated to Isabella Fenwick, specifically said that this underlying metaphor of the poem, in being Platonic and hence philosophical, "is far too shadowy a notion to be recommended to faith, *as more than an element in our instincts of immortality*" (my italics—RB), but as Wordsworth's remark indicates, the poem is concerned to use concepts of faith and concepts of philosophy mutually, for purposes of either philosophical or religious illumination, or of both at once, and I argue here that not so much a Platonic idealism, as a quasi-Wesleyan philosophical theology, is what best glosses his vocabulary and hence reveals best the unity of his seemingly disparate varieties of idiom. One finds, in other words, that the Ode in tone as well as content is at once generally Wesleyan and specifically Lockean.

Note, first, in passages familiar enough to need little comment, the Ode's Lockean assumption that identity is largely the function of experience. Beginning with the concluding lines of "My Heart Leaps Up," namely,

> The Child is Father of the Man;
> And I could wish my days to be
> Bound each to each by natural piety,

the Ode thus includes perhaps the aptest of all poetic summations of Lockean psychology; "The Child is Father of the Man" is a well-observed datum in Pickering's *John Locke and Children's Books in Eighteenth-Century England*. *Natural piety* is Lockean too, not so much perhaps by bespeaking demythologized, secular faith, as by connoting theistical natural religion. At any rate, even when Wordsworth makes poetry out of the least theological of his Lockean assumptions, his tone is more nostalgic for the ideal than despairingly secular:

> Earth fills her lap with pleasures of her own;
> Yearnings she hath in her own natural kind,
> And, even with something of a Mother's mind,
>   And no unworthy aim,
>   The homely Nurse doth all she can
> To make her Foster-child, her Inmate Man,
>   Forget the glories he hath known,
> And that imperial palace whence he came.
>
> (lines 77–84)

The Ode's all-but-exclusively-natural is balanced by its all-but-exclusively-spiritual. Even when speaking of nature, for example, Wordsworth employs language generally, if not specifically, Wesleyan: "glorious birth" (line 16), "glory" (line 18), "sing a joyous song" (line 19), and "radiance" (line 175). The "timely utterance" (line 23), moreover, over which many have labored—is the utterance the final lines of "My Heart Leaps Up"? or the words of the leech-gatherer in "Resolution and Independence"?[29]—is perhaps deliberately general to suggest the imageless realm of spiritual experience; my candidate for the referent accordingly is the "conversion"-experience in *Prelude* 4:

> . . . I made no vows, but vows
> Were then made for me; bond unknown to me
> Was given, that I should be, else sinning greatly,
> A dedicated Spirit.
>
> (lines 334–37)

This passage, referring to the summer of 1788 when the poet was eighteen, represents rebirth (see *W*"*NM*," pp. 95–100), and I suggest now
that the "vows" spoken for him, whether of spiritual rededication or dedication to poetry, or both, included the promise or certainly the hope of a
literary, if not religious, immortality that, whether religious or literary or
both, relieves his "grief" in the Ode (line 22) over the fleeting, mortality-
ridden nature of human experience. Be that as it may, his mention of the
"timely utterance" is followed promptly by his triumphant announcement that "The cataracts blow their trumpets from the steep" (line 25),
and although this image is natural, it appears to be a confirmation (by
nature-scripture?) of what the poet knows both from immediate revelation and from the sounding trumpet that in traditional revelation (1 Cor.
15:51) signals the change from death to life. The Ode's suggestion of unmediated spiritual experience is heightened still further if one reads literally, i.e., takes seriously the capitalization in, this comment from the Fenwick note: "Nothing was more difficult for me in childhood than to
admit the notion of death as a state applicable to my own being. . . . [I]t
was not so much from feelings of animal vivacity that *my* difficulty came
as from a sense of the indomitableness of the Spirit within me." *Spirit*
suggests both the poet's higher mind and the presence of God therein.

What brings the Ode's emphases on the spiritual and the natural together is its implied analogy between sense perception and immediate
revelation. Conversion, for example, is understood in natural terms,
e.g., "the sunshine" is a "glorious birth" (line 16), and although it is a
primarily somber and elegiac tone with which the Ode records that "the
Man" perceives the "celestial light" "die away, / And fade into the light of
common day" (lines 4, 75–76), the poet's ultimate conviction, namely
that "nature yet remembers / What was so fugitive" (lines 131–32), bespeaks his faith that somehow the celestial and natural kinds of light par-
ticipate in each other: the Ode's analogy between natural and spiritual is
thus "founded," in the words of Browne, "in the Very Nature of the
Things on both Sides of the Comparison." The "Child" (for whom
Hartley Coleridge is the original) is at once "best Philosopher" and
"Mighty Prophet! Seer blest!" in part because the historically immediate
spirit of philosophical theology made such a juxtaposition seem less vio-

lent at least to Wordsworth, if not necessarily to his readers in the twentieth century; the "Child," that is, despite being already "farther from the east" (line 71), appears still to enjoy the powers of a "spiritual sense" and a "perceptible inspiration":

> Thou, whose exterior semblance doth belie
> Thy Soul's immensity;
> Thou best Philosopher, who yet dost keep
> Thy heritage, thou Eye among the blind,
> That, deaf and silent, read'st the eternal deep,
> Haunted for ever by the eternal mind,—
> Mighty Prophet! Seer blest!
> On whom those truths do rest,
> Which we are toiling all our lives to find,
> In darkness lost, the darkness of the grave;
> Thou, over whom thy Immortality
> Broods like the Day, a Master o'er a Slave,
> A Presence which is not to be put by;
> Thou little Child, yet glorious in the might
> Of heaven-born freedom on thy being's height,
> Why with such earnest pains dost thou provoke
> The years to bring the inevitable yoke,
> Thus blindly with thy blessedness at strife?
> (lines 110–25)

Even the poet, for that matter, as far "from the east" as he is, yet affirms the "spiritual sense"'s efficacy:

> Our Souls have sight of that immortal sea
> Which brought us hither,
> Can in a moment travel thither, ...
> (lines 162–64)

The analogistic thinking underlying Wordsworth's conception of "our Souls"' "sight" is present as well in the Fenwick note, in which he uses an unmistakably Wesleyan idiom, and thus implies that the mythos of Christian experience had been at least as much in his mind, as he wrote the Ode, as the myth of preexistence: "[T]hough the idea [of preexistence] is not advanced in *revelation*, there is nothing there to contradict it, and *the fall of man* presents an *analogy* in its favor" (my italics—RB). Between Wordsworth and Wesley, here, is a particularly striking coincidence: a specific parallel between one's form of analogy and the other's. Remember first Wesley's explicit allusion in the letters to "Smith," to Augustine's two-part understanding of light: "I entered into my inward parts . . . and saw, with the eye of my soul . . . the unchangeable light of the Lord. . . . [T]he light was not of this common kind, which is obvious to all flesh." Just as Augustine is careful not to identify natural with spiritual light, so Wesley too undoubtedly thought that to do so would be to proceed too glibly and too metaphorically, but Wesley would also have seen a single "Nature" underlying "the Things on both Sides of the Comparison." Similarly, the Ode distinguishes between the "celestial light . . . of yore" (lines 4, 6) and the now dominant "light of common day" (line 76), but the Ode implies as well a single foundation of the two lights, for through a methodology that replaces the spiritual vision and quasi-philosophic certitude of childhood, the poet, in a spirit of perhaps his closest kinship with Wesley's philosophical theology, retains "the faith that looks through death, / In years that bring the philosophic mind" (lines 185–86). For him, therefore, "perpetual benediction" is still the legacy of "our past years" (lines 133–34).

Regarding Wordsworth's contribution to the sonnet form (of which he wrote more than 600 examples),[30] one thinks immediately in the present connection of his memorable lines on his daughter Catherine (who had died at the age of three):

> Surprised by joy—impatient as the Wind
> I turned to share the transport—Oh! with whom
> But thee, deep buried in the silent tomb,
> That spot which no vicissitude can find?
> Love, faithful love, recalled thee to my mind—
> But how could I forget thee? Through what power,
> Even for the least division of an hour,
> Have I been so beguiled as to be blind
> To my most grievous loss!—That thought's return
> Was the worst pang that sorrow ever bore,
> Save one, one only, when I stood forlorn,
> Knowing my heart's best treasure was no more;
> That neither present time, nor years unborn
> Could to my sight that heavenly face restore.

One of this poem's greatest strengths is its tough-minded refusal to take what would be, in such brief scope, an all too facile refuge in religious comfort. There is, to be sure, reflection of Wesley's experiential values, for just as Wesleyan Methodists enjoyed sudden influxes of Arminian transport so the poem's speaker writes, or appears to write, out of immediate spiritual experience: his "faithful love," distinct, say, from "love" alone, combines two of the spiritual graces to suggest that the loved one is spiritual being more than mere daughter of man. This pattern is undercut, however, or at least relegated to less than immediate importance, by the fact of loss so overwhelming that the speaker cannot, or will not, be consoled by any means, spiritual or other. Indeed, the content of this sonnet is so far from being unproblematically religious that it is, if not antireligious, then skeptical about religion to the point of irony. Any "power" is more diabolical than spiritual that would turn "the least division of an hour," not into a Wesleyan or even into a Blakean moment of infinity, but into a denial, rather, of Catherine's existence. Between this poem and Locke's thought is an especially apt parallel: a signal instance of Locke's emphasis on "the imperfections of the mind of man" is his argument that not even "grief and all our [other] nobler ideas" suffice to make man "able to think clearly and distinctly" on more than "one thing at once"; he adds that it is impossible for anyone to keep "one self-same single idea a long time alone in his mind";[31] and Wordsworth, for his part, translates such philosophical notions evidently into anger at himself, if not at God, for the minor endowment of mind that would allow him, however briefly, to forget that his daughter is dead.

In another mood, of course, the poet instructs men "how the mind of man becomes / A thousand times more beautiful than the earth / On which he dwells" (*Prelude* 14.448–50), but in "Surprised by Joy" Wordsworth's mood is like Wesley's in *his* more skeptical moments, i.e., quite another matter. Yes, the face is "heavenly." Yes, the father's "love" is "faithful." And yes, his "heart's best treasure" is laid up in the quasi-eternal heaven of his art. But the mind of this post-Lockean father is hardly able, even through the nobility of grief, to focus on the idea of Catherine long enough to create for that idea, much less for her, an eternity so much as quasi-Wesleyan. Wordsworth's assimilations of Wesleyan materials are usually less oblique, and more constructive, than in these lines, but this sonnet amounts to an experiment in which sudden, odelike turns are put to the service, not of beatific, breathtaking illuminations, but, in the press of grief's resurgence, of a desperate, almost unbearably futile searching for one who is gone.

The most characteristic of Wordsworth's forms, of course, is blank verse, and I note here the relevance of Wesley's philosophical theology to just three, but three important, blank verse passages: the lines portraying the Wanderer in Book 1 of *The Excursion*, the "Prospectus" to *The Recluse*, of which *The Excursion* forms the second, only completed part, and the lines from Book 5 of *The Prelude* in which the poet dreams of an apocalyptic flood.

There is much about the poet's dream, in *Prelude* 5.50–165, to suggest that it was of only natural origin, for the passage contains something of Wesley's uncertainty regarding which dreams "arise from natural, which from supernatural, influence" (recall "Human Life a Dream"), and one detects in these lines particular awareness of Locke's early modern, pro-topsychological explanation of dreams as "made up of the waking Man's Ideas, though, for the most part, oddly put together" (*Essay* 2.1.17; Nidditch, p. 113). The poet, lines 58–61, had been

> seated in a rocky cave
> By the sea-side, perusing, so it chanced,
> The famous history of the errant knight
> Recorded by Cervantes,

and these predream ideas explain, in Lockean terms, both how the Arab Bedouin could "become the knight / Whose tale Cervantes tells" (lines 122–23) and how the Bedouin could bear "underneath one arm / A stone, and in the opposite hand a shell" (lines 78–79).[32] The dream's ideas, moreover, are put together so oddly that they are almost more psychological than Lockean and almost more naturalistic than philosophical: the stone, for example, was somehow also the book of "Euclid's Elements" (line 88); the shell, moreover, was somehow also the book of prophetic poetry: "An Ode, in passion uttered, which foretold / Destruction to the children of the earth / By deluge, now at hand" (lines 96–98); the figure on the dromedary was not simply the Arab, and not simply Don Quixote, but "Of these was neither, and was both at once" (line 125); and none of these odd equivalencies, finally, fazes the dreamer: "[S]trange as it may seem, / I wondered not" (lines 110–11). Of such is the most modern, i.e., "scientific," understanding of dream-logic.

The dream, though, seems supernatural as well: for one thing, the dreamer had been musing "On poetry and geometric truth" as representatives of "lasting life" (lines 65–66); for another, when "sleep seized" him, his "senses yielded" (lines 69–70), presumably to an extrasensuous realm; the shell, moreover, prophesies apocalypse; the dreamer, significantly, has "a perfect faith" in all that passed (line 114); the dreamer "prayed" (line 116) to share the Bedouin's enterprise of seeking, by burying the books of geometry and poetry, to save them from destruction; and finally, the dreamer accords "reverence" to this unearthly "being," who is employed in the especially quasi-religious work of preserving "immortal verse, / Shakespeare, or Milton, labourers divine" (lines 150, 164–65). Wordsworth's ambivalence towards the dream—is it supernatural? natural? somehow both?—is itself an indication of the philosophically theological dimension, i.e., the richly both/and logic, of the passage. The more Whitefieldian than Wesleyan message ("Destruction to the children of the earth" [line 97]) arises indirectly from, or at least is understandable according to, sense experience, for the dream seems to function as spiritual sense and perceptible inspiration. The shell, for example, as "prophetic blast of harmony" (line 95), makes unmistakably clear its message from another world, and the shell speaks to this world according to a sense-based mode of appeal: "Of a surpassing brightness," "so beautiful in shape, / In colour so resplendent" (lines 80, 90–91), the shell attracts the eye of the soul, if not the natural eye, and its "articulate sounds" (line 94) strike the spiritual, if not natural, ear. This methodology, then, is both sensationalistic and rational: the poet "*heard* that instant in an unknown tongue, / Which yet I *understood*, articulate sounds" (lines 93–94. My italics—RB). His method here is more like that of Wesley's English doctrines, finally, than the sense-independent rationalism of Descartes: "Geometric truth," to be sure, is laid alongside "poetry" as the twin achievements of "Bard and Sage" (lines 42, 65), and as Geoffrey Durrant has shown, Wordsworth respected the mathematical, and largely Cartesian, model of intellect as transcendent,[33] but the geometric book

> that held acquaintance with the stars,
> And wedded soul to soul in purest bond
> Of reason, undisturbed by space or time,
>
> (lines 103–5)

receives rather less emphasis than the other, more "sensuous" (line 43) book, i.e., the book of poetry, which

> Had voices more than all the winds, with power
> To exhilarate the spirit, and to soothe,
> Through every clime, the heart of human kind.
>
> (lines 107–9)

Poetry, then, warming man's heart by filling his spiritual senses and aspiring to a properly enthusiastic glossolalia, i.e., "an unknown tongue, /

Which yet I understood," bespeaks generally evangelical sensibility as well as specifically Wesleyan methodology. Poetry, for Wordsworth, is an ever new dispensation to be perceived, spiritually, as inspiration.

The "Prospectus," published at the end of the Preface to *The Excursion,* can be thought of as the program for all of Wordsworth's poems.[34] As such, it seems at first to be exclusively philosophical in its fundamental concept of what poetry should do:

> [M]y voice [writes the poet] proclaims
> How exquisitely the individual Mind
> (And the progressive powers perhaps no less
> Of the whole species) to the external World
> Is fitted:—and how exquisitely, too—
> Theme this but little heard of among men—
> The external World is fitted to the Mind;
> And the creation (by no lower name
> Can it be called) which they with blended might
> Accomplish:—this is our high argument.
>
> (lines 62–71)

Subject/object interaction proved fertile to the literary mind during the Romantic period even more than in the eighteenth century. And yet in that word *proclaims* lies something of an evangelical purpose.

Indeed, not excluding the searching syntax and language of sense perception, there is nothing either non- or anti-Wesleyan in this most inclusive of Wordsworth's blank verse utterances. There is, for example, an anti-Cartesian and stubbornly English, i.e., a Wesleyan as well as Lockean, wakefulness in his insistence that nothing "scooped up / By help of dreams"

> can breed such fear and awe
> As fall upon us often when we look
> Into our Minds, into the Mind of Man—
> My haunt, and the main region of my song.
>
> (lines 37–41)

There is, moreover, in addition to such religious diction as the just-quoted *haunt, awe,* and *fear,* an at least partly religious goal in his declaration that sense perception is the method of regaining Paradise:

> Paradise, and groves
> Elysian, Fortunate Fields—like those of old

Sought in the Atlantic Main—why should they be
A history only of departed things,
Or a mere fiction of what never was?
For the discerning intellect of Man,
When wedded to this goodly universe
In love and holy passion, shall find these
A simple produce of the common day.

(lines 47–55)

There is a kerygmatic center as well as an implied distinction between the natural and spiritual modes of "sense" perception in his determination to "arouse the sensual from their sleep / Of Death, and win the vacant and the vain / To noble raptures" (lines 60–62). Finally, and most importantly from the present perspective, between his "Prospectus" and Wesley's "Great Privilege" is a striking and philosophically theological parallel: when, writes Wesley, "the Spirit or breath of God is immediately inspired, breathed into the new-born Soul," and when, he continues, "the same breath which comes from, returns to, God"—when, he concludes, "spiritual respiration" is reciprocal—"the senses of the soul" are fully "awake" and fully "capable of discerning spiritual good and evil"; similarly, not only is Wordsworth "intent to weigh / The good and evil of our mortal state" (lines 8–9), but he also hopes to awaken the sensual, and these are the corollaries of his determination to "breathe in worlds / To which the heaven of heavens is but a veil" (lines 29–30). The "Prospectus," then, like "The Great Privilege," suggests that through immediate revelation God and man are ensphered, or rather that just as man's wakeful involvement with sense data puts him almost at one with what he needs to know about the natural world, so his spiritual "sense perception" puts him almost at one with what he needs to know of a world elsewhere: in its philosophically theological dimension, in other words, the "Prospectus" affirms a bold principle that confidence in immediate revelation is groundable.

Wordsworth's methodological continuum from natural to revealed religion is so fully Wesleyan in his portrait of the Wanderer that here I conclude this section. Just as Wesley's embrace of revelation and his view of nature, i.e., "divine in origin and continuance," were both strangely facilitated by his philosophical empiricism, so the methodology of *Excursion* I maintains an all but sense grounded coexistence, complementarity, between nature religion on the one hand and scriptural theology on the other, for underlying the Wanderer's religion, revealed as well as natural, is an implicitly Lockean method or at least a poetic language of object and subject:

> A Herdsman on the lonely mountain-tops,
> Such intercourse was his, and in this sort
> Was his existence oftentimes *possessed.*
> O then how beautiful, how bright, appeared
> The written promise! Early had he learned
> To reverence the volume that displays
> The mystery, the life which cannot die;
> But in the mountains did he *feel* his faith.
> All things, responsive to the writing, there
> Breathed immortality, revolving life,
> And greatness still revolving; infinite:
> There littleness was not; the least of things
> Seemed infinite; and there his spirit shaped
> Her prospects, nor did he believe,—he *saw.*
>
> (1.219–32)

Sufficiently Lockean, here, is the sense perception, i.e., the sight-and-consciousness, with which the Wanderer reads nature scripture, and his natural religion, being consistent with the Bible, is theistical and therefore deeply felt without being improperly enthusiastic. His experience of immediate revelation, moreover, though not explicitly linked to the analogy of sense perception, is not far therefrom: his "mind" is "filled with inward light," and with "graces," and his "graces" are "unrevealed and unproclaimed" not so much because they are somehow either unkerygmatically expressed or nondivine in origin, but simply because they pertain to one "of whom the busy world hears least" (lines 93–95). Wordsworth, for his part, proclaims the genuine, sufficiently evangelical quality of the Wanderer's spiritual experience, for this experience, attendant as it is upon the Wanderer's conjoint loves of the Bible and the book of nature, completes the picture of him as Romantic personification of Wesley's philosophical theology.

In a brief, summary consideration of Wordsworth's prose I stress that the same poet who claims in the Preface to *Lyrical Ballads* (2d ed., 1800) to be only "a man speaking to [other unsophisticated] men" reconciles such sympathy for popular culture with a richly strange combination of transcendental and empirical modes of thought. In other words, Wesley's Lockean conviction that the word corresponds to the thing, albeit through the idea, and that language therefore should be "plain," "simple," and as little as possible metaphorically arbitrary, is more than vaguely predictive of the argument in the Preface that, in "humble and rustic life," "the passions of men are incorporated with the beautiful and permanent forms of nature," and that these "passions," therefore, "speak a plainer and more emphatic language; because in that condition of life our elementary feelings co-exist in a state of greater simplicity." Wordsworth's frequent allusions to scripture are not the least of the overtly metaphorical aspects of his language,[35] but he claims, in the Preface, that "I have at all times endeavoured to look steadily at my subject; consequently, there is I hope in these Poems little falsehood of description," and he adds that "this practice has necessarily cut me off from a large portion of . . . figures of speech. . . ." Like Wesley, then, Wordsworth felt that metaphor too often undermines the capacity of language for communicating and representing truths of whatever kind, whether natural or spiritual, for in both the Preface and the poetry is an implication that through analogy the things of this world correspond to spiritual things: Wordsworth says in the Preface and indicates by the poetry that "the Poet will lend his divine spirit to aid the transfiguration" of science, from "the remotest discoveries of the Chemist, the Botanist, or Mineralogist," to a quasi-spiritual "Being" "familiarised to men," and made "a dear and genuine inmate" of their households. Just as Wesley's language-for-many-people contains a Lockean dimension, so the methodological dimension of Wordsworth's language is more than compatible with his evangelistic desire to be understood. Wesley is the one figure who comes near being the model for Wordsworth's ability to convey to an increasingly widespread audience a complex message creative in its tension between "the language of the sense" (cf. line 108 of "Tintern Abbey") and otherworldly glimpses of "the light that never was, on sea or land" (cf. line 15 of "Elegiac Stanzas: Suggested by a Picture of Peele Castle").

Coleridge

Coleridge, besides being poet, was both philosopher and theologian. Hence the centrality of his position here. Starting from what has been said of his thought and adding what has been said of his poetry in its intellectual contexts I pursue a two-part question: how did he synthesize the faith and philosophy of his time and place? and did such a synthesis form the conceptual framework of his poetry? It is conceivable, in other words, that a means of considering his poetry and thought both separately and together is Wesley's philosophical theology, and, insofar as an essay permits, I accordingly argue that Wesley's philosophical theology is a means indeed of seeing steadily and whole this more multifaceted than merely motley genius of English Romanticism. Coleridge, more than Wesley perhaps, and perhaps even more than Browne, was exponent of philosophical theology, and the philosophical theology of Coleridge, like Wesley's in both import and detail, is of a piece with the poetry.

Coleridge's philosophy is generally placed not only in English but also in German contexts, and such intellectual binationality, of course, should not only be acknowledged but explained as well. Gian Orsini, in regard to German contexts, expands upon René Wellek's chapter on Coleridge and Kant and counts Kant the major influence:[36] after 1799, Orsini shows, Coleridge not only used vocabulary, phrasing, and general arguments from *Critique of Pure Reason* but also accepted major tenets thereof, such as, most notably, the transcendental aesthetic, the doctrine of categories, the transcendental unity of apperception, and the transcendental dialectic. The Germans are so obvious in Coleridge's prose indeed that the issue of plagiarism arises: Norman Fruman has disturbed Coleridgeans with his numerous accusations.[37] As to English contexts of Coleridge's thought, Wellek, for his part, has recently declared not only that "the question of Coleridge's relation to German thought seems far from being answered in a comprehensive and systematic manner," but also, and wisely, that "the whole English ancestry of Coleridge's ideas needs closer examination."[38] L. J. Swingle, for one, has envisioned Coleridge's importance to Romantic empiricism:[39] arguing, for example, that "the Lockean philosophical tradition, with its practical investigation of the notion of 'idea,'" cut English Romantics off from the Cartesian expectation of "clear and distinct ideas," Swingle cites "Frost at Midnight," by Coleridge, as a prime example of the English Romantic tendency to ask not "how the mind *should* operate" but "how the mind *does* operate" in the presence of particular objects. Finally, Arthur O. Wlecke comes close to saying that the criticism of Coleridge worked with, as well as against, the scientific temper of Locke; Wlecke suggests, in particular, that Coleridge's phenomenological apperceptions of "translucence," in his "description of a symbol as characterized 'above all by the translucence of the eternal through and in the temporal,'"

> partially grew out of the habit of British empirical psychology after Locke of discussing thinking as a kind of seeing, and therefore of discussing ideas as if they were somehow objects of sight. . . . [W]hen Coleridge uses the term "translucence" in his explanation of the symbol, it would seem as if he has not quite escaped the

Lockean habit. . . . [W]e might say that his metaphor of "translucence" is an attempt to mediate between the Lockean way of discussing ideas as if they were objects of sight and his own belief that certain ideas cannot be so explained, that certain ideas ought not to be submitted to the "despotism of the eye." . . . According to Coleridge . . . the symbol-making power of the mind implicitly refutes a basic methodological assumption of Lockean epistemology; but his use of the term "translucence" almost conceals this refutation.[40]

Coleridge's preoccupation with Kant necessarily bespeaks an attempt to synthesize neotranscendentalism and empiricism. The philosophy of Coleridge, in other words, remains largely English.

Studies of his theology, to date, tend to begin and end far from his English past: Charles Sanders, James Boulger, and J. Robert Barth, for three, explore Coleridge's affinities with Victorian and European theologians from Schleiermacher through Kierkegaard, Newman, Sterling, and Maurice to Teilhard de Chardin of the twentieth century.[41] But evangelicalism, like empiricism, is native to Coleridge: what Sanders, for example, calls the "vigorously practical" orientation of Coleridge's ethics, what Boulger, moreover, calls the "existential" bias of Coleridge's antirationalist polemics, and, finally, what Barth recognizes as the Christological, Pauline core of Coleridge's thought, all find immediate analogues in such key elements of evangelical sensibility as, respectively, practical charity, testimonial faith, and the call to an imitation of Christ.

F. C. Gill, relating Coleridge to the Methodist revival, establishes his high estimate of much Wesleyana: this estimate is found among the poems and letters and such prose works as *Table Talk, Aids to Reflection, Lay Sermons,* and *Biographia Literaria.* Gill, for example, not only indicates Coleridge's espousal of universal love, perfection, the new birth, "the old-fashioned 'plan of salvation,'" original sin, immediate revelation, and justification by faith, but also documents his admiration of the Methodists themselves: for their singing, for their being, in his words, "in the main directly opposed to an anti-Christian rationalism," and for their being, generally, and again in his words, "a new influx of living waters," and "an agency permitted by God in the restoration of our Church."[42] For Wesley, and specifically for his argument that faith is the gift of God, Coleridge has only the highest praise:

> I venture to avow it as my conviction, that . . . the Christian faith is what Wesley . . . describes. . . . It is either the identity of the reason and the will (the proper spiritual part of man), in the full

energy of each, consequent on a divine rekindling, or it is not at all. Faith is as real as life; as actual as force; as effectual as volition. It is the physics of the moral being. (*Table Talk*, as quoted in *The Romantic Movement and Methodism*, p. 169)

Coleridge's evangelical sensibility, as I have elsewhere contended, can be understood as a tense but fruitful "blend of self-mastery and consciousness of redemption" (see *W*"*NM*," pp. 38–39): in five letters, written (to Thomas Poole) from February 6, 1797, to February 19, 1798, he expresses his admiration for the sincerity and power of Methodist spiritual autobiography and outlines his plan to write his own autobiography according to the Methodists' model of heady self-consciousness tempered by the claim of disciplined humility. His desire to write his life, like his desire to master himself, and like his discipline, through which he accomplished much, can be understood according to the revival's Puritan strain of self-conquest through self-examination and introspective moralizing. An equally Wesleyan strain of the revival is found, implicitly, in the letter in which he expresses his desire to emulate the "Perfection" of his brother George's "moral character": this desire derives, I think, not so much from the perfectibilitarian secularity of the French Revolution's halcyon days as from the doctrine of Christian perfection so dear to Wesley and so widely understood throughout the Anglo-American world, for this doctrine, complementing the optimistic Arminian belief in possible redemption for all, justifies the spiritual exaltation that, stopping short of fanaticism, and even of egotistical sublimity, characterizes Coleridge at his best. His distinctly evangelical traits, at any rate, form what Hazlitt has in mind in "My First Acquaintance with Poets" (1823), in which he remembers young man Coleridge's preaching as a "revival of the primitive spirit of Christianity, which was not to be resisted." Hazlitt, for one who was in a position to know, understood Coleridge's religious sensibility as commandingly neo-Apostolic, if not as deliberately Wesleyan: Coleridge's youthful Unitarianism was evidently near enough to the Evangelical Movement's zealous Dissenting branch, of which Wesley's influence formed the trunk.

What has not been noted heretofore is that the English ancestry of Coleridge's thought, as of Wordsworth's and Blake's on the one hand, and, as I shall show, as of Shelley's and Keats's on the other, includes a branch both evangelical and empirical, with the interesting difference that Coleridge, as philosophical theologian, presented his "religious sense" even more systematically, and certainly more discursively than did they theirs. His definition of faith as "the physics of the moral being"

(i.e., something "real as life," "actual as force," and "effectual as volition"), together with his concept that faith should be not antirational certainly but "directly opposed to an anti-Christian rationalism," grow directly out of his praise for Wesley and all things Wesleyan, and it is
tempting, on the basis of partial exploration here, to think that such a
philosophical view of faith is more than merely consistent with the philosophy of religion whereby Wesley aligns faith with the rational experi-
entialism of John Locke. Coleridge's conclusion, in *Aids to Reflection*, that
"the Christian faith is the perfection of human *intelligence*" (my italics—
RB), together with his insistence in *Lay Sermons* that "the words of the
Apostle are literally and *philosophically* true: We (that is, the human race)
live by faith" (my italics—RB), are so far from divagating from his more
than merely "natural" "Methodism" that together they indicate the intellectual center thereof. Gill, on the basis of these statements from Coleridge's prose, concludes that his "aim, broadly speaking, was that of
Wesley in a more philosophic sense" (*The Romantic Movement and Methodism*, p. 176), but I am more than merely suggesting that Coleridge's aim
was Wesleyan even, nay, especially, in being philosophic, for it is surely
on the basis of a strangely philosophic-and-theological admiration for the
revival that his inscription on the flyleaf of the annotated *Life of Wesley*,
for example, is to be understood:

> It will not be uninteresting to [you] to know [writes Coleridge
> to Southey], that the one or the other volume [of Southey's *Life*]
> was the book more often in my hands than any other in my ragged
> book-regiment, and that to this work . . . I was used to resort
> whenever sickness and languor made me feel the want of an old
> friend, of whose company I could never be tired. How many and
> many an hour do I owe to this *Life of Wesley*; and how often have I
> argued with it, questioned, remonstrated, been peevish, and asked
> pardon—then again listened, and cried Right! Excellent!—and in
> yet heavier hours intreated it, as it were, to continue talking to
> me—for that I heard and listened, and was soothed, though I could
> make no reply.[43]

Only the broadest attraction, intellectual as well as emotional, could have
drawn such encomium from even the effusive pen of Coleridge.

I am not only convinced, then, of Coleridge's more or less conscious
concern to interfuse faith and philosophy, for this is common knowledge, but I am also persuaded that his philosophical faith is substantially
Wesleyan, for it is clear, significantly, that his attempted synthesis of

evangelicalism and empiricism contributes much more than has been noticed to the dialectical tension not only of his prose but also of his poetry.
Thomas McFarland's studies take the philosophy, theology, and poetry
together, and in their various contexts, and Reeve Parker's study of *Coleridge's Meditative Art*, as a way of understanding the poetry, affirms the
worth of Coleridge's religio-scientific thought.[44] Parker, however, is
more interested in seventeenth- than in eighteenth-century contexts, and
McFarland, though seeing the possibility that Coleridge was never able
to subscribe wholeheartedly to the philosophy of pantheism in part because of his off-and-on attraction to the "heat" and "stove" of Methodism, does not undertake to relate that basic sympathy for Methodism to
the poetry and philosophy or even to the rest of his religious knowledge.
He thought well enough of both the revival and its leader's intellectual
stature to devote considerable effort to marginalia for Southey's *Life*. It is
time, now, to determine just how far Coleridge understood the fundamental point common to evangelicalism and empiricism alike: experience provides criteria for deciding what is true. In his observation about
"the great book of [God's] servant Nature," for example—

> That in its obvious sense and literal interpretation it declares the
> being and attributes of the Almighty Father, none but the fool in
> heart has ever dared gainsay: But . . . it is the poetry of human na-
> ture to read it likewise in a figurative sense, and to find therein cor-
> respondences and symbols of the spiritual world[45]

—one finds shades of the analogical, i.e., more symbolical than metaphoric, mode whereby Wesley and Browne, for two, see nature as participant in divinity; and one suspects, accordingly, that Coleridge employs in his poetry too the spiritual as well as natural methodology
espoused by evangelicals and useful to an age skeptical but desirous of
knowing the divine once more. It is feasible here to indicate that in the
poetry indeed is the fullest version in Coleridge, and perhaps in any other
Romantic, of an evangelical faith in tandem with the philosophy of
empiricism.

To say nothing for the moment of their philosophic dimension, the
poems relate to evangelical faith. Elinor Shaffer has illustrated the value
of German higher criticism, and hence of a religious context, for interpreting them, but her focus rests upon a few, as related to Eichhorn and
Michaelis,[46] and it is time to see that Coleridge's knowledge of a timely,
quintessentially English faith helps to illuminate many. John Coulson and
Barth in his more recent book have established the connection between

Coleridge's faith and his poetics, theory and practice,[47] but Coulson, arguing that Coleridge intends his nonrational language of faith to express the presence of God, is not concerned to notice the historical relevance of what evangelicals, not unreasonably, felt to be God's ongoing work in the world, and Barth, though interested in eighteenth-century contexts, gives passing reference to the revival and does not mention the fact that key Coleridgean emphases, "the role of the human will in religious experience" and "a free commitment of the self in faith" (*The Symbolic Imagination*, p. 136), were watchwords of Arminian evangelicals, both Anglican and Nonconformist. Barth points out (p. 136) that these emphases enabled Coleridge to achieve "a new release of feeling" and hence a "change in poetic sensibility"; his art, then, proceeds from something of a conversion psychology, to wit,

> For never guiltless may I speak of him,
> The Incomprehensible! save when with awe
> I praise him, and with Faith that inly *feels*;
> Who with his saving mercies healèd me,
> A sinful and most miserable man. . . .
>   ("The Aeolian Harp," lines 58–62)

The revival's terms and concepts are generally reflected in the poetry, for many passages are pervaded by the love and joy in then current spiritual autobiography. (For "the fruits of the Spirit" as a major pattern of Methodist lore, see *W*"*NM*," pp. 70, 72–73, 126, 134–38, and passim.) "The Aeolian Harp"'s "faith that inly *feels*," and "saving mercies"; the "Soul" that "seeks to hear," the "Heart" that "listens," and the concluding prayer, to wit, "Let thy Kingdom come!," of "Reflections on having Left a Place of Retirement"; the conviction, in "Frost at Midnight," that God will "mould" the "spirit" of Hartley Coleridge "and by giving make it ask"; the hope, of "Fears in Solitude," that "the sweet words / Of Christian promise . . . / Might stem destruction" in an England threatened by moral corruption, as well as by the threat of Napoleonic invasion; and the veneration, in "Lines written in the Album at Elbingerode, in the Hartz Forest," for "That man's sublimer spirit, who can feel / That God is everywhere!"—all these evangelical patterns are especially implicit, and often explicit, in "This Lime-Tree Bower My Prison," wherein the evangelical revival's spiritual vocabulary modulates Coleridge's transition from a description of nature (or rather from a theistical natural religion) to a personal testimony (to his friend Charles Lamb) of immediate revelation from the Spirit of God:

> Ah! slowly sink
> Behind the western ridge, thou glorious Sun!
> Shine in the slant beams of the sinking orb,
> Ye purple heath-flowers! richlier burn, ye clouds!
> Live in the yellow light, ye distant grove!
> And kindle, thou blue Ocean! So my friend
> Struck with deep joy may stand, as I have stood,
> Silent with swimming sense; yea, gazing round
> On the wide landscape, gaze till all doth seem
> Less gross than bodily; and of such hues
> As veil the Almighty Spirit, when yet he makes
> Spirits perceive his presence.
>   A delight
> Comes sudden on my heart, and I am glad
> As I myself were there!
>   (lines 32–45)

This idiom of the graces, I think, is the most central indication of how much the Wesleyan language of experience helped Coleridge in his effort at once to celebrate his visionary moments and to distinguish them from solipsism.

Finally, "Christabel"'s theme of depravity, together with both the peculiarly Protestant independence of the Mariner's soul-struggle and the diction of beatitude in "Kubla Khan," are examples of the often noted but not yet fully described preoccupations of a poet whose generally religious and particularly evangelical background helped him to find the means of coping with and sometimes transcending his moods of metaphysical despair and epistemological timidity.[48] His philosophic caution, indeed, may be part of what led to the particularly evangelical and generally religious preoccupations of his poetry. "Poetic faith," after all, is in his terms a "willing suspension of disbelief," and thus subsumes a skeptical method more than merely reminiscent of empirical philosophy's.

Coleridge's "poetic faith," in other words, is not just religious but even skeptical in just as Wesleyan as, say, Lockean a sense. In "The Aeolian Harp," for instance, is found not just the deeply felt testimony of "saving mercies" but even one of Romanticism's most explicit examples of subject/object interpenetration:

> O! the one Life within us and abroad,
> Which meets all motion and becomes its soul,
> A light in sound, a sound-like power in light, . . .
>   (lines 26–28)

The poem, then, instead of being flawed by its division between the supernatural language of grace and the language of natural perception, achieves an experientialist dialectic between the two. The "one Life," though exclusively on a horizontal plane and though religious only in being quite pantheistical, is embodied in a "light" and "motion" connotatively spiritual as well as denotatively Newtonian. One thinks, in this connection, of the "presence" in "Tintern Abbey," i.e., "a motion and a spirit" whose "dwelling is the light of setting suns": the spiritual dimension of such language, in Coleridge as in Wordsworth, is more than merely pantheistic, for not merely does it precede but it also anticipates, provides the occasion for and even attends evangelical insights. One thinks, regarding Coleridge, of Colin Clarke's already quoted but eminently repeatable line of reasoning regarding the strangely religious-and-empirical aspect of "Tintern Abbey":

> The "mystical" moments in "Tintern Abbey" are validated by, and find their primary analogue in, quite ordinary sensory experiences in which the visible scene and the observer's mind at once confront each other (preserving their distinctions) and interpenetrate deeply. . . . The flashes of insight into an invisible or more ultimate world seem an inevitable consequence of the way substance and spirit are ambiguously and mysteriously implicated in the simplest act of perception.

For another, and the final, example, one finds in "Reflections on Having Left a Place of Retirement" that Coleridge highlights in the penultimate verse paragraph an at once evangelical and empirical, and hence a thoroughly Wesleyan, phraseology announcing the holistic purpose of his life:

> I therefore go, and join head, heart, and hand,
> Active and firm, to fight the bloodless fight
> Of Science, Freedom, and the Truth in Christ.
> (lines 60–62)

No more than Wesley does it faze Coleridge to blend the language of religious fundamentalism, e.g., Arminian as well as political *Freedom*, with the most basic, most hard-core diction of empirical methodology.

Shelley

No one, to my knowledge, has found occasion to apply Wesleyan terms to the work of Shelley, but in *Shelley's Myth of Metaphor* John

Wright has demonstrated the proximity of Shelleyan poetics to Lockean language theory, and Earl Wasserman in *The Subtler Language* has come close to characterizing the poetry as empirical-transcendental dialectic.[49] Accordingly, what I do is twofold: I supplement with Wesleyan-Lockean perspective Wasserman's insights into both the Lockean and the ideal philosophical aspects of "Adonais" and "Mont Blanc," and to the Lockean context in which Wright understands "A Defence of Poetry," I add that context's Wesleyan part. In Shelley's theory, and in a sample of his practice, transcendental/empirical tension responds to Wesleyan-Lockean analysis.

Shelley's Myth of Metaphor is concerned, primarily, with how the "Defence" resists *Essay* 3, and before adding the present perspective to Wright's study as an illustration of its seminality, it may be helpful to epitomize his argument. Its cogency demands encapsulation here.

Wright understands, first of all, that Locke's antimetaphorical bias was so near the heart of "the then generally received opinion about language and knowledge" (p. 11) that it constitutes what Shelley had to take into account. Wright aptly paraphrases Locke's view of metaphor thus: "[Metaphor is] a beguiling species of equivocation, delightful and useful rhetorically for purposes of persuasion and illustration but in the last analysis an enemy to instruction and sound judgment" (p. 13). Wright's paraphrase continues:

> The real foundation of all (secular) instruction . . . is that complex of Reason and Nature which can be called the world system. The basic unit of instruction in the universe of discourse which has the world system as its object is the univocal statement or proposition which can be cashed in, like a bank note, for phenomena. Such a transaction constitutes a claim to knowledge.

This point of view, as Wright points out, is clearly reflected even in such a moderate Lockean as Isaac Watts, whose *Logic* (1736) declares: "[W]here the Design of the speaker or writer is merely to *explain*, to *instruct*, and to lead into the knowledge of the naked truth, he ought, for the most part to use plain and proper words, if the Language affords them, and not to deal much in Figurative speech" (as quoted in Wright, p. 14).

Wright emphasizes, however, that Shelley abominated this view of language, for the "Defence" insists, as Wright paraphrases, that "metaphor is a direct instrument and form of human knowledge—it is the mode of apprehension and expression by which imagination creates experience" (*Shelley's Myth of Metaphor*, p. 11). Specifically, Wright argues (p. 13 and passim) that "Shelley sought to depose the universe of discourse in favor of a universe of poetry: an imaginative cosmos at once more adequately centered in immediate experience and more open to creative myth at the circumference of human knowledge." Wright is especially convincing, I think, in making the contrast between some early lines of the "Defence" and an important passage from the *Essay*. Here is the *Essay*:

> Judgment . . . lies . . . in separating carefully one from another ideas wherein can be found the least difference, thereby to avoid being misled by similitude, and by affinity to take one thing for another. This is a way of proceeding quite contrary to metaphor and allusion, wherein for the most part lies that entertainment and pleasantry of wit which strikes so lively on the fancy, and therefore is so acceptable to all the people; because its beauty appears at first sight, and there is required no labor of thought to examine what reason or truth there is in it. (*Essay* 2.11.2, as quoted in Wright, p. 14)

And here is the "Defence":

> Reason is the enumeration of quantities already known; imagination is the perception and value of those quantities, both separately and as a whole. Reason respects the differences, and imagination the similitudes of things.

Shelley, then, connects rather than separates, or, as Wright observes,

> Shelley turns one of the central principles of the Baconian-Lockean theory of knowledge against the theory of mind it started from: reason or judgment becomes the instrument only, not the agent of knowledge; imagination produces all the materials and constitutes the bloom of human knowledge. . . . [F]or Shelley—the metaphysical fiction of correspondence between mind and Nature is overthrown by the genius of experience itself. . . . [M]etaphor is a direct agent of human knowledge which plucks out and perpetuates the apprehensions of things or relations of things otherwise invisible to or overlooked by the human mind at any point in its individual or cultural history. (*Shelley's Myth of Metaphor*, pp. 18–20)

Shelley's assimilation of and departure from Lockean attitudes are important beyond their implications for reading his poetry, for his "myth of metaphor," as Wright makes clear, anticipates a theory among now active philosophers of science, namely that "metaphors or models are necessary and not merely heuristic elements of theoretical discovery and explanation of certain kinds." [50]

Wesleyan–Lockean analysis, despite or perhaps because of the "Defence"'s conformity to what Wright says of it, is the next tool for understanding Shelleyan theory historically. "[Poetic] language," declares the "Defence," "is vitally metaphorical; that is, it marks the before unapprehended relations of things and perpetuates their apprehension, until the words which represent them become, through time, signs for portions or classes of thought instead of pictures of integral thoughts," but one should note, here, that Shelley is not opposing the *Lockean* concept of metaphor to the Lockean concepts of reason and judgment, for the *vitally* metaphorical language of which he speaks is a far cry from the "mists and uncertainties" of the "specious *Tropes* and *Figures*" of which the empiricists warned. [51] Indeed, his way of elaborating his meaning tends in its very form to be more analogical than metaphorical: "Reason is to imagination as the instrument to the agent, as the body to the spirit, as the shadow to the substance." Insofar as his kind of metaphor implies a correspondence between spiritual things and the things of this world, his concept is nearly analogical, and thus less anti-Lockean than quasi-Wesleyan. Moreover, his definitions of poetry as "something divine" and as "at once the center and circumference of knowledge; it is that which comprehends all science, and that to which all science is referred," are empirically methodological as well as decidedly religious. Consider, finally, the following passage which not only juxtaposes the age's poetry with the empirical mainstream of its philosophy but also uses, in so doing, evangelical idiom and thus implies that poetry of the early modern era in England is both effective and substantial in part because it is based on and tacitly assumes the analogy between sense perception and methodistical faith:

> For the literature of England, an energetic development of which has ever preceded or accompanied a great and free development of the national will, has arisen as it were from a *new birth*. In spite of the low-thoughted envy which would undervalue contemporary merit, our own will be a memorable age in intellectual achievements, and we live among such philosophers and poets as surpass beyond comparison any who have appeared since the last national struggle for civil and *religious liberty*. The most unfailing herald, companion, and follower of the *awakening* of a great people *to work a beneficial*

change in opinion or institution, is poetry. ("Defence." My italics—RB)

This quasi-Wesleyan language of faith, if not (to alter Wright's phrase) this quasi-Wesleyan "myth of analogy," is characteristic of the "Defence." Not only does Shelley understand his age's poetry as quasi-evangelical in both efficacy and origin, but he also justifies, in biblical allusions of evangelical flavor, the poets themselves (Cowper? Coleridge? Byron?), who though not always "personally . . . the happiest, the best, the wisest, and the most illustrious of men" were men saved, finally, in a more than reminiscential evangelical way: "Their errors have been weighed and found to have been dust in the balance; if their sins were as scarlet, they are now white as snow: they have been washed in the blood of the mediator and redeemer, Time" (cf. Rev. 7:14, 1 John 1:7, and Isa. 1:18). Shelley's admiration for much of what the revival stood for, as well as his enthusiasm for a poetry therein, seem to underlie, may well have motivated, and are, in any case, sufficiently evident in his observation that the "abolition of domestic slavery, and the emancipation of women from a great part of the degrading restraints of antiquity, were among the consequences of [the poetry of the Christian and chivalric systems]." With Wright's argument, then, one agrees as far as it goes. Yes, the "philosophic alternative" to Locke's essentially antipoetical mood lay, for Shelley, "in agnostic scientific operationalism, and in a psychological and cultural phenomenalism which respects mind as maker and for what it makes" (*Shelley's Myth of Metaphor*, p. 23), but, despite Shelley's agnosticism, or perhaps because of it, what even Wright recognizes as Shelley's "synthesis of idealism and empiricism" (*Shelley's Myth of Metaphor*, p. 11) includes transcendental as well as phenomenal forms of the ideal. Against Earl Wasserman, who "ascribes a species of transcendentalism to Shelley's poetry," Wright argues (p. 9) that "we need to read his works . . . without sacrificing the indeterminacy which animated them and, as he thought, haunted him like Actaeon's hounds," but the indeterminacy of then current skeptical method is by no means inconsistent with the transcendentalism of Wesley's philosophical theology, and, as Wright himself acknowledges, rather against his argument, "A Defence of Poetry" (if not the poems from which it arose) is "an inspired synthesis of conformable elements of empiricism and platonism" (*Shelley's Myth of Metaphor*, p. 1).

Thus Wright begins, oddly enough, where Wasserman and many other students of Shelley end, namely with the view that Shelley's transcendentalism coexists, somehow, with his skeptically empirical method.[52] With regard now to Wasserman's view and by way of arguing not coexistence so much as symbiosis, I extricate from Wright's demurrer *The Subtler Language* in particular, for *The Subtler Language*'s interpretation of the poetry as interlocution both methodologically empirical and transcendental is both prelusive and initiatory to my view, immediately historical, that Shelley's empiricism is as Wesleyan as Lockean.

Wasserman recognizes, first of all, that Shelley's empiricist understanding was both thorough and his own. Properly aware, of course, of the sense in which "the parts of a poem" are "not available for philosophic analysis," Wasserman is careful to observe that the "philosophic systems a poem evokes cannot constitute the statement the poem makes, but can only establish the relational system by which the poem conducts its integrative act," but he argues persuasively that at the center of Shelley's art is Shelley's transformation of empirical method into "Intellectual Philosophy," according to which

> the known data of the mind and their unknowable outer causes dissolve into a higher unity which can be defined discursively only by the double assertion that reality is that which is the source of our impressions and at the same time is those impressions aroused by an outer something. Neither definition is sufficient, for each independently is false; reality must be defined from both positions simultaneously. . . . Subject and object have no real existence apart from their interdependence. . . . Subject and object live in each other. (*The Subtler Language*, pp. 198, 202–3)

Thus Wasserman paraphrases, in particular, Shelley's subject/object methodology.

This methodology provides "the relational system" by which "Mont Blanc" "conducts its integrative act," or so Wasserman argues. *The Subtler Language*, with regard to the opening clause ("The everlasting universe of things / Flows through the mind"), reveals that four especially subject/object-oriented passages from Shelley's essay "On Life" form a telling context. Here are the passages:

> Each [life or being] is at once the centre and the circumference, the point to which all things are referred, and the line in which all things are contained.

> Life and the world, or whatever we call that which we are and feel, is an astonishing thing.

[As children, what a] distinct and intense apprehension had we of the world and of ourselves! . . . We less habitually distinguished all that we saw and felt, from ourselves. They seemed, as it were, to constitute one mass. . . . Those who are subject to the state called reverie feel as if their nature were dissolved into the surrounding universe, or as if the surrounding universe were absorbed into their being. They are conscious of no distinction. And these are states which precede, or accompany, or follow an unusually intense and vivid apprehension of life.

The difference is merely nominal between those two classes of thought which are vulgarly distinguished by the names of ideas or of external objects. (as quoted in *The Subtler Language*, pp. 203–4)

These passages, Wasserman contends, represent Shelley's repeated struggle both in "On Life" and throughout the prose "to capture in the unyielding dualistic language of discourse the paradox inherent in his monistic interpretation of the internal and external" (*The Subtler Language*, p. 203). Wasserman adds that such "unity of opposing perspectives obliterates the distinction between subject and object," so that "in writing that life and the world 'is,' Shelley . . . is denying the dualism of mind and world" (pp. 203, 204). Wasserman concludes, with regard to "Mont Blanc"'s beginning, that such "true unity of reality requires a linguistic approximation that thing and thought be assimilated into each other by one constituting the subject and the other the predicate of the same sentence: 'The everlasting universe of things / Flows through the mind'" (p. 204). Thus, Shelley's "linguistic approximation" of mind/world is finally sought for in the poetry, though Wasserman is of course aware that no more than the prose does "Mont Blanc" at every point bring off the effect of identity between object and subject:

[The artificial linguistic fusion of the inner and the outer] has a propensity to separate again into its contrary terms, the world of things and the world of thoughts. That is, the temporary interfusion of the antithetical worlds in the first poetic paragraph leads directly to the subject matter of the second, of which the first twenty-two lines depict a presumably real and independent external universe, and the last fifteen lines a self-existent mind. (*The Subtler Language*, p. 209)

It is on the basis of verse paragraphs three and four that Wasserman, in the words of Wright, "ascribes a species of transcendentalism to

Shelley's poetry." In a note to *Queen Mab* and in the essay "On a Future State" Shelley appears to adopt an entirely untranscendental concept of causation:

> [W]hen we use the words *principle, power, causes* &c., we mean to express no real being, but only to class under those terms a certain series of co-existing phenomena. . . .

> [T]he only idea we can form of causation is a constant conjunction of similar objects and the consequent inference of one from another. (as quoted in *The Subtler Language*, p. 215)

"For Shelley's day," writes Wasserman of these passages, "the problem of power, or causation, had been raised most provocatively by Hume, who denied the possibility of an empirical knowledge of power. Since we can experience only succession, it must be the imagination, he held, that converts the observation of succession into the notion of causation." But Wasserman adds the transcendentalist point that, in the essay "On Morals," Shelley "exceeded Hume's thesis," "for although ['On Morals'] denies the possibility of experiencing Power," concludes Wasserman, it "allows no doubt of [Shelley's] own conviction of its real existence." Here is "On Morals":

> [T]he existence of a Power bearing the same relation to all that we perceive and are, as what we call a cause does to what we call effect, [was never the subject] of sensation, and yet the laws of mind almost universally suggest, according to the various dispositions of each, a conjecture, a persuasion, or a conviction of [its] existence. The reply is simple: these thoughts are also to be included in the catalogue of existence; they are modes in which thoughts are combined. (as quoted in *The Subtler Language*, p. 216)

Such prose, Wasserman argues, underlies paragraphs three and four's development of "Mont Blanc"'s poetic faith, namely, that "Power dwells apart in its tranquillity, / Remote, serene, and inaccessible" (lines 96–97).

The "species of transcendentalism" implied by these lines, though hardly reminiscent of Wesley's personal God, is quite reminiscent of such Wesleyan emphases as "perceptible inspiration" and the "spiritual sense," theistical natural religion, Lockean, rather than Humean, empiricism, and skeptical yet religious methodology, all of which, separately and together, illuminate the philosophical and theological "species of transcendentalism" in "Mont Blanc": its Wesleyan context broadens the scope, and sharpens the focus, of Wasserman's classic and still useful study.

Consider, first, the matter of skeptical method. Since, as Wasserman puts it (p. 227), the mountains in "Mont Blanc" "only reveal that Cause is infinitely remote from its first palpable manifestation; that the timeless is entirely 'apart' from the first in time," Shelley's "Intellectual Philosophy," as Shelley puts it in "On Life," "establishes no new truth, . . . [and] gives us no additional insight into our hidden nature, neither its action nor itself. . . . It makes one step towards this object: it destroys error and the root of error . . ." (as quoted in *The Subtler Language*, p. 229). This philosophy, in "Mont Blanc," does not claim much more than negative results:

> Thou hast a voice, great Mountain, to repeal
> Large codes of fraud and woe; not understood
> By all, but which the wise, and great, and good
> Interpret, or make felt, or deeply feel.
>
> (lines 80–83)

Shelley's implication here that the intuition of common men is sufficient, without the actions of the great or the teachings of the wise, for the vast majority of the human race to question any form of theoretical certitude is strikingly parallel to Wesley's belief in "Thoughts upon Necessity" that a skeptical method leading to faith is, or rather can be, an almost natural property of all men: "It is not easy for a man of common understanding, especially if unassisted by education, to unravel these finely woven schemes [of Kames and Hartley], or show distinctly where the fallacy lies. But he knows, he feels, he is certain, they cannot be true. This more than merely resonates not only with Shelley's prose, to wit, "a conjecture, a persuasion, or a conviction . . .," but also, and even more importantly, with Shelley's principle in both prose and poetry, to wit, that skepticism is efficacious even though it lead to no dramatic *cogito*: skepticism, for him as for Wesley, precludes the absolute in any dogma and leads to truth that makes one free.

The full range of Wesley's philosophical theology, and not just its skeptical component, is a more fully English means of reading "Mont Blanc" than the narrowly empirical means employed by Wasserman and by Pulos before him. Their confinement of Shelley's thought to the contexts of Hume and Sir William Drummond, for example, overlooks the fact that much of "Mont Blanc" is conformable, signally, to the relatively untroubled subject/object interactions of empiricism's Lockean beginning and Wesleyan continuation. Just as there is a Wesleyan, or at least a Lockean, objectivity in "On Life"'s view that "the basis of all things" cannot be "mind," so there is similarly commonsensical objectivity in "Mont Blanc"'s "clear universe of things around" (line 40), and although in both poem and essay is a Berkeleian, if not Cartesian, subjectivity, to wit, "I seem as in a trance sublime and strange / To muse on my own separate phantasy" ("Mont Blanc," lines 35–36) and "Nothing exists but as it is perceived" ("On Life"), there is in both poem and essay more Wesleyan-Lockean balance of subject and object than any intentional emphasis on subjectivity alone. Wasserman's observation that "Shelley reflects" empiricism's tendency "to encourage the psychologizing of reality by stripping it of material attributes and to leave man most unsure of what exists outside his own mind and yet stimulates it" is at any rate short of the mark. Not only does Shelley's essay accord equal weight to internal and external, but the poem, for its part, could not be clearer in its faith, quasi-Wesleyan as well as quasi-Lockean, that the "universe of things around" is in "unremitting interchange" with "My own, my human mind" (lines 37, 39–40).

This thought/thing interchange seems especially Lockean, and especially Wesleyan, as it carries over into the poem's transcendental theme of "Power." It is no wonder that the Lockean concept thereof has not figured, as has the Humean, in modern critical understanding of "Mont Blanc," for Locke's chapter on power (2.21) is among the most difficult sections of the *Essay*, but this chapter's pertinence to late eighteenth- and early nineteenth-century philosophical and religious sensibilities is strongly suggested by Wesley's devotion of more space to it, despite its difficulty, than to any other section of the *Essay* by far, i.e., thirty-six pages of the abridgment over the ten months from August 1782 through May 1783. It is the case, therefore, that a partly Wesleyan as well as fully Lockean concept of power lay closer to Shelley's time than did the concept to be found in Hume.

For Hume, *power* denotes the decidedly nonanthropomorphic essence of an imagined but unexperienced First Cause, but *power*, for Locke, denotes man's liberty of will, and I suggest strongly that for Shelley this word connotes what man and God hold in common, namely, a going out of self more than merely reminiscent, in man, if not in God, of Arminian free will. *Power*, to rely on MacLean's summary of its Lockean signification, is a

simple idea. . . . Having explained the origin of this idea [in sensation and reflection], Locke then discusses the numerous complex

ideas that are built upon it, for example, the idea of liberty, which is
no more than the physical power to do what the mind has the mental power to will. . . . [L]iberty may stand as a satisfactory example
of a complex idea, or mode, originating in the simple idea of power
which sensation and reflection have furnished. (*John Locke and English Literature of the Eighteenth Century*, pp. 91–92)

Power, to rely on Wasserman's summary of its Shelleyan signification,
has as its nature the "inexorable necessity of acting": "to act is its essence"
(*The Subtler Language*, pp. 227, 230). In "Mont Blanc," then, "Power" is
active as Locke says man is active and since the poem illustrates man's
activity in seeking "Power," the poem implies that man is godlike and
that "Power" is accessible at least indirectly. "Power," finally, is more
theistical than deistical, for Shelley no sooner mentions its remoteness
than he insists (lines 98–100) that

> *this*, the naked countenance of earth,
> On which I gaze, even these primaeval mountains
> Teach the adverting mind,

and, if these lines do not quite suggest that "Power" relates to the world
as subject to object, neither do they quite rule out the possibility that
earth's countenance figuratively, if not really and analogically, reflects
"Power"'s truth. Unlike Wesley's God, of course, Shelley's "Power" is, in
the words of Wasserman, "neither [good nor evil]," but there is something Wesleyan, as well as Lockean, in the experiential nature of the
poem's philosophical and religious quest in process, or, as Wasserman, in
a not un-Wesleyan as well as fully Lockean way, puts it, "Since reality
[for Shelley] resides in neither subject nor object, but in both simultaneously, it truly resides in the verb, which implicates both subject and object; in the searching, which contains both the searcher and the sought"
(*The Subtler Language*, pp. 221, 230).

I do not hold, then, with Wasserman, that "Mont Blanc" describes
"Power" as "beyond the experiential knowledge of man" (*The Subtler
Language*, p. 227). True, Shelley implies an unbridgeable gulf between
"Power" and the summit of Mont Blanc, as symbol of the first in time,
for he merely raises and does not presume to answer the methodological
question of origins:

> —Is this the scene
> Where the old Earthquake-daemon taught her young

Ruin? Were [the summit's shapes] their toys? or did a sea
Of fire, envelope once this silent snow?
None can reply—. . . .

(lines 71–75)

Shelley adds, however, that "all seems eternal now" (line 75), and this appearance of eternity emerges, clearly, from his imagined but sense-based and tough-minded description of the summit as, for example, a "desart peopled by the storms alone" (line 67). He refuses to seek revelation by such means as death and dreams, but rather, with a Lockean-Wesleyan wakefulness, he looks for transcendency with the eye of his imagination opened wide:

Some say that gleams of a remoter world
Visit the soul in sleep—that death is slumber,
And that its shapes the busy thoughts outnumber
Of those who wake and live. —I look on high; . . . .

(lines 49–52)

This "looking," I suggest, yields part of Shelley's experiential, i.e., conscious, knowledge.

Indeed, the "looking" amounts to his "perceptible inspiration" and his "spiritual sense." Not only does his faith accord with theistical natural religion, but his vision of eternity attends the mind's reconstitutions of sense experience, and it should be said of the poem's last paragraph (1) that its analogy to sense perception is everywhere apparent and (2) that its quality of revelation is immediate:

Mont Blanc yet gleams on high:—the power is there,
The still and solemn power of many sights,
And many sounds, and much of life and death.
In the calm darkness of the moonless nights,
In the lone glare of day, the snows descend
Upon that Mountain; none beholds them there,
Nor when the flakes burn in the sinking sun,
Or the star-beams dart through them:—Winds contend
Silently there, and heap the snow with breath
Rapid and strong, but silently! Its home
The voiceless lightning in these solitudes
Keeps innocently, and like vapour broods
Over the snow. The secret Strength of things

Which governs thought, and to the infinite dome
Of Heaven is as a law, inhabits thee!
And what were thou, and earth, and stars, and sea,
If to the human mind's imaginings
Silence and solitude were vacancy?

(lines 127–44)

With much of what Wasserman says of this passage, one agrees:

> [Shelley's] suddenly renewed vision of the heights divulges that the
> Power is the quality-less essence of experiential qualities: still,
> gleaming, silent, innocent, solitary. It is all that Shelley meant by
> the words, "the intense inane": a vacancy that nevertheless holds in
> itself the potentiality of all that is. . . . What remains in order that
> the poet's experience be meaningful is that he conjoin his imagina-
> tive knowledge of the noumenal with his experiential knowledge of
> the phenomenal. . . . Shelley's term "imaginings" . . . is his secular
> correlative for Christian "faith," faith in the supernatural revela-
> tions of the unknowable God who is essence. . . . [T]he restless
> activity, turbulent sound, and destruction and vitality of the phe-
> nomenal world are, at the noumenal level, silence, stillness, and in-
> nocence. (*The Subtler Language*, pp. 236–38)

But one need not understand the poem's conclusion in terms either so
Kantian or so secular. "The deep truth is imageless" is a line from *Prometheus Unbound* that (like "the intense inane" from that work) may indeed
be intended to convey the ineffability of the noumenon, and may even
reflect (at several removes) the Cartesian distrust of sense experience as an
avenue to truth, but the closest parallel to this quintessential distillation
of Shelley's thought, perhaps, or at least to the last verse paragraph of
"Mont Blanc," is the almost more Brownean than Wesleyan realization
that, though the spiritual realm cannot be linked metaphorically with the
world of nature, it can be hinted at, in language, through analogy.
Wasserman drives, without quite arriving, at such an analogical view: he
variously observes (1) that "the poet seeks . . . revelations . . . without
really abandoning his empirical ontology" and (2) that the poet "can have
the data of his imaginative experience and yet keep his empirically
grounded philosophy" (*The Subtler Language*, pp. 224–25). One thinks
finally, though, of not so much the Cartesian and Kantian parallels as the
poetic parallel of T. S. Eliot's more theological than philosophic and
more analogical than metaphoric lines from "Ash Wednesday": [T]he un-
stilled world still whirled / About the center of the silent Word."

Wasserman's discussion of "Adonais," resting like his discussion of "Mont Blanc" upon his perception of creative tension between Shelley's transcendental aspirations and his empirical ontology, is aptly summed up in a single selection from *The Subtler Language*'s view of this three-part poem:

> The first movement [i.e., stanzas 1–17] . . . had implied that matter is the ultimate reality, since vitality is not; the second [i.e., 18–37] had distinguished vitality from spirit, or mind, the first passing through an endless cycle and the second ending in annihilation. This stanza [i.e., 38] then reverts to the materialism of the first movement ("Dust to the dust") and opposes it to the revelation that it is spirit, or mind, that is eternal, not because it is cyclical, but because it is resurrected. (*The Subtler Language*, pp. 317–18)

The method of Wasserman's argument is perhaps best illustrated by his tracing of Shelley's atmosphere image through the poem's three sections; compare, for example, some famous lines from section three with what Wasserman says of them:

> The One remains, the many change and pass;
> Heaven's light forever shines, Earth's shadows fly;
> Life, like a dome of many-coloured glass,
> Stains the white radiance of Eternity,
> Until Death tramples it to fragments.
> (lines 460–64; stanza 52)

> The "dome," of course, is a metaphor for the sky, the earth-surrounding atmosphere that establishes the milieu for mortal existence: it is therefore like life. Because this atmospheric dome diffracts the rays of the sun it stains the radiance of eternity, which is outside the atmosphere. . . . (*The Subtler Language*, p. 339)

Seeing stanza 52 as "one of the points of final revelation towards which all the previous related imagery had been driving and in which that imagery attains its full significance," Wasserman illustrates the point (e.g., pp. 337, 340, 341) by (1) citing examples of the atmosphere image in sections one and two and (2) showing that this "related imagery" structures the poem's underlying dialectic. The atmosphere in section one, for example, suggests mortality without hope:

> Within the twilight chamber spreads apace,
> The shadow of white Death, and at the door

> Invisible Corruption waits to trace
> His extreme way to her dim dwelling-place; . . .
> (lines 65–68; stanza 8)

But the atmosphere in section two suggests mortality relieved somewhat by a muted but prefiguring hope, namely that the radiant light of eternity will break through the dome of earth:

> *As long as* skies are blue, and fields are green,
> Evening must usher night, night urge the morrow,
> Month follow month with woe, and year wake year to sorrow.
> (lines 187–89; stanza 21. My italics—RB)

It remains now to indicate wherein Wesleyan-Lockean analysis amplifies what Wasserman says; I confine myself here to the mention of some parallels between Shelley's use of the atmosphere image and Wesley's. It is not simply that both Wesley and Shelley enumerated the atmosphere's constituent parts, i.e., dew, rain, and "other vapours," nor is it simply that they both associated the atmosphere with "various diseases" and "death itself," but it is intriguingly, and most importantly, that their similar atmospherics measure their similar understandings and their similar expressions of immediate revelation. Consider, for example, parallels, both verbal and thematic, between "The Scripture Way of Salvation" and the last two stanzas of "Adonais." Here is Shelley:

> That Light whose smile kindles the Universe,
> That Beauty in which all things work and move,
> That Benediction which the eclipsing Curse
> Of birth can quench not, that sustaining Love
> Which through the web of being blindly wove
> By man and beast and earth and air and sea,
> Burns bright or dim, as each are mirrors of
> The fire for which all thirst; now beams on me,
> Consuming the last clouds of cold mortality.

> The breath whose might I have invoked in song
> Descends on me; my spirit's bark is driven,
> Far from the shore, far from the trembling throng
> Whose sails were never to the tempest given;
> The massy earth and sphered skies are riven!
> I am borne darkly, fearfully, afar;
> Whilst burning through the inmost veil of Heaven,

> The soul of Adonais, like a star,
> Beacons from the abode where the Eternal are.
>   (lines 478–95; stanzas 54 and 55)

And here is Wesley:

> We have a prospect of the invisible things of God; we see the *spiritual world*, which is all round about us, and yet no more discerned by our natural faculties than if it had no being: And we see the eternal world; piercing through the veil which hangs between time and eternity. Clouds and darkness then rest upon it no more, but we already see the glory which shall be revealed.

The differences, of course, are several, not the least being that one is poetry and the other prose, but both passages clearly associate the dissipation of atmosphere with immediate revelation of eternity, and the lack of sensationalistic diction in Shelley's lines is reminiscent of *plerophory*, whereby Wesley, in counterpoint to sensationalistic *elenchos*, describes the mind oriented aspect of immediate revelation as a fullness, i.e., a "mystical consciousness of unhindered, unclouded favour with God."

Just as Wesley, then, makes the point in "Thoughts upon Necessity" that color produced by the atmosphere is "a real material thing" ("there is no illusion in the case, unless you confound the perception with the thing perceived"), and just as Wesley draws a parallel between such material reality and the spiritual world ("you have no illusion in the natural world to countenance that you imagine to be in the moral") so Shelley in "Adonais" everywhere draws a more or less systematic and more or less conscious analogy between the immediacies of spiritual experience and the mediacies of sense perception. I agree, in other words, with Wasserman's view

> that the conclusion of the elegy is not a plea for suicide, but a prayer that the limited spiritual existence expand into a pure and infinite spiritual life; that in mortal life one's soul may so brightly mirror the fire of the One that this fire will burn bright and so consume "the last clouds of cold mortality." The emphasis is not upon the destruction of the mortal self, but upon the enlargement of the earthly soul until "Heaven's light," which burns bright in proportion as the earthly soul mirrors it, will remove the mortal atmosphere. . . . It is because of the present purification of the poet's earthbound soul that the "breath whose might I have invoked in song / Descends on me"; . . . (*The Subtler Language*, pp. 338–39)

I add only that Shelley's at least semitranscendent "Intellectual Philosophy" is understandable according to contexts not only of philosophy from Plato to Hume and Drummond but also of philosophical theology from Locke to Browne and Wesley. The advice that both Wesley and Shelley give, after all, is to cultivate a strangely empirical faith. Here is Shelley:

> Clasp with thy panting soul the pendulous Earth;
> As from a centre, dart thy spirit's light
> Beyond all worlds, until its spacious might
> Satiate the void circumference: then shrink
> Even to a point within our day and night;
> And keep thy heart light lest it make thee sink
> When hope has kindled hope, and lured thee to the brink.
>
> (lines 417–21; stanza 47)

And here is Wesley: "Stand upon the edge of the world ready to take wing; having your feet on earth and your eyes and heart in heaven" (Telford, 3:148).

To conclude, now, Shelley's recognition of the revival's social importance, together with his respect for the sincerity of its participants, are far from the only parts of the methodistical spirit of religion that informs his work and which coexists with his skeptical method. One of the most frequent objects of his attacks, of course, was Christianity as system and institution, but "in his moments of most intense feeling," as Newman Ivey White has pointed out, "he believed in a God of Love,"[53] and both his God of Love and his religious feeling are at times put forward in an unmistakably testimonial, and even Arminian, language of faith. Since "Hymn to Intellectual Beauty," along with "Adonais" and "Mont Blanc," are arguably indispensable to understanding Shelley's work,[54] the "Hymn" should serve as my final example of his evangelical and empirical tone. In the beginning stanza, i.e., all in the space of just twelve lines, both the experiential method and the tentative quality of his yearning culminate in and are prelusive to reverential/evangelical idiom:

> The awful shadow of some unseen Power
>   Floats tho' unseen among us; visiting
>   This various world with as inconstant wing
> As summer winds that creep from flower to flower;
> Like moonbeams that behind some piny mountain shower,
>   It visits with inconstant glance
>   Each human heart and countenance;

Like hues and harmonies of evening,
  Like clouds in starlight widely spread,
  Like memory of music fled,
  Like aught that for its grace may be
Dear, and yet dearer for its mystery.

(lines 1–12)

"Thy light alone," prays Shelley to the "Hymn"'s more than semitranscendent "Power," "gives grace and truth to life's unquiet dream" (lines
32, 36), and Shelley remembers, as did the Wesleyans, a call experience
palpably religious:

  When musing deeply on the lot
Of life, at that sweet time when winds are wooing
  All vital things that wake to bring
  News of birds and blossoming,
  Sudden, thy shadow fell on me;
I shrieked, and clasped my hands in ecstacy!

I vowed that I would dedicate my powers
  To thee and thine: have I not kept the vow?

(lines 55–62)

This language, indeed, is sufficiently Wesleyan to temper the poem's
overly careful, timid methodology.

Keats

Keats's attraction to coexistence between empiricism and grace helps
to account for his nostalgia for the latter and for the presence of the two
in his poetry: empiricism and grace, together, make up the experiential
richness of his poetic world. The next step, in other words, for those
who study Keats is to explore his "skepticism" and "religion of beauty"
in relation to each other.[55] Robert M. Ryan, in *Keats: The Religious Sense*,
reexamines Keats's intellectual milieu and establishes, as never before, his
respect and admiration for religious points of view as well as for "scientific empiricism."[56] What needs further investigation is how far his allegiance to induction combines with his methodistical, and hence equally
experiential, allegiance to the "holiness of the Heart's affections."[57] In his
sensibility, I look for a Romantic version of John Wesley's theology of
experience, i.e., his both/and logic of empiricism and grace. Keats was
not able to reconcile, as Wesley did, the Lockean "theory of mind" with

"the possibility of . . . supernatural influences on the personality,"[58] but Keats was at last like Wesley and like Locke in being alternately, or even both, tough-minded and tender-minded.

This alternation, if not this simultaneity, is evident from the beginning of Keats's career. Consider, first, his early "naturalism," i.e., his imitation of usual natural surroundings; *poetry of earth*, distinct, say, from *poetry of mind*, or for that matter from anything else ideal, occurs in a poem at once one of his most naturalistic and one of his earliest:

> The poetry of earth is never dead:
>   When all the birds are faint with the hot sun,
>   And hide in cooling trees, a voice will run
> From hedge to hedge about the new-mown mead;
> That is the Grasshopper's—he takes the lead
>   In summer luxury,—he has never done
>   With his delights; for when tired out with fun
> He rests at ease beneath some pleasant weed.
> The poetry of earth is ceasing never:
>   On a lone winter evening, when the frost
>   Has wrought a silence, from the stove there shrills
> The Cricket's song, in warmth increasing ever,
>   And seems to one in drowsiness half lost,
>   The Grasshopper's among some grassy hills.
>   ("On the Grasshopper and the Cricket"; December 1816)

"To My Brother George" (1817) includes among "the living pleasures of the bard" "the mysteries" not of the supernatural, but simply of nature's "night" (line 67):

>   . . . the dark, silent blue
> With all its diamonds trembling through and through,
> Or the coy moon, when in the waviness
> Of whitest clouds she does her beauty dress,
> And staidly paces higher up, and higher.
>   (lines 57–61)

Keats adds, however, that the moon is "like a sweet nun in holy-day attire" (line 62), and as though remembering the sky as symbol of transcendency, he stresses the thoroughly transcendental, and indeed religious, message uttered by the dying bard:

> "What though I leave this dull, and earthly mould,
> Yet shall my spirit lofty converse hold
> With after times. . . .
>
> .   .   .   .
>
> The sage will mingle with each moral theme
> My happy thoughts sententious; he will teem
> With lofty periods when my verses fire him,
> And then I'll stoop from heaven to inspire him."
>
> (lines 69–71, 77–80)

Even "On the Grasshopper and the Cricket," balancing a faint concept of flesh as grass with a consoling (albeit natural kind of) immortality, is not without idealistic coloration.

In the early poetry, indeed, the ideal gets the better lines and hence the greater degree of Keats's involvement. Although the emphasis in "Sleep and Poetry" (1817) lies upon poetry not as mediator of otherworldly truth but rather as at once "a lovely tale of human life" (line 110) and "a friend / To soothe the cares, and lift the thoughts of man" (lines 246–47), it should be remarked that the latter function, at least, is as humanistic as earthly. "I Stood Tip-toe," published in 1817, is effective only when transcendental in tone; the following passage, for example, resting upon the traditional allegorization of the love between Endymion and Cynthia as "the celestial contemplation of an astronomer"[59] and containing speculations about the originator of that myth, is perhaps Keats's most triumphant and certainly one of his most untroubled, affirmations of the ideal:

> Where had he been, from whose warm head out-flew
> That sweetest of all songs, that ever new,
> That aye refreshing, pure deliciousness,
> Coming ever to bless
> The wanderer by moonlight? to him bringing
> Shapes from the invisible world, unearthly singing
> From out the middle air, from flowery nests,
> And from the pillowy silkiness that rests
> Full in the speculation of the stars.
> Ah! surely he had burst our mortal bars;
> Into some wond'rous region he had gone,
> To search for thee, divine Endymion!
>
> (lines 181–92)

"Full in the speculation of the stars," blending concrete with abstract diction, well represents how poets have traditionally evoked the transcendent: Douglas Bush seems right in his edition of the poems and letters when he describes the passage as a "direct statement of Keats's—and other romantic poets'—central quest, the attaining, through the imagination, of supra-human or supra-rational intuitions of spiritual reality" (p. 310). The passage's nonrational but not antirational tone, i.e., its references to blessing, singing, and, above all, the invisible world, bespeaks apprehension of spiritual reality, and theism is overt in the lines, elsewhere in the poem, that employ an idiom of natural religion: "For what has made the sage or poet write / But the fair paradise of Nature's light" (lines 125–26).

Ideal and actual find simultaneous expression in a familiar passage from *Endymion* (1817); these sixty-five lines (1.777–842) "helped a little to redeem *Endymion*, in [Keats's] own opinion, as he tried energetically to turn to other writing." [60] I quote enough of this long passage to make my point.

The ideal, therein, is expressed at times with a deliciousness all too characteristic of the early Keats. The passage's characteristically Keatsean mythological allusiveness, moreover, expresses a more Hellenic than Hebraic ideal. And the question "Wherein lies happiness?" (line 777) is far indeed both from the traditional question of eternal life and from the then especially timely question of salvation.

Keats's answer to this question, however, is not only one of the most generally transcendental but also one of the most particularly religious passages in all of his poetry:

> In that which becks
> Our ready minds to fellowship divine,
> A fellowship with essence; till we shine,
> Full alchemiz'd, and free of space. Behold
> The clear religion of heaven! . . .
> .   .   .   .
> Feel we these things?—that moment have we stept
> Into a sort of oneness, and our state
> Is like a floating spirit's. . . .
>   (lines 777–81, 795–97)

These lines, indeed, are evangelical in tone. Note, for example, Keats's emphasis on man's spiritual state, his reliance on emotion as access to faith, his use of such words as "shine," and such phrases as "religion of heaven" and "fellowship divine," and, not least, his announcement of immediate revelation: "Behold the clear religion of heaven!" Whatever "becks / Our ready minds," of course, is not anything so evangelical as the Holy Spirit, but since "Ghosts of melodious prophecyings rave / Round every spot where trod Apollo's foot" (lines 789–90), poetry substitutes for, if not gives access to, spiritual inspiration, and even when Keats describes as happiness's "chief intensity" not communion with the Ghost of God so much as cultivation of such secular and humanist values as "love and friendship" (lines 800–801), he recommends them in terms generally spiritual and specifically evangelical. "Love," for example, like graces emanating from the Spirit, sheds "influence" (line 807), and thereby engenders a "novel sense" (line 808) reminiscent, if not conscious, of the "spiritual sense" in Wesleyan lore. "Friendship," like the Spirit and the twice-born soul, sends out "steady splendour" (lines 804–5). And in Keats's lines on love alone—

> . . . [I]n the end,
> Melting into its radiance, we blend,
> Mingle, and so become a part of it. . . .
>
> . . . .
>
> [L]ove, although 'tis understood
> The mere commingling of passionate breath,
> Produce[s] more than our searching witnesseth:
> (lines 812–14, 835–37)

—is a particularly tender-minded sense of mystery, if not a "Wesleyan" interpenetration of subject and object: *witnesseth, searching,* and *radiance* suffuse with especially evangelical ideality the otherwise exclusively natural *love* of which Keats speaks.

The empirical complement to such a peculiarly English form of the transcendental is conveyed, for example, by the methodological idiom implicit in "Full alchemiz'd" (line 780): over the notion of alchemy hovers an analogy between a supernatural "science" and experimental chemistry. Keats felt, as he wrote the sixty-five lines, "a regular stepping of the Imagination towards a Truth," and after he wrote them, he felt "set before me at once the gradations of Happiness even like a kind of Pleasure Thermometer" (see Perkins, p. 1, 146n). An instrument of science, then, though not such a measure of spiritual experience as Wesley's "spiritual sense," serves metaphorically to measure something equally subjective. Keats, to be sure, favors love and friendship over the transcendental experience of "oneness" (line 796): "But there are / Richer entanglements" (lines 797–98). But the passage as a whole, like the thermometer image, suggests that the contrast between supernatural mystery on the one hand, and love and friendship on the other, is of two different places along a continuum from natural to spiritual experience, rather than of two different concepts, one fruitful and one deluded.

On March 25, 1818, Keats wrote "Epistle to John Hamilton Reynolds," which, though never intended for publication, constitutes, nonetheless, a concentration of Keats's frame of mind at midcareer. Stuart Sperry is certainly right to describe Keats's final lines, in particular, as "uncompromisingly realistic and anti-romantic":[61]

> . . . '[T]was a quiet eve,
> The rocks were silent, the wide sea did weave
> An untumultuous fringe of silver foam
> Along the flat brown sand; I was at home
> And should have been most happy,—but I saw
> Too far into the sea, where every maw
> The greater on the less feeds evermore.—
> But I saw too distinct into the core
> Of an eternal fierce destruction,
> And so from happiness I far was gone.
> Still am I sick of it, and tho', to-day,
> I've gathered young spring-leaves, and flowers gay
> Of periwinkle and wild strawberry,
> Still do I that most fierce destruction see,—
> The shark at savage prey,—the hawk at pounce,—
> The gentle robin, like a pard or ounce,
> Ravening a worm,—Away ye horrid moods!
> Moods of one's mind! You know I hate them well.
> You know I'd rather be a clapping bell
> To some Kamschatkan missionary church,
> Than with these horrid moods be left i' the lurch.—
>
> (lines 89–109)

The "Epistle," though, is not entirely without an idealistic answer to the question of art's function. The realism of the lines just quoted, for example, is softened immediately thereafter: "I'll dance, / And from detested moods in new romance / Take refuge" (lines 110–12). Earlier, in lines anticipating the nature of such "new romance" as "Isabella; or, The Pot of Basil" and "The Eve of St. Agnes," is an interplay of actual and ideal:

> O that our dreamings all of sleep or wake,
> Would all their colours from the sunset take:
> From something of material sublime,
> Rather than shadow our own soul's day-time
> In the dark void of night. For in the world
> We jostle. . . .

(lines 67–72)

The "Epistle," then, constitutes an inclusive poetic version of Keats's thought.

Material sublime, as Sperry points out (p. 126), expresses "the desire of the imagination to possess the best of both worlds, the ethereal and the concrete," and this desire yields the accommodation achieved in the best of Keats's poetry. With regard to the "Epistle," of course, concrete finally outweighs ethereal: the "Epistle" is everywhere uneasy about the "drift" of art "into one-sidedness and subjectivity," i.e., about art's "continued tendency to refine away too much that is fundamental to our general awareness of life" (Sperry, p. 126). The "fullness or complexity" of Keats's "condition of awareness," writes Sperry (p. 125), "exceeds the powers of any particular work of art to harmonize or satisfy." At few points can Keats be said ever to have slighted the "wealth of human knowledge and experience that provides the substratum of all aesthetic apprehension" (Sperry, p. 125), but a species of transcendentalism is traceable even in the methodologically rigorous and intellectually un-compromising "Epistle," for Wesley's thought parallels and helps to gloss this particular assimilation of idealism within preponderating awareness of actuality. With regard, in other words, not only to the "Epistle," but also to the other poems, I suggest (1) that Keats's imagination was often able "to possess the best of both worlds," and (2) that the way in which it did so amounted to his version of the sufficiently transcendental, or at any rate variously ideal, and at the same time quasi-empirical "sense perception" to be found in Wesleyan sensibility.

The point, of course, is not to claim that Methodism was a source of the poetry. Nor is it my purpose to argue that Methodism directly influenced Keats. His transcendentalism came, in part, from Plato.[62] And Keats's empiricism came from Locke. Methodism, however, was decidedly "in the air," and can be invoked not only on the side of Keats's transcendentalism and of his empiricism, but also of them both together, on their experiential common ground. The experiential theology of Wesley, in other words, is an especially timely, especially near, and especially inclusive means of glossing the mix of tough and tender to be found in Keats's work, for Keats's point of view included not only a peculiarly English form of transcendentalism, and not only a peculiarly English form of the naturalistic, but also a peculiarly English dialectic of the two, and no one more than Wesley provides so heuristic, so close, an analogue to that dialectic. Keats, in his characteristic state of Negative Capability, "when man is capable of being in uncertainties, Mysteries, doubts, without any irritable reaching after fact & reason,"[63] was in one sense further than any other Romantic poet from direct contact with and sympathy for the certainties of Wesleyan fundamentalism, but, in another sense, and for the very same reason of Negative Capability, he was even closer than any other to certain aspects of Wesleyan method. Wesley showed himself capable of skeptical method, i.e., uncertainties and doubts, precisely because *mystery* with a capital *m*, i.e., not mysticism so much as *mysterium tremendum*, was for him at the center of all experience, both mental and physical, and Wesley is like Keats too in mastering "fact & reason" without irritably reaching after them.

Consider then the "Epistle" in these terms. No one could have held the value of "jostling" in "the world" any higher than Wesley did. No one more than he could have been empirically oriented enough to insist that even the dreams of one's sleep, to say nothing of one's waking "dreams," should take on the full aspect of external reality. No one more than he could have been the model for Keats's proclamatory, kerygmatic "clapping bell" of a "missionary church" near the outermost corner of the earth, in eastern Siberia on the Bering Sea. No one more than Wesley could have been as "sick" as Keats of creation's groanings from the "eternal fierce destruction" of death, since Wesley alleviated those groanings during countless waking hours. No one more than Wesley could have shared Keats's "horror of a subjective *enfer*,"[64] for no one, before Keats, asserted more than Wesley a radically Lockean, indeed a proto-Keatsean, objectivity over against the "delightful fairy vision" of Addison. No one more than Wesley, finally, could have managed nonetheless the sort of warmth to be found in the "Epistle"'s admixture of sublime to material.

As for the other poetry, Keats resumed, after the "Epistle," a similar methodistical exploration of the "material sublime." The ideal, for example, to which Porphyro (previously all too actual, and even all too lustfully corporeal) aspires, is expressed by generally evangelical and particularly Wesleyan means:

> Ah, silver shrine, here will I take my rest,
> After so many hours of toil and quest,

A famish'd pilgrim, — *saved* by *miracle.*
("The Eve of St. Agnes," lines 337–39.
My italics—RB)

Jack Stillinger, of course, describes the preconversion Porphyro as "corporeal"[65] and suggests that in Keats's career, tough-mindedness wins out
to the near devaluation of tender-mindedness. Of the odes, for example,
Stillinger states the following general view:

> Characteristically, the speaker . . . begins in the real world (A),
> takes off in mental flight to visit the ideal (B), and then—for a vari-
> ety of reasons, but most often because he finds something wanting
> in the imagined ideal or because, being a native of the real world, he
> discovers that he does not or cannot belong permanently in the
> ideal—returns home to the real (A'). But he has not simply arrived
> back where he began (hence "A'" rather than "A" at the descent), for
> he has acquired something—a better understanding of a situation, a
> change in attitude toward it—from the experience of the flight, and
> he is never again quite the same person who spoke at the beginning
> of the poem.[66]

With regard to "Psyche," at least, if not to "Nightingale" and "Melancholy," "experience of the flight" is an insufficient phrase for the cause of
Keats's "change in attitude," for it is not just the having dared to aspire. It
is also the having entertained, apart from aspiration considered as mere
process, such goals of process as heaven rather than earth, immortality
rather than mortality, eternity rather than time, spirituality rather than
materiality, the unknown rather than the known, the infinite rather than
the finite, and romance rather than realism.

Consider, to begin with, "Ode to Psyche"'s final stanza:

Yes, I will be thy priest, and build a fane
    In some untrodden region of my mind,
Where branched thoughts, new grown with pleasant pain,
    Instead of pines shall murmur in the wind:
Far, far around shall those dark-cluster'd trees
    Fledge the wild-ridged mountains steep by steep;
And there by zephyrs, streams, and birds, and bees,
    The moss-lain Dryads shall be lull'd to sleep;
And in the midst of this wide quietness
A rosy sanctuary will I dress

With the wreath'd trellis of a working brain,
   With buds, and bells, and stars without a name,
With all the gardener Fancy e'er could feign,
   Who breeding flowers, will never breed the same:
And there shall be for thee all soft delight
   That shadowy thought can win,
A bright torch, and a casement ope at night,
   To let the warm Love in!

(lines 50–67)

Insofar, of course, as these lines are at all religious, they are so partly at the remove of a rather too studied allusiveness to Greek mythology. But their immediate Wesleyan context is a means of explaining their peculiar modernity. For in this stanza is empiricism strikingly Wesleyan in tone. "Who can deny," asks Wesley in "Thoughts upon Necessity," "that not only the memory, but all the operations of the soul, are now dependent on the bodily organs, the brain in particular? . . . Our judgments . . . will and passions also, . . . alternately depend on the fibres of the brain" (Jackson, 10:469–70). It is a "working brain," similarly, and mere "shadowy thought," on which the poet must rely for the will and judgment to create the "soft delight" of passionate verse.

An at-once oddly modern and oddly Wesleyan quality, in other words, governs the proximity between ideal and actual in this stanza. Its content is not so Hartleian that it precludes the triumphantly ideal image of the window of love. That figure, in turn, notwithstanding implications of sexuality, is precisely reminiscent of the "spiritual sense" in Wesley's "Letter to the Rev. Dr. Conyers Middleton":

Does not every thinking man want a window, not so much in his neighbour's, as in his own, breast? He wants an opening there, of whatever kind, that might let in light from eternity. He is pained to be thus feeling after God so darkly and uncertainly; to know so little of God, and indeed so little of any beside material objects. He is concerned, that he must see even that little, not directly, but in the dim, sullied glass of sense; and consequently so imperfectly and obscurely, that it is all a mere enigma still.

Now, these very desiderata faith supplies. (Jackson, 10:74–75)

Keats's casement, in its context of the stanza's modestly empirical method, is a muted version of Wesley's hope, despite, or perhaps because of, the limits of natural perception that a window on divine love, i.e., the "spiritual sense," will relieve the darkness and uncertainty of one's search for God. Keats's image of the mind as "untrodden region," moreover, does not so much declare Cartesian consciousness to be the subject of modern poetry as it remembers tabula rasa. For just as Wesley bases mind's capacity for religious knowledge not upon some innate or inherent idea of self-transcendence, but rather upon quasi-empirical acquirement of revelation, so Keats seeks to ground his faith not in some already known capacity of mind, but rather in its potentialities. And just as Wesley, through sensuous experience in "the very world which is the world / Of all of us," finds himself not quite knowing but almost rationally persuaded of a world of the spirit, so Keats is confident of finding an ideal, if not otherworldly, "Love," despite, or perhaps because of, his collateral enterprise of writing a poetry of earth. The quasi-Wesleyan idealism of "Psyche"'s last stanza raises the possibility of immediately historical, as well as historically nostalgic, connotations of such diction as *prophet*, *choir*, *sing*, *holy*, and *vows* (lines 36, 38, 43, 44, 49).

As for the other odes, I glance at their most "Wesleyan" elements, noting that their actualities even make up sufficiently "Wesleyan" as well as indispensable components of Keats's philosophically theological dialectic. "Ode on Melancholy"'s intense realism, i.e., its rejection of such dream inducing agents as "Wolf's-bane" and "nightshade" (lines 2, 4), is no less "Wesleyan" than Wesley's Lockean view of dreaming as unreliable access to the supernatural: Keats does not want "shade to shade" to come "too drowsily, / And drown the wakeful anguish of the soul" (lines 9–10). This high regard for wakefulness suggests that "wake" is the desired answer to the rhetorical question with which "Ode to a Nightingale" concludes: "Do I wake or sleep?" (line 80); the poet, I think, would not want any part of the nightingale's world were it possible to reach it only through the sleep of oblivion or even through the sleep of dreams. The poet's wakefulness, moreover, if not his quasi-Wesleyan sobriety, suggests that "a waking dream" is the desired answer to the rhetorical question comprising "Nightingale"'s penultimate line: "Was it a vision, or a waking dream?" (line 79). It takes nothing away from the "waking dream"'s spiritually methodological status to observe that it is not a "vision" in the sense of medieval dream vision, for in Wesley's terms one's most visionary moments are so conscious that they are recordable in journals. Keats's wakefulness then in the context of Wesley's need not merely imply the tough-mindedness of a naturalized imagination but may signal, in addition, total concentration on some single idealism to create the impression of eternity in the midst of time. Regarding Keats's premium on "the wakeful anguish of the soul," one thinks, on the one hand, of such a parallel as Freud's willingness to experience his cancer without benefit of painkiller, but one thinks, on the other, of the *soul*'s wakeful anguish in Wesleyan lore, for one thinks, specifically, of Wesley's analogy in "The Great Privilege of those that are born of God" between "all the bodily senses . . . now awakened, and furnished with their proper objects" and "all the senses of the soul . . . now awake, and capable of discerning spiritual good and evil." Finally, though "To Autumn" rests content, in its last stanza, with the actual rather than the ideal, Keats softens down the features of death even here with a strangely untroubled and in the present context not un-"Wesleyan" series of vertical and hence semi-transcendent images:

> Where are the songs of Spring? Ay, where are they?
>   Think not of them, thou hast thy music too,—
> While barred clouds bloom the soft-dying day,
>   And touch the stubble-plains with rosy hue;
> Then in a wailful choir the small gnats mourn
>   Among the river sallows, borne aloft
>   Or sinking as the light wind lives or dies;
> And full-grown lambs loud bleat from hilly bourn;
>   Hedge-crickets sing; and now with treble soft
> The red-breast whistles from a garden-croft;
>   And gathering swallows twitter in the skies.
>   (lines 23–33)

In sum, one may reaffirm the ideal in Keats's poetry without denying its grasp of actualities. One need not veer so far from the tough-minded interpretation that one completely embraces *The Finer Tone* in which Earl Wasserman takes an all but exclusively transcendental approach to the poetry.[67] Nor need one come so near Wesley's thought that one sees in Keats's poetry an analogical quasi-identity between perception of the natural world and receptivity to spiritual influx: the poetry, after all, never more than implies that these two ways of "knowing" are founded in the same creation, derived from the same Source, and therefore really related. On the other hand, one need not accept Stillinger's point in his essay on the odes (p. 2) that the boundary between the actual and the ideal "separates" them therein. Rather, in the odes and other poems, that boundary is a place of quasi-analogical interpenetration. Keats, like Wesley, reaffirms in no uncertain terms Locke's indication that the sense image, as well as the thing sensed, is almost mind independently real, so that one's experience in the natural world can hardly resemble Addisonian romance, but Keats is careful in "The Eve of St. Agnes," for example, not only to include as something incontrovertible the "haggard-seeming" (line 344) phenomena of life and death, but also to convert such evangelical idealisms as salvation by miracle into some of the most delicious, and hence both substantial and ideal, descriptions in all of English poetry. In "Epistle to John Hamilton Reynolds," similarly, Keats not only trusts his impressions of nature to the point of drawing out their most painful implications, but also, and partly for that reason, solidly rededicates himself to a poetry of the material *sublime*.

To put the matter another way: Keats's vocabulary and his ideas are much illuminated by John Wesley's thought and language, for an honorific, straightforward, and nonironic evangelical idiom coexists with and is indeed part of Keats's empirical language. A philosophically theological dialectic, then, lies near the heart of his poetic quest: his evangelical vocabulary, though frame of reference more than sign of faith, enriches his confrontation of the actual. Recent criticism emphasizes that confrontation, and is in fact so far from tender-minded that it places Keats among the most inflexibly empirical temperaments of the early modern world; Stillinger, for example, epitomizes his argument thus:

> [I]n the over-all view, [Keats's] significant poems center on a single basic problem, the mutability inherent in nature and human life, and openly or in disguise they debate the pros and cons of a single hypothetical solution, transcendence of earthly limitations by means of the visionary imagination. If one were to summarize the career in a single sentence, it would be something like this: Keats came to learn that the kind of imagination he pursued was a false lure, inadequate to the needs of the problem, and in the end he traded the visionary for the naturalized imagination, embracing experience and process as his own and man's chief good. ("Imagination and Reality in the Odes of Keats," p. 2)

"Keats came to learn," indeed, "that the kind of imagination he pursued was a false lure, inadequate to the needs of the problem." But he held, nevertheless, to a language of transcendency. And he was in the odd position of lending authority to his naturalized imagination by means of his nostalgia for visionary imagination. His conclusions, moreover, though hardly Wesleyan in their substance, were describably so in their methodology, for he "made it new" specifically by basing his poetry, more or less consciously, upon a tentative but satisfyingly mysterious, and not even quite merely hypothetical, spiritual "sense." His nature is the more capacious for this procedure.

Overemphasis of the actual in his poetry comes often and naturally enough from those interested in the Lockean context of Romanticism. But my approach is partly Lockean. And a faulty assumption underlies the view, widespread, that the Lockean theory of mind is in no way reconcilable with the concept of grace. This view not only misses the religious emphases within Locke's theory, but also overlooks the religious uses to which the theory was put by such as Wesley, for whom it was not often, or even ever, a question of either empiricism or grace, but rather, and distinctively, a matter of both empiricism and grace. Keats's poetry, finally, supports the view that he introduced the naturalized imagination. But not even of him should it be said that the naturalized imagination emerges with any great sense of either intellectual gain or broadened poetic horizons. And he was in some ways less tough-minded than Wesley, whose empirical attitudes were radical.

Although the religious language of second-generation English Romantics was more attenuated than that of the first generation, even the second generation came well before religious language was often used either only casually or with little regard for its various historical nuances.[68] The religious sensibility of Keats, notably, compels consideration. Responsive, though unsponsored, his religious inclinations emerged from his milieu: Benjamin Bailey, "a student of theology and candidate for Holy Orders," was "a more impressive spokesman for orthodoxy than any other of Keats's close acquaintances," and from the beginning of his career, in his Leigh Hunt circle of friends, Keats found sympathetic access to "every major tendency in English religious life . . . from enthusiastic piety to skeptical irreverence."[69] The hallmarks of Benjamin Robert Haydon's "highly emotional religion," for example—admiration for "the abolition of African Slavery, the institution of Charities & Hospitals," and the general "amelioration of human Conditions" (Ryan, p. 90)— could only have developed from the timely enterprise of evangelical practical charity.

On the empirical side, Ryan offers a sketch of Keats's medical teacher Astley Cooper, of whom it was said not long before his death that "his general influence on the practice of surgery in this country has, perhaps, been most evident in the great share he has had in establishing pure induction as the only means of a just diagnosis" (pp. 63–64). Ryan demonstrates that Cooper's watchword, "Don't Speculate. Observe," pertains to Keats's doctrine of Negative Capability. Keats's role of medical doctor, and thence of poetic "physician to all men" (*The Fall of Hyperion*, line 90), is from the empiricist point of view the closest he came to being Wesleyan, since one of Wesley's chief roles was to disseminate a basic "physick" that he knew would do no harm, and which he hoped would do good to bodies, if not to minds and spirits.

The religious sense—more accurately, I think, than *material sublime*—conveys the ratio of Keats's empirical method to his religious thought: his religious thought is subordinate to—but subsumed within and consistent with—the medical orientation of his empiricism. One might explore, further, his "skepticism" and "religion of beauty" not only in relation to each other, but also in their Wesleyan-Lockean context of philosophical theology.

One might begin, for example, with "Written upon the Top of Ben Nevis":

> Read me a lesson, Muse, and speak it loud
>   Upon the top of Nevis, blind in mist!
> I look into the chasms, and a shroud
>   Vaporous doth hide them,—just so much I wist
> Mankind do know of hell; I look o'erhead,
>   And there is sullen mist,—even so much
> Mankind can tell of heaven; mist is spread
>   Before the earth, beneath me,—even such
> Even so vague is man's sight of himself!
>   Here are the craggy stones beneath my feet,—
> This much I know that, a poor witless elf,
>   I tread on them,—that all my eye doth meet
> Is mist and crag, not only on this height,
>   But in the world of thought and mental might!

Sperry, tough-minded in approach, regards this sonnet as quintessential Keats.[70] Ryan, who acknowledges in Keats strangely simultaneous degrees of the actual and the ideal, sees in these lines only the unideal skepticism of "metaphysical difficulties" and "helpless bewilderment."[71] Is this tough-minded poem particularly evangelical precisely, if only, because of its tough-mindedness? I think so.

I suggest, in other words, that an at least nostalgic loyalty to religious ideas coexists, even here, with the almost bitterly skeptical tone. The ending, in its near denial of the *cogito*, is not even so affirmative as solipsism. But in Keats's confident "I tread on them" is, more than a subject/object interpenetration, an ascendancy of mind in nature. And the stones he walks on seem to possess what John Crowe Ransom, for one, missed in the poetry of Shelley, namely, "thick *dinglich* substance."[72] The poem, in short, probes skeptically, but finds some solid ground. If it does not build up quite to any idea of order fully religious, neither is its state of unbelief entirely static, for its method, far from simply rejecting the Christian cosmology of heaven and hell, entertains it, rather as a doctrinal and still felt (though hardly palpable) element of a deeply felt, experiential quest for truth. The sonnet's language, in sum, is experiential theology's: though "blind in mist," Keats can say "This much I know"; and, of the "evidence" (similarly "inward") of immediate revelation, Wesley concludes "One thing I know; I was blind, but now I see" (Jackson, 10:75–76).

The progression in Keats is not so much from blindness to vision, of course, as from blindness to insight. But his various perspectives, sense-based and shifting though they are, are new. And though not quite his substitute for immediate revelation, they ground his almost more than rational, and hence not less than ideal, methodology. His substitute for traditional revelation, of course, is poetry. But whereas in such an early poem as "On First Looking into Chapman's Homer" (October 1816) the written word is held to "speak out loud and bold," even when once removed from Homer's authentic tongue, the Muse in "Written upon the Top of Ben Nevis" (June 1818) is taunted for not "speak[ing] loud." Keats, clearly, came to expect neither the word of poetry, nor, by implication, the book of nature, to speak as "loud and clear" as Wesley told Middleton the Bible does.[73] Neither, though, was even the later Keats wholly without the "lively impression" of an "inward evidence." For the "Ben Nevis" sonnet, religious as well as philosophical, implies, like Wesley, that an inner voice is more "intimately present," and therefore more authoritative, than the evidences of both nature and the written word.

A *Methodological Postscript*

Wesley's methodology incorporates both *The Procedure* and the *Essay*. His works make them manifestoes of his Methodism. His message spread his method. His method formed part of what attracted Southey to him. Southey's *Life of Wesley* is a marriage between Wesley's thought and English Romantic prose. *The Life of Wesley*, therefore, suggests the possibility of connections between Wesleyan experience, in its disciplinary range, and the experiential emphasis of English Romantic literature. Such turns out to be the case indeed.

Wesley's thought and expression, in other words, together form not only a heuristic way in, but also a close analogue, to the works of Blake, Wordsworth, Coleridge, Shelley, and Keats. Coleridge stands closest to this quintessentially native context: in his method are especially explicit signs of the Wesleyan method "in the air" that all these poets breathed. In additon to *Zeitgeist*, then, and in addition to heuristic/analogistic criticism is the question of influence. This question is answered affirmatively thus: Blake, Wordsworth, Coleridge, Shelley, and Keats owe something of their theory, and much of their practice, to the relation between John Wesley and John Locke. This mix, then, is English Romantic method.

"The peculiar difficulty of dialectical writing," observes Fredric Jameson, "lies . . . in its holistic, 'totalizing' character: . . . as though with each new idea you were bound to recapitulate the entire system."[1] I have not, of course, written dialectically in Jameson's sense. But I have, at various points, recapitulated my system. Here is a final, full recapitulation: empiricism and evangelicalism exhibit complementary trusts in experience; these two cultural movements converge in English Romantic consciousness; they give content, and perhaps even form, to English Romantic poetry; together they constitute the most illuminating of all contexts in which that poetry emerges from the Enlightenment; English Romantic poets resolve the dichotomy of mind and matter; these poets thus transform the "spirit" of empiricism; experimental method and methodical faith together inform their minds; they theologize empiricism; they ground transcendentalism; they balance religious myths, and religious morality, with scientific reverence for fact and detail; they ally their empirical tempers with their disciplined spirits; they benefit, in their search of a soul, from the second apostolic era; that era supports their encounters with the *numinosum*; they envision spiritualized nature, and hence paradise regained; they envision it in accordance with evangelical readings of creation's book; the natural and revealed forms of religion together give expression at once to these poets' yearning for renewal of spirit and to their theism; and *poetry of experience*, therefore, is an apt phrase for the way evangelical as well as empirical features of their works come together. *The Poetry of Experience*, of course, is the title of Robert Langbaum's study of *The Dramatic Monologue in Modern Literary Tradition*. Though Langbaum's meaning of *experience* is primarily philosophical, and not theological at all, his term is wonderfully apt for the Romantic mainstream of "modern literary tradition" in England.

Not only, then, have I established for Wesleyan studies an interdiscipline by which criticism of Wesley's language facilitates the broadest possible view of his thought, but I have also shown that his thought and expression counterpoint, and largely account for, the poets' languages of philosophy and faith. For purposes of the present postscript, the latter aspect of that demonstration is more important. It remains, in other words, to indicate how my approach is useful, first in further understanding belles-lettres, and second in providing perspective on modern theoretical criticism of Romantic art.

With regard, first, to part 2 of this two-part purpose: my study has attempted to be cognizant of recent critical theory and to resist, thus, the fact that (as Joseph Wittreich puts it) "historical and contextual studies [lag] behind interpretation." [2] Attracted, like Foucault, to the eighteenth century, but without quite accepting his perception of "an essential rupture in the Western world" at that time, [3] I show continuity between the eighteenth and nineteenth centuries. Foucault, moreover, though questioning the idea of tradition, speaks of "the history of opinions" as a "level" of inquiry that would undoubtedly reveal "a tangled network of influences" from Hobbes, through Berkeley, Leibniz, and Condillac, to the Ideologues.[4] (Derrida's interest in the eighteenth century is similar: witness the discussion of Condillac in *L'Archéologie du frivole*.) I untangle a parallel network of influences. My practice bears too upon "the structuralist vision of an interdisciplinary methodology and the integration of various humanistic fields."[5] One thinks, for instance, of *Sade, Fourier, Loyola*, in which Roland Barthes juxtaposes theology with both philosophy and an especially decadent body of belles-lettres. Implicit in my title is the phenomenological assumption of particular consciousnesses underlying particular canons: Poulet embarks upon a "project of mimetically duplicating the *cogito*," or intentionality, of an author,[6] and so, as it were, do I.

My assumption, then, that English Romantic poetry can be well understood against a particular native tradition is not naively practical. My approach is well supplemented by Anne K. Mellor's *English Romantic Irony*, which recognizes that English Romantic indeterminacy is balanced by English Romantic optimism. Often, Mellor works against Paul de Man, who, contra M. H. Abrams's neglect of German Romanticism, reads into English Romanticism the decidedly deconstructing *romantische ironie* of Friedrich Schlegel: Schlegel, according to de Man, carries on the "dialectic of self-determination and self-invention which . . . leads to no synthesis."[7] Mellor realizes that English Romanticism lies near, if not to such a German Romantic irony, then to the irony in English empiricism, and one recalls, in this connection, Stuart Sperry's empiricist perspective, which finds not just in Keats, but in English Romanticism generally, "concerns and questions . . . that cannot be brought to any final determination."[8] Mellor, though, seems closer to the mark than either Sperry or de Man: she mediates between the deconstructions of de Man and the reconstructions of Abrams, and in the import of her attack on de Man, she is close to the Wesleyan-Lockean approach, for she faults him, among other things, for arbitrarily privileging allegory, with its discontinuity between signifier and signified, over symbolic discourse, which maintains an analogical link not only between word and thing but also between word and the things of God. More importantly, she faults de Man for overemphasizing the indeterminacy of Schlegel, whom she, for her part, reads as a prophet of "abundant becoming" as much as "chaotic process."[9] Her terms, then, like mine, allow the English Romantics to entertain two different ideas at the same time without being paralyzed by the irony of irony. My terms, however, in space and even in time, are closer to the English poets than hers, for notwithstanding her title, her view of Romantic irony is Schlegel's and not English: the Wesleyan-Lockean approach, added to *English Romantic Irony*, would give the title additional force and at the same time preserve the insight of the book, namely that distrust, among the English poets, leads somehow to commitment.

Mellor examines Byron, whereas I only conceive of doing so, but although she reads Keats, she leaves out Blake, Wordsworth, and Shelley; Tilottama Rajan, too, though omitting Wordsworth, Blake, and Byron, often parallels my argument. Emphasizing text as much as subtext, and nowhere insisting that subtext replaces text, Rajan acknowledges everywhere in *Dark Interpreter: The Discourse of Romanticism* that English Romanticism in particular, if not Romanticism in general, is "less decisive in its commitment to self-irony" than deconstruction would permit.[10] "Although it is possible to envisage a deconstructed poetry," she observes, "it does not seem possible to write it. Irony can never purge itself of a certain sentimentality. By its very existence as an articulate rather than a mute structure, a poem resists the knowledge of its own impotence, and wakes 'just enough of life in death / To make Hope die anew!'" Here (pp. 241–42) Rajan quotes Coleridge's "Love's Apparition and Evanishment" (lines 27–28). One thinks, in this connection, of Harold Bloom's argument that poems "resist" deconstruction, i.e., that they claim more than mystery and more than the realities of demystification.[11] Regarding English Romanticism as "stubbornly idealistic in its assumptions," Rajan turns, however, like Mellor, "to German theory . . . for a vocabulary which can name the specters that haunt an ideal art."[12] To find these specters one need hardly go so far as Schiller, Schopenhauer, and Nietzsche, for in the form of skeptical method such specters haunt the immediate atmosphere, i.e., the Lockean as well as Wesleyan milieux. The idealism of English Romanticism is stubborn in the sense not so much of being narrowly naive as of tenaciously maintaining interaction between radical skepticism and quasi-empirical faith.

Geoffrey Hartman's *Criticism in the Wilderness*, finally, gives moral support. Hartman's mode is "enigma not kerygma" (p. 244), whereas mine, emphatically, is enigma and kerygma. But his acknowledgment that the irony of irony turns into the ideology of irony is both refreshing and pertinent to my drift: "Indeterminacy as a 'speculative instrument' should influence the way literature is read, but by modifying the reader's awareness rather than by imposing a method. To methodize indeterminacy would forget the reason for the concept" (p. 269). The goal of criticism, observes Hartman, is "to understand understanding through the detour of the writing/reading experience" (p. 244). My experience, here, of reading and writing about Keats, Shelley, Coleridge, Wordsworth, Blake,

Wesley, Perronet, Browne, Pendarves, and Locke is my means of puzzling out, or even proclaiming, that the "human understanding" as understood by them is the understanding as it is. Be that as it may, one is far (as Hartman says) from going back to Arnold's division between criticism and creation, for one participates with Hartman in a philosophical criticism whose relation to art is symbiotic, not parasitic.

To art and philosophical criticism, however, one should add theological criticism. Hartman, I think, agrees. Acknowledging that among secularized Jewish interpreters, e.g., Benjamin, Bloom, and Derrida, sacred and profane intermix and cannot be disentangled, Hartman argues that any critic is dangerous who either presumes to disentangle the two or pretends that the "ghost" of religious feeling does not exist. Benjamin, troping theology as the "hunchback in the puppet" of dialectical materialism, leads Hartman to describe the critic in general as "cousin to the little hunchback. The romantic or religious passion, in all its calculating if displaced strength, may be the hump he can't shake off. . . . This *kakadaimon* is what literary criticism should acknowledge once more. Otherwise it may be drawn into the demon's service" (*Criticism in the Wilderness*, p. 84). G. Douglas Atkins, for one, regards the "Yale School" as intent upon the "Dehellenization of literary criticism," i.e., the subordination of order, logic, decorum, and reason to the speculative hermeneutics of Hebraic thought.[13]

"The English tradition in criticism," writes Hartman, "is sublimated chatter" (p. 199). Be that as it may, and though I contribute to a quasi-Continental collapsing of distinctions among philosophy, criticism, and literature, I do not finally "cross over" from England to the Continent, for I cannot ignore such insular contexts as may be helpful, nor do I fail to include theology within the broad view of discourse that should prevail at the present time. I remain close enough to Anglo-American origins to avoid furthering what Hartman calls the "Neo-Orientalism" of Nietzschean, Derridean style (Hartman, p. 134). I have not wished to be even so Asiatic as the English Carlyle. In adding English theology and English philosophy to criticism and belles-lettres, however, I weave a *bricolage* of text indeed. "Criticism," writes Hartman, "is not independent of the fictional drive. The more insidious question is whether any critic has value who is only a critic: who does not put us in the presence of 'critical fictions' or make us aware of them in the writings of others. . . . [The stimulating critic is one] who overextends his art, having decided that his role is creative rather than judicious" (*Criticism in the Wilderness*, p. 201). I would only add: "Or rather both judicious and creative."

In sum, then, and once more to employ Hartman's terms, English Romanticism's "religious passion" should be recognized, but is not "demonic," for it is, in my terms, sensationalistic and even rational and hence sufficiently commensurable with intellectual criteria to be less than, say, enthusiastic. In a spirit of nonideological, though methodological, inquiry, and at the risk of being too conscious of method even for a study of it, I declare, at last, that a byword for approaching the English Romantics should be "method more, theory less." The bent for theory in literary criticism will always require the complementary understanding of past sensibilities that comes only through research. The present research has more than merely indicated that Wesley's importance for late eighteenth- and early nineteenth-century thought and letters lay in his promise of a common land, and a common language, of spiritual and natural experience. Not only Coleridge, and not only Wordsworth and Blake, but also Keats and Shelley breathed in an England at once empiricist and evangelical, and they sometimes more or less directly fashioned from Wesley's religious and philosophical discourse the "awful doubt" and "mild faith," to borrow the language of "Mont Blanc," with which they kindled and enlightened their uncommon common readers. Thus, these poets' experiential sensibilities together constitute an understanding of the positive, optimistic aspect of Romanticism and show, indeed, wherein that aspect retains an edge against Romanticism seen as fundamentally nihilistic; "in a sense," writes Gerald Graff,

> both sides are right. The opposing theories of Romanticism do not really conflict, since they are not talking about the same aspects of the subject. Those who see Romanticism as positive and optimistic [notably, M. H. Abrams and René Wellek] base their view largely on what the romantics themselves consciously intended—to respect common truth and the artist's responsibility to his community. Those who by contrast see romanticism as nihilistic [e.g., Morse Peckham, J. Hillis Miller, and Harold Bloom] base their views on the logical consequences of romantic ideas, independent of intentions.[14]

The intentionality of English Romanticism, its sense of community, and its common truth are both strong and interrelated insofar as philosophical theology within Wesley's community and in his mind is helpful towards reading Blake, Wordsworth, Coleridge, Shelley, and Keats: their "need for reticulation," to borrow Thomas McFarland's terms, finally controls the "fragmentations" of which they are heroically aware.[15] "Fragmentations" succeeding them, moreover, should be traced to them only with the care and qualification that the idea of faith as a "trend of feeling" should be traced to Wesley.

With regard, finally, to part 1 of my two-part purpose, I anticipate the application of my method to Cowper, Southey, Hazlitt, and Lamb, who are presences, already, in these pages.

Lamb's perception of Wordsworth's "natural methodism" is sufficient basis, perhaps, for hypothesizing that Lamb himself combined evangelical tendencies with the naturalizing, i.e., the empiricizing, thereof. Bernard Barton, in describing Lamb as "the very sort of character likely to be completely misunderstood by superficial observers," remarked that "a cold philosophical sceptic might . . . set him down as a crack-brained enthusiast,"[16] but the context of Wesley's philosophical theology leaves room for a quasi-enthusiasm consistent with skepticism. Nothing necessarily contradictory is in the facts that Lamb was at once "the very reasonable Romantic" and a man whose faith, evangelical fashion, was "actable religion."[17]

As for Hazlitt, he was not only attracted to Locke and Hobbes, but also possessed of a distinctively "Puritan nature," and, as Ronald Blythe points out, Hazlitt's "awakening to faith had about it much of the detail of the classic [say rather: timely] Christian conversion."[18] These facts, of course, were possibly merely warring in the feisty Hazlitt. But my terms of analysis seem warrant enough for testing, if not correcting, John Kinnaird's assumption that especially in Hazlitt, among Romantics, transcendentalism and empiricism were "irreconcilable."[19]

Hazlitt and Lamb, as masters of the familiar essay, had a common touch that put them on the verge of, if not over into, bonnes-lettres. This fact in itself aligns them with the writings of Wesley in their pragmatic function. Southey too occupied a position on or near the boundary between bonnes-lettres and belles-lettres. He not only wrote poetry, but also produced such popular prose as one finds in *The Life of Wesley*, and one will likely find in his prose generally, if not in his poetry, both the Lockean-Wesleyan content of the *Life* and the Wesleyan form of clear-cut messages written for many people.

Cowper fits the paradigm well. His reputation as evangelical laureate is secure. One has, moreover, MacLean's demonstration of Cowper's Lockean attitudes.[20] One will likely find in his works generally the combination of empiricism and evangelicalism to be found in the following passage from *The Task*:

> Philosophy, baptized
> In the pure fountain of eternal love,

> Has eyes indeed; and viewing all she sees
> As meant to indicate a God to man,
> Gives *Him* his praise, and forfeits not her own.
> Learning has borne such fruit in other days
> On all her branches; piety has found
> Friends in the friends of science, and true prayer
> Has flowed from lips wet with Castilian dews.
> Such was thy wisdom, Newton, child-like sage;
> Sagacious reader of the works of God,
> And in His word sagacious.[21]

The compatibility, here, between faith and scientific empiricism forms no small part of this Cowperian version of the spiritual "sense."

One thinks, with regard again to High Romanticism, of John Clare in poetry and Thomas De Quincey in prose. Alethea Hayter remarks of De Quincey that his "revelations were confined to his own interior life. In this aspect, the nearest parallel to De Quincey's *Confessions* was the Methodist or Evangelical narratives of religious conversion, in which men who, after a wandering and dissatisfied youth, had found salvation, told of their personal experience in the hope of helping others."[22] On the other hand, or rather by the same token, is De Quincey's philosophic as well as aesthetic distinction between "the literature of power" and "the literature of knowledge."[23] As for Clare, John Barrell is interested in his theme of perception,[24] and Greg Crossan explores his religious temperament.[25] Mark Minor has gone so far as to conclude that Clare's "'final' rejection of the Methodists [i.e., in 1824], after at least ten years of periodic and intense association with them and with other Dissenters, may have represented part of a symbolic break with his and his society's past. Whether he realized it or not, this break was to have profound consequences for all his future poetry."[26] Evangelical and empirical idioms, then, whether ironical or meant, lie sufficiently near the center of what Clare and De Quincey say to justify (1) pursuing with regard to their works the method tested here and (2) inquiring whether the not so marginal marginalia and the quite revealing glosses of Wesley's philosophical theology await at the edges of English Romantic texts in general, prose as well as poetry.

One thinks, accordingly, of such another poet as Byron and such a fiction writer as Jane Austen. In 1809, she wrote to her sister, "I do not like the Evangelicals," but, in 1814, she exclaimed to Fanny Knight, "I am by no means convinced that we ought not all to be Evangelicals, & am at least persuaded that they who are so from Reason and Feeling, must be happiest and safest."[27] This progression of attitude, in light especially of the fact that "Reason and Feeling" is reminiscent of the sensationalistic and rational continuum, suggests that Wesley's thought, broadly considered, is a means of understanding the substance of the more or less explicitly proevangelical qualities of *Mansfield Park* (1814).[28] Byron, for his part, maintained ironic distance from both faith and philosophy, but it should be remembered, nonetheless, that he was somehow at once a "skeptic" and a "believer": what E. W. Marjarum calls "our bewildering state of confusion" over the seemingly incongruous blend of Calvinism and philosophic skepticism in Byron's poetry could even be cleared up in the light of Wesley's philosophical theology.[29] Byron's statement in *Don Juan* 15.91, i.e., that he "was bred a moderate Presbyterian," relates him to the English Nonconformity that Wesley helped to leaven. Byron's puzzling, and perhaps not entirely ironic, plan to make Don Juan end up as a Methodist, together with his respect for Dr. James Kennedy, whose medical mission work to the West Indies followed upon the Methodists' efforts there, provide possible explanations for the experiential joy of Byron's faith as he defined it for Dr. Kennedy: "Devotion is the affection of the heart, and this I feel; for when I view the wonders of creation, I bow to the Majesty of Heaven; and when I feel the enjoyments of life, health, and happiness, I feel grateful to God for having bestowed these upon me."[30] This diluted but apparently sincere version of heart religion (assuming, for the moment, the truth of Kennedy's reporting) is sufficiently experiential, indeed, to complement Edward Bostetter's view of Byron's poetry as in the "empirical tradition."[31] But Byron's testimony, both as given to Kennedy and as implicit in such a writing as Canto 4 of *Childe Harold's Pilgrimage*, is sufficiently religious to cast doubt upon Bostetter's conclusion that the external world is Byron's only reality; I have in mind Byron's suggestion in his lines on the Roman Coliseum of a divine forgiveness of his enemies:

> Though from our birth the faculty divine
> Is chain'd and tortured—cabin'd, cribb'd, confined,
> And bred in darkness, lest the truth should shine
> Too brightly on the unprepared mind,
> The beam pours in, for time and skill will couch the blind.

> . . . [T]he moonbeams shine
> As 'twere its natural torches, for divine
> Should be the light which streams here to illume
> This long-explored but still exhaustless mine

Of contemplation; and the azure gloom
Of an Italian night, where the deep skies assume

Hues which have words, and speak to ye of heaven,

. . . .

. . .[T]here is that within me which shall tire
Torture and Time, and breathe when I expire;
Something unearthly, which they deem not of,
Like the remember'd tone of a mute lyre,
Shall on their soften'd spirits sink, and move
In hearts all rocky now the late remorse of love.

(Stanzas 127, 128, 129, and 137)

One thinks for now, though, primarily of the five poets. Consider some parting comments on the first-generation three.

Concerning Coleridge's "Abstract Self," Edward Kessler has recently argued that it distrusts the world as illusory and that it seeks, therefore, to get "beyond metaphor";[32] one adds to this that getting beyond metaphor and regarding the world as less than ultimate do not, according to the Wesleyan-Lockean terms with which Coleridge was familiar, mean abandoning the language of sense perception, as if that were possible. Coleridge, insofar as he identified with Wesley's thought, went beyond metaphor not so much to escape the world as to develop a world-based language of analogy. Jerome McGann has recently reaffirmed the critical usefulness of "The Ancient Mariner"'s immediate historical context: McGann argues, specifically, that the "Rime"'s "process of textual evolution" has "a religious, a Christian, and ultimately a redemptive meaning," and, moreover, that the poem finds "a new birth of freedom" for "Christian ideas" "in reaction to the revolutionary intellectual developments of the Enlightenment."[33]

One adds to this that such fruitful tension is to be found not simply in German Higher Criticism, where McGann, following Elinor Shaffer, finds it, but closer to home in Wesley's philosophical theology. One thinks next of Charles Sherry's approach to Wordsworth's transcendentalism through Plato's anamnesis.[34] This approach is especially helpful with regard to the central and seriously intended "clouds of glory" in the "Intimations Ode," but, adding to Sherry's analogue criticism the present criticism of contexts and influences, one discovers not simply *that* Wordsworth remembers the divine, but even something, at least, about *what* he remembers thereof.

One thinks, finally, of Leopold Damrosch's capacious caveat against

Blake scholarship's tendency "to organize dilemmas into diagrams," and one welcomes Damrosch's argument, large-minded, that "potent contradictions lie at the heart" of Blake's epistemology, psychology, ontology, and aesthetics, and, moreover, that "the never-ending struggle to reconcile" these contradictions "gives his work its peculiar energy and value." [35] One adds, though, that the present terms of understanding Blake specifically blend epistemology, psychology, ontology, and aesthetics, and find in these systems more tension and more continuum than contradictions.

Did the evangelical testimony and the empirical philosophy of eighteenth-century England, with their complementary trusts in experience, come together to form a sensibility culturally powerful not simply from the age of Johnson, through English Romanticism's formative years, to the end of High Romanticism in England, but even beyond, to post-Victorian literature there? I am thinking, for example, of the Midlands Methodism in *Sons and Lovers* and in *Lady Chatterly's Lover*. In *To the Lighthouse*, Virginia Woolf is fascinated with Cowper's "Castaway." And Forster, though he "could not swallow" his evangelical heritage, "revered" the Clapham Sect. [36] As late as Forster, Woolf, and Lawrence, then, evangelical patterns are to be found, and the view that Wesleyan background is either too low class or too unfashionable, or both, to be an influence on Victorian letters is beginning to change, and change dramatically. [37] As for post-Romantic England's empiricist sensibility, empiricist assumptions are commonplace in literature of the Victorian period, if not thereafter; to take just one example, Bernard J. Paris has firmly established George Eliot's empiricist point of view as central to her mainstream identity. [38] Her "evangelicalism," moreover, is precise enough to be represented by her sympathetic portrait in *Adam Bede* of Diana Morris's Methodist preaching. The peculiarly English quality of George Eliot's religio-philosophical temperament finds a more or less directly Wesleyan source insofar as, for example, she admired and saw no contradiction in the "Worldliness and Other-worldliness" of Edward Young's eighteenth-century evangelical poetry. [39]

Did evangelicalism and empiricism exert blended impact not just in England but in America and Germany as well? Schelling, Fichte, Hardenburg, and Harms, besides incorporating, as Kant did, the English philosophy of experience into their own philosophies, responded favorably to Schleiermacher's attempt "to lead an age weary with and alien to religion back to its very mainsprings, and to reweave religion threatened with oblivion into the incomparably rich fabric of the burgeoning intellectual life of modern times"; and Rudolf Otto, for one, not only stresses Schleiermacher's identity as philosopher of religion, but also acknowledges the coincidence of Methodism and Schleiermacher's pietist back-ground.[40] Moreover, the deeply Protestant and empirically philosophical roots of Herman Melville have attracted lines of recent inquiry: A. Carl Bredahl's emphasis on Melville's "angles of vision" and T. Walter Her-bert, Jr.,'s emphasis on the dismantled world of Melville's Calvinism are especially reconcilable.[41] One recalls here the similarities and the links be-tween Wesley's philosophical theology and that of Jonathan Edwards. The blended impact of evangelicalism and empiricism has little to do, of course, with such a large and important category as Catholic fiction, Anglo-American or other; one notes well Flannery O'Connor's animad-versions against experience.[42] The blend of which I speak, though, has a great deal to do with the experiential part of modern Protestant, and modern Protestant oriented, literature, Anglo-American or other.

I do not wish, in thus casting a wide net, to detract in any way from the complexity of any given writer. Indeed, I insist that the literature to which my method applies is more than amply interpreted, if not more than adequately explained, by that method's own complexity. And I must, with quasi-Wesleyan if not neo-Kantian relief, juxtapose against Derrida's unceasing dialectic, T. Walter Herbert, Jr.,'s neo-Lockean (if not neo-Kantian and quasi-Wesleyan) line of recent thought:

> Logical arrangements of abstractions have, indeed, an extraordi-nary power to carry what Alfred Schutz called "the accent of real-ity." When we take ideas to be fully adequate, they have an absolute transparency, seeming to bring us directly into contact with the re-ality of the thing deliberated. For this reason, it is entirely possible for an idea, like an image or a story, to have the symbolic function of establishing a communion between the mind and the thing rep-resented. It is true that images and stories have a thick polysemous texture and can embody rich vistas and dimensions of indeter-minacy; and it may further be true that they do justice better than ideas to the great mystery of things. But one sometimes suspects that, amid the clamor in behalf of noncognitive modes of expression as the fundamental shapers of human experience, there is a secret impulse to preserve the cognitive realm as a transcendent domain where in point-blank univocal definitive ideas we can characterize the behavior of the thoughtless.[43]

Be this as it may, and notwithstanding the limits of my method, both the transition from neoclassic to Romantic and the arc from Romantic to modern are touched by the method of John Wesley. My perspective on

Wesleyan historiography and my program for studies in Romanticism determine that his lifelong interpretation of one of the most important documents of the Enlightenment assured the depth and breadth, and hence the altogether satisfying complexity, not of the Enlightenment alone, but of the entire era of modernity. My discovery, in sum, is twofold: first, a bipartite approach to Wesley—i.e., at once an analysis of his thought and a criticism of his language; and second, a new—if not renewing—historical criticism of English Romanticism in particular, and Romanticism in general.

Appendix A

Wesley and Edwards: A Hypothesis

John Wesley was a founder of the Religious Enlightenment, which as I conceive it was cofounded by Jonathan Edwards. It is time, in other words, to attempt a study of Wesley and Edwards together, for they were on the same side of important dependencies. I propose in particular that the Great Awakening as led by Edwards and Wesley's revival as defined at once by English and American Methodism and by the Methodist-inspired Evangelical Movement within the Church of England comprise a single phenomenon in their common debt to the Enlightenment philosophy of John Locke.

Caveats are in order here. Perry Miller's view of Edwards as "more a product of the new thought of the Enlightenment than Puritan traditionalism" is baldly stated, if not overstated; for William J. Wainwright has recently argued against Miller to good effect, that "Edwards's reflections on types were not influenced by the new science."[1] It is necessary, moreover, to disclaim for Edwards any agreement with Wesley's views about providence in general and predestination in particular: Edwards knew George Whitefield and was, like Whitefield, anti-Arminian. Finally, though Wesley rejoiced in Edwards, Edwards was not at all well acquainted with Wesley.

"The new thought of the Enlightenment," however, especially its Lockean manifestation, is a promising basis for comparing them. With regard to Edwards, it does not seem likely that Miller's view will simply go away, for Sacvan Bercovitch is concerned in part to approach Miller's work with new respect.[2] Conrad Cherry takes the balanced view that Edwards defended "religious experience" by drawing upon Enlightenment thought and traditional theology alike.[3] Miller's argument, then, is more likely to be refined and qualified than refuted altogether. Norman Fiering's *Jonathan Edwards's Moral Thought and Its British Context*[4] undertakes to refute in particular Miller's emphasis on Locke's influence, but Fiering's inquiry into the British roots of Edwards's thought amounts to a refinement of Miller's efforts insofar as Locke was a formative influence on many British moralists.

For present purposes, the most valuable view of Edwards's theology is *The Philosophical Theology of Jonathan Edwards* by Douglas J. Elwood, for Elwood argues that Edwards "drank at the fountain of Lockean psychology" and thereby "recast the Reformation theology in an intellectual framework compatible with new understanding of . . . the ways of the mind."[5] Elwood's approach, then, is reminiscent of H. Richard Niebuhr's existentialist and more psychological than abstractly intellectual interpretation of Edwards; Edwards's sermons on hellfire, Niebuhr writes, represent

> intense awareness of the precariousness of life's poise, of the utter insecurity of men and of mankind which are at every moment as ready to plunge into the abyss of disintegration, barbarism, crime and the war of all against all, as to advance toward harmony and integration. He recognized what Kierkegaard meant when he described life as treading water with ten thousand fathoms beneath us.[6]

But Elwood is mainly careful to establish the fact that *philosophical theology* is a more accurate label for Edwards's thought than *theology* alone. (The title of my second chapter indicates my debt to Elwood's terms of analysis.) *The Philosophical Theology of Jonathan Edwards* should be considered, here, if for no other reasons than the following parallels between its argument and my point of view. First, Elwood realizes that insofar as Locke represents the Enlightenment, the Enlightenment need not be thought of as entirely nonreligious, for Elwood argues in particular that Locke wanted not only to liberate "the physical sciences from outmoded habits of disputation," but also to "preserve practical piety from the unnecessary sophistication of dogmatic theology." Elwood roundly concludes, moreover, that Locke never dreamed his philosophy would lead to "the eventual division of philosophy and theology as seen in radical empiricism and logical positivism."[7] (Bercovitch, despite the bibliographical thoroughness of *The American Jeremiad*, does not take *The Philosophical Theology of Jonathan Edwards* into account, and perhaps for that reason reaches the narrow conclusion that Edwards was indebted to Locke not for theology and not for philosophy so much as for the economic and political ideas of "self-interest" and "possessive individualism.")[8]

Joseph Haroutinian, asserting the importance of Elwood's book, observes of Edwards that "those impressed by his spirituality have done no justice to his intelligence, and those impressed by his intelligence have been impervious to his sense of divine things." [9] Thus Haroutinian credits Elwood with recognizing that Edwards's religious "sense" not only arises from his revivalist fervor, but is also precisely analogous to the sensationalistic, and hence "psychological," emphasis of Lockean epistemology. And thus Haroutinian implies that Edwards's "epistemology" of faith includes a more or less precisely Lockean intellectualistic strain. At any rate, in its emphasis on the Lockean ways of Edwards's mind, Elwood's study shows that Edwards's sense perception of natural things formed the model for his "sense perception" of the divine, and Wesley's *hearing ear* and *seeing eye* ("emphatically so called"), when considered in Elwood's light, raise the distinct possibility that in theologizing what was philosophically current, Edwards was not alone among revival leaders of the age.

There is ample warrant for bringing Wesleyan perspective to bear on Jonathan Edwards, or even for establishing Wesleyan/Edwardsean study. The present book, with its chapters on "Young Man Wesley's Lockean Connection" and "Wesley's Philosophical Theology," constitutes preparation for seeing that the experiential philosophy of Locke is perhaps the most fully explanatory basis for such study.

One reason for comparing Wesley with Edwards in Lockean terms would be to explore the intellectual sense in which the Great Awakening and Wesley's revival formed a single movement. Elisabeth Jay, to be sure, wishes to isolate Methodism from "Anglican Evangelicalism," to say nothing of the Great Awakening. [10] But Charles Foster has made a good beginning toward establishing connections between Wesley's revival and that of Edwards. [11] I point out in "Johnson's Wesleyan Connection" (p. 166) that "Robert Southey in his *Life of Wesley* (1820) devotes a lengthy chapter, based on information from [Wesley's sister] Martha Hall, to the rapid rise, temperate tone, and restraining influence of Methodism in America, asserting that the revival preserved a link between America and England even during the Revolution." As Henry May puts it, "the similarities, differences, and reciprocal influence of British and American evangelistic movements need further analysis," and May points to Reginald Ward's American- and English-oriented studies of "comparative religious responses to the French Revolution." [12]

Another purpose in yoking the Locke-related theologies of Wesley and Edwards would be to pursue the implications of such yoking for the Anglo-American accent of Romanticism. Little is more common in American studies, of course, than for Edwards to serve as theological gloss on writers as late as Emily Dickinson. My first book, *Wordsworth's*

"Natural Methodism," shows that Wesley serves as a similar gloss at least on Wordsworth, and since the present pages show that Wesley illuminates the simultaneously philosophical and religious languages of Blake, Wordsworth, Coleridge, Shelley, and Keats, one is ready to examine whether the similarly experiential and thence similarly philosophical theologies of Wesley and Edwards together constitute an appropriately historical as well as satisfyingly interdisciplinary means of understanding, quite synoptically, the literatures of the United States and England during the early modern era. A joint binational contribution to Romanticism emerges from the hardly anticlerical, and indeed religious as well as philosophical, nature of the Anglo-American Enlightenment.

Henry May indulges in a rather conventional description of the Enlightenment as consisting of all those who believe that "we understand nature and man best through the use of our natural faculties," but with regard to my phrase *Religious Enlightenment* it should be said even now that May offers an unconventional and intriguing "working definition" of the Enlightenment as somehow essentially "religious."[13] Going so far as to quote Jesus ("I am the way, the truth, and the life") in conjunction with the Enlightenment, May nonetheless nowhere elaborates on the sense in which the adjective *religious* is appropriate. To recall his statement that "Wesley, Blake, and (despite Perry Miller's arguments to the contrary) Jonathan Edwards" should be excluded from the Enlightenment, it is by no means clear to me why Edwards and Wesley, to say nothing for the moment of Blake, could not be central to both the Moderate, Lockean Enlightenment of which May speaks and the Religious Enlightenment that he dimly envisions. Wesley and Edwards were the intellectual leaders of their respective revivals; their revivals met to span the Anglo-American world; their respective leaderships were each shaped by each man's respect for Locke's *Essay*; and it is therefore at least a good hypothesis that the Anglo-American Enlightenment included as one of its distinguishing modes the Religious Enlightenment of which I speak.

Appendix B

Wesley's Abridgment of Browne's Procedure: *An Item in the Methodist Archives*

In 1977, following two years of negotiations between the University of Manchester and the Methodist Conference, the Collection of the Methodist Archives and Research Centre moved from Epworth House, London, and its modest facilities, to the Rylands Library, where cataloguing will make the Collection fully accessible to students of Methodism in particular and religious culture in general. The abridgment, then, forms part of an unfinished process.

D. W. Riley has amply classified this material, which, besides medallions, portraits, busts, walking sticks, lovefeast cups, and other souvenirs, includes autograph letters, diaries, journals, minutes, pamphlets, periodicals, hymnbooks, class tickets, circuit plans, brochures, and assorted Nonconformist writings among its 26,000 printed works and 600 shelving feet of manuscripts. "Now," writes Riley, "with the financial assistance of the Methodist Conference, it is hoped that catalogues and handlists of the Archives will be published and that the work begun at Epworth House over twenty years ago will be brought to a successful conclusion."[1] The Eighteenth-Century Short-Title Catalogue Project at the British Library, which has been at work since 1976, is cataloguing the similarly abundant evangelical materials at Oxford and Cambridge: the Glaisher and Madden Collections at Cambridge, and the Johnson and Harding Collections at the Bodleian, include, for example, publications by Cheap Repository Tracts, the Religious Tract Society, and the Society for the Propagation of Christian Knowledge.

Thus, the abridgment is just one among many out-of-the-way, but by no means necessarily unimportant, items. Green merely mentions it,[2] and Eayrs, despite being aware of Wesley's familiarity with *The Proce-dure*,[3] does not mention the manuscript at all. It is a tribute to Wesleyan scholarship that the abridgment has been noticed: Hindley, with his inter-est in Wesley's philosophical studies as a background to his theology, mentions the manuscript. However, Hindley is not completely familiar with it, for he says that Wesley's selections are "almost verbatim" (p. 102). Yet Wesley, precisely by avoiding duplication, excised verbiage in *The Procedure*; the following comparison typifies his condensation:

> Before I speak of the particular Properties of these Ideas of Sensa-tion, it will be convenient to observe these three things in general concerning them. (*The Procedure*, p. 57)
>
> Before we speak of v Properties of Ids of Sensae, it $\frac{1}{w}$ be proper to observe three ths: . . . (The manuscript, p. 13)

Wesley's version, illustrating his abbreviations and shorthand, reduces twenty-five words to eighteen, uses less than half the characters, and keeps Browne's sense. Hindley says, moreover, that Wesley's omissions amount to "large sections" (p. 102); yet only one "large section"—*Proce-dure* 3—is left out; and the method of abridgment, while allowing a three-fourths reduction (from 477 pages), represents a high proportion of the content: the excerpt just quoted, for example, does full justice to a transitional passage. Finally, Hindley states that "original additions" are "infinitesimal in extent and trivial in substance" (p. 102). But I can find no additions at all: additions, original or not, are hardly what an abridg-ment calls for.

What Hindley says, then, suggests the need for another, closer look at the manuscript.

Appendix C

Wesley's "Remarks upon Mr. Locke's 'Essay on Human Understanding'": A Table of Reference

Wesley's "Remarks upon Mr. Locke's 'Essay on Human Understanding'" includes five sustained responses (one to Book 1, and four to Book 2), and twenty-four annotations (fourteen to Book 3, and ten to Book 4). The *Essay* passages thus reacted to are followed here by correlations between Nidditch and Jackson:

1.1.4–7 (from the "Introduction")
(See Nidditch, pp. 44–47, and the second, third, and fourth paragraphs of the "Remarks": Jackson, 13:455–56.)

2.10.3–9 (from "Of Retention")
(See Nidditch, pp. 150–54, and Jackson, 13:456, third paragraph.)

2.11.2, 13 (from "Of Discerning, and other Operations of the Mind")
(See Nidditch, pp. 156–57, 160–61, and Jackson, 13:456, fourth and fifth paragraphs.)

2.21.31, 41 (from "Of Power")
(See Nidditch, pp. 250–51, 258, and Jackson, 13:456, last paragraph, and 457, first paragraph.)

2.27.8 (from "Of Identity and Diversity")
(See Nidditch, pp. 332–34, and Jackson, 13:457, second paragraph, through 460, first complete paragraph.)

3.1.6 (from "Of Words or Language in General")
(See Nidditch, p. 404, and Jackson, 13:460, fifth complete paragraph. The second through fourth complete paragraphs lament the anti-Aristotelianism and faulty definitions in Books 3 and 4, and state Wesley's preference for Books 1 and 2.)

3.2 ("Of the Signification of Words")

(See Nidditch, pp. 404–8, and Jackson, 13:460, last complete paragraph.)

3.3.10 (from "Of General Terms")
(See Nidditch, pp. 412–13, and Jackson, 13, the paragraph at the bottom of 460 and the top of 461.)

3.3.15
(See Nidditch, p. 417, and Jackson, 13:461, first complete paragraph.)

3.3.19
(See Nidditch, pp. 419–20, especially p. 419, and Jackson, 13:461, second complete paragraph.)

3.4.9 (from "Of the Names of simple Ideas")
(See Nidditch, p. 423, and Jackson, 13:461, third and fourth complete paragraphs.)

3.5.9 (from "Of the Names of mixed Modes and Relations")
(See Nidditch, pp. 433–34, and Jackson, 13:461, fifth complete paragraph.)

3.6.36 (from "Of the Names of Substances")
(See Nidditch, p. 462, and Jackson, 13:461, sixth complete paragraph.)

3.6.38
(See Nidditch, pp. 462–63, especially p. 463, and Jackson, 13:461, last complete paragraph.)

3.7 ("Of Particles")
(See Nidditch, pp. 471–73, and Jackson, 13, the paragraph at the bottom of 461 and the top of 462.)

3.9.13 (from "Of the Imperfection of Words")
(See Nidditch, pp. 482–83, especially p. 482, and Jackson, 13:462, first and second complete paragraphs.)

3.10.6 (from "Of the Abuse of Words")
(See Nidditch, pp. 493–94, and Jackson, 13:462, third complete paragraph.)

3.10.18
(See Nidditch, p. 500, and Jackson, 13:462, fourth complete paragraph.)

3.10.21
(See Nidditch, pp. 502–3, especially p. 502, and Jackson, 13:462, fifth complete paragraph.)

4.3.6 (from "Of the Extent of Humane Knowledge")
(See Nidditch, pp. 539–43, especially p. 540, and Jackson, 13:462, sixth complete paragraph.)

4.6.8 (from "Of Universal Propositions, their Truth and Certainty")

(See Nidditch, pp. 582–83, and Jackson, 13:462, seventh and eighth complete paragraphs.)

4.6.11

(See Nidditch, pp. 585–86, and Jackson, 13:462, last paragraph.)

4.6.13

(See Nidditch, p. 588, and Jackson, 13:463, first paragraph.)

4.7 and .8 ("Of Maxims"; "Of Trifling Propositions")

(See Nidditch, pp. 591–617, and Jackson, 13:463, second paragraph.)

4.14.3 (from "Of Judgment")

(See Nidditch, p. 653, and Jackson, 13:463, third, fourth, and fifth paragraphs.)

4.16 ("Of the Degrees of Assent")

(See Nidditch, pp. 657–68, and Jackson, 13:463, sixth paragraph.)

4.16.11

(See Nidditch, p. 665, and Jackson, 13:463, seventh paragraph.)

4.17.2 (from "Of Reason")

(See Nidditch, p. 668, and Jackson, 13:463, eighth paragraph.)

4.17.4

(See Nidditch, pp. 670–78, and Jackson, 13:463, ninth paragraph, and the paragraph at the bottom of 463 and the top of 464.)

Appendix D

Wesley's "Extracts from Mr. Locke": A Table of Reference

The following table identifies the *Essay* passages that Wesley included in particular numbers of *The Arminian Magazine*. Numbers that include remarks are shown by stars. Page numbers in the left column refer to Nidditch.

Essay	*The Arminian Magazine*
1.1.4–7 (pp. 44–47)	5 (January 1782), 27–30★
2.7.3–6 (pp. 129–31)	(February), 85–88
2.9.11–15 (pp. 147–49)	(March), 144–46
2.10.3–9 (pp. 150–54)	(April), 190–95★
2.11.2, 13 (pp. 156–57, 160–61)	(May), 247–49★
2.13.21–24 (pp. 175–78)	(June), 307–10
2.15.10–12 (pp. 203–4)	(July), 361–63
2.21.5–13 (pp. 236–40)	(August), 413–17
2.21.14–16 (pp. 240–41)	(September), 476–78
2.21.17–24 (pp. 241–46)	(October), 528, 534
2.21.25–29 (pp. 247–49)	(November), 585–87
2.21.47–48 (pp. 263–64)	(December), 646–48★
2.21.49–50 (pp. 265–66)	6 (January 1783), 30–31
2.21.51–53 (pp. 266–68)	(February), 86–89
2.21.56–57 (pp. 270–72)	(March), 136–38
2.21.58–60 (pp. 272–74)	(April), 197–99
2.21.61–63 (pp. 274–76)	(May), 254–56
2.23.12 (pp. 302–3)	(June), 310–12
2.23.13 (pp. 303–4)	(July), 366–68
2.23.22–24 (pp. 307–9)	(August), 418–20
2.23.25–29 (pp. 309–12)	(September), 480–84

2.23.30−32 (pp. 312−14)   (October), 534−36
2.27.8 (pp. 332−35)   (November), 590−94*
2.33.1−6 (pp. 394−96)   (December), 650−52
2.33.7−9 (pp. 396−97)   7 (January 1784), 32−33
2.33.10−14 (pp. 397−99)   (February), 91−92
2.33.15−17 (pp. 399−400)   (March), 148−49
2.33.18 (pp. 400−401)   (April), 201−2

Wesley did not excerpt Books 3 and 4. But in the May number (pp. 254−
56), he published his remarks on 3.1.6, 3.2, 3.3.10, 3.3.15, 3.3.19, 3.4.9,
3.5.9, 3.6.36, 3.6.38, 3.7, 3.9.13, and 3.10.6. And in the June number
(pp. 314−16), he published his remarks on 3.10.18, 3.10.21, 4.3.6, 4.6.8,
4.6.11, 4.6.13, 4.7−8, 4.14.3, 4.16, 4.16.11, 4.17.2, 4.17.4. (See, again,
Appendix C.) In the May number (p. 254), he speaks of his disappoint-
ment in the "second volume," meaning Books 3 and 4; therefore, he
must have used the two-volume sixth edition (1710), which differs only
slightly from Nidditch's copy text, i.e., the fourth edition (1700). See the
discussion in Nidditch, p. x.

Notes

An Orientation

1. Gene W. Ruoff and L. J. Swingle, "From the Editors." These remarks represent Ruoff's and Swingle's introduction to a special issue on British Romantic fiction.

2. See, for example, John Murray Todd, *John Wesley and the Catholic Church*; Maximin Piette, *John Wesley in the Evolution of Protestantism*; and Robert Clarence Monk, *John Wesley: His Puritan Heritage*. See also William R. Cannon, *The Theology of John Wesley, with Special Reference to the Doctrine of Justification*; Harald Gustave Ake Lindstrom, *Wesley and Sanctification: A Study of the Doctrine of Salvation*; Arthur S. Yates, *The Doctrine of Assurance: with Special Reference to John Wesley*; Granville C. Henry, "John Wesley's Doctrine of Free Will"; and Leo George Cox, *John Wesley's Concept of Perfection*. Frederick Hunter, in view of such diversity, sees Wesley as a pioneer of ecumenical thought in his *John Wesley and the Coming Comprehensive Church*. Wesley was an eclectic traditionalist who mined the variety of Christian thought from the Middle Ages to the eighteenth century. He found time even on horseback, and indeed especially there, to express at his portable writing desk his theological perspective; see at Epworth House, City Road, London, the writing desk itself, designed to face the rear: the horse knew the circuit by heart.

3. Frank Baker, *John Wesley and the Church of England*, p. 3. The term *Anglican*, in use only occasionally during the eighteenth century, is employed here throughout as Baker employs it: in accordance with its current usage as a synonym for "pertaining to the Church of England."

4. Bernard Semmel's study, *The Methodist Revolution*, emphasizes Wesley's Arminian thought. Biographies such as Luke Tyerman's *The Life and Times of John Wesley* and Richard Green's *John Wesley, Evangelist* stressed his impact on religious life. One assortment of studies was social in emphasis: see Maldwyn Lloyd Edwards, *John Wesley and the Eighteenth Century: A Study of His Social and Political Influence*; J. H. Whiteley, *Wesley's England: A Survey of Eighteenth-Century Social and Cultural Conditions*; Robert Featherstone Wearmouth, *Methodism and the Working Class Movements of England, 1800–1850*, and *Methodism and the Common People of the Eighteenth Century*.

5. For a recent discussion of this well-known conversation, see Frank Baker, "John Wesley and Bishop Butler: A Fragment of John Wesley's Manuscript Journal, 16th to 24th August 1739."

6. They did so in 1795. Wesley's puzzling relationship to the Anglican community is perhaps best epitomized by Joseph Beaumont: "Mr. Wesley, like a strong and skilful rower, looked one way, while every stroke of his oar took him in the opposite direction." See Benjamin Gregory, *Sidelights on the Conflicts of Methodism*, p. 161.

7. J. Clifford Hindley, "The Philosophy of Enthusiasm," p. 106. See also Frederick Dreyer, "Faith and Experience in the Thought of John Wesley." I am delighted to find in this recent essay an ally; Dreyer, concluding that "philosophy [e.g., that of Locke and David Hume] in the end . . . explains what [Wesley's] religion meant," is quite consistent with my own attempt to place Wesley's thought in the context of his age.

8. For Wesley's account of his conversion, see Curnock, 1:475–76. Holland, though "in union with the Brethren," and though "he ranked in the Moravian Church as the first 'Congregation Elder'," was also a member of the Church of England; see Curnock's full discussion: 1:475–76n. Wesley does not identify Holland as the "one" who "was reading Luther's preface," but Curnock's argument in support of Holland is persuasive.

9. See Hindley, "The Philosophy of Enthusiasm," pp. 99–109, 199–210, especially 108. For Wesley's Moravian contacts (from February 7, 1738, when Peter Böhler arrived in London, to May 4, 1738, when Böhler departed for America), see Curnock, 1:436–60.

10. The following studies are classics: S. G. Dimond, *The Psychology of the Methodist Revival: An Empirical and Descriptive Study*; Umphrey Lee, *John Wesley and Modern Religion*; G. C. Cell, *The Rediscovery of John Wesley*; and J. S. Rattenbury, *The Conversion of the Wesleys: A Critical Study*.

11. Robert L. Moore, *John Wesley and Authority*.

12. John Telford, *The Life of John Wesley*, pp. 162–63.

13. See Hindley, "The Philosophy of Enthusiasm," p. 99, and A. J. Ayer, *Language, Truth and Logic*.

14. See Alfred H. Body, *John Wesley and Education*, especially pp. 33, 52, 56–61. Of his curriculum at Kingswood, Wesley wrote that "Whoever goes carefully through this course will be a better scholar than nine in ten of the graduates at Oxford and Cambridge" (ibid., p. 61). A. G. Ives, *Kingswood School in Wes-*

ley's Day and Since, especially pp. 19, 240–41, 247, engagingly recasts Body's argument for the Lockean basis of Wesley's experiment at Kingswood.

Ives and Body, though making a sizable number of points concerning the relation between Wesley and Locke, do not make the Lockean background a major feature of their approaches, and each, therefore, finally resembles George Eayrs, whose *John Wesley: Christian Philosopher and Church Founder* asserts that Locke was among the authors whom Wesley "read and studied" (p. 22), but nowhere pursues the question of Wesley's debt to the *Essay*. See especially my third chapter, however, for further acknowledgment of Eayrs's otherwise useful study.

15. Samuel F. Pickering, Jr.'s recent study, *John Locke and Children's Books in Eighteenth-Century England*, is preceded by his similarly instructive, and similarly delightful book, *The Moral Tradition in English Fiction, 1785–1850*.

16. Martin Schmidt, *John Wesley: A Theological Biography* 2 (pt. 1):73.

17. See Basil Willey, "On Wordsworth and the Locke Tradition," pp. 296–309; and Hartman, *Wordsworth's Poetry 1787–1814*, pp. 33–69.

18. Moritz Schlick, *Problems of Ethics*.

19. Pyrrho's philosophy is known primarily through the poetical fragments of Timon of Phlius; see Leon Robin, *Pyrrhon et le Scepticisme Grec*.

20. Alexander Campbell Fraser, in annotating *Essay* 4.16.12, quotes Bacon's essay: see Fraser's edition 2:381n.

21. See, for example, the discussion in R. N. Stromberg, *Religious Liberalism in Eighteenth-Century England*, pp. 38–66. See also John Toland, *Christianity Not Mysterious*, pp. 86–87; Anthony Collins, *A Discourse of Free-thinking*, pp. 20, 25, 33, 44, 50–52, 99, 177; and Matthew Tindal, *Christianity as old as the Creation*, pp. 268, 394.

22. See Thomas Bray's *Bibliotheca Parochialis; or a Scheme of such Theological and Other Heads, as seem requisite to be perus'd, or Occasionally consulted, by the Reverend Clergy. Together with the Books which may be profitably Read on each of these Points*, p. 40.

23. See Andrew Baxter, *An Enquiry into the Nature of the human soul: Wherein the immateriality of the soul is evinced from the principles of reason and philosophy*; and Bishop Joseph Butler, *The Analogy of Religion, Natural and Revealed, to the constitution and course of Nature*. The word *materialism*, among many eighteenth-century English scientists and doctors, was not wholly incompatible with the notion of *spirit*: these materialists believed in the reality of some etherealized substance, and they distinguished between themselves and those Newtonian *mechanists* who explained life as exclusively physical, e.g., as a system of pulleys. See Robert E. Schofield, *Mechanism and Materialism: British Natural Philosophy in An Age of Reason*, especially pp. 91–114. Butler, Baxter, and Berkeley, clearly, worried about incompatibility between the material and the spiritual.

24. See Catharine Cockburn, *Remarks upon the principles and reasonings of Dr. Rutherforth's Essay on the nature and obligations of virtue, in vindication of the contrary principles and reasonings inforced in the writings of the late Dr. Samuel Clarke*; see also her earlier work, *A Defence of the Essay on human understanding, written by Mr. Lock—In answer to some Remarks on that essay* [by Sir Thomas Burnet].

25. See Butler's *Analogy* 1.1.17, as quoted in Kenneth MacLean, *John Locke and English Literature of the Eighteenth Century*, p. 52. See also Hindley, "The Philosophy of Enthusiasm," p. 202, and MacLean, pp. 27, 62, 73, 101, 152, 162. Nonconformist writers as diverse, and as widely separated in time, as Thomas Tryon in his *Letters . . . Philosophical, Theological, and Moral* and Samuel Pike in his *Philosophia Sacra: or, The Principles of Natural Philosophy. Extracted from Divine Revelation* shared the Lockean attitudes of that more famous Nonconformist, Isaac Watts, and fed like him into a mainstream Christian thought that was increasingly "ecumenical" in part because of the almost universal desire to take theological account of Locke's empiricism.

26. MacLean quotes, for example, *Essay* 2.23.3 (see MacLean, *John Locke and English Literature of the Eighteenth Century*, p. 121); moreover, he quotes (pp. 96–97, 137) *Essay* 2.23.28, 32 and 4.12.10.

27. Horton Davies, *Worship and Theology in England from Watts and Wesley to Maurice, 1690–1850*, pp. 143–254, especially p. 184.

28. See Donald Greene, *The Age of Exuberance: Backgrounds to Eighteenth-Century English Literature*.

29. For Wesley's admiration of Butler's thought, see, for example, Curnock, 3:232; 5:265. For V. H. H. Green's comments see *The Young Mr. Wesley: A Study of John Wesley and Oxford*, pp. 10–11, 303.

30. For a discerning application of this Lockean view, see Hugh Sykes Davies, "Wordsworth and the Empirical Philosophers," pp. 157–62. Compare this with the discussion of synchronicity in M.-L. von Franz, "The Process of Individuation," pp. 226–27. For Wesley's bibliomancy as a sufficiently theological guide in spiritual experience see Frederic Greeves, "John Wesley and Divine Guidance." For a recent, authoritative discussion of providential theology in the eighteenth century, see Aubrey Williams, *An Approach to Congreve*, especially pp. 31–34.

31. See Francis Gallaway, *Reason, Rule, and Revolt in English Classicism*, pp. 10, 25–26, 55–56, 161–62 and *passim*. Gallaway's classic study has been reprinted (New York: Octagon Books, 1965).

32. Green, *The Young Mr. Wesley*, p. 2 and *passim*.

33. An exclusively sensationalistic empiricism, for example, is more or less explicitly assumed to comprise the entire Lockean background to *Gulliver's Travels* (1726). Irvin Ehrenpreis bases his argument that Gulliver gradually grows "irrational" on a view that the *Essay* describes man as sensationalistic rather than rational: subordinating Locke's definition of reason as man's "real essence" to his designation of "sensible shape" as man's "nominal essence," Ehrenpreis implies that the senses make up the more philosophically tenable, if not the more desirable and the more intended, component of Locke's epistemology. See Irvin Ehrenpreis, "The Meaning of Gulliver's Last Voyage." Ehrenpreis's interpretation of the *Essay* has been pushed further, and further applied to Swift, by W. B. Carnochan; see *Lemuel Gulliver's Mirror for Man*, pp. 118–65, especially pp. 123, 133. David B. Morris and Patricia Meyer Spacks in their studies of Pope interpret the *Essay* as primarily sensationalistic; assume that Pope thus interpreted it; and suggest that Pope, unlike Swift, embraced a primarily sensationalistic epistemology. See Spacks, *An Argument of Images: The Poetry of Alexander Pope*, pp. 42, 84, 112;

and Morris, "The Kinship of Madness in Pope's *Dunciad*," especially pp. 813, 819, 831. Michael V. DePorte goes even further than Morris and Spacks in implying that among eighteenth-century English authors there was an increasing tendency to interpret and endorse Locke's philosophy as nonrational. Locke's point that irrationality is not easily cured, rather than Locke's argument that rationality can be maintained, is in DePorte's view central to Sterne's perspective in *Tristram Shandy*, which according to DePorte everywhere suggests that reason is easily lost and indeed that extreme irrationality constitutes a norm of behavior; see especially DePorte's "Digressions and Madness in *A Tale of a Tub* and *Tristram Shandy*," especially 50–52. For arguments acknowledging, if not a Lockean, then a more than rational strain in Sterne, see Arthur Hill Cash, "The Sermon in *Tristram Shandy*," p. 395; and Melvyn New, *Laurence Sterne as Satirist: A Reading of* Tristram Shandy.

34. For a discussion of the a priori rationalists in England, see, for example, Robert Bernard Schuda, "A Study of Laurence Sterne's Sermons: Yorkshire Background, Ethics, and Index." William Wollaston, John Balguy, and Richard Price are also notable among the figures in Schuda's helpful analysis.

35. ". . . [A]nd the measure of heaven itself," Sterne adds, "is but the measure of our present appetites and concoctions"; see Laurence Sterne, *The Life and Opinions of Tristram Shandy, Gentleman* 2:593, edited by Melvyn New and Joan New.

36. "It is so difficult," adds Nicoll, "to feel that the fashion of this world passeth away and yet at the same time to do one's utmost in it and to care for everything"; see T. H. Darlow, *William Robertson Nicoll: Life and Letters*, p. 348.

37. Green, *The Young Mr. Wesley*, pp. 10–11, 303.

38. Francis McConnell, *John Wesley*, p. 326.

39. See M. H. Abrams's "Structure and Style in the Greater Romantic Lyric."

40. Samuel T. Coleridge, *The Friend* 3:261–62. Coleridge's statement, of course, anticipates the modern loss of balance between subject and object, i.e., the modern victory of the subjective: see, for example, David Bleich's chapter on "The Subjective Paradigm" in *Subjective Criticism*, pp. 10–37. Modern criticism could rediscover a subject/object balance by drawing, for example, on dialectical biology, which, like Locke, attempts "to break down the alienation of subject and object"; dialectical biology, that is,

insist[s] on the interpenetration of gene, organism, and environment. Thus, in place of the metaphor of adaptation of organisms to a preexistent environmental "niche," dialectical biology emphasizes the way in which organisms define and alter their environment in the process of their life activities. Organism and environment are both in a constant state of becoming, mutually determining each other.

See R. C. Lewontin, "The Corpse in the Elevator," p. 37, a review of *Against Biological Determinism* and *Towards a Liberatory Biology*, both edited by Steven Rose.

41. See the concise summation in Frank Thilly, *A History of Philosophy*, pp. 1–4.

42. See the discussion in MacLean, *John Locke and English Literature of the Eighteenth Century*, p. 15.

43. Henry May, for example, finds in general that "people whose ultimate authority is either scripture or faith do not belong in the Enlightenment," and in particular that "Wesley, Blake, and (despite Perry Miller's arguments to the contrary) Jonathan Edwards" should be excluded; see *The Enlightenment in America*, pp. xiv, 402. Paul Hazard, assuming that Wesley was "anti-rationalist" and hence enthusiastic, asserts that he set about to end the age of reason; see *European Thought in the Eighteenth Century: From Montesquieu to Lessing*, p. 454. In "Johnson's Wesleyan Connection," pp. 146–47, I focus on the Calvinist/Arminian controversy as a means of suggesting that the differences between Wesley and George Whitefield are considerable, but students of the Enlightenment tend to lump Wesley with Whitefield, and, assuming that Wesley (like Whitefield) was not particularly intellectual, they erroneously conclude that he was un-"enlightened." Basil Willey, in *The Eighteenth-Century Background: Studies on the Idea of Nature in the Thought of the Period*, pp. 108–9, writes that "Wesley and Whitefield range[d] the world, converting their ten thousands, not by rational ethical suasion, but by impassioned appeals to the heart," but Wesley's "Earnest Appeal to Men of Reason and Religion," by the title alone, challenges Willey's assumption that appeals to emotion and the moral arguments of reason are necessarily mutually exclusive. Peter Gay, in *The Enlightenment, An Interpretation: The Rise of Modern Paganism*, pp. 254, 346, (1) condescends to all eighteenth-century Methodists (they would have been "at home," Gay sneers, "in twelfth-century Chartres"); (2) associates Wesley with their enthusiastic excesses (neither Wesley nor Whitefield should be lumped with enthusiastic Methodists); (3) identifies Wesley, erroneously, with the strictures of Whitefield against Tillotson and the Latitudinarians; and (4) erroneously concludes that "philosophical religion" was held by Wesley, as well as Whitefield, to be "their worst enemy." Even one so proficient in the varieties of eighteenth-century religious experience as E. P. Thompson has not advanced any further than students of the Enlightenment beyond the view of Wesley as unenlightened: in his review of Donald Davie's *A Gathered Church: The Literature of the English Dissenting Interest*, Thompson declares that "the Wesleys," John and Charles, "turned their backs" upon "rational modes" and were thus "self-consciously *anti*-enlightenment"; see *The Modern Language Review* 75 (1980): 165. Thompson is right, of course, to take on Davie for identifying the Wesleys with Dissent; from my point of view, moreover, Thompson is right to conceive of "rational modes" in a country where the Enlightenment was chiefly Lockean. But it is worth pointing out that, in addition to the forgivable error of lumping John with Charles, whose intellectual gifts, sometimes as rich as those of John, were at no time so varied, Thompson commits the (no less forgivable) error of overlooking the self-evidently possible relation between Wesley's *experience* of faith and the philosophy of *experience* underlying the Enlightenment. For a study of an Arminian (and therefore proto-

Methodist?) background to the English Enlightenment, see Rosalie L. Colie, *Light and Enlightenment: A Study of the Cambridge Platonists and the Dutch Arminians.*

Wesley's "intellectual position," as set forth in his "Appeals to Men of Reason and Religion" and his lengthy treatise on "Original Sin" (1757), is mentioned in Sir Leslie Stephen's *History of English Thought in The Eighteenth Century*, 2:409. But Stephen's main points are that Wesley's "strength lies almost entirely in the sphere of practice," and that his importance, accordingly, lies in providing "the religious reaction" to the eighteenth-century emphasis on the intellect (2:409, 418–19).

44. See Albert M. Lyles, *Methodism Mocked: The Satiric Reaction to Methodism in the Eighteenth Century.* I have quoted the charge leveled against Wesley himself by the Rev. Thomas Church in 1744; see John Wesley, *Wesley's Standard Sermons*, edited by Edward H. Sugden, 2:84–85. A good example of the polemics, though not one cited by Lyles, is William Warburton's scorn of Wesley's bibliomancy. Warburton, as a means of laughing at a passage from the Journal, thinks it sufficient to quote it:

> In the evening, being sent for to her again, I was unwilling, indeed afraid to go; thinking it would not avail, unless some, who were strong in faith, were to wrestle with God for her. I opened my Testament on these words—I was afraid, and went and hid my talent in the earth. [Cf. Matt. 25:25.] I stood reproved, and went immediately.

See William Warburton, *The Doctrine of Grace; or, the Office and Operations of the Holy Spirit Vindicated from the Insults of Infidelity and the Abuses of Fanaticism* 8:335.

45. See, for example, *Essay* 4.19 (Nidditch, pp. 697–706). See also my *Wordsworth's "Natural Methodism,"* p. 71. Wesley's *Dictionary* defines "enthusiast" as "a religious madman, one that fancies himself inspired," and "inspiration" as "that secret influence of the Holy Ghost which enables man to love and serve God."

46. Curnock, 3:54. See also Jackson, 1:216; 3:34; 6:471–72; 8:105–6, 110, 405, 432–34, 445–68; 9:1–14, 22–28.

47. See Telford, 5:383; Jackson, 2:49, 3:465, 503; and 4:458. See also Monk, *John Wesley: His Puritan Heritage.*

48. Jackson, 7:271; Wesley included Hume within "the great triumvirate" of *philosophes* who preached the religion of humanity. Far from simply lumping Hume and Locke together, as empirical philosophers, Wesley distinguished between them, and, equally clearly, he preferred Locke, down to the most particular issues. For example, Wesley's pejorative phrase *the casual involuntary association of our ideas* (see Sugden, ed., *Wesley's Standard Sermons* 2:26) suggests (in the adjectives *casual* and *involuntary*) that Wesley intended to recommend *association of ideas* as understood by Locke rather than by Hume: Hume, like Hobbes, Dryden, Watts, and Hartley, regarded the concept positively, as an instrument for improving knowledge, whereas Locke regarded it negatively, as a detriment to judgment and as "a sort of madness" (*Essay* 2.33; Nidditch, pp. 394–401). See Chinmoy Bannerjee, "*Tristram Shandy* and the Association of Ideas"; and MacLean, *John*

Locke and English Literature of the Eighteenth Century, pp. 128–30. For further discussion of Wesley's relationship to Hume, which was well informed and sometimes even implicitly positive, see chapter 2.

49. See, for example, Telford, 2:346; 5:373.

50. May, *The Enlightenment in America*, p. 107.

51. For Wesley's admiration of Berkeley's *Alciphron* (1728) and the works of John Norris, see, for example, Curnock, 1:125–26, 345; 5:458; and Telford, 3:163; 5:110; and 7:228. For the interrelationship of Descartes, Malebranche, Berkeley, and Norris, see, for example, A. A. Luce, *Berkeley and Malebranche: A Study in the Origins of Berkeley's Thought*, pp. 70–75. For Wesley's praise of *De la Recherche de la Vérité* (1674–78), see, for example, Curnock, 8:277. Scholars can welcome the following: Nicolas Malebranche, *The Search after Truth*, trans. Thomas M. Lennon and Paul L. Olscamp.

52. See Hazard, *European Thought in the Eighteenth Century*, pp. vi, 31, 41–43, and Gay, *The Enlightenment, An Interpretation*, pp. 11–12; Nidditch (p. xxxvii) cites Pierre Coste's French translation of the *Essay* (1700) and Ezekiel Burridge's Latin translation (1701).

53. May, *The Enlightenment in America*, pp. 38, 246–47, 337, 347.

54. Pocock, though generally distinguishing between the continental and insular traditions, discovers one surprising interconnection: he finds eschatological patterns among the *philosophes* as well as the Puritans. See J. G. A. Pocock, "Post-Puritan England and the Problem of the Enlightenment." The broadest and most thorough demonstration of the *Essay*'s influence in England remains MacLean's *John Locke and English Literature of the Eighteenth Century*. Nidditch does not exaggerate in observing that "perhaps no other modern work of discursive prose has sold so well and steadily in the course of centuries" (p. xxxiv): the *Essay* after its first appearance went through five additional editions—in 1694, 1695, 1700, 1706, 1710—and was subsequently reprinted every three or four years until the middle of the nineteenth century.

55. See Gay, *The Enlightenment, An Interpretation*, p. x. See also Appendix A.

56. Going beyond a study of the Enlightenment alone, to a study of how Romanticism grew out of the Enlightenment, I shall indicate, moreover, that Wesley's age of Lockean as well as religious illumination extended to British Romanticism. Rousseau's passion, Diderot's vitalism, Hume's skepticism, Voltaire's blend of empiricism and a priori reason, and, clearly not least, Locke's blend of a posteriori reason and sense-based methodology, all form the uncompacted Enlightenment, and Wesley's transmutation of Locke's empiricism formed another, equally prophetic, element of the Enlightenment, namely, the Religious Enlightenment which, diffused throughout the atmosphere of late eighteenth- and early nineteenth-century England, formed in turn a condition whereby English Romanticism, uncompacted but describable, aspired to the state of its chief precursor and prime exemplar: Blake was in the world, but not of it.

57. Consider, for example, *Essay* 4.9.3 (Nidditch, pp. 618–19):

> As for *our own Existence*, we perceive it so plainly, and so certainly, that it neither needs, nor is capable of any proof. For nothing can be more evi-

dent to us, than our own Existence. *I think, I reason, I feel Pleasure and Pain*; Can any of these be more evident to me, than my own Existence? If I doubt of all other Things, that very doubt makes me perceive my own *Existence*, and will not suffer me to doubt of that. For if I know *I feel Pain*, it is evident, I have as certain a Perception of my own Existence, as of the Existence of the Pain I feel: Or if I know *I doubt*, I have as certain a Perception of the Existence of the thing doubting, as of that Thought, which I call *doubt*. Experience then convinces us, that *we have an intuitive Knowledge of our own Existence*, and an internal infallible Perception that we are. In every Act of Sensation, Reasoning, or Thinking, we are conscious to our selves of our own Being; and, in this Matter, come not short of the highest degree of *Certainty*.

The skeptical method of this passage, calling into doubt what can be doubted, is reminiscent of Descartes, too: see his *Discourse on Method*.

58. See the discussion in Luce, *Berkeley and Malebranche*, pp. 70–75. Locke, by contrast, gives what Luce calls "a psychology of idea," and, though Luce adds that Locke also gives "a metaphysic by means thereof," Luce concludes that Locke "attempts no metaphysic of the idea itself." Luce, in sum, distinguishes between "the reality of the idea-thing," a reality urged in Cartesian "mentalism," and psychological Lockean "ideism." Or in other words, Cartesian thought is distinct from empiricism insofar as Lockean reason is finally an a posteriori extension of the senses quite different in its sensuous moorings from Descartes's a priori brand of reasoning.

Perhaps the first modern definition of *psychology*, incidentally, is that of David Hartley, who calls it "the theory of the human Mind, with that of the intellectual Principles of Brute Animals"; see *Observations on Man, His Frame, His Duty, and His Expectations*, p. 354. At the time of Locke, the definition was linked to the myth of Psyche: "Psucologie, which Treats of the Soul," is contrasted with "Anatomy, which treats of the Body"; see Blancard's *Physical Dictionary* (2d ed., 1693), as quoted in the *Oxford English Dictionary*, s.v. "Psychology." Samuel Johnson, perhaps, was unknowingly perceiving a psychological dimension to the *Essay*, and unknowingly pioneering the psychological interpretation of it, when he referred to his own period of history as an age when, "sometimes with nice discernment" (as in the *Essay*?), "but often with idle subtility" (as in *Observations on Man*?), "Speculation" attempts "to analyze the mind," "trace the passions to their sources," "unfold the seminal principles of vice and virtue," and "sound the depths of the heart for the motives of action"; see the discussion of Johnson's preface to the plays of Shakespeare in MacLean, *John Locke and English Literature of the Eighteenth Century*, p. 13.

59. See T. Walter Herbert, *John Wesley as Editor and Author*, pp. 46–71; and George Lawton, *John Wesley's English: A Study of His Literary Style*.

60. Frank Baker, general editor, *The Oxford Edition of Wesley's Works*. This edition is in the process of highlighting the various categories of Wesley's writings. The editors, devoting themselves to such topics as Wesley's poetry, not all of which is hymns, can finally be classed among students of his language; Herbert,

gathering Wesley's harvest "as Editor and Publisher," is trained in the study of literature. Besides Cragg's presentation of the "Appeals to Men of Reason and Religion," Baker's edition of the early letters has appeared. Albert C. Outler's edition of the sermons, heavily annotated, is forthcoming.

61. I am grateful to Samuel Rogal for communicating with me about his work.

62. See the discussion in James L. Golden, "John Wesley on Rhetoric and Belles Lettres," p. 255.

63. See Jackson, 8:300, 336–37; 10:255–58; and 11:493–95.

64. See Friedrich Nietzsche, "European Nihilism," in Book I of *The Will to Power*, p. 7; and *Werke in Drei Bänden*, ed. Karl Schlechta, 3:881.

65. For a Deconstructionist manifesto, see J. Hillis Miller, "The Critic as Host," pp. 217–53.

66. See Lawton, *John Wesley's English*, especially chapter 1 ("Wesley's Vocabulary and the Evangelical Mission," pp. 15–25) and chapter 2 ("Emergence of a Distinctive Terminology," pp. 26–35).

67. Golden, "John Wesley on Rhetoric and Belles Lettres," pp. 250–64.

68. For the empirical assumptions of such "new rhetoricians," see Marsha Kent Savage, "Archibald Alison and the Spiritual Aesthetics of William Wordsworth"; and Byron Keith Brown, "Wordsworth's Affective Poetics: Rhetorical Theory and Poetic Revolution." See also Golden, "John Wesley on Rhetoric and Belles Lettres," pp. 263–64.

69. See, for example, Kathleen Walker MacArthur, *The Economic Ethics of John Wesley*; Robert N. Kingdon, "Laissez-faire or Government Control: A Problem for John Wesley"; and Alfred Wesley Hill, *John Wesley Among the Physicians: A Study of Eighteenth-Century Medicine.* Herbert, in *John Wesley as Editor and Author*, discerns immediacy in Wesley's political language.

70. See the discussion in MacLean, *John Wesley and English Literature of the Eighteenth Century*, p. 5.

71. Theodore Roszak, "In Search of the Miraculous."

72. Hans Aarsleff, *From Locke to Saussure: Essays on the Study of Language and Intellectual History*. See also D. W. Harding's classic study, *Experience into Words: Essays on Poetry*; and Italo Calvino's recent essay, "The Written and the Unwritten Word." Fascinated by the all but irreconcilable challenges of the writer, namely, "to use a language responsible only to itself" and "to use a language in order to reach the silence of the world," Calvino concludes:

> In a certain way, I think we always write about something we don't know, we write to give the unwritten world a chance to express itself through us. Yet the moment my attention wanders from the settled order of the written lines to the movable complexity no sentence is able to hold entirely, I come close to understanding that on the other side of the words there is something words could mean.

73. Derek Bickerton, *Roots of Language*.

74. These remarks form part of Edward Dowden's contribution to a special

issue of the *Pall Mall Gazette*, as cited in E. D. Hirsch, Jr., *The Aims of Interpretation*, pp. 141–42.

75. Hirsch, *The Aims of Interpretation*, pp. 140–42.

76. For the relevant bibliography, see Brantley, *Wordsworth's "Natural Methodism,"* p. 175. See also Stephen Prickett, *Romanticism and Religion: The Tradition of Coleridge and Wordsworth in the Victorian Church*. I am intrigued, in this connection, by Norman Nicholson's statement that the evangelical revival "was, in fact, not so much a symptom of the Romantic Movement as the Movement itself in so far as it affected a large class and section of the population. . . . For these the Revival was all they ever saw or heard of Romanticism": see *William Cowper*, p. 10.

77. Langbaum's study, *The Poetry of Experience*, is subtitled *The Dramatic Monologue in Modern Literary Tradition*.

78. The fundamentalist absolute trust in the New Testament, of course, which is the hallmark of many evangelicals who followed Wesley, as well as of most who did not, is incompatible with an acknowledgment of "the priority of experience," and so makes such a phrase less suitable than "the importance of experience" not only to eighteenth-century evangelicals in general, but also to Wesleyan evangelicals in particular. For the latter, however, and certainly for Wesley himself, experience was important indeed. See chapter 1 for a philosophically theological perspective on, and definition of, the "evangelical faith" of which young Wesley read deeply. Wesley's own evangelical faith, as I show in chapter 2, reflected that definition and perspective.

79. "Romantic origins" is Leslie Brisman's phrase: see his *Romantic Origins*. Brisman argues that the various Romantic quests for origins of society, language, sexuality, and "the growth of the soul" are motivated by "the desire to know correctly a state which no longer exists, and the desire to express one's awareness of the fictionality of such a state" (p. 11); Brisman is indebted to Deconstructionist criticism. For theoretical criticism's relation to my point of view, see especially my conclusion.

One. *Young Man Wesley's Lockean Connection*

1. Green is aware that theology, even in the early part of the century, took the *Essay* into account, and often took it to be true: Deists, Unitarians, and Latitudinarians, for example, were influenced by what Green calls "the foundation" of the *Essay*, i.e., "the certainty of God's existence"; see V. H. H. Green, *The Young Mr. Wesley: A Study of John Wesley and Oxford*, pp. 2–5. In 1703, to be sure, the heads of Oxford colleges had agreed that "tutors should not read [the *Essay*] with their pupils": for the *Essay's* controversial early days at Oxford, see John Andrew Hamilton's article on Locke in the *Dictionary of National Biography*. But among Wesley's friends at Oxford he counted John Burton, later vicar of Buckland, who tried to introduce the *Essay* into the curriculum: for Green's account of Wesley's friendship with Burton, see Green, *The Young Mr. Wesley*, p. 73. And it could be said that Locke, as the most important philosopher of the day, was all but necessarily prominent in Wesley's early milieu.

Wesley, besides reading the above-mentioned theologians, studied some who were not so philosophical: Edward Synge, Archbishop King, Robert Nelson,

William Lowth, John Ellis, William Law, George Hickes, Jeremy Taylor, Thomas à Kempis, St. Francis de Sales, Justin Martyr, and St. Augustine. But Wesley's early interest in the relation between empiricism and theology is especially well indicated by his study of George Cheyne's *Philosophical Principles of Religion.* And Wesley's early interest in scientific empiricism is indicated by his study of Newton's *Opticks* and Robert Boyle's *The Sceptical Chymist.* See Green, *The Young Mr. Wesley,* especially pp. 305–19.

2. See Telford, 1:24. See also Locke's *The Reasonableness of Christianity* and his fourth Book of the *Essay* (especially chapters 17 ff.), and compare them with Richard Fiddes, *Theologia Speculativa: or; the first part of a body of divinity under that title, Wherein are explain'd the principles of natural and revealed religion,* especially p. 95. The very phrasing of the Anglican Fiddes's definition is to be found, ironically enough, in the Deist John Toland's *Christianity Not Mysterious,* p. 138.

3. This letter is quoted from my transcription of the manuscript, which is in the John· Rylands University Library of Manchester. Telford's transcription (Telford, 1:22) errs in adding quotation marks to Wesley's definition of belief as "Assent to a Proposition upon Rational Grounds." Wesley's words, indeed his (or at least put together in his own way), illustrate his engagement in philosophical theology.

4. Natural religion, i.e., religion founded on the laws of nature (distinct from the Bible and the Spirit's ministrations), evinces differing views of divine involvement in natural laws; Deism, with its emphasis on transcendency, constitutes the extreme form of natural religion. Of Locke's natural religion, which, assuming no great gap between God and creation, is theistical, here is a typical statement:

> We are able, by our Senses, to know, and distinguish things; and to examine them so far, as to apply them to our Uses, and several ways to accommodate the Exigences of this Life. We have insight enough into their admirable Contrivances, and wonderful Effects, to admire, and magnify the Wisdom, Power, and Goodness of their Author.
>
> (*Essay* 2.23.12; Nidditch, p. 302)

For early usages of *natural religion,* see Samuel Freiher von Pufendorf, *Of the Nature and Qualification of Religion in Reference to Civil Society*; Pufendorf, *The Law of Nature and Nations: or, A general system of the most important principles of morality, jurisprudence, and politics;* and Pufendorf, *The Whole Duty of Man According to the Law of Nature.*

George Lawton, in *John Wesley's English: A Study of His Literary Style* (especially pp. 20, 24, 195), argues that Wesley's language was theistical in part because "the language of the philosophy of his time was largely theistical." It is true, of course, that several of Wesley's characteristic expressions ("only Agent," "Cause and Lord of All," "Governor of the World," "Great Creator") blend theism with deistical cosmology. It is true, too, that Wesley resembled the Deists in emphasizing reason and evidence as ingredients of faith. But not the least difference between him and them is his sufficiently natural-religionist but nonetheless theistical belief in God's activity in creation. For Wesley's definition of Deism (as "infidelity denying the Bible") see his *The Complete English Dictionary* and the discussion in G. H. Vallins, *The Wesleys and the English Language*, p. 34.

For Locke's "fundamental theism," see the discussion in Nidditch, pp. ix ff.

5. The date of the manuscript's completion (as quoted above) appears on p. 103. I am indebted to Aubrey Williams for encouraging me to think of Peter Browne, *The Procedure, Extent, and Limits of Human Understanding* as important. It has long been recognized, of course, that Browne's career as a conscientious Churchman was a not insignificant episode of English Church history. His episcopate, like that of Berkeley, adumbrates the practical charity of Wesley's revival; for Browne's benevolence supported such proto-Wesleyan causes as "Physick and advice to the sick," "Books to the poorer clergy," relief of common beggars, and prison visitation; and his high standard of episcopal duty was in contrast to the negligence of some of his fellow bishops: in 1714, there were only two resident bishops in the province of Armagh. See Richard Mant, *A History of the Church of England, from the Reformation to the Union of the Churches of England and Ireland Jan. 1, 1801* 2:156; and C. A. Webster, *The Diocese of Cork: With Illustrations.*

6. Wesley's diary for September 1730 shows him reading *The Procedure*, and on October 3, he referred to his abridgment, "which I hope to have finished shortly." "Shortly" turned into eighty-two more days. See Telford, 1:56n, 57.

7. Many thanks to David Riley, assistant librarian at Rylands. During my visit there, in the summer of 1978, he was especially helpful as a guide through the Colman Collection, which, incidentally, includes the letters to Susanna, and he kindly allowed me to microfilm Wesley's manuscript abridgment; the microfilm is at the Graduate Research Library, University of Florida, Gainesville. See also Appendix B.

8. Many thanks to Professor Heitzenrater for corresponding with me about his project in transliteration.

9. J. Clifford Hindley, "The Philosophy of Enthusiasm," p. 108. Browne, as Hindley points out (pp. 101–5, 199, 201, 203), posits three sources of knowledge, (1) the direct evidence of sense perception, (2) "self-consciousness" or "the immediate feeling or consciousness of what is transacted in our mind," and (3) "mediate" knowledge derived from argumentation and demonstration. Hindley suggests that Wesley, if not Browne, saw a connection between this epistemology and Christian experience: "Wesley . . . was tempted to carry Browne's empiricism into the religious sphere: knowledge of God's saving grace is like sense-perception, in which an external reality (the Holy Spirit) impresses itself on our mind" (Hindley, p. 204). Theology, of course, has always tended to take on the coloring of philosophy, or even, as in the case of Aquinas, to become identical with it, but what emerges from my pursuit of Hindley's suggestion is that at no time before or since the eighteenth century did the interdiscipline of theology and philosophy flourish more luxuriantly than it did then.

10. That principle had swayed Browne as early as 1697, when Narcissus Marsh, Archbishop of Dublin, asked Browne to counter John Toland's Deist argument, derived in part from Locke, that there is nothing in Christianity either

beyond or contrary to reason. Browne, in "A Letter in Answer to a Book entitled 'Christianity Not Mysterious'" (May 1697), obliged by drawing on Locke to argue against "all those who set up for Reason and Evidence in opposition to Revelation and Mysteries"; Browne held that mysteries and revelation, though beyond reason, are not necessarily contrary thereto: indeed, they appeal to reason insofar as they constitute evidence. Browne's "Answer" was well received: Toland boasted that he made Browne a bishop, and in the same sense it could be said that Toland made Browne Provost of Trinity College, Dublin, where he was instrumental in creating a place for Locke's *Essay* to be read by such as Berkeley. In sum, then, Locke taught Browne that the mysteries of revelation, though nonrational, are neither contrary to reason nor antirational; see A. R. Winnett, *Peter Browne: Provost, Bishop, Metaphysician*, especially pp. 11–19, 102–43, 166–88.

Winnett's study answers the call of Berkeley's biographer, Alexander Campbell Fraser, for an intellectual as well as ecclesiastical biography of Berkeley's fellow bishop and philosophic peer; for Winnett not only analyzes the philosophical theology in *The Procedure* and in *Things Divine and Supernatural conceived by Analogy with Things Natural and Human* but also characterizes Browne's dispute with Berkeley. Berkeley interpreted Browne's thought as being so inflexible in its empiricism as to preclude religious knowledge. During the early 1730s, polemical battles between the two bishops centered on the odd paradox in religious philosophy that God must be both like and unlike man—both near and so far away as to seem utterly unknowable. This dispute, of course, impeded the influence of Browne's thought, but the full range thereof, as the abridgment shows, enjoyed an immediate reception in the mind of Wesley. For Fraser's comment see his *Life and Letters of George Berkeley, D.D.*, p. 18. Swift, writing to Pope after Browne's death, called Browne "the most speculative author of this age, and as scholars tell me, excellent in his way, but I never read much of his works": see Harold Williams, ed., *The Correspondence of Jonathan Swift* 4:385. Wesley would have agreed with the "scholars," and, indeed, he was among them insofar as he, too, esteemed Browne's speculative faith as both an excellent and a timely intellectual foundation.

11. See A. R. Winnett, *Peter Browne: Provost, Bishop, Metaphysician*, especially pp. 9–11. Thus *The Procedure* elaborates Browne's "Answer" to *Christianity Not Mysterious*; whereas Toland emphasizes part of Lockean method to argue for one kind of natural religion, Browne emphasizes all of Lockean method to argue for another.

12. See Winnett, *Peter Browne*, especially pp. 234 ff. Winnett perhaps overemphasizes Browne's sensationalistic (distinct from rational) dimension; Winnett is intent upon substantiating J. W. Yolton's statement that *The Procedure* draws from Locke's "sensationalist side": see J. W. Yolton, *John Locke and the Way of Ideas*, p. 195. Frank Thilly, in *A History of Philosophy* (p. 354), goes too far in placing Browne with Etienne de Condillac and Charles de Bonnet among Locke's followers who "explain all mental processes, reflection as well as the higher faculties, as transformed sensations": "Reflection and the powers of the understanding," adds Thilly, "are reduced [in Browne's view] to sensation." But the *Essay*

and *The Procedure* share sensationalistic as well as rational idioms. At the end of *The Procedure*, for example, Browne reinforces his view that even the mind,

> in all its noblest efforts and most lofty flights, must ever have a steady eye to the earth from whence it took its rise . . . for when once it . . . attempts a direct flight to the heavenly regions, then it falls headlong to the ground, where it lies grovelling in superstitions or infidelity. (*The Procedure*, p. 477)

Thus *The Procedure* concludes that the mind should be restrained by the senses, even in religious claims; compare this conclusion with *Essay* 2.1.24:

> All those sublime Thoughts, which towre above the Clouds, and reach as high as Heaven it self, take their Rise and Footing here: In all that great Extent wherein the mind wanders, in those remote Speculations, it may seem to be elevated with, it stirs not one jot beyond those Ideas, which Sense or Reflection, have offered for its Contemplation. (Nidditch, p. 118)

Far from being completely "grounded," however, the sense-tempered reason of Browne took a Locke-directed, indirect "flight to the heavenly regions."

13. See, for example, *Procedure* 1, *passim*, and *Procedure* 2, p. 250. The verse, for that matter, lies at least on the periphery of the sometimes theological philosophy of Locke; for insofar as Heb. 11:1 offers what Hindley (p. 207) calls "the same" account of faith as the one given in *Essay* 4.16 ("Of the Degrees of Assent"), Locke appears to have worked with the biblical definition. In any case, the following quotations (from 4.16.4, 5) especially capture the epistemological spirit consistent with, if not implicit in, that definition:

> For where is the Man, that has uncontestable Evidence of the Truth of all that he holds, or of the Falshood of all he condemns; or can say, that he has examined, to the bottom, all his own, or other Men's Opinions? The necessity of believing, without Knowledge, nay, often upon very slight grounds, in this fleeting state of Action and Blindness we are in, should make us more busy and careful to inform our selves, than constrain others.
>
> . . . .
>
> But to return to the grounds of Assent, and the several degrees of it, we are able to take notice, that the Propositions we receive upon Inducements of Probability, are of two sorts; either concerning some particular Existence, or, as it is usually termed, matter of fact, which falling under Observation, is capable of humane Testimony, or else concerning Things, which being beyond the discovery of our Senses, are not capable of any such Testimony. (Nidditch, pp. 660–61)

These passages, like Heb. 11:1, are concerned with a paradox: the unseen, though "upon very slight grounds," must often serve as "evidence" of truth, whether religious or philosophical. *Essay* 4.16 and Heb. 11:1 imply that faith, like belief, approaches the probable and hence the philosophically acceptable, or in other words that the assent to revelation is all but necessarily based on an analogy with sense perception.

14. See, for example, Winnett, *Peter Browne*, pp. 164–65. Browne's doctrine, moreover, along with Sir William Hamilton's "great principle" that "the Unconditioned is incognizable and inaccessible," formed the starting point of Dean H. L. Mansell's paradoxical view that man cannot know the nature of God but seeks, nevertheless, to understand Him in terms of human experience: see Mansell, *The Limits of Religious Thought examined in eight lectures preached before the Univ. of Oxford in the year 1858 on the foundation of the late Rev. J. Bampton*, p. 246.

Victor Harris and Earl R. Wasserman, though recognizing the importance of analogy in eighteenth-century English thought, give Browne's doctrine passing reference. Wasserman asserts that Browne added only "the subtleties of the Thomistic system" to Bishop William King's argument that "an analogical knowledge of incomprehensibles is sufficient for human existence": see "Nature Moralized: The Divine Analogy in the Eighteenth Century," especially pp. 54–55. And Harris, in "Allegory to Analogy in the Interpretation of Scriptures," especially p. 20, lumps Browne with Bishop Butler, observing that both of them used analogy (i.e., "not a figurative and mysterious [allegory] but a natural and intelligible correspondence between nature and spirit") to establish Christianity as "something more than a piece of allegorical fiction."

15. Wilbur Howell and John Wright go too far, perhaps, in implying that Locke's linguistic habit of mind is so "scientific" and so purely denotative as to preclude comparisons of any kind: see Wright, *Shelley's Myth of Metaphor*, pp. 14–27; and Howell, "John Locke and the New Rhetoric." See also Perry Miller, "Edwards, Locke, and the Rhetoric of Sensation," pp. 103–23; and Kenneth MacLean, *John Locke and English Literature of the Eighteenth Century*, pp. 63, 104, 110–11.

16. In distinguishing between Browne's doctrine and that of St. Thomas Aquinas, Anders Jeffner comes close to arguing that Browne's amounts to an inevitably proto-modern refinement of the medieval concept; whereas "in St. Thomas" much is predicated through "the assumption of the Neo-Platonist scale of being," in Browne's view there is no "assumption of a known relation between God and the world," and there is a "delimitation of what can be predicated of God." See Jeffner, *Butler and Hume on Religion: A Comparative Analysis*, p. 185. Don Cupitt observes that Browne's doctrine anticipates Karl Barth's rejection of Thomistic doctrine in favor of an *analogia fidei* resting on revelation. See Cupitt, *Christ and the Hiddenness of God*, pp. 78–79.

17. See, for example, Phillip Harth, *Swift and Anglican Rationalism: The Religious Background of A Tale of a Tub*, pp. 20, 30, 151–52, and Gerald R. Cragg, *From Puritanism to the Age of Reason*, pp. 69 ff. Robert South, when he preaches on the Spirit, sees the Spirit's operations as restricted primarily to New Testament times:

> . . . [S]ome will be apt to enquire, how long these extraordinary and miraculous Gifts continued in the Church. . . . [T]heir Duration was to be

proportioned to the need, which that new Religion had of such Creden-
tials, and Instruments of Confirmation. . . . [T]here is an Omnipotence required to maintain, as well as first to set up the Christian Church, yet it
does not therefore follow that this Omnipotence must still exert itself to
the same Degree, and after the same way, in one Case, that it does in the
Other.

See South, "The Christian Pentecost . . . Preach'd at Westminster-Abbey, 1692,"
3:410–50, especially 418–19. In the case of John Tillotson, such titles as "The
Distinguishing Character of a good and a bad Man," "The Example of Jesus in
doing Good," and "The Wisdom of Religion" are typical of his homiletical tone
and emphasis. See *The Works of the Most Reverend Dr. John Tillotson, Late Lord
Archbishop of Canterbury: Containing Two Hundred and Fifty Four Sermons and Discourses on Several Occasions* 1:294–318, 353–73; and 5:142–58.

18. See Warburton's attack on Wesley's position in *The Doctrine of Grace: or, the
Office and Operations of the Holy Spirit vindicated from the Insults of Infidelity and the
Abuses of Fanaticism.*

19. *Essay* 4.19.5; Nidditch, p. 699. See also MacLean's discussion of Locke's
view of revelation in *John Locke and English Literature of the Eighteenth Century,*
pp. 136–37, 140.

20. From *Paradise Lost,* for example, he kept the phrase "Can make a Heaven
of Hell," but commented that "this is fit rant for a stoic or a Devil." See John
Wesley, *An Extract from Milton's* Paradise Lost: *With Notes*; and Oscar Sherwin,
"Milton for the Masses: John Wesley's Edition of *Paradise Lost.*" The abridgments
signify the characteristic intensity of Wesley's reading but not always his reading
tastes. For a portrait of Wesley-the-reader's vivid decidedness, see T. Walter Herbert, *John Wesley as Editor and Author,* especially pp. 75–79.

21. The main new point of Book 3 is that Locke errs in forming an idea of God
by enlarging human qualities and faculties to infinity; see, for example, *The Procedure,* p. 452. It is consistent with Wesley's appeals to reason and with his heart-
religion to think that young Wesley omitted 3 in part because he was temperamen-
tally willing to follow Locke, and for that matter Browne in 2.7–9, in trusting
human qualities and faculties as a means of acquiring religious knowledge.

22. *Procedure* 3, "A Summary of the Natural Order and Whole Procedure of
the Intellect," repeats such Lockean concepts as the tabula rasa, sensation, and
compound and complex ideas. Perhaps Wesley omitted it not so much because he
disagreed with it, as because its argument is sufficiently well represented by his
version of *Procedure* 1.

23. *Essay* 4.19.4; Nidditch, p. 698. For Wesley's version of *Procedure* 2.7 ("Of
the farther Improvement of Knowledge by Relations revealed"—pp. 290–301)
see the manuscript, pp. 71–77; for his version of 2.8 ("Of Revealed Relations entirely new"—pp. 302–29) see pp. 78–87; and for 2.9 ("Of the Improvement of
Morality by Revelation"—pp. 330–52) see pp. 88–103. Wesley omitted 2.10
("Of Spirit, Soul, and Body"—pp. 353–81).

24. See pp. 71–72 and 90–91 of the manuscript.

25. See the manuscript, pp. 23–25, 28–30; *Procedure* 1.6 ("A Third Property that [Ideas] are Immediate"—pp. 103–7); and 1.9 ("The Difference between Divine Metaphor, and Divine Analogy"—pp. 132–46).

26. Wesley's version of 2.6 ("Of the Different Kinds of Knowledge and Evidence"—pp. 214–89) occupies pp. 37–71 of the manuscript. (Pp. 30–37 of the manuscript are allotted to *Procedure* 1.1–5, in which Browne simply appropriates such Lockean concepts as judgment, abstraction, and relation: Wesley's pages correlate with pp. 147, 150, 175, 179, 180, 182, 184, 195, 196, 200, 202, 204, 205, and 210 of *The Procedure*.) For Locke's definition see: *Essay* 4.19.4; Nidditch, p. 698.

27. See, for example, chapter 2 ("Of Sense, and the Ideas of Sensation"—pp. 55–72), chapter 4 ("The Several Properties of Ideas of Sensation"—pp. 87–98), chapter 5 ("A Second Property of Ideas of Sensation, that they are Simple"—pp. 99–102), chapter 6 ("A Third Property that they are Immediate"—pp. 103–7), chapter 7 ("That they are Direct"—pp. 108–18), and chapter 8 ("A Fifth Property, that they are Clear and Distinct"—pp. 119–31). Compare these chapters with the following sections of the *Essay*: 2.2. ("Of Simple Ideas"), .3 ("Of Simple Ideas of Sensation"), .5 ("Of Simple Ideas of Divers Senses"), .6 ("Of Simple Ideas of Reflection"), .7 ("Of Simple Ideas of Sensation and Reflection"), .29 ("Of Clear and Obscure, Distinct and Confused Ideas"); and 4.17 ("Of Reason").

In only two sections of *Procedure* 1 do Browne's topics fail to reflect explicit headings of the *Essay*: chapter 3 ("Of our Idea of Spirit, and of God in particular"—pp. 73–86) and chapter 9 ("The Difference between Divine Metaphor, and Divine Analogy"—pp. 132–46). And the latter reflects a Lockean topic; see the discussion above.

28. See pp. 11–30 of the manuscript; in sections varying from one to three pages, Wesley represents each of the nine chapters of *Procedure* 1. Wesley allots his first pages to Browne's "Introduction to the Whole Design": *The Procedure*, pp. 1–48.

29. See the abridgment's versions (pp. 46, 49–50, 52–53, 55, 69) of *The Procedure* (pp. 247, 249, 253, 258–60, 263, 287). See also *The Procedure*, pp. 248, 257, 282, 285. For Wesley's thirteen lines see the manuscript, p. 49.

The following passage, closely resembling the one from 2.6, is typical of what does appear in the manuscript:

> If it is here objected, that I place the distinguishing Character of Evangelical Faith in the Act of the Will, Subsequent to that Assent of the Intellect which is properly Knowledge; and not in the Assent of the Mind to Things Incomprehensible, which seems to be the very thing that makes it Properly Faith. I answer, that the Assent of the Mind to the Reality and Existence of Things Incomprehensible, is not to be Excluded from the Nature of Evangelical Faith, for it must Mediately and Ultimately refer to what is Incomprehensible. But then this is of an after and Secondary Consideration; and the true Nature of a Religious Faith is to be clearly stated

and resolved in respect of what is Directly and Immediately understood and comprehended, before any thing which is neither understood nor comprehended can come into the Account, or be esteemed a necessary Ingredient of it either in Natural or Reveal'd Religion. (*The Procedure*, p. 258; cf. the manuscript, p. 52.)

30. Carl F. H. Henry, "The Concerns and Considerations of Carl F. H. Henry," p. 21.

31. *Essay* 4.16.10; Nidditch, p. 664. Locke is careful, of course, to set up criteria for testimony:

In the Testimony of others, is to be considered, 1. The Number. 2. The Integrity. 3. The Skill of the Witnesses. 4. The Design of the Author, where it is a Testimony out of a Book cited. 5. The Consistency of the Parts, and Circumstances of the Relation. 6. Contrary Testimonies. (*Essay* 4.16.4; Nidditch, p. 656)

32. See the entries in the *Oxford English Dictionary*. The one for *proposition*, for example, includes the following illustration: "1866 *Liturgy Ch. Sarum 67 note*, A proposition of Christ under the sacramental veils, to receive the adoration of the faithful." For the "loaves of proposition" see Exod. 25:30.

33. See Henry Edward Manning, *The Temporal Mission of the Holy Ghost; or, Reason and Revelation*, pp. i, 13. The *Oxford English Dictionary*, under *evangelical* (1.b), includes the following illustration: "1730 Berkeley *Serm*. Wks. 1871 IV 641 Not lip-worship nor will-worship, but inward and evangelical."

34. The *Oxford English Dictionary*, however, stresses a narrow meaning of evangelical: by 1791, it had come to signify "those Protestants who hold that the essence of the Gospel consists in the doctrine of salvation by faith in the atoning death of Christ, and deny the saving efficacy of either good works or the sacraments." This definition does not fit Wesley. It fits, pretty well, Whitefield, the Evangelical party of Anglican priests, and the rigid Calvinists in Dutch Reformed, Presbyterian, and Baptist congregations.

35. This quotation from Matthew Arnold's *Culture and Anarchy* is cited in the *Oxford English Dictionary*'s definition of *evangelical*. See also Matthew Arnold, *Literature and Dogma: An Essay Towards a Better Apprehension of the Bible*, in *The Works of Matthew Arnold* 7:345–46, 348.

36. See, for example, Jackson, 6:46; 7:231, 326; 8:276; 9:496; 12:58, 62. Note, in particular, the rational and sensationalistic "epistemology" implicit in the following hymn, in which Charles Wesley alludes to Heb. 11:1:

> The things unknown to feeble sense,
>   Unseen by reason's glimmering ray,
> With strong commanding evidence
>   Their heavenly origin display.

> Faith lends its realizing light,
>   The clouds disperse, the shadows fly;
> The Invisible appears in sight,
>   And God is seen by mortal eye. (Jackson, 8:352)

37. Browne, in what can be called a philosophy of traditional revelation, suggests that the Bible anticipates a Lockean natural religion. In *Procedure* 2.7–9, for example, both nature and the Bible point to monotheism: "Both reason and revelation," writes Browne, "shew us there can be but one God," and therefore "we can own and worship but one" (p. 313). By arguing, moreover, that God "created all things by the Word," made man "of the earth," assured "the union of matter and spirit" in man's "living soul," and continues as upholder of all things "through his providence" (pp. 292–93), Browne suggests that details of traditional revelation do not strain rational inference and, indeed, accord with the religion of any theist.

38. See Isaac Watts, "On Mr. Lock's Annotations upon several Parts of the New Testament, left behind him at his death," pp. 205–7. Watts accuses Locke of a cold response to revealed truth.

39. Locke's view of analogy gained additional support from "Pope and Bolingbroke of the left, and Addison and Thompson representing the center"; see MacLean, *John Locke and English Literature of the Eighteenth Century*, pp. 142–43.

40. I thank Alan Grob for corresponding with me about this point.

Two. Wesley's Philosophical Theology

1. Hindley speculates that this doctrine, first enunciated during the 1740s, arose from the conversion. The doctrine, he adds, constitutes "a brave first attempt to plot a course through the problems raised (and the solutions offered) by a consideration of religious experience in the no-man's-land of philosophical theology": J. Clifford Hindley, "The Philosophy of Enthusiasm," p. 209.

2. See J. H. Van den Berg, *The Changing Nature of Man: Introduction to a Historical Psychology*, especially p. 229.

3. Friedrich Schleiermacher, *The Christian Faith*, p. 8.

4. See Jackson, 12:56n. These letters were recognized as important and published by Henry Moore in his nineteenth-century biography of Wesley: *The Life of the Rev. John Wesley* 2:95, 475 ff.

5. Consider, for example, a work reprinted often: Philip Doddridge, *The Rise and Progress of Religion in the Soul*. Doddridge's partly Lockean theory of religious education was embodied in his school at Harborough, and both his school and his theory influenced Wesley's partly Lockean experiment at the Kingswood School. See, for example, Luke Tyerman, *The Life and Times of the Rev. John Wesley* 1:490.

6. Telford, 2:60n. Translated by Thomas Jackson; Wesley quoted the Latin.

7. John Wesley, *Primitive Physick: or, an Easy and Natural Method of Curing Most Diseases*, p. vii. Subsequent references to this edition appear in the text. For a discussion of *Primitive Physick*, which foreshadowed the empirical emphasis of

nineteenth-century medicine, see G. S. Rousseau, "John Wesley's *Primitive Phys- ick* (1747)."

8. Lewis Thomas, *The Lives of a Cell: Notes of a Biology Watcher*, p. 35.

9. Ephraim Chambers, *Cyclopedia*, s.v. "Diffusion," as quoted in Earl Wasser- man, *The Subtler Language: Critical Readings of Neoclassic and Romantic Poems*, p. 330n.

10. Compare Charles de Bonnet's *Contemplation de la Nature* and Wesley's abridgment of it in the *Survey*; see a widely available edition (Philadelphia: Jonathan Pounder, 1816), 2:187–345. Subsequent references to this edition appear in the text.

T. H. Huxley, of course, is responsible for the dogma that religion and scien- tific empiricism do not mix, but, whereas Huxley finds in de Bonnet a precursor for this split, Wesley clearly finds de Bonnet's decidedly proto-evolutionary biology so far from being a threat to faith as to be an aid thereto. See, for exam- ple, the discussion of Huxley and de Bonnet in George Eayrs, *John Wesley: Chris- tian Philosopher and Church Founder*. See also, in *Protestant Thought Before Kant*, A. C. McGiffert's intriguing suggestion that the scientific attitudes of modern re- ligious ideas should be traced to such thought; Wesley should be seen as a fore- runner of such religious empiricism.

11. Jackson, 13:490–91. For a discussion of the not always sympathetic re- sponse to Newtonian physics, see Herbert Leventhal, *In the Shadow of the Enlighten- ment: Occultism and Renaissance Science in Eighteenth-Century America*, pp. 177–99.

12. See, for example, the discussion in Earl Shorris's review of Hannah Arendt's *Life of the Mind*.

13. The 1777 abridgment differs from the manuscript in omitting one of *The Procedure*'s substantial chapters, namely, "Of the Improvement of Morality by Revelation," and its two shortest sections: "Introduction to the Whole Design" and "Introduction to this Treatise." See *The Procedure*, pp. 1–54, 302–52; the manuscript, pp. 1–12, 84–103; and the *Survey* 2:438–62.

The abridgment appears in the *Survey*'s third edition (London: Fry, 1777), copies of which are (for example) at Yale University, Emory University, Garrett Theological Seminary, and Southern Methodist University, as well as the Bod- leian and the John Rylands University Library of Manchester.

14. See Appendix C.

15. It is pertinent, here, to recall Wesley's admiration of Isaac Watts's *Logick; or, The right use of reason in the enquiry after truth*, an updating of Aristotle's logic; Ar- istotle's balance between reason and evidence is reflected in Watts's combination of a modestly inductive approach to "Affairs of Science and Human Life" and a modestly idealistic approach to the "Powers and Operations" of the intellect. See the discussion in Kenneth MacLean, *John Locke and English Literature of the Eigh- teenth Century*, p. 15.

16. See Jean-Paul Sartre, *L'Être et le néant: Essai d'ontologie phénoménologique*, p. 66; and the translation and discussion in Thomas McFarland, *Romanticism and the Forms of Ruin: Wordsworth, Coleridge, and Modalities of Fragmentation*, p. 131.

17. See Frank Wilbur Collier, *John Wesley among the Scientists*; Alfred Wesley Hill, *John Wesley among the Physicians: A Study of Eighteenth-Century Medicine*; Robert E. Schofield, "John Wesley and Science in 18th Century England"; William W. Sweet, "John Wesley and Scientific Discovery"; K. Stoolz, "John Wesley and Evolution: Reply to W. W. Sweet"; W. J. Turrell, *John Wesley, Physician and Electrotherapist*; and Alfred A. Weinstein, "John Wesley, Physician and Apothecary."

18. For Wesley's praise of Addison, see Jackson, 14:469; for Wesley's simultaneously philosophic and experiential phraseology, see Curnock, 3:284; for his admiration of travel literature, see Telford, 4:325; and for a discussion of these points, and of Wesley's thorough use of Proverbs and Ecclesiastes, see George Lawton, *John Wesley's English: A Study of His Literary Style*, especially pp. 103, 143, 192, 291.

19. See the discussion in MacLean, *John Locke and English Literature of the Eighteenth Century*, p. 139.

20. As quoted in Robert Southey, *The Life of Wesley; and the Rise and Progress of Methodism* 2:74. Subsequent references to Southey's *Life* (first published in 1819) are to this edition (i.e., the 2d).

21. The latter group was moderate in that it disagreed with Locke on the nature of animals: Johnson, Watts, Young, and Addison held that animals perform by instinct, not by reasoning and understanding. By Henry Fielding's time, Lockeans who were radical on this issue were popularly known as "brutes." See Fielding's *Covent-Garden Journal*, No. 4., as discussed in MacLean, *John Locke and English Literature of the Eighteenth Century*, pp. 69–73.

22. Watts goes on:

> . . . but that antecedently to all the Effects of Custom, Experience, Education, or any other contingent Causes, as the Mind is necessarily ordained and limited by its Creator to have such and such appointed Sensations or Ideas raised in it by certain external Motions of the Matter or Body to which it is united, and that while the Organs are good and sound it cannot have others, so 'tis also inclined and almost determined by such Principles as are wrought into it by the Creator, to believe some Propositions true, others false; and perhaps also some Actions good, others evil.

See Isaac Watts, *Philosophical Essays*, Essay 4, sec. 3, as quoted in MacLean, *John Locke and English Literature of the Eighteenth Century*, p. 23.

23. Sir Leslie Stephen, *History of English Thought in the Eighteenth Century* 1:161; 2:419–20, 454.

24. See, for example, the discussion of Berkeley in MacLean, *John Locke and English Literature of the Eighteenth Century*, p. 140. See also Swift's reverent acceptance of the mysteries of nature along with those of religion and his argument that the senses do not take one beyond color, size, and shape, in Swift, *A Tale of a Tub* (edited by Temple Scott, 1:120), and Swift, "On the Trinity" (*Prose Works*, edited by Temple Scott, 4:133, 137) as cited and discussed in MacLean, *John Locke*

and English Literature of the Eighteenth Century, p. 137. And finally, compare Laurence Sterne, *Tristram Shandy*, Bk. 4, ch. 17:

> We live amongst riddles and mysteries—the most obvious things, which come in our way, have dark sides, which the quickest sight cannot penetrate into; and even the clearest and most exalted understandings amongst us find ourselves puzzled and at a loss in almost every cranny of nature's works

with *Essay* 4.12.10:

> Experiments and historical observations we may have, from which we may draw advantage of ease and health, and thereby increase our stock of conveniences for this life; but beyond this I fear our talents reach not, nor are our faculties, as I guess, able to advance

as cited and discussed in MacLean, pp. 137–38.

25. "What is the barrier between man and brutes," asks Wesley, "—the line which they cannot pass? It is not reason. . . . But it is this: man is capable of God; the inferior creatures are not." Herein Wesley concurs with "Milton, Locke, Young"; see MacLean's discussion (pp. 80–81) of Southey, *The Life of Wesley*, 2:74. Wesley's view of nature as both organic and divine is cited in Lawton, *John Wesley's English*, p. 24.

26. Wesley, of course, was on one occasion capable of an almost a priori reason with regard to the Bible; he equated "reasoning with flesh and blood" with "doubt" or "evil reasoning," and distinguished between such reasoning and the "Pure" reason "rooted in Divine Revelation" (Telford, 4:248). But Lockean reason figured in his "wish to be in every point, great and small, a scriptural, rational Christian" (Telford, 8:112); for Wesley's discussion of scripture as "the best means of rational conviction," see Jackson, 7:255.

27. See Telford, 3:332. These remarks, addressed to Law himself in January 1756, at a time of Wesley's philosophically theological development when his philosophically theological taste in reading became a common emphasis in his journal. In 1758, for example, he deplored therein what he regarded as insufficient scriptural documentation in the otherwise "ingenious" and "sensible" interdisciplinary inquiries of John Hutchinson in *Moses's Principia* and Robert Spearman in *An Enquiry after Philosophy and Theology*. See Curnock, 4:261; 5:353.

28. Other instances are "*Wisdom*" and "*Glory*"; Locke goes on to say that these "Words . . . are frequent enough in every Man's Mouth; but if a great many of those who use them, should be asked what they mean by them, they would be at a Stand, and not know what to answer. . . ." In the fourth number of *Covent-Garden Journal*, Fielding discusses this passage from *Essay* 3; see MacLean, *John Locke and English Literature of the Eighteenth Century*, p. 113.

29. See James Boswell, *Life of Johnson*, 1:293.

30. Wesley elsewhere keeps something of the same idea; he boasts that he "squared his life by reason and grace" (Telford, 7:228). Here, though, in the trigonometrical figure an almost Cartesian concept of reason lends interiority to grace.

31. See, for example, the discussion in Lawton, *John Wesley's English*, pp. 16, 209. The English moralists succeeding Locke, e.g., Lord Shaftesbury, Francis Hutcheson, David Hume, Adam Ferguson, and Adam Smith, "subscribed to the immediacy and quasi-sensuous character of moral knowledge" (Frank Thilly, *A History of Philosophy*, pp. 355–56); but this "moral sense," though sensationalistically Lockean like the "spiritual sense" of Wesley, is primarily intuitional and does not include in its experiential dimension any quasi-sensuous encounter with the Spirit. Wesley's "spiritual sense," then, is indeed a distinctive development of Lockean method.

32. Ernest Lee Tuveson, *The Imagination as a Means of Grace: Locke and the Aesthetics of Romanticism*, p. 2.

33. *Essay* 2.7.5, as quoted in MacLean, *John Locke and English Literature of the Eighteenth Century*, p. 82. MacLean (pp. 169–70) stresses Watts's subscription to Locke's view that perfect knowledge is something that "the spirits of just men made perfect" shall have (*Essay* 4.17.14; cf. Heb. 12:23). In *Essay* 4.14.2, Locke observes that it is "highly rational to think, even were revelation silent in the case, that, as men employ those talents God has given them here, they shall accordingly receive their rewards at the close of the day, when their sun shall set, and night shall put an end to their labours." See the discussion in MacLean, p. 151. See MacLean (p. 27) for a discussion of Berkeley's Locke-derived notion that virtue is not natural to man.

34. MacLean's summary (p. 91) of *Essay* 2.14.3, 4.

35. See Ronald A. Knox, *Enthusiasm: A Chapter in the History of Religion, with Special Reference to the Seventeenth and Eighteenth Centuries*, pp. 256 ff., 537.

36. Thilly, *A History of Philosophy*, p. 449. "With Hamann and Herder," adds Thilly, "Jacobi broadens the scope of experience to include the vision of realities which the critical philosophy had placed beyond the reach of human understanding."

37. Richard Green, in *The Works of John and Charles Wesley: A Bibliography*, p. 192, quotes the part of the headnote in which Wesley identifies the abridgment as "an Appendix on the Human Understanding written chiefly on the plan of Dr. Brown, late Bishop of Cork."

38. See J. A. Faulkner, "Wesley the Mystic."

39. Henry Bett, in *The Spirit of Methodism*, pp. 144 ff., points out that such a work as Wesley's letter to Middleton anticipates Schleiermacher's doctrine of a special "Religious Sense" whereby spiritual experience is possible for early modern man. George Eayrs, it is true, in *John Wesley: Christian Philosopher and Church Founder* (pp. 181–82) points out some important differences between the two men. For example, Wesley holds that "divine revelation culminated in Jesus Christ," whereas Schleiermacher

seems sometimes to make Christian experience the judge of Jesus Christ, as thus: "Who is Jesus Christ? The revealer of God, the Saviour. Why? Christian consciousness declares it. How does Christ reveal God and save men? Christian consciousness has no answer, and it is unnecessary to raise these questions."

Eayrs points out, moreover, that "Schleiermacher gave little or no recognition to the Person and work of the Holy Spirit, God in action," whereas "Wesley's contribution was notable for the treatment of this Christian truth," and one may add that Wesley could hardly have agreed with Schleiermacher that, as Eayrs puts it, "the religious feeling is *a priori*." Finally, however, Eayrs (like Bett) sees similarities. Eayrs points out, for example, that the following attributes of Schleiermacher are those of Wesley as well:

> . . . [R]eligion is not the acceptance of a dogmatic faith, nor the practice of religious observances, but a vital experience of God. It is direct contact with God in one's emotional and moral nature, which is deeper than thought. . . . Schleiermacher held that the common element in all the varied expressions of piety which distinguishes religion from all other feelings—that is to say, the essence of religion—is this: that we are conscious of ourselves as absolutely dependent, or, in other words, in relation to God. . . . The religious experience of the individual must be developed and tested in a Christian community.

See Eayrs, *John Wesley: Christian Philosopher and Church Founder*, pp. 182–83; Eayrs goes so far as to say that "the philosophy and theology of Wesley may be said to have gained a central place in later thought through the influence" of Schleiermacher (p. 181). See also the valuable, albeit scattered, suggestions in Martin Schmidt, *John Wesley: A Theological Biography* 1:57, 142; 2 (pt. 1): 34, 172; 2 (pt. 2): 33, 215, 223, 288.

40. As quoted in McFarland, *Romanticism and the Forms of Ruin*, p. 45.

Three. Wesley's Intellectual Influence

1. W. E. H. Lecky, *A History of England in the Eighteenth Century* 2:521.

2. See James L. Golden, "John Wesley on Rhetoric and Belles Lettres," p. 250.

3. Augustine Birrell, *The Collected Essays & Addresses of the Rt. Hon. Augustine Birrell, 1880–1920* 1:324–25.

4. *The Gentleman's Magazine* 69 (March 1791): 283.

5. See V. H. H. Green, *The Young Mr. Wesley: A Study of John Wesley and Oxford*, pp. 218–25.

6. The letter is quoted in the Right Honourable Lady Llanover, ed., *The Autobiography and Correspondence of Mary Granville, Mrs. Delany: with interesting reminiscences of King George the Third and Queen Charlotte* 1:269.

7. Maldwyn Lloyd Edwards, *My Dear Sister: The Story of John Wesley and the Women in His Life*, p. 22.

8. Green, *The Young Mr. Wesley*, pp. 106, 120, 204–25, 231, 266, 279, 292–94, especially 206.

9. She moved there after sojourning in Ireland from September 1731, to April 1733. In the summer of 1731, Wesley asked her whether he was "too strict, with carrying things too far in religion?" (Telford, 1:92). In July of 1734, apparently feeling unworthy of Wesley, but clearly signaling her loss of interest in him, she wrote: "I am so sincerely sorry for the ill impression I have given you of myself that I shall shun you as a criminal would a judge" (Telford, 1:164). He got the point: "I sincerely thank you for what is past" (Telford, 1:165). On June 9, 1743, she married Dr. Patrick Delany, Dean of Down, and after his death in 1768 became the friend of the King and Queen; Edmund Burke described her as "the fairest model of female excellence of the days that were passed": see "Delany, Mary," in the *Dictionary of National Biography*. As Mrs. Delany, in 1783, Mary reminisced about the Wesleys distantly indeed:

> These brothers joined some other young men at Oxford, and used to meet of a Sunday evening and read the Scriptures, and find out objects of charity to relieve. This was a *happy beginning*, but the vanity of being singular and growing *enthusiasts* made them endeavour to gain proselytes and adopt that system of religious doctrine which many reasonable people thought pernicious.

See Lady Llanover, ed., *The Autobiography and Correspondence of Mary Granville, Mrs. Delany* 6:175.

As Mary Pendarves she must have detected Wesley's touching awkwardness as early as August 1730, when, after he had given her about all he had to give, i.e., a sermon manuscript, she called him affectionately but with rather pointed wit "Primitive Christianity" (Telford, 1:50). Her thank you for the abridgment (written in February 1731) vaguely pleads a lack of time as the reason for both her lateness and her hurry: "I should sooner have endeavoured" to write, said she, "if I could have found the time. . . . I have not time now to enlarge my letter" (Telford, 1:77). And there is even a note of irony: "How happy we should have been to have heard it read by one who so well knows to recommend everything he approves of!"

10. See, for example, Luke Tyerman, *The Life and Times of John Wesley* 1:37–39, 146–49, 169; 2: 45–56, 111–15. The awkward business with Sophia Hopkey, the disastrous relationship with Molly Vazeille, and the promising but ill-fated friendship with Grace Murray are all more or less precisely anticipated by certain features of his friendship for Mary Pendarves.

11. See Green, *The Young Mr. Wesley*, p. 191.

12. See John Wynne, D.D., *An Abridgment of Mr. Locke's Essay concerning Human Understanding*. Wynne omits Book 1 because its denial of innate ideas is sufficiently evident from what he includes: see his rationale in "The Dedication." But the abridgment includes most of the *Essay's* introduction, and represents (1) all chapters of *Essay* 2 (see Wynne, pp. 1–8, 9–145), (2) the first eleven chapters of

Essay 3 (see Wynne, pp. 146–210), and (3) the first twenty-one chapters of Book 4 (see Wynne, pp. 211–371).

13. For Wesley and the Oxford Movement, see, for example, my *Wordsworth's "Natural Methodism,"* pp. 4, 5, 10, 174–75. For Wesley's influence on Claphamites (William Wilberforce, Thomas Clarkson, Granville Sharp, Zachary Macaulay, James Steven, Henry Thornton, John Shore, and Charles Grant), see Ernest Marshall Howse, *Saints in Politics: The Clapham Sect and the Growth of Freedom,* especially pp. 10, 30 ff., 69, 95, 102, 105.

14. See *Essay* 4.3.6 and the discussion in Kenneth MacLean, *John Locke and English Literature of the Eighteenth Century,* p. 124. It is "not much more remote from our Comprehension to conceive," writes Locke (among similar things), "that GOD can, if he pleases, superadd to Matter a Faculty of Thinking, than that he should superadd to it another Substance, with a Faculty of Thinking"; see Nidditch, p. 541. Locke meant, of course, that *gray* matter thinks, but (as MacLean points out) he was taken to mean that even *rocks* think.

15. François Marie Arouet de Voltaire, *Letters concerning the English Nation,* pp. 100–104.

16. See R. W. Chapman's edition of Johnson's *Rasselas,* pp. 214–18, as cited and discussed in MacLean, *John Locke and English Literature of the Eighteenth Century,* pp. 126–28.

17. See Isaac Watts, *Philosophical Essays,* Essay 5, sec. 3, and the discussion in MacLean, *John Locke and English Literature of the Eighteenth Century,* p. 50.

18. See Vincent Perronet, *Some Enquiries, A Vindication of Mr. Locke,* and *A Second Vindication of Mr. Locke,* and MacLean's paraphrase of *Essay* 2.27.16 (*John Locke and English Literature of the Eighteenth Century,* p. 100). Butler, despite his general fear that Locke leads to materialism, is glad to find in Locke's doctrine of identity an argument for immortality: see *Analogy* 1.1.15 and the discussion in MacLean, pp. 101–2. For a recent, wide-ranging discussion of Locke's doctrine and its influence, see Christopher Fox, "Locke and the Scriblerians: The Discussion of Identity in Early Eighteenth Century England"; Fox (p. 12) mentions but does not elaborate upon Perronet.

19. John Wesley, *A Plain Account of the People Called Methodists,* p. 4.

20. See William Hunt's article on Perronet in the *Dictionary of National Biography.* As soon as Henry Piers, vicar of Bexley, introduced Perronet to Wesley on August 14, 1744, Wesley expected "to have cause of blessing God for ever for the acquaintance begun this day" (Curnock, 3:145). Such cause he had indeed: Perronet bravely defended Charles during an anti-Methodist riot at Shoreham; Perronet regularly invited John to preach there, in both Church and rectory; Perronet faithfully advised the brothers on their marriages and occasional disagreements; and Perronet frequently attended Methodist Conferences. Moreover, he effectively encouraged his own family to assume revival leadership: sons Edward and Charles became itinerants; daughter Damaris founded Shoreham's Society; and William Briggs, son-in-law, was Wesley's secretary and book steward. See, besides the *Dictionary of National Biography,* Curnock, 3:303n; 5:249, 348–49.

21. To wit: Vincent Perronet, *Some Remarks on a late Anonymous Piece, Intitled,*

The Enthusiasm of Methodists and Papists, compared. In a Letter to the Author; An Earnest Exhortation to the Strict Practice of Christianity. Drawn up chiefly For the Use of the Inhabitants of the Parish of Shoreham in Kent; and *Some Strictures on a Few Places of the late Reverend Mr. Hervey's Letters to the Reverend Mr. John Wesley. By a Clergyman.* In 1749 and 1752, Perronet published second and third letters to the "anonymous author," i.e., Bishop Lavington.

22. His argument, published in *The Wesley Banner*, 1:125, was constructed in the days following August 7, 1770, when the issue came to a head in the 27th Conference; see Curnock, 5:381n.

23. Hunt concludes, rather obviously, that Perronet's "religious character" and "great piety" were the bases of Wesley's admiration for him. Telford, without elaborating the point, does acknowledge that Perronet "was a scholar as well as a saint" (Telford, 2:292).

24. Wesley, *A Plain Account of the People called Methodists*, p. 4.

25. For Wesley's admiration of Watts, see, for example, Curnock, 1:66, and my *Wordsworth's "Natural Methodism,"* pp. 5, 67–68, 70–71, 88–89, 173. A shared admiration of Locke is explicit between Perronet and Watts. Watts, for his part, wrote to Perronet on February 26, 1742, to pay

> Honour to the Papers which you had wrote in Defence of Mr Locke. . . . I . . . pay superior respect to . . . the memory of Mr. Locke, so that I trust nothing shall ever induce me . . . to injure the reputation of that great man.

See Vincent Perronet, "Memoirs of the Rev. Vincent Perronet, A.M.," p. 54. Perronet, for his part, was delighted to receive both this letter and, as a gift from Watts, a copy of *Philosophical Essays.* On the flyleaf of this copy, which I have seen in the British Library, Perronet writes that

> Dr *Watts* was a very pious and learn'd Man. He had some peculiar Notions to himself in relation to certain points of Philosophy.
> Some of his Objections to the great Mr *Locke* I took notice of in my *Second Vindication* of that Philosopher.
> Dr Watts upon this occasion, sent me this Piece, with a most obliging Letter: in which, he excuses himself from replying on account of his great Infirmities.

The copy is the third edition (London: James Blackstone, 1742).

26. Remarks of the editor in Perronet, "Memoirs of the Rev. Vincent Perronet, A.M.," p. 57.

27. See Telford, 3:206.

28. For Wesley's thirty-year span of favorable references to *The Procedure*, see Telford, 13:163n, 368n; 5:270; 6:113; and Jackson, 9:506–7; 12:293, 296; 13:463.

29. Here is the Journal entry for Sunday, January 6, 1788:

Prayed, read; 8 the preachers; 9:30 prayers, 2 Kings xxiii.3, communion; 1 dinner; 2 prayed, tea; 3 the Covenant, read narrative; 8 supper, within, prayer; 9:30. (Curnock, 7:351)

30. See Telford, 1:77.

31. See Telford, 1:165.

32. See Appendix D.

33. Jackson, 13:458. Cf. *Essay* 2.23.8 (Nidditch, pp. 332–34). Wesley's last sentence suggests that he meant to keep his distance from the Cartesian doctrine of innate ideas, but his elevation of consciousness above moment-by-moment awareness amounts to a Descartes-related and hence proto-phenomenological insight. Foucault, it is true, distinguishes between "the modern *cogito*" of Heidegger's existentialist brand of phenomenology, i.e., "the constantly renewed interrogation as to how thought can reside elsewhere than here, and yet so very close to itself," and the Cartesian *cogito*'s concern "to reveal thought as the general form of all . . . thoughts"; see Michel Foucault, *Les Mots et Les Choses*, trans., *The Order of Things: An Archaeology of Human Sciences*, p. 324. But Poulet, though "not a throwback to seventeenth-century France and its intellectual climate," reveals, among other things, "obvious Cartesian affinities" that may also be found in Husserl's transcendental form of modern phenomenology; on November 25, 1961, Poulet wrote to J. Hillis Miller:

I should readily consider that the most important form of subjectivity is not that of the mind overwhelmed, filled, and so to speak stuffed with its objects, but that there is another [kind of consciousness] which sometimes reveals itself on this side of, at a distance from, and protected from, any object, a subjectivity which exists in itself, withdrawn from any power which might determine it from the outside, and possessing itself by a direct intuition. . . . As you have seen, in this I remain faithful to the Cartesian tradition.

See the discussion in Frank Lentricchia, *After the New Criticism*, pp. 65–66.

34. John Wesley, "Extracts from Mr. Locke," *The Arminian Magazine* 7 (January 1784): 32.

35. T. Walter Herbert, *John Wesley as Editor and Author*, p. 42.

36. See the discussion in H. F. Mathews, *Methodism and the Education of the People, 1791–1851*, p. 85.

37. James Lackington, *The Confessions of J. Lackington, late bookseller, at the Temple of the Muses*, pp. 182–83.

38. See J. H. Whiteley, *Wesley's England: A Survey of Eighteenth Century Social and Cultural Conditions*, p. 320.

39. James Boswell, *Boswell: Life of Johnson*, ed. R. W. Chapman, corrected by J. D. Fleeman, p. 327.

40. Edwards, *My Dear Sister*, pp. 91, 93.

41. Ibid., pp. 80–81, 92, 117.

42. See Nathaniel Brown, *Sexuality and Feminism in Shelley.*

43. See Perronet's "Memoirs," pp. 56 ff.; and Telford, 5:216; 7:278.

44. See, besides Grace Elizabeth Harrison's *Son to Susanna: The Private Life of John Wesley,* J. H. Rigg's *The Living Wesley, as he was in his youth and in his prime,* and John Telford's *The Life of John Wesley,* pp. 236–44. V. H. H. Green, discussing the Cotswold circle, speculates about Wesley's romantic feelings for Sally Kirkham; see *The Young Mr. Wesley,* pp. 204–5, 231, 266, 279, 292n, 293–94.

45. See Green, *The Young Mr. Wesley,* p. 138.

46. "Scribbling women" is a characteristic phrase of the Rev. Richard Polwhele in *The Unsex'd Females: A Poem.*

47. Edwards, in *My Dear Sister* (p. 84) makes a similar suggestion.

48. Herbert, *John Wesley as Editor and Author,* pp. 17–18.

49. See W. L. Doughty, *John Wesley, Preacher.*

50. George Lawton, *John Wesley's English: A Study of His Literary Style,* pp. 246–47.

51. *The Proceedings of the Wesley Historical Society* 2:138, as quoted in Lawton, *John Wesley's English,* p. 249.

52. R. Wilberforce Allen, *Methodism and Modern World Problems,* with an introduction by Sir Josiah Stamp, p. 82.

53. See Leslie Shepard, *The History of Street Literature,* p. 48.

54. See the discussion in Mathews, *Methodism and the Education of the People,* p. 176.

55. See G. S. Rousseau, "John Wesley's *Primitive Physick* (1747)."

56. Oliver Goldsmith, *A History of the Earth, and Animated Nature.* "I had not read over the first volume of this," writes Wesley,

> when I almost repented of having wrote anything on the head. It seemed to me, that had he published this but a few years sooner, my design would have been quite superseded, since the subject had fallen into the hands of one who had both greater abilities and more leisure for the work. (Jackson, 14:302)

57. See Mathews, *Methodism and the Education of the People,* p. 171. The *Arminian Magazine,* under its various names, boasts "the longest record of continuous publication of all the religious journals in the world"; see Herbert, *John Wesley as Editor and Author,* p. 34.

58. Mathews, *Methodism and the Education of the People,* pp. 178–79.

59. James Lackington, *Memoirs of the first forty-five years of the life of James Lackington,* p. 227.

60. See Victor E. Neuberg, *Popular Literature: A History and Guide,* especially pp. 259 ff.

61. See Thomas Bray, *Bibliotheca Parochialis; or a Scheme of such Theological and Other Heads, as seem requisite to be perus'd, or Occasionally consulted, by the Reverend Clergy;* and the article on Bray in the *Dictionary of National Biography.* Neuberg

(*Popular Literature*, p. 252) finds "puzzling" what he calls Wesley's "neglect of the tract," but Wesley's goal was nothing less than for substantial works, too, to be best-sellers. For studies of pre-Wesleyan literacy in England, see, for example, Mary Gwladys Jones, *The Charity School Movement: A Study of Eighteenth-Century Puritanism in Action*; Dudley W. Bahlman, *The Moral Revolution of 1688*; and David Cressy, *Literacy and the Social Order: Reading and Writing in Tudor and Stuart England*.

62. Herbert, *John Wesley as Editor and Author*, pp. 40, 45.

63. Green, *The Young Mr. Wesley*, pp. 11–12.

64. Douglas J. Elwood, *The Philosophical Theology of Jonathan Edwards*, pp. 56, 154.

65. See Whiteley, *Wesley's England*, p. 351.

66. Lackington, *Confessions*, pp. 182–83, 184.

67. As quoted in Mathews, *Methodism and the Education of the People*, p. 74.

68. J. H. Rigg, *Wesleyan Methodist Reminiscences Sixty Years Ago*, p. 42.

69. Lackington, *Memoirs*, pp. 256–57.

70. As quoted in Mathews, *Methodism and the Education of the People*, p. 41.

71. See Mathews, *Methodism and the Education of the People*, pp. 32, 35, 71, and chapter 2 of Frank Smith, *A History of English Elementary Education, 1760–1902*.

72. See Henry Bett, *The Spirit of Methodism*, p. 163.

73. See Brantley, *Wordsworth's "Natural Methodism,"* p. 34.

74. Mathews, *Methodism and the Education of the People*, p. 80.

75. For bibliography and discussion, see, for example, Neuberg, *Popular Literature*, pp. 265–97, and Robert K. Webb, *The British Working Class Reader 1790–1848: Literacy and Social Tension*.

76. Mathews, *Methodism and the Education of the People*, pp. 99–104.

77. The quoted phrase is from *The Life of Thomas Cooper*, p. 59, as cited in Mathews, *Methodism and the Education of the People*, pp. 99–104. See also J. L. and Barbara Hammond, *The Age of the Chartists, 1832–1854: A Study of Discontent*, especially p. 248.

78. Élie Halévy, *A History of the English People* 3:192. See also Amy Cruse, *The Victorians and their Reading*, p. 66, and A. E. Dobbs, *Education and Social Movements, 1700–1850*.

79. See Marilyn Gaull, "From Wordsworth to Darwin," especially p. 40. See also Roger Sharrock, "The Chemist and the Poet: Sir Humphry Davy and the Preface to *Lyrical Ballads*."

80. As quoted in Will Durant, *The Story of Philosophy: The Lives and Opinions of the Greater Philosophers*, p. xxv.

81. As quoted in Durant, *The Story of Philosophy*, p. xxvi.

82. See the final chapter of Richard Green's *John Wesley, Evangelist*.

83. See Cragg, pp. 37–38. On November 9, 1779, Wesley told John Bredin, a Methodist preacher in Ireland: "At every new place you may give the *Earnest Appeal* to the chief man in the town" (Telford, 6:362).

84. See the discussion in Tyerman, *The Life and Times of John Wesley* 2:298–99.

85. See, for example, Frank Wilbur Collier, *Back to Wesley*, and F. Louis Bar-

ber, *The Philosophy of John Wesley*. Wesley's abridgment of Charles de Bonnet's *The Contemplation of Nature* (1764) occupies vol. 4, chaps. 2, 3, and 4, of the 1777 *Survey of the Wisdom of God in the Creation*.

86. See especially George Eayrs, *John Wesley: Christian Philosopher and Church Founder*, pp. 75, 262–63, and Curnock, 4:192. Rigg, moreover, in *The Living Wesley*, gives attention to Wesley as thinker, and both *The Living Wesley* (p. 184) and *The Proceedings of the Wesley Historical Society* (4:109) acknowledge Peter Browne as an influence on Wesley's thought. John Snaith, a Primitive Methodist minister, argues throughout *The Philosophy of Spirit* that "Wesley was without an equal as a philosopher and evangelist" (p. 211).

87. Caldecott, "The Religious Sentiment: An Inductive Enquiry, illustrated from the Lives of Wesley's Helpers," as quoted in Eayrs, *John Wesley: Christian Philosopher and Church Founder*, p. 263.

88. Green, *The Young Mr. Wesley*, p. 1.

89. Frank Baker, preparing the bibliographical volume for *The Oxford Edition of Wesley's Works*, tells how Wesley abridged (for example) Jonathan Edwards's *A Faithful Narrative of the Surprising Work of God in the Conversion of Many Hundred Souls in Northampton* (1737):

> It seems likely that he worked through the volume, pen in hand, during his preaching tour of Cornwall in the Spring of 1744, handing the amended copy to Farley on arrival in Bristol at the end of April. He probably went on similarly to abridge Edwards's *Distinguishing Marks* during his tour of the midlands and the north, handing this to William Strahan after his return to London in June. . . .

See Frank Baker, *A Union Catalogue of the Works of John and Charles Wesley*, pp. 6–7. This catalogue, considerably fuller than Richard Green's bibliography (1906), will serve until the bibliographical volume appears. About Wesley's abridgments, incidentally, Baker makes a point immediately pertinent to my argument: "[T]hese works are highly important to a correct estimate of Wesley's own thought, as well as of his literary activities and general influence."

As early as 1734, Wesley wrote out by hand his abridgment of John Norris's *Treatise on Christian Prudence*, and, in 1775, he wrote out a very large part of his edition of Samuel Johnson's *Taxation No Tyranny* (retitled *A Calm Address to Our American Colonies*). I am grateful to T. Walter Herbert for this information.

90. That abridgment was of Norris's *Christian Prudence*; see Baker, *A Union Catalogue*, p. 21.

91. The quoted phrase is the subtitle of Walter J. Ong's "Peter Ramus and the Naming of Methodism." Ong argues that Wesley's *Compendium of Logic* includes "telling reminiscences of Ramism," and that Ramus's explicitly monomethodological preference, during the 1540s and 1550s, for logic and science over "the flowers of rhetoric," has much to do with "the plain style" of Wesleyan preaching, which, at least as Wesley practiced it, was methodical not simply in advocating "orderly routine," but in reflecting, itself, "specifically logical routine." Ong's

argument parallels and is consistent with my emphasis on the Lockean method whereby Wesley learned to align language with sense perception. I am grateful to Professor Ong for communicating with me about this point.

92. Elisabeth Jay, for example, in *The Religion of the Heart: Anglican Evangelicalism and the Nineteenth-Century Novel* (pp. 16–50) emphasizes the differences between Methodism and Evangelical Anglicanism particularly in the areas of church polity and social status.

93. For an impressive argument that nineteenth-century Evangelical Anglicanism was descended from the ministries of Wesley and Whitefield, see Richard D. Altick, *Victorian People and Ideas: A Companion for the Modern Reader of Victorian Literature*, pp. 167 ff. Robert Southey both understood the revival broadly and gave it a Wesleyan name: "The Wesleyans, the Orthodox dissenters of every description, and the Evangelical churchmen may all be comprehended under the generic name of Methodists." See "Periodical Accounts relative to the Baptist Missionary Society," *The Quarterly Review* 1 (1809): 193–226, especially 195. The *Oxford English Dictionary* (s.v. "evangelical" 2 b) identifies the author of this article as Robert Southey. Even Jay acknowledges in *The Religion of the Heart* (p. 17) that "many of the early Evangelicals," e.g., Henry Venn and William Grimshaw, "did sympathize with the aims and methods of Methodism, and accepted the blanket title of 'methodist,' though with increasing reluctance." For the relation between Methodism and Nonconformism, see most notably Horton Davies, *Worship and Theology in England from Watts and Wesley to Maurice, 1690–1850*, pp. 143–254. I am grateful to Frank Baker for communicating with me about Wesley's influence in America; see also my Appendix A.

94. Thomas McFarland, *Romanticism and the Forms of Ruin: Wordsworth, Coleridge, and Modalities of Fragmentation*, pp. 301, 305.

95. See Telford, 7:376.

96. See the first section of *Original Letters, by the Rev. John Wesley and his Friends, illustrative of his early History, with other curious Papers. Communicated by the late Rev. S. Badcock; to which is prefixed, an Address to the Methodists. By Joseph Priestly, L.L.D.F.R.S.* Edited by Joseph Priestley.

97. See the discussion in MacLean, *John Locke and English Literature of the Eighteenth Century*, p. 154.

98. Robert Southey's *The Life of Wesley; and the Rise and Progress of Methodism*, 2 ed., 1:v–x, acknowledges the following: Samuel Drew, *Life of Thomas Coke* (1817); Joseph Benson, *Life of the Rev. John William de la Flechère* (1817); Charles Wesley, *Sermons* (1816); *The Works of the Rev. John Fletcher* (1815); Jonathan Crowther, *Portraiture of Methodism* (1815); William Myers, *Life and Writings of the Late Rev. William Grimshaw* (1813); John Nelson, *Journal* (1813); the second edition of Whitefield's *Memoirs* (1813); *Minutes of the Methodist Conference* (1812); James Morgan, *Life and Death of Mr. Thomas Walsh, Minister of the Gospel* (1811); John Ffirth, *Experience and Gospel Labours of the late Rev. Benjamin Abbott* (1809); *The Works of the Rev. John Wesley* (1809); Thomas Coke, *History of the West Indies* (1808–11); Joseph Nightingale, *Portraiture of Methodism* (1807); John Whitehead, *Life of the Rev. John Wesley* (1805); William Myers, *Chronological History of the Peo-*

ple Called Methodists (1803); *The Works of Augustus Toplady* (1794); *Extracts of the Journals of the Rev. Dr. Coke's Five Visits to America* (1793); Dr. Coke and Henry Moore, *Life of the Rev. John Wesley* (1792); *Original Letters by the Rev. John Wesley . . . to which is prefixed an Address to the Methodists. By Joseph Priestly, L.L.D.F.R.S.*; and, clearly not least, "*The Arminian Magazine* (now called the *Methodist Magazine*) from its commencement" in 1777.

99. See *Transactions of the Wordsworth Society* 6 (May 10, 1884): 226.

100. See Southey, *The Life of Wesley; and Rise and Progress of Methodism*, 3d ed. with notes by the late S. T. Coleridge. Coleridge writes, for example (1:184), that Arminian Methodism "has been the occasion, and even the cause, of turning thousands from their evil deeds, and . . . has made . . . bad and mischievous men peaceable and profitable neighbours and citizens."

Four. Romantic Method

1. John Kinnaird, *William Hazlitt: Critic of Power*, p. 47.

2. Margaret Bottrall, *The Divine Image: A Study of Blake's Interpretation of Christianity*, p. 98.

3. See Morton B. Paley, *Energy and the Imagination: A Study of the Development of Blake's Thought*, pp. 146–47, and Bottrall, *The Divine Image*, p. 98. See also Bernard Blackstone, *English Blake*, p. 385n, where Blackstone compares Blake's theme of "instantaneous conversion," in *The Everlasting Gospel*, with "the theory and practice of Wesley's and Whitefield's revivalist movements."

4. See especially England's chapters on "Wesley's Hymns for Children and Blake's *Songs*," "*Hymns for the Nation* and *Milton*," "Enthusiasm without Mysticism," and "*Short Hymns* and *Jersualem*," in England and John Sparrow, *Hymns Unbidden: Donne, Herbert, Blake, Emily Dickinson, and the Hymnographers*, pp. 44–112.

5. See Jacob Bronowski, *A Man Without a Mask*, pp. 100–101, 103–5, 107–8, 121–22.

6. J. G. Davies, *The Theology of William Blake*, pp. 27–28.

7. Morton B. Paley, "Cowper As Blake's Spectre." See also Lodwick Hartley, "Cowper and the Evangelicals: Notes on Early Biographical Interpretations."

8. Geoffrey Keynes, ed., *The Complete Writings of William Blake*, p. 845.

9. "Christ died for all" was frequently on Wesley's lips; see my "Johnson's Wesleyan Connection," pp. 146–47.

10. Blackstone, *English Blake*, pp. 166, 168; Bottrall, *The Divine Image*, p. 98.

11. D. J. Sloss and J. P. R. Wallis, *The Prophetic Writings of William Blake* 2:92. Gerald E. Bentley, Jr., points out that *before* Blake's protracted Felpham "conversion" (culminating in November 1802) "he was using the Christian myth, as he used others, as a subsidiary of his own myth"; see *Vala or the Four Zoas*, p. 174.

12. See Morton Paley, "Cowper As Blake's Spectre," p. 249.

13. I borrow from the phraseology of Coleridge who in chapter 13 of *Biographia Literaria* speaks of the object as "one and the same thing with our own immediate self-consciousness."

14. Paley, *Energy and Imagination*, p. 223. Paley adds that Blake carries Berke-

ley "to a point where the Bishop does not wish to go": "an analogy between the world as an idea in the mind of God and the work of art as an image in the mind of the artist." The connection between Berkeley and Blake is beginning to receive the attention it deserves. See, for example, the discussion of Blake's marginalia to Berkeley's *Siris* in Michael Davis, *William Blake: A New Kind of Man*, p. 69. See also Kathleen Raine's brief study, *Berkeley, Blake and the New Age*.

15. For the phrase "Imagination or Spiritual Sensation," see Blake's letter to the Rev. Dr. John Trusler, August 23, 1799, in David V. Erdman, ed., *The Poetry and Prose of William Blake*, pp. 676–77. For the phrase "inside out," and for Blake's informed as well as finally unsympathetic attitude toward Newton, see Donald Ault, *Visionary Physics: Blake's Response to Newton*.

16. See the discussion in Davis, *William Blake*, p. 69.

17. Commenting, for example, on the differences between *Poetical Sketches* and *Songs of Innocence*, Hirsch concludes:

> The inspiration was a brilliant and liberating one which exploited the natural association between pastoral imagery and Christian symbolism and accorded perfectly with Blake's expanding conception of his prophetic vocation in lyric poetry.

Thus Hirsch implies Blake's dependence on what Milton, in "Lycidas," had done before. See E. D. Hirsch, *Innocence and Experience: An Introduction to Blake*, p. 27.

18. "The poem," writes Hirsch (ibid., p. 29), "subtly expresses a religious perspective in which man and God are not simply analogous but essentially one."

19. One can never surely know: William Gifford, editor of *The Quarterly*, omitted the phrase (and Lamb's elaboration of it) from Lamb's review of *The Excursion*. Lamb regretted the omission and, expressing the regret to Wordsworth, apparently thought that the phrase would have met with the poet's approval:

> I regret . . . that I did not keep a copy [of the review]. I am sure you would have been pleased with it, because I have been feeding my fancy for some months with the notion of pleasing you.

See E. V. Lucas, ed., *The Letters of Charles Lamb to which are added those of his sister Mary Lamb* 2:149.

20. Colin Clarke, *Romantic Paradox: An Essay on the Poetry of Wordsworth*, pp. 1–2.

21. In the attempt to identify man's ruling passions, "the wisest may mistake, / If second qualities for first they take": see Pope's *Moral Essays* 1:210–11. It is clearly on the basis of primary and secondary qualities that Sterne distinguishes between appearance and substance in religion:

> . . . [S]o strong a propensity is there in our nature to sense—and so unequal a match is the understanding of the bulk of mankind, for the impres-

sions of outward things—that we see thousands who every day mistake the shadow for the substance, and was it fairly put to the trial would exchange the reality for the appearance. ("Pharisee and Publican": *Sermons* 1:79)

See the citations and discussion in Kenneth MacLean, *John Locke and English Literature of the Eighteenth Century*, pp. 95–96.

22. For secondary qualities, see, in Lane Cooper, ed., *A Concordance to the Poems of William Wordsworth*, the following words and their variations: *colour*: ¼ column, p. 150; *sound*: 3½ columns, pp. 901–3; *taste*: ¼ column, p. 970; and *touch*: 1 column, p. 1009. Variations of smell, i.e., *odour*, *aroma*, etc., account for less than ¼ column. For primary qualities, see the following words and their variations: *solid*: ¼ column, p. 891; *broad/abroad/extend/figure*: 1½ columns, pp. 3, 103, 271, 308; *motion/move*: 4½ columns, pp. 625, 630–31; and *number*: ½ column, p. 662. It is true, of course, that *light* frequently occurs: 4¾ columns, pp. 532–35. But *object* and *objects* take up 1½ columns, pp. 663–64, to only ¼ column, p. 948, for *subject* and its variations.

23. See H. W. Piper, *The Active Universe: Pantheism and the Concept of Imagination in the English Romantic Poets*, especially pp. 16–19.

24. Geoffrey Hartman, *The Unmediated Vision: An Interpretation of Wordsworth, Hopkins, Rilke, and Valéry*, p. 36.

25. Hugh Sykes Davies and George Watson, *The English Mind: Studies in the English Moralists Presented to Basil Willey*, p. 160. Davies alludes to the *Essay* (2.12.1 and 2.33.5) and to David Hartley's *Observations on Man, His Frame, His Duty, and His Expectations* (1.90).

26. Alan Grob, for example, is untempted, even by my *Wordsworth's "Natural Methodism,"* to add theology to his Lockean approach: see his review in *The Wordsworth Circle* and his *The Philosophic Mind: A Study of Wordsworth's Poetry and Thought, 1797–1805*.

27. L. J. Swingle, "On Reading Romantic Poetry."

28. See Geoffrey Durrant, *Wordsworth and the Great System: A Study of Wordsworth's Poetic Universe*; Durrant also brings out Wordsworth's usage, both in this poem and generally, of Newton's optics.

29. See Jack Stillinger's summary of the scholarship in Stillinger, ed., *William Wordsworth: Selected Poems and Prefaces*, p. 538.

30. See Lee M. Johnson, *Wordsworth and the Sonnet*.

31. See the discussion of the *Essay* 2.14.13 and 4.1.8 in MacLean, *John Locke and English Literature of the Eighteenth Century*, p. 123.

32. I know of no Lockean approaches to this passage, but it has attracted considerable attention. For a summary of the criticism, see Melvyn New, "Wordsworth's Shell of Poetry." New argues, intriguingly, that the shell, "of the tortoise, out of which the lyre was first made," bespeaks "Wordsworth's faith in the redemptive and restorative powers of poetry." Theresa M. Kelley, in "Spirit and Geometric Form: The Stone and the Shell in Wordsworth's Arab Dream," focuses especially on Euclid's *Elements* and Francis Bacon to argue that, in the Arab

dream, Wordsworth "rejected the narrow experimentalism of contemporary scientific practice, but included science in his prophetic narrative of deluge, books, and burying treasure" (p. 564).

33. Wordsworth's love of mathematics dates from his days at Cambridge; see Durrant, *Wordsworth and the Great System*, and *Prelude* 5.

34. Indeed, the "Prospectus" can be thought of as the program for much of modern poetry. See M. H. Abrams, *Natural Supernaturalism: Tradition and Revolution in Romantic Literature*.

35. See, for example, Frances Ferguson, *Wordsworth: Language as Counterspirit* and "Bible" in the index to *Wordsworth's "Natural Methodism."*

36. See Gian Orsini, *Coleridge and German Idealism: A Study in the History of Philosophy, with unpublished materials from Coleridge's manuscripts*. See also René Wellek, *Immanuel Kant in England, 1793–1838*.

37. See Norman Fruman, *Coleridge, The Damaged Archangel*; and two reviews in particular: Thomas McFarland, "Coleridge's Plagiarisms Once More," *Yale Review* and John Beer's review of *Coleridge, The Damaged Archangel*.

38. See René Wellek, "Coleridge's Philosophy and Criticism," in Frank Jordan, Jr., ed., *The English Romantic Poets: A Review of Research and Criticism*, especially pp. 215–16.

39. Swingle, "On Reading Romantic Poetry," especially 978–80. See also, for just one other example, Earl Wasserman, "The English Romantics: The Ground of Knowledge."

40. Arthur O. Wlecke, *Wordsworth and the Sublime*, p. 155. For a summary of the empiricist/idealist balance in Coleridge's thought, see Frederick J. Copleston, *A History of Philosophy*, Vol. 8 (*Modern Philosophy: Bentham to Russell*), Part 1 (*British Empiricism and the Idealist Movement in Great Britain*), pp. 176–81.

41. See J. Robert Barth, *Coleridge and Christian Doctrine*; James Boulger, *Coleridge as Religious Thinker*; and Charles Sanders, *Coleridge and the Broad Church Movement: Studies in S. T. Coleridge, Dr. Arnold of Rugby, J. C. Hare, Thomas Carlyle and F. D. Maurice.*

42. F. C. Gill, *The Romantic Movement and Methodism: A Study of English Romanticism and the Evangelical Revival*, especially pp. 170–77.

43. See Robert Southey, *The Life of Wesley; and Rise and Progress of Methodism*, 3d ed. with notes by the late S. T. Coleridge; and Gill, *The Romantic Movement and Methodism*, p. 169.

44. See also Thomas McFarland's *Coleridge and the Pantheist Tradition*, in addition to Reeve Parker's study, *Coleridge's Meditative Art*, and Thomas McFarland's *Romanticism and the Forms of Ruin: Wordsworth, Coleridge, and Modalities of Fragmentation.*

45. See Samuel T. Coleridge, *The Statesman's Manual* (Appendix B), as quoted in Richard E. Brantley, *Wordsworth's "Natural Methodism,"* p. 146.

46. Elinor Shaffer, *"Kubla Khan" and the Fall of Jerusalem: The Mythological School in Biblical Criticism and Secular Literature, 1770–1880.*

47. See J. Robert Barth, *The Symbolic Imagination: Coleridge and the Romantic Tradition*; I am indebted to Robert Barth for his early encouragement of my ap-

proach to Coleridge. See also John Coulson, *Newman and the Common Tradition: A Study in the Language of Church and Society.*

48. For parallels between the psychological and intellectual anxieties of Coleridge, see the introduction ("Fragmented Modalities and the Criteria of Romanticism") and chapter 2 ("Coleridge's Anxiety") of McFarland's *Romanticism and the Forms of Ruin.* For "The Ancient Mariner" as a portrait of evangelical psychology, see Lionel Stevenson, "'The Ancient Mariner' as a Dramatic Monologue"; Stevenson's assessment of the Mariner's character as superstitious seems overly negative and reflects bias against the evangelical temper. For "Kubla Khan" as Coleridge's *Paradiso,* see G. Wilson Knight, *The Starlit Dome: Studies in the Poetry of Vision.* Ever since Dr. James Gillman's interpretation of Geraldine, in his biography of Coleridge, the theme of evil in "Christabel" has often seemed preeminent. Gerald E. Enscoe, to be sure, in *Eros and the Romantics: Sexual Love as a Theme in Coleridge, Shelley and Keats,* sees Geraldine as partly salutary in her effects on Christabel. But Harold Bloom, in *The Visionary Company: A Reading of English Romantic Poetry,* p. 210, sees Geraldine as an "apparent triumph of evil." And Bloom's position represents mainstream interpretation; see, for example, Edward E. Bostetter, "Christabel: The Vision of Fear"; John Beer, *Coleridge the Visionary;* and Lawrence D. Berkoben, "Christabel: A Variety of Evil Experience."

49. See, besides *The Subtler Language: Critical Readings of Neoclassic and Romantic Poems,* Earl Wasserman's more recent (but not methodologically dissimilar) studies: *Shelley's* Prometheus Unbound: *A Critical Reading;* and *Shelley: A Critical Reading.* John Wright's study, *Shelley's Myth of Metaphor,* amounts to an extension (if not a refinement) of Wasserman's approach.

50. See, for example, Mary B. Hesse, "The Explanatory Function of Metaphor," pp. 252 ff.; Wright, *Shelley's Myth of Metaphor,* p. 20; and, most recently, Roger S. Jones, *Physics as Metaphor.*

51. Thomas Sprat, *The History of the Royal Society of London,* p. 112, as quoted in Wright, *Shelley's Myth of Metaphor,* p. 14.

52. See, for example, C. E. Pulos, *The Deep Truth: A Study of Shelley's Skepticism.* Pulos's perception that Shelley's skepticism gives rise to his idealism is consistent with the context of Wesley's philosophical theology. Lloyd Abbey, in *Destroyer and Preserver: Shelley's Poetic Skepticism,* finds little common ground between the two dimensions of Shelley's thought. On the one hand, Abbey argues that Shelley thinks anything beyond "phenomenal reality" "impossible either to know or to portray" (p. 8), but Abbey realizes, on the other hand, that Shelley is tempted by a "concept of imagination as a faculty of intuitive reason, transcending the uncertainties of phenomenal illusion and intuiting a noumenal reality inaccessible to the senses" (p. 13).

53. Newman Ivey White, *Shelley* 1:104–6. "Behind much of Shelley's poetry," writes Timothy Webb, "it is possible to detect a variety of literary traditions centered on religious experience. His reputation as an atheist has tended to obscure the fact that, though his opinions were heterodox, his sensibility was profoundly religious." See Webb, *Shelley: A Voice Not Understood,* p. 37.

54. These three poems and "A Defence of Poetry" are in Donald Reiman's list

of eleven works that should be read by anyone "wishing to understand Shelley." See Reiman, *Percy Bysshe Shelley*, p. 7.

55. I have in mind Ronald A. Sharp's terminology in *Keats, Skepticism, and the Religion of Beauty*. I supplement Sharp's nonhistorical approach.

56. Robert M. Ryan, *Keats: The Religious Sense*, especially p. 63. Not even Clarence Thorpe in *The Mind of John Keats* is as thorough as Ryan in unearthing materials pertinent to Keats's frame of mind. Since Ryan does not criticize the poetry systematically, one might read his volume as companion not only to the present discussion but also to Sharp's *Keats, Skepticism, and the Religion of Beauty*.

57. Hyder E. Rollins, ed., *The Letters of John Keats, 1814–1821* 1:184.

58. Ernest Lee Tuveson, *Imagination as a Means of Grace: Locke and the Aesthetics of Romanticism*, p. 3.

59. Douglas Bush, ed., *Keats: Selected Poems and Letters*, p. 310.

60. David Perkins, ed., *English Romantic Writers*, p. 1, 146n.

61. Stuart Sperry, *Keats the Poet*, p. 129.

62. Bush, in this connection, calls Keats's Pleasure Thermometer "Platonic-Romantic." Keats "could speak," writes Bush, "of 'the eternal Being, the Principle of Beauty' (letter to Reynolds, April 9, 1818) and of 'The mighty abstract Idea I have of Beauty in all things' (letter to George and Georgiana Keats, Oct. 21, 1818)." See Bush, ed., *Keats: Selected Poems and Letters*, p. 319.

63. See the letter to George and Thomas Keats, 21, 27 (?) December 1817, in Rollins, ed., *The Letters of John Keats* 1:192–93.

64. Sperry, *Keats the Poet*, p. 128.

65. Jack Stillinger, "The Hoodwinking of Madeline: Scepticism in 'The Eve of St. Agnes.'"

66. "Imagination and Reality in the Odes of Keats," in Stillinger, ed., *Twentieth Century Interpretations of Keats's Odes*, p. 3.

67. Wasserman's study of Keats, *The Finer Tone*, is subtitled *Keats's Major Poems*.

68. I have in mind E. Leroy Lawson's *Very Sure of God: Religious Language in the Poetry of Robert Browning* and Ward Hellstrom's *On the Poems of Tennyson*. Hellstrom shows Tennyson's particular knowledge of Liberal Anglican thought, and Lawson shows Browning's compatibility with such thinkers as Paul Tillich, Jürgen Moltmann, and Harvey Cox. Josephine Miles, notably, puts the casual use of religious language in the 1840s; see *The Primary Language of Poetry in the 1740s and the 1840s*. Sharp, acknowledging Wordsworth's "Natural Methodism" as a means of understanding Wordsworth's belief in "a reality that transcended this world," observes that "by contrast with Keats, Wordsworth is considerably more traditional"; see Sharp, *Keats, Skepticism, and the Religion of Beauty*, pp. 14, 169.

69. Ryan, *Keats: The Religious Sense*, pp. 71, 115. One needs to supplement Ryan's book, for Ryan's argument, like those of Blackstone and Bottrall with regard to Blake, is flawed by the reduction of "Methodism and Evangelicalism" to "their emphasis on sin and guilt" (Ryan, p. 80).

70. Sperry, *Keats the Poet*, p. 133.

71. Ryan, *Keats: The Religious Sense*, pp. 174–75.

72. As quoted in Wasserman, *The Subtler Language*, pp. 205–6.

73. See Jackson, 10:75–76, from which I quote as well in my next two sentences.

A Methodological Postscript

1. Fredric Jameson, *Marxism and Form: Twentieth Century Dialectical Theories of Literature*, p. 13.

2. Joseph A. Wittreich, Jr., *Visionary Poetics: Milton's Tradition and His Legacy*, p. xxi.

3. Michel Foucault, *The Order of Things*, p. 50.

4. Ibid., p. 63.

5. Frank Lentricchia, *After the New Criticism*, pp. 108–9.

6. Ibid.

7. Paul de Man, "The Rhetoric of Temporality," p. 202.

8. Stuart Sperry, *Keats the Poet*, p. 245.

9. See, besides *English Romantic Irony*, Anne K. Mellor's review of David Simpson, *Irony and Authority in Romantic Poetry*. Simpson, following de Man, interprets *romantische ironie* as more epistemologically than ontologically nihilistic and is thus one-sided in approaching English Romanticism.

10. Tilottama Rajan, *Dark Interpreter: The Discourse of Romanticism*, p. 21.

11. Harold Bloom, "Poetic Crossing: Rhetoric and Psychology."

12. Rajan, *Dark Interpreter*, pp. 19, 28.

13. G. Douglas Atkins, "Dehellenizing Literary Criticism."

14. Gerald Graff, *Literature Against Itself: Literary Ideas in Modern Society*, p. 39.

15. Thomas McFarland, *Romanticism and the Forms of Ruin: Wordsworth, Coleridge, and Modalities of Fragmentation*, especially pp. vi–vii.

16. E. V. Lucas, ed., *Bernard Barton and his Friends: A Record of Quiet Lives*, p. 114.

17. See Dudley Wright, "The Religious Opinions of Charles Lamb." See also George L. Barnett, *Charles Lamb*, especially pp. 17–42.

18. Ronald Blythe, ed., *William Hazlitt: Selected Writings*, pp. 17, 29, 35.

19. John Kinnaird, *William Hazlitt: Critic of Power*, p. 47.

20. Kenneth MacLean, *John Locke and English Literature of the Eighteenth Century*, especially pp. 28, 38n, 72.

21. As quoted in George Eayrs, *John Wesley: Christian Philosopher and Church Founder*, p. 251.

22. See Thomas De Quincey, *Confessions of an English Opium Eater*, edited by Alethea Hayter, pp. 17 ff.

23. See, for example, the discussion in Hugh Sykes Davies, *Thomas De Quincey*, pp. 16 ff.

24. See John Barrell, *The Idea of Landscape and the Sense of Place, 1730–1840: An Approach to the Poetry of John Clare*.

25. See Greg Crossan, *A Relish for Eternity: The Process of Divinization in the Poetry of John Clare*.

26. Mark Minor, "John Clare and the Methodists: A Reconsideration."

27. R. W. Chapman, ed., *Jane Austen's Letters to her sister Cassandra*, pp. 256, 410. I am indebted to Professor James Thompson for correspondence about Jane Austen.

28. See, for example, the discussion in Avrom Fleishman, *A Reading of* Mansfield Park: *An Essay in Critical Synthesis.*

29. E. W. Marjarum, *Byron as Skeptic and Believer*, especially p. ix.

30. See James Kennedy, *Conversations on Religion, with Lord Byron and others, held in Cephalonia, a short time previous to his lordship's death*, p. 11.

31. Edward Bostetter, "Masses and Solids: Byron's View of the External World."

32. See especially chapter 4 of Edward Kessler's *Coleridge's Metaphors of Being.*

33. Jerome McGann, "The Meaning of the Ancient Mariner," especially p. 60.

34. Charles Sherry, *Wordsworth's Poetry of the Imagination.*

35. Leopold Damrosch, *Symbol and Truth in Blake's Myth*, especially pp. 3–4.

36. Wilfred Stone, *The Cave and the Mountain: A Study of E. M. Forster*, pp. 24–71.

37. See, for example, the chapters on George Eliot in Vineta Colby's recent studies: *Yesterday's Woman: Domestic Realism in the English Novel* and *The Singular Anomaly: Women Novelists of the Nineteenth Century.* See also (besides Elisabeth Jay's *The Religion of the Heart: Anglican Evangelicalism and the Nineteenth-Century Novel*): George Landow, *The Aesthetic and Critical Theories of John Ruskin*; Valentine Cunningham, *Everywhere Spoken Against: Dissent in the Victorian Novel*; Samuel Pickering, Jr., *The Moral Tradition in English Fiction, 1785–1850*; Carl Dawson, *Victorian Noon: English Literature in 1850*; and Robert F. George, "The Evangelical Revival and Charlotte Brontë's *Jane Eyre.*"

38. Bernard J. Paris, *Experiments in Life: George Eliot's Quest for Values.*

39. See George Eliot, "Worldliness and Other-worldliness: The Poet Young."

40. Schleiermacher himself praised the English "popular interest in missions and the spread of the Bible"; see Friedrich Schleiermacher, *On Religion: Speeches to its Cultured Despisers*, p. 230. See also Rudolf Otto's introduction to *Über die Religion: Reden an die Gebildeten unter ihren Verächtern*, 5. durchgeschene Auflage.

41. See T. Walter Herbert, Jr., Moby Dick *and Calvinism: A World Dismantled* and A. Carl Bredahl, *Melville's Angles of Vision.*

42. Flannery O'Connor writes:

Grace can't be experienced in itself. An example: when you go to Communion, you receive grace but you experience nothing; or if you do experience something, what you experience is not the grace but an emotion caused by it. . . .

. . . Ideal Christianity doesn't exist, because anything the human being touches, even Christian truth, he deforms slightly in his own image. Even the saints do this. . . .

I know that the writer does call up the general and maybe the essential through the particular, but this general and essential is still deeply embedded in mystery. It is not answerable to any of our formulas. It doesn't rest finally in a statable kind of solution. It ought to throw you back on the living God. Our Catholic mentality is great on paraphrase, logic, formula, instant and correct answers. We judge before we experience and never trust our faith to be subjected to reality, because it is not strong enough. And maybe in this we are wise. . . .

I am more and more impressed with the amount of Catholicism that fundamentalist Protestants have been able to retain.

See Flannery O'Connor's letters to "A" (April 4, 1958) and to Sister Mariella Gable (May 4, 1963) in Sally Fitzgerald, ed., *The Habit of Being: Letters Edited and with an Introduction*, pp. 275, 516–17, 518.

43. T. Walter Herbert, Jr., *Marquesan Encounters: Melville and the Meaning of Civilization*, p. 16. See also Richard Rorty, "Philosophy as a Kind of Writing: An Essay on Derrida."

Appendix A

1. See William J. Wainwright, "Jonathan Edwards and the Language of God," pp. 519–30. For a sampling of Miller's argument, see *Errand into the Wilderness* and "Jonathan Edwards and the Sense of the Heart," pp. 123–45.

2. See Sacvan Bercovitch, *The American Jeremiad*.

3. See Conrad Cherry, *The Theology of Jonathan Edwards*, especially pp. 1–6. For a sampling of the debate, see John Opie, ed., *Jonathan Edwards and the Enlightenment*.

4. Norman Fiering, *Jonathan Edwards's Moral Thought and Its British Context*.

5. Douglas J. Elwood, *The Philosophical Theology of Jonathan Edwards*, p. 159.

6. Waldo Beach and H. Richard Niebuhr, eds., *Christian Ethics: Sources of the Tradition*, p. 380.

7. Elwood, *The Philosophical Theology of Jonathan Edwards*, p. 124.

8. Bercovitch, *The American Jeremiad*, pp. 107–8.

9. Joseph Haroutinian's remark appears in the foreword to Elwood's book.

10. See Elisabeth Jay, *Religion of the Heart: Anglican Evangelicalism and the Nineteenth-Century Novel*, especially p. 17. Her study depends upon J. D. Walsh's narrow view of the history; see Walsh, "Origins of the Evangelical Revival," pp. 132–62.

11. See Charles Foster, *An Errand of Mercy*.

12. Henry May, *The Enlightenment in America*, p. 402.

13. Ibid., p. xiv.

Appendix B

1. D. W. Riley, "Notes and News." The souvenirs, as Riley points out, are included in such individual collections as the Sidney Lawson and the Edmund S. Lamplough.

2. V. H. H. Green, *The Young Mr. Wesley: A Study of John Wesley and Oxford*, p. 220.

3. George Eayrs, *John Wesley: Christian Philosopher and Church Founder*, p. 22.

Sources

Baker, Frank, ed. *See* Wesley, John.

Baxter, Andrew. *An Enquiry into the Nature of the human soul: Wherein the immateriality of the soul is evinced from the principles of reason and philosophy.* London: James Bettenham, 1730.

Blake, William. *The Poetry and Prose of William Blake.* With commentary by Harold Bloom. Edited by David V. Erdman. Garden City, N.Y.: Doubleday, 1965.

de Bonnet, Charles. *Contemplation de la Nature.* Amsterdam: Chez Marc-Michel Rey, 1764. Reprint. 2 vols. Philadelphia: Jonathan Pounder, 1816.

Boswell, James. *Boswell: Life of Johnson.* Edited by R. W. Chapman. Corrected by J. D. Fleeman. London: Oxford University Press, 1970.

———. *Life of Johnson.* Edited by G. Birkbeck Hill and revised by L. F. Powell. 6 vols. Oxford: Clarendon Press, 1934–50.

Boyle, Robert. *The Sceptical Chymist.* London: Printed for J. Crooke, 1661.

Bray, Thomas. *Bibliotheca Parochialis; or, a Scheme of such Theological and Other Heads, as seem requisite to be perus'd, or Occasionally consulted, by the Reverend Clergy. Together with the Books which may be profitably Read on each of these Points.* London: R. Wilkin and W. Hawes, 1707.

Browne, Peter. *The Procedure, Extent, and Limits of Human Understanding.* 2d ed. London: W. Innys, 1729.

———. *Things Divine and Supernatural Conceived by Analogy with Things Natural and Human.* London: W. Innays and R. Manby, 1733.

Bush, Douglas, ed. *See* Keats, John.

Butler, Bishop Joseph. *The Analogy of Religion, Natural and Revealed, to the constitution and course of Nature.* London: James, John, and Paul Knapton, 1736.

Chambers, Ephraim. *Cyclopaedia; or, An universal dictionary of arts and sciences.* London: J. and J. Knapton, 1728.

Cheyne, George. *Philosophical Principles of Religion.* 3d ed. London: George Strahan, 1716.

Cockburn, Catharine. *A Defence of the Essay on human understanding, written by Mr. Lock—In answer to some Remarks on that essay [by Sir Thomas Burnet].* London: W. Turner, 1702.

————. *Remarks upon the principles and reasonings of Dr. Rutherforth's Essay on the nature and obligations of virtue, in vindication of the contrary principles and reasonings inforced in the writings of the late Dr. Samuel Clarke.* London: J. and P. Knapton, 1747.

Coleridge, Ernest Hartley, ed. *See* Coleridge, Samuel T.

Coleridge, Samuel T. *The Friend: A Series of Essays, in Three Volumes, to aid in the formation of fixed principles in politics, morals, and religion, with literary amusements interspersed.* 3 vols. London: R. Fenner, 1818.

————. *Poetical Works of Coleridge, including poems and versions of poems herein published for the first time.* Edited by Ernest Hartley Coleridge. 1912. Reprint. London and New York: Oxford University Press, 1969.

Collins, Anthony. *A Discourse of Free-thinking.* London, N.p., 1713.

Cragg, Gerald R., ed. *See* Wesley, John.

Curnock, Nehemiah, ed. *See* Wesley, John.

Doddridge, Philip. *The Rise and Progress of Religion in the Soul.* London: J. Waugh, 1745.

Erdman, David V., ed. *See* Blake, William.

Fiddes, Richard. *Theologia Speculativa: or; the first part of divinity under that title, Wherein are explain'd the principles of natural and revealed religion.* London: B. Lintot, 1718.

Fraser, Alexander Campbell, ed., *See* Locke, John.

Goldsmith, Oliver. *A History of the Earth, And Animated Nature.* 7 vols. London: J. Nourse, 1774.

Hartley, David. *Observations on Man, His Frame, His Duty, and His Expectations.* 1749. Reprint. Gainesville, Florida: Scholars' Facsimiles and Reprints, 1966.

Hutchinson, John. *Moses's Principia.* London: J. Bettenham, 1724.

Ingpen, Roger, and Walter E. Peck, eds. *See* Shelley, Percy Bysshe.

Jackson, Thomas, ed. *See* Wesley, John.

Keats, John. *Keats: Selected Poems and Letters.* Edited by Douglas Bush. New York: Riverside Editions, 1959.

Kennedy, James. *Conversations on Religion, with Lord Byron and others, held in Cephalonia, a short time previous to his lordship's death.* London: J. Murray, 1830.

Lackington, James. *The Confessions of J. Lackington, late bookseller, at the Temple of the Muses.* London: R. Edwards, 1804.

————. *Memoirs of the first forty-five years of the life of James Lackington.* London: Printed for and sold by the author, 1791.

Llanover, Right Honourable Lady, ed. *The Autobiography and Correspondence of Mary Granville, Mrs. Delany: with interesting reminiscences of King George the Third and Queen Charlotte.* 2 vols. London: R. Bentley, 1862.

Locke, John. *An Essay concerning Human Understanding.* Edited by Alexander Campbell Fraser. 2 vols. Oxford: Clarendon Press, 1894.

———. *An Essay concerning Human Understanding.* 1690. Edited by Peter H. Nidditch. Oxford: Clarendon Press, 1975.

———. *The Reasonableness of Christianity. As Delivered in the Scriptures.* London: A. and J. Churchill, 1695.

———. *Some Thoughts concerning Education.* London: A. and J. Churchill, 1693.

———. *Two Treatises of Government.* London: A. and J. Churchill, 1694.

Malebranche, Nicolas. *The Search After Truth.* Translated by Thomas M. Lennon and Paul L. Olscamp. Columbus: Ohio State University Press, 1980.

Mant, Richard. *A History of the Church of Ireland, from the Reformation to the Union of the Churches of England and Ireland Jan. 1, 1801.* 2 vols. London: J. W. Parker, 1840.

Newton, Isaac. *Opticks.* London: S. Smith and B. Walford, 1704.

Nidditch, Peter H., ed. *See* Locke, John.

Perronet, Vincent. *An Earnest Exhortation to the Strict Practice of Christianity. Drawn up chiefly For the Use of the Inhabitants of the Parish of Shoreham in Kent.* 1746. 2d ed. "enlarged." London: J. Oliver, 1750.

———. "Memoirs of the Rev. Vincent Perronet, A.M." *The Methodist Magazine, For the Year 1799: Being a continuation of The Arminian Magazine, First Published by the Rev. John Wesley, A.M.* Vol. 22. London: for G. Whitefield, January–April 1799.

———. *A Second Vindication of Mr. Locke, Wherein his Sentiments relating to Personal Identity are clear'd up from some Mistakes of the Rev. Dr. Butler, in his Dissertation on that Subject. And the various Objections rais'd against Mr. Locke, by the learned Author of An Enquiry into the Nature of the Human Soul, are consider'd. To which are added Reflections on some Passages of Dr. Watts's Philosophical Essays.* London: Fletcher Gyles, 1738.

———. *Some Enquiries, Chiefly relating to Spiritual Beings: In which the Opinions of Mr. Hobbes, With Regard to Sensation, Immaterial Substance, and the Attributes of the Deity, Are taken Notice of. And wherein likewise is examined, how far the Supposition of an Invisible Tempter, is defensible on the Principles of Natural Reason. In Four Dialogues.* London: F. Gyles, J. and P. Knapton, and J. Roberts, 1740.

———. *Some Reflections, By Way of Dialogue, on the Nature of Original Sin, Baptismal Regeneration, Repentance, the New Birth, Faith, Justification, Christian Perfection, or Universal Holiness, and the Inspiration of the Spirit of God.* London: J. and P. Knapton and J. Roberts, 1747.

———. *Some Remarks on a late Anonymous Piece, Intitled, The Enthusiasm of Methodists and Papists, compared. In a Letter to the Author.* London: J. Roberts, 1749.

———. *Some Strictures on a Few Places of the late Reverend Mr. Hervey's Letters to the Reverend Mr. John Wesley. By a Clergyman.* London: N.p., 1766.

———. *A Vindication of Mr. Locke, from the charge of giving Encouragement to Scepti-*

cism and Infidelity, and from several other Mistakes and Objections of the Learned Author of the Procedure, Extent, and Limits of Human Understanding. Wherein is likewise Enquired, Whether Mr. Locke's True Opinion of the Soul's Immateriality was not mistaken by the Learned Mons. Leibnitz. London: James, John, and Paul Knapton, 1736.

Pike, Samuel. *Philosophia Sacra: or, The Principles of Natural Philosophy. Extracted from Divine Revelation.* London: J. Buckland, 1753.

Polwhele, Rev. Richard. *The Unsex'd Females: A Poem.* London: Cadell and Davies, 1798.

Priestley, Joseph, ed. *Original Letters, by the Rev. John Wesley and his Friends, illustrative of his early History, with other curious Papers. Communicated by the late Rev. S. Badcock: to which is prefixed, an Address to the Methodists. By Joseph Priestley, L.L.D.F.R.S.* Birmingham: Thomas Pearson, 1791.

von Pufendorf, Samuel Freiher. *The Law of Nature and Nations: or, A general System of the most important principles of morality, jurisprudence, and politices.* 1684. Translated by Basil Kennet. London: J. and J. Bonwicke, 1749.

———. *Of the Nature and Qualification of Religion in Reference to Civil Society.* Translator anonymous. 1687. London: Printed by E. E. for A. Roper and A. Bosvile, 1698.

———. *The Whole Duty of Man According to the Law of Nature.* Translator anonymous. 1673. London: Printed by Benjamin Motte for Charles Harper, 1691.

Schleiermacher, Friedrich. *On Religion: Speeches to its Cultured Despisers.* Translated by John Oman. 1799. Reprint. New York: Harper, 1958.

———. *The Christian Faith. (Der Christliche Glaube.)* 1821. Translated by D. M. Baillie. Edited by H. R. MacKintosh and J. S. Stewart. 1928. Reprint. Edinburgh: T. and T. Clark, 1948.

de Selincourt, Ernest, ed. *See* Wordsworth, William.

Shelley, Percy Bysshe. *The Complete Works of Percy Bysshe Shelley.* Edited by Roger Ingpen and Walter E. Peck. 10 vols. London: Ernest Benn, 1965.

South, Robert. "The Christian Pentecost . . . Preach'd at Westminster-Abbey, 1692." In *Sermons upon several Subjects and Occasions,* 6th ed. 11 vols. London: J. Bettenham, 1727.

Southey, Robert. *The Life of Wesley; and the Rise and Progress of Methodism.* 2d ed. 2 vols. London: Longman, Hurst, Rees, Orme, and Brown, 1820.

———. *The Life of Wesley; and Rise and Progress of Methodism.* 3d ed. with notes by the late S. T. Coleridge. 2 vols. London: A. Knox, 1846.

Spearman, Robert. *An Enquiry after Philosophy and Theology.* Dublin: William Watson, 1757.

Sprat, Thomas. *The History of the Royal Society of London.* London: J. Martyn, 1667.

Sugden, Edward H., ed. *See* Wesley, John.

Telford, John, ed. *See* Wesley, John.

Tillotson, John. *The Works of the Most Reverend Dr. John Tillotson, Late Lord Archbishop of Canterbury: Containing Two Hundred and Fifty Four Sermons and Discourses on Several Occasions.* 12th ed. 10 vols. Dublin: S. Powell, 1734.

Tindal, Matthew. *Christianity as old as the Creation*. London: N.p., 1731.

Toland, John. *Christianity Not Mysterious*. London: Sam. Buckley, 1696.

Tryon, Thomas. *Letters . . . Philosophical, Theological, and Moral*. London: Geo. Conyers and Eliz. Harris, 1700.

Voltaire, François Marie Arouet de. *Letters concerning the English Nation*. Translated by John Lockman. London: Thiriot, 1733.

Warburton, William. *The Doctrine of Grace; or, the Office and Operations of the Holy Spirit Vindicated from the Insults of Infidelity and the Abuses of Fanaticism*. 1763. In *The Works of the Right Reverend William Warburton, D.D.* Edited by Richard Hurd. 12 vols. London: T. Cadell and W. Davies, 1811.

Watts, Isaac. *Logick: or, The right use of reason in the enquiry after truth*. London: John Clark and Richard Hett, 1725.

———. "On Mr. Lock's Annotations upon several Parts of the New Testament, left behind him at his death." In *Horae Lyricae*. 2d ed. London: J. Humfreys, 1709.

———. *Philosophical Essays*. 3d ed. London: James Blackstone, 1742.

Wesley, John. *The Appeals to Men of Reason and Religion and Certain Related Open Letters*. Edited by Gerald R. Cragg. Vol. 11 of *The Works of John Wesley*. Edited by Frank Baker. Oxford: Clarendon Press, 1975.

———. *A Compendium of Logic: translated and abridged from Aldrich*. Bristol: W. Pine, 1750.

———. *The Complete English Dictionary*. 2d ed. Bristol: W. Pine, 1763.

———. *An Extract from Milton's* Paradise Lost: *With Notes*. London: Henry Fenwick, 1763.

———. *The Journal of the Rev. John Wesley, A.M., Sometime Fellow of Lincoln College, Oxford, Enlarged from Original MSS., With Notes from Unpublished Diaries, Annotations, Maps, and Illustrations*. Edited by Nehemiah Curnock. 8 vols. London: Robert Culley, 1909.

———. *The Letters of the Rev. John Wesley, A.M., Sometime Fellow of Lincoln College, Oxford*. Edited by John Telford. 8 vols. London: The Epworth Press, 1931.

———. *A Plain Account of the People called Methodists*. Bristol: Felix Farley, 1749.

———. *Primitive Physick: or, an Easy and Natural Method of Curing Most Diseases*. 9th ed. London: Printed by W. Strahan, 1761.

———. *Sermons on Several Occasions. First Series. Consisting of Forty-four Discourses, Published in Four Volumes, in the Years 1746 1748, 1750, and 1760 (Fourth Edition, 1787); To which Reference is Made in the Trust-deeds of the Methodist Chapels, As Constituting, with Mr. Wesley's Notes on the New Testament, The Standard Doctrines of the Methodist Connexion*. London: The Epworth Press, 1944.

———. *A Survey of the Wisdom of God in the Creation: or a Compendium of Natural Philosophy*. 1777. Reprint. Philadelphia: Jonathan Pounder, 1816.

———. *Wesley's Standard Sermons*. Edited by Edward H. Sugden. London: The Epworth Press, 1960.

———. *Letters, I, 1721–1739*. Edited by Frank Baker. Vol. 25 of *The Works of John Wesley*. Edited by Frank Baker. Oxford: Clarendon Press, 1980.

————. *The Works of the Rev. John Wesley, A.M.* 14 vols. London: Wesleyan-Methodist Book-Room, n.d. This edition and the London 1872 edition re-issued by Zondervan in 1958 are reissues of the third edition, edited by Thomas Jackson, 1829–31.

Wordsworth, William. *The Poetical Works of William Wordsworth.* Edited by Ernest de Selincourt. 5 vols. Oxford: Clarendon Press, 1940–49. 2d ed. of vol. 2 (1952) and vol. 3 (1954) revised by Helen Darbishire.

————. *The Prelude: or, Growth of a Poet's Mind.* Edited by Ernest de Selincourt. Oxford: Clarendon Press, 1959. 2d ed. revised by Helen Darbishire. Unless otherwise indicated, quotations from *The Prelude* are from the 1850 version.

Wynne, John. *An Abridgment of Mr. Locke's Essay concerning Human Understanding.* 1695. 3d ed. London: A. Churchill, 1721.

Secondary References

Aarsleff, Hans. *From Locke to Saussure: Essays on the Study of Language and Intellectual History*. Minneapolis: University of Minnesota Press, 1982.

Abbey, Lloyd. *Destroyer and Preserver: Shelley's Poetic Skepticism*. Lincoln: University of Nebraska Press, 1979.

Abrams, M. H. *Natural Supernaturalism: Tradition and Revolution in Romantic Literature*. New York: W. W. Norton, 1971.

———. "Structure and Style in the Greater Romantic Lyric." In *From Sensibility to Romanticism*. Edited by F. W. Hilles and Harold Bloom. New York: Oxford University Press, 1965.

Allen, R. Wilberforce. *Methodism and Modern World Problems, with an introduction by Sir Josiah Stamp*. London: Methuen & Co., 1926.

Altick, Richard D. *Victorian People and Ideas: A Companion for the Modern Reader of Victorian Literature*. New York: Norton, 1973.

Arnold, Matthew. *Literature and Dogma: An Essay Towards a Better Apprehension of the Bible*. In *The Works of Matthew Arnold*. 15 vols. London: Macmillan & Co., Limited, 1903.

Atkins, G. Douglas. "Dehellenizing Literary Criticism." *College English* 41 (1980): 769–79.

Ault, Donald. *Visionary Physics: Blake's Response to Newton*. Chicago: University of Chicago Press, 1974.

Ayer, A. J. *Language, Truth and Logic*. London: V. Gollancz, 1936.

Bahlman, Dudley W. *The Moral Revolution of 1688*. New Haven: Yale University Press, 1957.

Baker, Frank. *A Union Catalogue of the Works of John and Charles Wesley*. Durham, N.C.: The Divinity School, Duke University, 1966.

———. "John Wesley and Bishop Butler: A Fragment of John Wesley's Manuscript Journal, 16th to 24th August 1739." *Proceedings of the Wesley Historical Society* 42 (May, 1980): 93–100.

———. *John Wesley and the Church of England*. Nashville: Abingdon Press, 1970.

Bannerjee, Chinmoy. "*Tristram Shandy* and the Association of Ideas." *Texas Studies in Language and Literature* 15 (1973–74): 693–706.

Barber, F. Louis. *The Philosophy of John Wesley*. Toronto: The Ryerson Press, 1923.

Barnett, George L. *Charles Lamb*. Boston: Twayne, 1976.

Barrell, John. *The Idea of Landscape and the Sense of Place, 1730–1840: An Approach to the Poetry of John Clare*. Cambridge: Cambridge University Press, 1972.

Barth, J. Robert, S.J. *Coleridge and Christian Doctrine*. Cambridge: Harvard University Press, 1969.

———. *The Symbolic Imagination: Coleridge and the Romantic Tradition*. Princeton: Princeton University Press, 1977.

Barthes, Roland. *Sade, Fourier, Loyola*. Paris: Éditions du Seuil, 1971.

Beach, Waldo and H. Richard Niebuhr, eds. *Christian Ethics: Sources of the Tradition*. New York: Ronald, 1955.

Beer, John. *Coleridge the Visionary*. London: Chatto & Windus, 1959.

———. Review of *Coleridge, The Damaged Archangel*, by Norman Fruman. *Review of English Studies* 24 (1973): 346–53.

Bentley, Gerald E., Jr., ed. *Vala or the Four Zoas*. Oxford: Clarendon Press, 1963.

Bercovitch, Sacvan. *The American Jeremiad*. Madison: University of Wisconsin Press, 1978.

Berkoben, Lawrence D. "Christabel: A Variety of Evil Experience." *Modern Language Quarterly* 25 (1964): 400–411.

Bett, Henry. *The Spirit of Methodism*. London: The Epworth Press, 1937.

Bickerton, Derek. *Roots of Language*. Ann Arbor: Karoma Publishers, Inc., 1982.

Birrell, Augustine. *The Collected Essays & Addresses of the Rt. Hon. Augustine Birrell, 1880–1920*. 3 vols. London and Toronto: J. M. Dent and Sons, 1922.

Blackstone, Bernard. *English Blake*. 1949. Reprint. Hamden, Connecticut: Archon Books, 1966.

Bleich, David. *Subjective Criticism*. Baltimore: The Johns Hopkins University Press, 1978.

Bloom, Harold. "Poetic Crossing: Rhetoric and Psychology." *The Georgia Review* 30 (Fall 1976): 495–524.

———. *The Visionary Company: A Reading of English Romantic Poetry*. Garden City, N.Y.: Doubleday, 1961.

Blythe, Ronald, ed. *William Hazlitt: Selected Writings*. 1970. Reprint. Hammondsworth, England: Penguin Books, 1982.

Body, Alfred H. *John Wesley and Education*. London: The Epworth Press, 1936.

Bostetter, Edward E. "Christabel: The Vision of Fear." *PQ* 36 (1957): 183–94.

———. "Masses and Solids: Byron's View of the External World." *Modern Language Quarterly* 35 (1974): 257–71.

Bottrall, Margaret. *The Divine Image: A Study of Blake's Interpretation of Christianity.* Rome: Edizioni di Storia e Letteratura, 1950.

Boulger, James. *Coleridge as Religious Thinker.* New Haven: Yale University Press, 1961.

Brantley, Richard E. "Johnson's Wesleyan Connection." *Eighteenth-Century Studies* 10 (Winter 1976/77): 143–68.

———. *Wordsworth's "Natural Methodism."* New Haven: Yale University Press, 1975.

Bredahl, A. Carl. *Melville's Angles of Vision.* Gainesville: University of Florida Press, 1972.

Brisman, Leslie. *Romantic Origins.* Ithaca: Cornell University Press, 1978.

Bronowski, Jacob. *A Man Without a Mask.* 1944. 3d ed. London: Secker and Warburg, 1947.

Brown, Byron Keith. "Wordsworth's Affective Poetics: Rhetorical Theory and Poetic Revolution." Ph.D. diss., University of Florida, 1981.

Brown, Nathaniel. *Sexuality and Feminism in Shelley.* Cambridge: Harvard University Press, 1979.

Caldecott, Alfred. "The Religious Sentiment: An Inductive Enquiry, illustrated from the Lives of Wesley's Helpers." *Proceedings of the Aristotelian Society of London* 8 (1909): 11–47.

Calvino, Italo. "The Written and the Unwritten Word." Translated by William Weaver. *The New York Review of Books* 30 (May 12, 1983): 38–39.

Cannon, William R. *The Theology of John Wesley, with Special Reference to the Doctrine of Justification.* Nashville: Abingdon-Cokesbury Press, 1946.

Carnochan, W. B. *Lemuel Gulliver's Mirror for Man.* Berkeley and Los Angeles: University of California Press, 1968.

Cash, Arthur Hill. "The Sermon in *Tristram Shandy*." *ELH* 31 (1964): 395–417.

Cell, G. C. *The Rediscovery of John Wesley.* New York: Henry Holt, 1935.

Chapman. R. W., ed. *Jane Austen's Letters to her sister Cassandra and others.* Oxford: Clarendon Press, 1932. Reprint. 1979.

Cherry, Conrad. *The Theology of Jonathan Edwards.* New York: Doubleday, 1966.

Clarke, Colin. *The Romantic Paradox: An Essay on the Poetry of Wordsworth.* New York: Barnes & Noble, 1963.

Colby, Vineta. *The Singular Anomaly: Women Novelists of the Nineteenth Century.* New York: New York University Press, 1970.

———. *Yesterday's Woman: Domestic Realism in the English Novel.* Princeton: Princeton University Press, 1974.

Colie, Rosalie L. *Light and Enlightenment: A Study of the Cambridge Platonists and the Dutch Arminians.* Cambridge: Cambridge University Press, 1957.

Collier, Frank Wilbur. *Back to Wesley.* New York and Cincinnati: Methodist Book Concern, 1924.

———. *John Wesley among the Scientists.* New York: Abingdon Press, 1928.

Cooper, Lane, ed. *A Concordance to the Poems of William Wordsworth.* 1911. Reprint. New York: Russell & Russell, 1965.

Copleston, Frederick J., S.J. *A History of Philosophy.* 9 vols. Garden City, N.Y.: Doubleday, 1966.

Coulson, John. *Newman and the Common Tradition: A Study in the Language of Church and Society*. Oxford: Clarendon Press, 1970.

Cox, Leo George. *John Wesley's Concept of Perfection*. Kansas City: Beacon Hill Press, 1964.

Cragg, Gerald R. *From Puritanism to the Age of Reason: A Study of Changes in Religious Thought Within the Church of England, 1660 to 1700*. Cambridge: Cambridge University Press, 1950.

Cressy, David. *Literacy and the Social Order: Reading and Writing in Tudor and Stuart England*. Cambridge and New York: Cambridge University Press, 1980.

Crossan, Greg. *A Relish for Eternity: The Process of Divinization in the Poetry of John Clare*. Salzburg: Institut für Englische Spräche und Literatur, Universität Salzburg, 1976.

Cruse, Amy. *The Victorians and their Reading*. Boston and New York: Houghton Mifflin Co., 1935.

Cunningham, Valentine. *Everywhere Spoken Against: Dissent in the Victorian Novel*. Oxford: Clarendon Press, 1975.

Cupitt, Don. *Christ and the Hiddenness of God*. London: Lutterworth Press, 1971.

Damrosch, Leopold. *Symbol and Truth in Blake's Myth*. Princeton: Princeton University Press, 1980.

Darlow. T. H. *William Robertson Nicoll: Life and Letters*. London: Hodder and Stoughton, 1926.

Davie, Donald. *A Gathered Church: The Literature of the English Dissenting Interest*. London and Henley: Routledge, 1978.

Davies, Horton. *Worship and Theology in England from Watts and Wesley to Maurice, 1690–1850*. Princeton: Princeton University Press, 1961.

Davies, Hugh Sykes. *Thomas De Quincey*. Harlow, England: Longman, 1964.

———. "Wordsworth and the Empirical Philosophers." In *The English Mind: Studies in the English Moralists Presented to Basil Willey*. Edited by Hugh Sykes Davies and George Watson. Cambridge: Cambridge University Press, 1964.

Davies, J. G. *The Theology of William Blake*. Oxford: Clarendon Press, 1948.

Davis, Michael. *William Blake: A New Kind of Man*. Berkeley and Los Angeles: University of California Press, 1977.

Dawson, Carl. *Victorian Noon: English Literature in 1850*. Baltimore: The Johns Hopkins University Press, 1979.

de Man, Paul. "The Rhetoric of Temporality." In *Interpretation: Theory and Practice*. Edited by Charles S. Singleton. Baltimore: The Johns Hopkins University Press, 1969.

DePorte, Michael V. "Digressions and Madness in *A Tale of a Tub* and *Tristram Shandy*." *The Huntington Library Quarterly* 34 (November 1970): 43–57.

Derrida, Jacques. *L'Archéologie du frivole*. Paris: Donoel/Gonthier, 1976.

Dimond, S. G. *The Psychology of the Methodist Revival: An Empirical and Descriptive Study*. London: Oxford University Press, 1926.

Dobbs, A. E. *Education and Social Movements, 1700–1850*. London and New York: Longmans, Green, and Co., 1919.

Doughty, W. L. *John Wesley, Preacher*. London: The Epworth Press, 1955.

Dreyer, Frederick. "Faith and Experience in the Thought of John Wesley." *The American Historical Review* 88 (February 1983): 12–30.

Durant, Will. *The Story of Philosophy: The Lives and Opinions of the Greater Philosophers.* New York: Washington Square Press, 1970.

Durrant, Geoffrey. *Wordsworth and the Great System: A Study of Wordsworth's Poetic Universe.* London: Cambridge University Press, 1970.

Eayrs, George. *John Wesley: Christian Philosopher and Church Founder.* London: The Epworth Press, 1926.

Edwards, Maldwyn Lloyd. *John Wesley and the Eighteenth Century: A Study of His Social and Political Influence.* London: G. Allen & Unwin, 1933.

———. *My Dear Sister: The Story of John Wesley and the Women in His Life.* Manchester, England: Penwork, 1980.

Ehrenpreis, Irvin. "The Meaning of Gulliver's Last Voyage." *A Review of English Literature* 3 (July 1962): 18–38.

Eliot, George. "Worldliness and Other-worldliness: The Poet Young." *Westminster Review* 67 (January 1857): 1–42.

Elwood, Douglas J. *The Philosophical Theology of Jonathan Edwards.* New York: Columbia University Press, 1960.

England, Martha, and John Sparrow. *Hymns Unbidden: Donne, Herbert, Blake, Emily Dickinson, and the Hymnographers.* New York: The New York Public Library, 1966.

Enscoe, Gerald E. *Eros and the Romantics: Sexual Love as a Theme in Coleridge, Shelley and Keats.* The Hague: Mouton, 1967.

Faulkner, J. A. "Wesley the Mystic." *London Quarterly and Holborn Review* 153 (1930): 145–60.

Ferguson, Frances. *Wordsworth: Language as Counterspirit.* New Haven: Yale University Press, 1977.

Fiering, Norman. *Jonathan Edwards's Moral Thought and Its British Context.* Chapel Hill: University of North Carolina Press, 1981.

Fitzgerald, Sally, ed. *The Habit of Being: Letters Edited and with an Introduction.* By Flannery O'Connor. New York: Vintage Books, 1980.

Fleishman, Avrom. *A Reading of* Mansfield Park: *An Essay in Critical Synthesis.* Minneapolis: University of Minnesota Press, 1967.

Foster, Charles. *An Errand of Mercy.* Chapel Hill: University of North Carolina Press, 1960.

Foucault, Michel. *Les Mots et Les Choses.* 1966. Translation, *The Order of Things: An Archaeology of Human Sciences.* New York: Vintage Books, 1973.

Fox, Christopher. "Locke and the Scriblerians: The Discussion of Identity in Early Eighteenth-Century England." *Eighteenth-Century Studies* 16 (Fall 1982): 1–25.

von Franz, M.-L. "The Process of Individuation." In *Man and His Symbols,* by Carl Jung et al. New York: Dell, 1968.

Fraser, Alexander Campbell. *Life and Letters of George Berkeley, D.D.* Oxford: Clarendon Press, 1871.

Fruman, Norman. *Coleridge, The Damaged Archangel*. New York: George Braziller, 1971.

Gallaway, Francis. *Reason, Rule, and Revolt in English Classicism*. New York: Charles Scribner's Sons, 1940.

Gaull, Marilyn. "From Wordsworth to Darwin." *The Wordsworth Circle* 10 (Winter 1979): 33–48.

Gay, Peter. *The Enlightenment, An Interpretation: The Rise of Modern Paganism*. New York: Knopf, 1967.

George, Robert F. "The Evangelical Revival and Charlotte Brontë's *Jane Eyre*." Ph.D. diss., University of Florida, 1981.

Gill, F. C. *The Romantic Movement and Methodism: A Study of English Romanticism and the Evangelical Revival*. London: The Epworth Press, 1937.

Golden, James L. "John Wesley on Rhetoric and Belles Lettres." *Speech Monographs* 28 (November 1961): 250–64.

Graff, Gerald. *Literature Against Itself: Literary Ideas in Modern Society*. Chicago: University of Chicago Press, 1979.

Green, Richard. *John Wesley, Evangelist*. London: The Religious Tract Society, 1905.

———. *The Works of John and Charles Wesley: A Bibliography*. London: Methodist Publishing House, 1906.

Green, V. H. H. *The Young Mr. Wesley: A Study of John Wesley and Oxford*. New York: St. Martin's Press, 1961.

Greene, Donald. *The Age of Exuberance: Backgrounds to Eighteenth-Century English Literature*. New York: Random House, 1970.

Greeves, Frederic. "John Wesley and Divine Guidance." *London Quarterly and Holborn Review* 162 (July 1937): 379–95.

Gregory, Benjamin. *Sidelights on the Conflicts of Methodism*. London: Cassell, 1898.

Grob, Alan. *The Philosophic Mind: A Study of Wordsworth's Poetry and Thought, 1797–1805*. Columbus: Ohio State University Press, 1973.

———. Review of *Wordsworth's "Natural Methodism,"* by Richard E. Brantley. *The Wordsworth Circle* 7 (1976): 173–78.

Halévy, Élie. *A History of the English People*. Translated by E. I. Watkin and D. A. Barker. London: E. Benn, 1912–47.

Hammond, J. L. and Barbara. *The Age of the Chartists, 1832–1854: A Study of Discontent*. London: Longmans, Green, and Co., 1930.

Harding, D. W. *Experience into Words: Essays on Poetry*. New York: Horizon Press, 1964.

Harris, Victor. "Allegory to Analogy in the Interpretation of Scriptures." *PQ* 45 (1966): 1–23.

Harrison, Grace Elizabeth. *Son to Susanna: The Private Life of John Wesley*. London: I. Nicholson and Watson, 1937.

Harth, Phillip. *Swift and Anglican Rationalism: The Religious Background of A Tale of a Tub*. Chicago: University of Chicago Press, 1961.

Hartley, Lodwick. "Cowper and the Evangelicals: Notes on Early Biographical Interpretations." *PMLA* 65 (1959): 719–31.

Hartman, Geoffrey. *Criticism in the Wilderness.* New Haven: Yale University Press, 1980.

———. *The Unmediated Vision: An Interpretation of Wordsworth, Hopkins, Rilke, and Valéry.* New Haven: Yale University Press, 1954.

——— *Wordsworth's Poetry 1787–1814.* New Haven: Yale University Press, 1964.

Hayter, Alethea, ed. *Confessions of an English Opium Eater.* By Thomas De Quincey. 1821. Reprint. Hammondsworth, England: Penguin Books, 1971.

Hazard, Paul. *European Thought in the Eighteenth Century: From Montesquieu to Lessing.* Cleveland and New York: The World Publishing Co., 1963.

Hellstrom, Ward. *On the Poems of Tennyson.* Gainesville: University of Florida Press, 1972.

Henry, Carl F. H. "The Concerns and Considerations of Carl F. H. Henry." *Christianity Today* 25 (March 13, 1981): 18–23.

Henry, Granville C. "John Wesley's Doctrine of Free Will." *London Quarterly and Holborn Review* 185 (1960): 200–204.

Herbert, T. Walter. *John Wesley as Editor and Author.* Princeton: Princeton University Press, 1940.

Herbert, T. Walter, Jr. *Marquesan Encounters: Melville and the Meaning of Civilization.* Cambridge: Harvard University Press, 1980.

———. *Moby Dick and Calvinism: A World Dismantled.* New Brunswick, N.J.: Rutgers, The State University Press, 1977.

Hesse, Mary B. "The Explanatory Function of Metaphor." In *International Congress for Logic, Methodology, and Philosophy of Science.* Edited by Y. Bar-Hillel. Amsterdam: North Holland Publication Co., 1965.

Hill, Alfred Wesley. *John Wesley among the Physicians: A Study of Eighteenth-Century Medicine.* London: The Epworth Press, 1958.

Hindley, J. Clifford. "The Philosophy of Enthusiasm." *The London Quarterly and Holborn Review* 182 (1957): 99–109, 199–210.

Hirsch, E. D., Jr. *The Aims of Interpretation.* Chicago: University of Chicago Press, 1975.

———. *Innocence and Experience: An Introduction to Blake.* New Haven: Yale University Press, 1964.

Howell, Wilbur. "John Locke and the New Rhetoric." *The Quarterly Journal of Speech* 53 (December 1967): 319–33.

Howse, Ernest Marshall. *Saints in Politics: The Clapham Sect and the Growth of Freedom.* Toronto: University of Toronto Press, 1952.

Hunter, Frederick. *John Wesley and the Coming Comprehensive Church.* London: The Epworth Press, 1968.

Ives, A. G. *Kingswood School in Wesley's Day and Since.* London: The Epworth Press, 1970.

Jameson, Fredric. *Marxism and Form: Twentieth Century Dialectical Theories of Literature.* Princeton: Princeton University Press, 1972.

Jay, Elisabeth. *The Religion of the Heart: Anglican Evangelicalism and the Nineteenth-Century Novel.* Oxford: Clarendon Press, 1979.

Jeffner, Anders. *Butler and Hume on Religion: A Comparative Analysis.* Stockholm: Diakonistyrelsense bokförlog, 1966.

Johnson, Lee M. *Wordsworth and the Sonnet.* Copenhagen: Rosenkilde and Bagger, 1973.

Jones, Mary Gwladys. *The Charity School Movement: A Study of Eighteenth-Century Puritanism in Action.* Cambridge: Cambridge University Press, 1938.

Jones, Roger S. *Physics as Metaphor.* Minneapolis: University of Minnesota Press, 1982.

Jordan, Frank, Jr., ed. *The English Romantic Poets: A Review of Research and Criticism.* 3d ed. New York: The Modern Language Association of America, 1972.

Kelley, Theresa M. "Spirit and Geometric Form: The Stone and the Shell in Wordsworth's Arab Dream." *Studies in English Literature* 22 (Autumn 1982): 563–82.

Kessler, Edward. *Coleridge's Metaphors of Being.* Princeton: Princeton University Press, 1979.

Keynes, Geoffrey, ed. *The Complete Writings of William Blake.* London: Oxford University Press, 1966.

Kingdon, Robert N. "Laissez-faire or Government Control: A Problem for John Wesley." *Church History* 26 (1957): 342–54.

Kinnaird, John. *William Hazlitt: Critic of Power.* New York: Columbia University Press, 1978.

Knight, G. Wilson. *The Starlit Dome: Studies in the Poetry of Vision.* London: Oxford University Press, 1941.

Knox, Ronald A. *Enthusiasm: A Chapter in the History of Religion, with Special Reference to the Seventeenth and Eighteenth Centuries.* New York: Oxford University Press, 1950.

Landow, George. *The Aesthetic and Critical Theories of John Ruskin.* Princeton: Princeton University Press, 1971.

Langbaum, Robert. *The Poetry of Experience: The Dramatic Monologue in Modern Literary Tradition.* London: Chatto & Windus, 1957.

Lawson, E. Leroy. *Very Sure of God: Religious Language in the Poetry of Robert Browning.* Nashville: Vanderbilt University Press, 1974.

Lawton, George. *John Wesley's English: A Study of His Literary Style.* London: George Allen & Unwin, 1962.

Lecky, W. E. H. *A History of England in the Eighteenth Century.* 8 vols. New York: D. Appleton, 1883.

Lee, Umphrey. *John Wesley and Modern Religion.* Nashville: Cokesbury Press, 1936.

Lennon, Thomas M., and Paul L. Olscamp, trans. *The Search After Truth.* By Nicholas Malebranche. Columbus: Ohio State University Press, 1980.

Lentricchia, Frank. *After the New Criticism.* Chicago: University of Chicago Press, 1980.

Leventhal, Herbert. *In the Shadow of the Enlightenment: Occultism and Renaissance*

Science in Eighteenth-Century America. New York: New York University Press, 1976.

Lewontin, R. C. "The Corpse in the Elevator," a review of *Against Biological Determinism* and *Towards a Liberatory Biology*, both edited by Steven Rose. *The New York Review of Books* 29 (January 20, 1983): 34–37.

Lindstrom, Harald Gustave Ake. *Wesley and Sanctification: A Study of the Doctrine of Salvation*. London: The Epworth Press, 1950.

Lucas, E. V., ed. *Bernard Barton and His Friends: A Record of Quiet Lives*. London: E. Hicks, Jr., 1893.

————. *The Letters of Charles Lamb to which are added those of his sister Mary Lamb*. London: J. M. Dent & Sons and Methuen & Co., 1935.

Luce, A. A. *Berkeley and Malebranche: A Study in the Origins of Berkeley's Thought*. 1934. Reprint. London: Oxford University Press, 1967.

Lyles, Albert M. *Methodism Mocked: The Satiric Reaction to Methodism in the Eighteenth Century*. London: The Epworth Press, 1960.

MacArthur, Kathleen Walker. *The Economic Ethics of John Wesley*. New York: Abingdon Press, 1936.

McConnell, Francis. *John Wesley*. New York: Abingdon, 1939.

McFarland, Thomas. *Coleridge and the Pantheist Tradition*. Oxford: Clarendon Press, 1969.

————. "Coleridge's Plagiarisms Once More." *Yale Review* 63 (Winter 1974): 152–84.

————. *Romanticism and the Forms of Ruin: Wordsworth, Coleridge, and Modalities of Fragmentation*. Princeton: Princeton University Press, 1981.

McGann, Jerome. "The Meaning of the Ancient Mariner." *Critical Inquiry* 7 (Autumn 1981): 35–67.

McGiffert, A. C. *Protestant Thought Before Kant*. New York: Charles Scribner's Sons, 1911.

MacLean, Kenneth. *John Locke and English Literature of the Eighteenth Century*. 1936. Reprint. New York: Russell & Russell, 1962.

Manning, Henry Edward. *The Temporal Mission of the Holy Ghost; or, Reason and Revelation*. 3d ed. London: Longmans, Green, and Co., 1877.

Mansell, H. L. *The Limits of Religious Thought examined in eight lectures preached before the Univ. of Oxford in the year 1858 on the foundation of the late Rev. J. Bampton*. Oxford and London: Printed by J. Wright for J. Murray, 1858.

Marjarum, E. W. *Byron as Skeptic and Believer*. Princeton: Princeton University Press, 1938.

Mathews, H. F. *Methodism and the Education of the People, 1791–1851*. London: The Epworth Press, 1949.

May, Henry. *The Enlightenment in America*. New York: Oxford University Press, 1976.

Mellor, Anne K. *English Romantic Irony*. Cambridge: Harvard University Press, 1980.

————. Review of *Irony and Authority in Romantic Poetry*, by David Simpson. *The Wordsworth Circle* 12 (Summer 1981): 196.

Miles, Josephine. *The Primary Language of Poetry in the 1740's and the 1840's*. Berkeley and Los Angeles: University of California Press, 1950.

Miller, J. Hillis. "The Critic as Host." In *Deconstruction and Criticism*. Edited by Geoffrey Hartman et al. New York: The Seabury Press, 1979.

Miller, Perry. "Edwards, Locke, and the Rhetoric of Sensation." In *Perspectives of Criticism*. Edited by Harry Levin. Harvard Studies in Comparative Literature, no. 20. Cambridge: Harvard University Press, 1950.

————. *Errand into the Wildernesss*. Cambridge: Harvard University Press, 1956.

————. "Jonathan Edwards and the Sense of the Heart." *Harvard Theological Review* 41 (April 1948): 123–45.

Minor, Mark. "John Clare and the Methodists: A Reconsideration." *Studies in Romanticism* 19 (Spring 1980): 31–50.

Monk, Robert Clarence. *John Wesley: His Puritan Heritage*. Nashville: Abingdon Press, 1966.

Moore, Henry. *The Life of the Rev. John Wesley*. 2 vols. New York: J. and J. Harper, 1824–25.

Moore, Robert L. *John Wesley and Authority*. Missoula, Montana: Scholars Press, 1979.

Morris, David B. "The Kinship of Madness in Pope's *Dunciad*." *PQ* 51 (1972): 813–31.

Neuberg, Victor E. *Popular Literature: A History and Guide*. London: Penguin Books, Ltd., 1977.

New, Melvyn. *Laurence Sterne as Satirist: A Reading of* Tristram Shandy. Gainesville: University of Florida Press, 1969.

————. "Wordsworth's Shell of Poetry." *PQ* 53 (Spring 1974): 275–81.

————, and Joan New, eds. *The Life and Opinions of Tristram Shandy, Gentleman*. By Laurence Sterne. 2 vols. Gainesville: University Presses of Florida, 1978.

Nicholson, Norman. *William Cowper*. London: J. Lehmann, 1951.

Nietzsche, Friedrich. "European Nihilism." In *The Will to Power*. New York: Vintage Books, 1968.

————. *Werke in Drei Bänden*. Edited by Karl Schlechta. Munich: Carl Hauser Verlag, 1966.

Ong, Walter J., S.J. "Peter Ramus and the Naming of Methodism." *Journal of the History of Ideas* 14 (April 1953): 235–48.

Opie, John, ed. *Jonathan Edwards and the Enlightenment*. Lexington, Mass.: D. C. Heath, 1969.

Orsini, Gian. *Coleridge and German Idealism: A Study in the History of Philosophy, with unpublished materials from Coleridge's manuscripts*. Carbondale: Southern Illinois University Press, 1969.

Otto, Rudolf, ed. *Über die Religion: Reden an die Gebildeten unter ihren Verächtern*. By Friedrich Schleiermacher. Göttingen: Vandenhoeck und Ruprecht, 1926.

Paley, Morton B. "Cowper as Blake's Spectre." *Eighteenth-Century Studies* 1 (1968): 236–52.

————. *Energy and the Imagination: A Study of the Development of Blake's Thought*. Oxford: Clarendon Press, 1970.

Paris, Bernard J. *Experiments in Life: George Eliot's Quest for Values*. Detroit: Wayne State University Press, 1965.

Parker, Reeve. *Coleridge's Meditative Art*. Ithaca: Cornell University Press, 1975.

Perkins, David, ed. *English Romantic Writers*. New York: Harcourt, Brace & World, 1967.

Pickering, Samuel F., Jr. *John Locke and Children's Books in Eighteenth-Century England*. Knoxville: University of Tennessee Press, 1981.

————. *The Moral Tradition in English Fiction, 1785–1850*. Hanover, N.H.: The University Press of New England, 1976.

Piette, Maximin. *John Wesley in the Evolution of Protestantism*. Translated by J. B. Howard. New York: Sheed and Ward, 1937.

Piper, H. W. *The Active Universe: Pantheism and the Concept of Imagination in the English Romantic Poets*. London: The Athlone Press, 1962.

Pocock, J. G. A. "Post-Puritan England and the Problem of the Enlightenment." In *Culture and Politics from Puritanism to the Enlightenment*. Edited by Perez Zagorin. Berkeley and Los Angeles: University of California Press, 1980.

Prickett, Stephen. *Romanticism and Religion: The Tradition of Coleridge and Wordsworth in the Victorian Church*. Cambridge: Cambridge University Press, 1976.

Pulos, C. E. *The Deep Truth: A Study of Shelley's Skepticism*. Lincoln: University of Nebraska Press, 1954.

Raine, Kathleen. *Berkeley, Blake and the New Age*. Ipswich, Mass.: Golgonooza Press, 1977.

Rajan, Tilottama. *Dark Interpreter: The Discourse of Romanticism*. Ithaca: Cornell University Press, 1980.

Rattenbury, J. E. *The Conversion of the Wesleys: A Critical Study*. London: The Epworth Press, 1938.

Reiman, Donald. *Percy Bysshe Shelley*. New York: Twayne Publishers, Inc., 1969.

Rigg, J. H. *The Living Wesley, as he was in his youth and in his prime*. London: C. H. Kelly, 1875.

————. *Wesleyan Methodist Reminiscences Sixty Years Ago*. London: R. Cully, 1904.

Riley, D. W. "Notes and News." *Bulletin of the John Rylands University Library of Manchester* 60 (Spring 1978): 269.

Robin, Leon. *Pyrrhon et le Scepticisme Grec*. Paris: Presses Universitaires de France, 1944.

Rollins, Hyder E., ed. *The Letters of John Keats, 1814–1821*. Cambridge: Harvard University Press, 1958.

Rorty, Richard. "Philosophy as a Kind of Writing: An Essay on Derrida." *New Literary History* 10 (1978): 141–60.

Rose, Steven, ed. *Against Biological Determinism*. New York: Schocken, 1982.

————, ed. *Towards a Liberatory Biology*. New York: Schocken, 1982.

Roszak, Theodore. "In Search of the Miraculous." *Harper's*, January 1981, pp. 54–62.

Rousseau, G. S. "John Wesley's *Primitive Physick* (1747)." *Harvard Library Bulletin* 16 (July 1968): 242–56.

Ruoff, Gene W., and L. J. Swingle. "From the Editors." *The Wordsworth Circle* 10 (Spring 1979): 130.

Ryan, Robert M. *Keats: The Religious Sense*. Princeton: Princeton University Press, 1976.

Sanders, Charles. *Coleridge and the Broad Church Movement: Studies in S. T. Coleridge, Dr. Arnold of Rugby, J. C. Hare, Thomas Carlyle and F. D. Maurice*. Durham, N.C.: Duke University Press, 1942. Reprint. New York: Russell & Russell, 1972.

Sartre, Jean-Paul. *L'Être et le néant: Essai d'ontologie phénoménologique*. Paris: Gaillimard, 1943.

Savage, Marsha Kent. "Archibald Alison and the Spiritual Aesthetics of William Wordsworth." Ph.D. diss., University of Florida, 1980.

Schlick, Moritz. *Problems of Ethics*. Translated by David Ryrin. Reprint. New York: Prentice-Hall, 1939.

Schmidt, Martin. *John Wesley: A Theological Biography*. 2 vols. New York: Abingdon Press, 1961.

Schofield, Robert E. "John Wesley and Science in 18th Century England." *Isis* 44 (1953): 331–40.

———. *Mechanism and Materialism: British Natural Philosophy in an Age of Reason*. Princeton: Princeton University Press, 1970.

Schuda, Robert Bernard. "A Study of Laurence Sterne's Sermons: Yorkshire Background, Ethics, and Index." Ph.D. diss., University of Wisconsin, 1975.

Semmel, Bernard. *The Methodist Revolution*. New York: Basic Books, 1973.

Shaffer, Elinor. *"Kubla Khan" and the Fall of Jerusalem: The Mythological School in Biblical Criticism and Secular Literature, 1770–1880*. Cambridge: Cambridge University Press, 1975.

Sharp, Ronald A. *Keats, Skepticism, and the Religion of Beauty*. Athens: University of Georgia Press, 1979.

Sharrock, Roger. "The Chemist and the Poet: Sir Humphry Davy and the Preface to *Lyrical Ballads*." *Notes and Records of the Royal Society of London* 17 (1962): 57–76.

Shepard, Leslie. *The History of Street Literature*. Detroit: Singing Tree Press, 1973.

Sherry, Charles. *Wordsworth's Poetry of the Imagination*. Oxford: Clarendon Press, 1980.

Sherwin, Oscar. "Milton for the Masses: John Wesley's Edition of *Paradise Lost*." *Modern Language Quarterly* 12 (1951): 267–85.

Shorris, Earl. Review of *Life of the Mind*, by Hannah Arendt. *Harper's*, August 1978, p. 84.

Simpson, David. *Irony and Authority in Romantic Poetry*. Totowa, N.J.: Rowman and Littlefield, 1979.

Sloss, D. J. and J. P. R. Wallis. *The Prophetic Writings of William Blake*. Oxford: Clarendon Press, 1926.

Smith, Frank. *A History of English Elementary Education, 1760–1902*. London: University of London Press, 1931.

Snaith, John. *The Philosophy of Spirit.* London and New York: Hodder and Stoughton, 1914.

Spacks, Patricia Meyer. *An Argument of Images: The Poetry of Alexander Pope.* Cambridge: Harvard University Press, 1971.

Sperry, Stuart. *Keats the Poet.* Princeton: Princeton University Press, 1973.

Stephen, Sir Leslie. *A History of English Thought in the Eighteenth Century.* 3d ed. 2 vols. Reprint. New York: G. P. Putnam's Sons, 1927.

Stevenson, Lionel. "'The Ancient Mariner' as a Dramatic Monologue." *Personalist* 30 (1949): 34–44.

Stillinger, Jack. "The Hoodwinking of Madeline: Scepticism in 'The Eve of St. Agnes.'" *Studies in Philology* 58 (1961): 533–55.

———, ed. *Twentieth Century Interpretations of Keats's Odes.* Englewood Cliffs, N.J.: Prentice-Hall, Inc., 1968.

———, ed. *William Wordsworth: Selected Poems and Prefaces.* New York: Riverside Editions, n.d.

Stone, Wilfred. *The Cave and the Mountain: A Study of E. M. Forster.* Stanford: Stanford University Press, 1966.

Stoolz, K. "John Wesley and Evolution: Reply to W. W. Sweet." *Christian Century* 50 (May 24, 1934): 663.

Stromberg, R. N. *Religious Liberalism in Eighteenth-Century England.* London: Oxford University Press, 1954.

Swingle, L. J. "On Reading Romantic Poetry." *PMLA* 86 (October 1971): 974–81.

Sweet, William W. "John Wesley and Scientific Discovery." *Christian Century* 40 (May 10, 1923): 591–92.

Telford, John. *The Life of John Wesley.* London: Hodder and Stoughton, 1886.

Thilly, Frank. *A History of Philosophy.* 3d ed. rev. by Ledger Wood. New York: Holt, Rinehart, and Winston, 1957.

Thomas, Lewis. *The Lives of a Cell: Notes of a Biology Watcher.* New York: Viking Press, 1974.

Thompson, E. P. Review of *A Gathered Church: The Literature of the English Dissenting Interest,* by Donald Davie. *The Modern Language Review* 75 (January 1980): 165.

Thorpe, Clarence. *The Mind of John Keats.* 1926. Reprint. New York: Russell and Russell, 1964.

Todd, John Murray. *John Wesley and the Catholic Church.* London: Hodder and Stoughton, 1958.

Turrell, W. J. *John Wesley, Physician and Electrotherapist.* Oxford: Blackwell, 1938.

Tuveson, Ernest Lee. *Imagination as a Means of Grace: Locke and the Aesthetics of Romanticism.* Berkeley and Los Angeles: University of California Press, 1960.

Tyerman, Luke. *The Life and Times of the Rev. John Wesley.* London: Harper and Brothers, 1870.

Vallins, G. H. *The Wesleys and the English Language.* London: The Epworth Press, 1957.

Van den Berg, J. H. *The Changing Nature of Man: Introduction to a Historical Psychology.* New York: Dell Publishing Co., 1964.

Wainwright, William J. "Jonathan Edwards and the Language of God." *Journal of the American Academy of Religion* 48 (December 1980): 519–30.

Walsh, J. D. "Origins of the Evangelical Revival." In *Essays in Modern English Church History: In Memory of Norman Sykes.* Edited by J. D. Walsh and Gareth Vaughan Bennett. New York: Oxford University Press, 1966.

Wasserman, Earl. "The English Romantics: The Ground of Knowledge." *Studies in Romanticism* 4 (1964): 17–34.

———. *The Finer Tone: Keats's Major Poems.* Baltimore: The Johns Hopkins University Press, 1953.

———. "Nature Moralized: The Divine Analogy in the Eighteenth Century." *ELH* 20 (1953): 39–76.

———. *Shelley: A Critical Reading.* Baltimore: The Johns Hopkins University Press, 1971.

———. *Shelley's* Prometheus Unbound: *A Critical Reading.* Baltimore: The Johns Hopkins University Press, 1965.

———. *The Subtler Language: Critical Readings of Neoclassic and Romantic Poems.* Baltimore: The Johns Hopkins University Press, 1959.

Wearmouth, Robert Featherstone. *Methodism and the Common People of the Eighteenth Century.* London: The Epworth Press, 1945.

———. *Methodism and the Working Class Movements of England, 1800–1850.* London: The Epworth Press, 1937.

Webb, Robert K. *The British Working Class Reader: 1790–1848: Literacy and Social Tension.* London: Allen & Unwin, 1955.

Webb, Timothy. *Shelley: A Voice Not Understood.* Highlands, N. Y.: Humanities Press, 1977.

Webster, C. A. *The Diocese of Cork: With Illustrations.* Cork: Guy and Co., 1920.

Weinstein, Alfred A. "John Wesley, Physician and Apothecary." *The Georgia Review* 10 (Spring 1956): 48–54.

Wellek, René. "Coleridge's Philosophy and Criticism." In *The English Romantic Poets: A Review of Research and Criticism.* Edited by Frank Jordan. 3d ed. New York: The Modern Language Association of America, 1972.

———. *Immanuel Kant in England, 1793–1838.* Princeton: Princeton University Press, 1931.

White, Newman Ivey. *Shelley.* New York: Alfred A. Knopf, 1940.

Whiteley, J. H. *Wesley's England: A Survey of Eighteenth-Century Social and Cultural Conditions.* London: The Epworth Press, 1938.

Willey, Basil. *The Eighteenth-Century Background: Studies on the Idea of Nature in the Thought of the Period.* 1940. Reprint. New York: Columbia University Press, 1964.

———. "On Wordsworth and the Locke Tradition." In *The Seventeenth-Century Background: Studies in the Thought of the Age in Relation to Poetry and Religion.* 1934. Reprint. London: Chatto & Windus, 1949.

Williams, Aubrey. *An Approach to Congreve.* New Haven: Yale University Press, 1979.

Williams, Harold, ed. *The Correspondence of Jonathan Swift.* 5 vols. Oxford: Clarendon Press, 1963–65.

Winnett, A. R. *Peter Browne: Provost, Bishop, Metaphysician.* London: S.P.C.K., 1974.

Wittreich, Joseph A., Jr. *Visionary Poetics: Milton's Tradition and His Legacy.* San Marino, California: Huntington Library, 1979.

Wlecke, Arthur O. *Wordsworth and the Sublime.* Berkeley and Los Angeles: University of California Press, 1973.

Wright, Dudley. "The Religious Opinions of Charles Lamb." *Open Court* 37 (November 1923): 641–47.

Wright, John. *Shelley's Myth of Metaphor.* Athens: University of Georgia Press, 1970.

Yates, Arthur S. *The Doctrine of Assurance: with Special Reference to John Wesley.* London: The Epworth Press, 1952.

Yolton, J. W. *John Locke and the Way of Ideas.* London: Oxford University Press, 1956.

Index

BT842070